The Fortifications of Paris

ALSO BY JEAN-DENIS G.G. LEPAGE
AND FROM MCFARLAND

French Fortifications, 1715–1815: An Illustrated History (2010)

Vauban and the French Military Under Louis XIV: An Illustrated History of Fortifications and Strategies (2010)

Aircraft of the Luftwaffe, 1935–1945: An Illustrated Guide (2009)

Hitler Youth, 1922–1945: An Illustrated History (2009)

The French Foreign Legion: An Illustrated History (2008)

German Military Vehicles of World War II: An Illustrated Guide to Cars, Trucks, Half-Tracks, Motorcycles, Amphibious Vehicles and Others (2007)

Medieval Armies and Weapons in Western Europe: An Illustrated History (2005)

Castles and Fortified Cities of Medieval Europe: An Illustrated History (2002; paperback 2010)

The Fortifications of Paris

An Illustrated History

Jean-Denis G. G. Lepage

McFarland & Company, Inc., Publishers
Jefferson, North Carolina, and London

Acknowledgments

The author wishes to thank
Jeannette à Stuling,
Simone and Bernard Lepage,
Eltjo de Lang and Ben Marcato,
Michèle Clermont,
Véronique Janty, John Beauval,
Florence Rigal and Erik Karstel.

The present work is a reprint of the illustrated case bound edition of The Fortifications of Paris: An Illustrated History, *first published in 2006 by McFarland.*

LIBRARY OF CONGRESS CATALOGUING-IN-PUBLICATION DATA

Lepage, Jean-Denis.
The fortifications of Paris :
an illustrated history / Jean-Denis G. G. Lepage.
p. cm.
Includes bibliographical references and index.

ISBN 978-0-7864-6100-4
softcover : 50# alkaline paper ♾

1. Fortification — France — Paris — History. I. Title.
UG430.P2.L45 2010 355.7'0944'361—dc22 2005020085

British Library cataloguing data are available

On the cover: Pol, Jean, and Herman de Limbourg, *The Belles Heures of Jean of France, Duke of Berry,* ink, tempera, and gold leaf on vellum 9⅜" × 6$^{11}/_{16}$", 1409 *(Cloisters Collection/Pictures Now)*

Manufactured in the United States of America

McFarland & Company, Inc., Publishers
Box 611, Jefferson, North Carolina 28640
www.mcfarlandpub.com

Contents

Part III. Bastioned Fortifications (1512–1874)

Part IV. Modern Fortifications (1874–1944)

Introduction

The fate of Paris has been determined by two main factors: its favorable geographical situation, a defensible island in the middle of a broad river; and the historical choice by the early kings of France to establish there the seat of power. A junction between natural conditions and human will, Paris is one of the most fascinating cities in the world. Having entered history in the year 52 B.C. via Julius Caesar's Gallic Wars, the city attracted at one and the same time politicians, clergy, scholars, craftsmen, merchants, tradesmen, financiers, artists and soldiers. All left their mark on the city's destiny, reflected by town planning, arts, religious and secular architecture and fortifications.

Written with the general reader in mind, this is a history of Parisian fortifications throughout the centuries. This history is, however, little known, as for a long time historians were content to dismiss fortifications as hardly worth serious study. The existence, role and location of the Parisian fortifications are only quickly mentioned in the countless books on and guides of the city, probably because they have disappeared or have become hidden behind the numerous and marvelous pieces of civil and religious architecture. The fortifications of Paris have played a significant role in the history of the city and of France. When they were demolished, they provided useful spaces for traffic lanes, avenues, public gardens, open squares and new speculative buildings. Their outline is still visible in the motorways.

So this book is at the same time a history of the city itself, that of France and that of warfare, as fortifications were the result of political situations and military conditions. The writing of such complicated and intertwined developments has demanded a measure of selectivity among many choices, and I hope that my readers will remember that oversimplification is an almost inescapable result of compression. Important historical developments have been summarized in a few lines or even in a single phrase. Many problems and controversial issues have been left unexplored, and in several cases their very existence had to simply be ignored. Significant personalities have suffered too—some are only sketched in a few strokes—and details which are apparently trivial but which are in fact full of significance also had to be neglected. I hope, however, that I have been able to maintain a sane balance among the development of the fortifications of Paris and that of warfare, the history of the city, and that of France, and to link those four closely related histories together coherently.

The time span considered begins with the hazy installation of a Celtic tribe in the Parisian basin and ends in August 1944—the last time Paris was involved in a major war fought on French soil.

A book of this kind is largely based upon the work of others, but I have thought it undesirable to encumber the text with an overly elaborated system of footnotes. Instead a select bibliography is provided at the end of the book to share my sources with readers.

I created the drawings and illustrations in this volume myself from numerous sources; when known, the major contributors to the depiction are named.

With the emphasis on the military history of Paris and France, the reader will be constantly confronted with ambition, greed, aggression, conflict, turmoil, battles, bloodshed, foreign and civil wars, revolutions, uprisings and repressions, conquests and invasions, glorious victories and catastrophic disasters. But this is only one side of the coin. France is also a nation of amazement and wonder, where many ideas were born useful for Europe and the world, a country that has produced civilization, masterpieces of art and culture, and a fascinating cultural diversity and richness. The French people — even if at odds with themselves— in the eyes of the outside world have a many-sided natural unity.

Let me now say a few words about fortification. The art of building defenses is an activity almost as old as the human race itself, traceable from the day when the first human raised a stockade to protect himself from wild beasts or aggressive neighbors. The time when the first fortresses appeared in prehistory is unknown, and the manner of their early development is still very much a subject for speculation. Humanity's prime concern of defending itself against attack may be termed biological but fortifications became increasingly more sophisticated. Sited strategically, a fortress can deter a potential attacker. It might control a key access point (mountain pass or river crossing) or dominate the hinterland. A fortress may also be used to control conquered territories; impose a system of government; and provide a central point from which a region can be administrated, a base for police surveillance, a place from which taxes and levies can be collected, and a stronghold from which new offensives can be launched. A fortress was also a daily reminder of the physical presence and strength of the ruler — in the case of Paris, the king of France.

Fortifications presented two main military advantages. First, they allowed a small force to resist a larger opposing force. Second, they allowed poorly trained troops to hold out against a better-trained aggressor. To defend a home, a village, a castle, a town, a country or an empire, the basic principle of fortification remains the same: to put a barrier between attacker and defender. The number of obstacles and the sophistication of their arrangements may vary a lot, but the principle is as valid for a Roman camp as for a Middle Age castle, a 17th century bastioned town, a ring of detached forts, or a network of concrete bunkers. Of course nature plays a key role in the shaping and placing of fortifications: in order to erect a barrier against an attacker, it is necessary to adopt, reinforce, extend and improve the defensive potential of natural obstacles. Therefore fortifications have always been erected on top of hills, mountains, or cliffs along marshes and rivers, and at any other place where nature made the progression of the enemy difficult — in the case of Paris, the small island of the Cité.

The aim of this book is both simple and ambitious: to shed light historically and technically on one neglected aspect of the development of Paris and to give a rather general overview of the subject as a reference for the professional and amateur historian.

A Note about Measurements

All measurements are given in metric units. Rough metric to U.S. conversions are:

2.5 centimeters (25 millimeters) to 1 inch
91 centimeters to one yard
1,609 m to one mile
1 kilogram to 2 lb 3 1/4 oz
1 metric ton to 2204 lbs
1 litre to 1.06 quarts

— *Jean-Denis G. G. Lepage*
Fall 2005
Groningen,
The Netherlands

PART I

From Lucotecia to Paris (300 B.C.–A.D. 987)

1

Geographical Situation of Paris

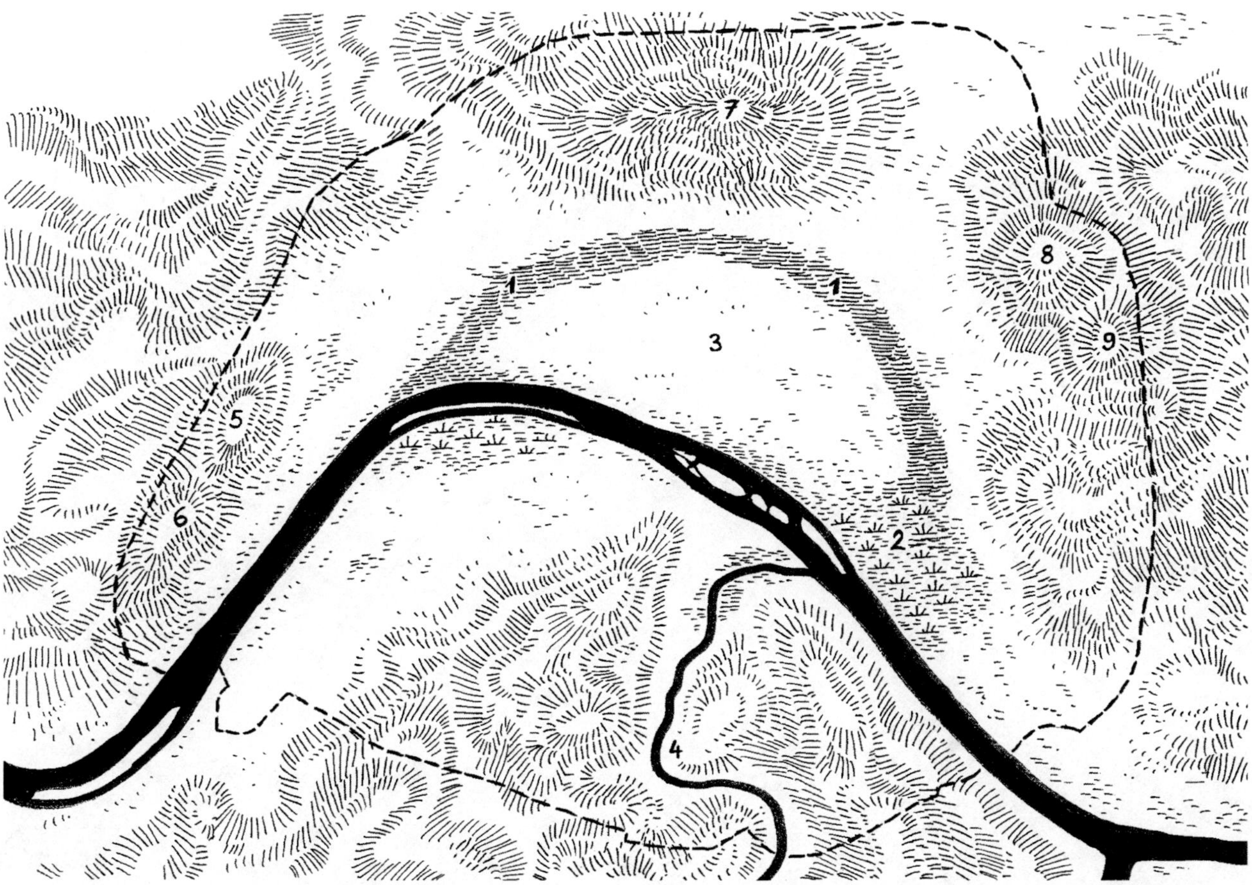

Geographical map of Paris. 1. Approximative flow of the Seine in the quaternary. 2. Le Marais (marsh). 3. The so-called Island Saint Martin, a slightly higher ground. 4. The Bièvre sinuating between several hills of middle height (Montagne Sainte Geneviève, Butte aux Cailles, and Montsouris). 5. Chaillot hill. 6. Passy hill dominating the plain of Vaugirard. 7. Montmartre, the highest point (129 m) in the north, today crowned with the Sacré Coeur Basilique. 8. Belleville hill. 9. Ménilmontant hill. The dotted line indicates the administrative limits of the city today. Except in the valley along the Seine, all space was covered with forests, of which two parks remain: the Bois de Boulogne in the west, and the Bois de Vincennes in the east.

The *île de la Cité*— the very origin of the development of Paris— occupies a privileged geographical position. This is one of the essential reasons for its development, since it benefits from a remarkable river system, being situated on the River Seine between its confluences with the Marne upstream and the Oise downstream. At this point, the crossing of the River Seine was facilitated by the existence of a group of small islands, reducing the river to two comparatively narrow arms. On the right bank, the Seine originally divided up into two beds, the present one and another farther to the north; in the Quaternary (geological period about 4 million years B.C.), this old arm curved at the foot of the hills Belleville, Montmartre and Chaillot. On the right bank there was also a small affluent river called the Bièvre, named after the beavers that populated it. The Bièvre took its source near Versailles and mouthed in the Seine near the present bridge of Austerlitz.

Archaeological evidence including graves, weapons, tools and other artifacts reveals that the region of Paris was populated as early as 4000 B.C. Those early Parisians, emerging from a primitive background, were hunters using weapons; their methods and equipment slowly but constantly improved, they learned to build themselves shelter, to use fire, and to clothe themselves. They transmitted ideas and experience by speech, buried their dead with ceremony and created art of both a decorative and a magical character. Evidence of prehistory in the Parisian region is abundant, not because of extra large-scale human settlements but because the sites have been dug over and over and endlessly excavated for building purposes over the centuries.

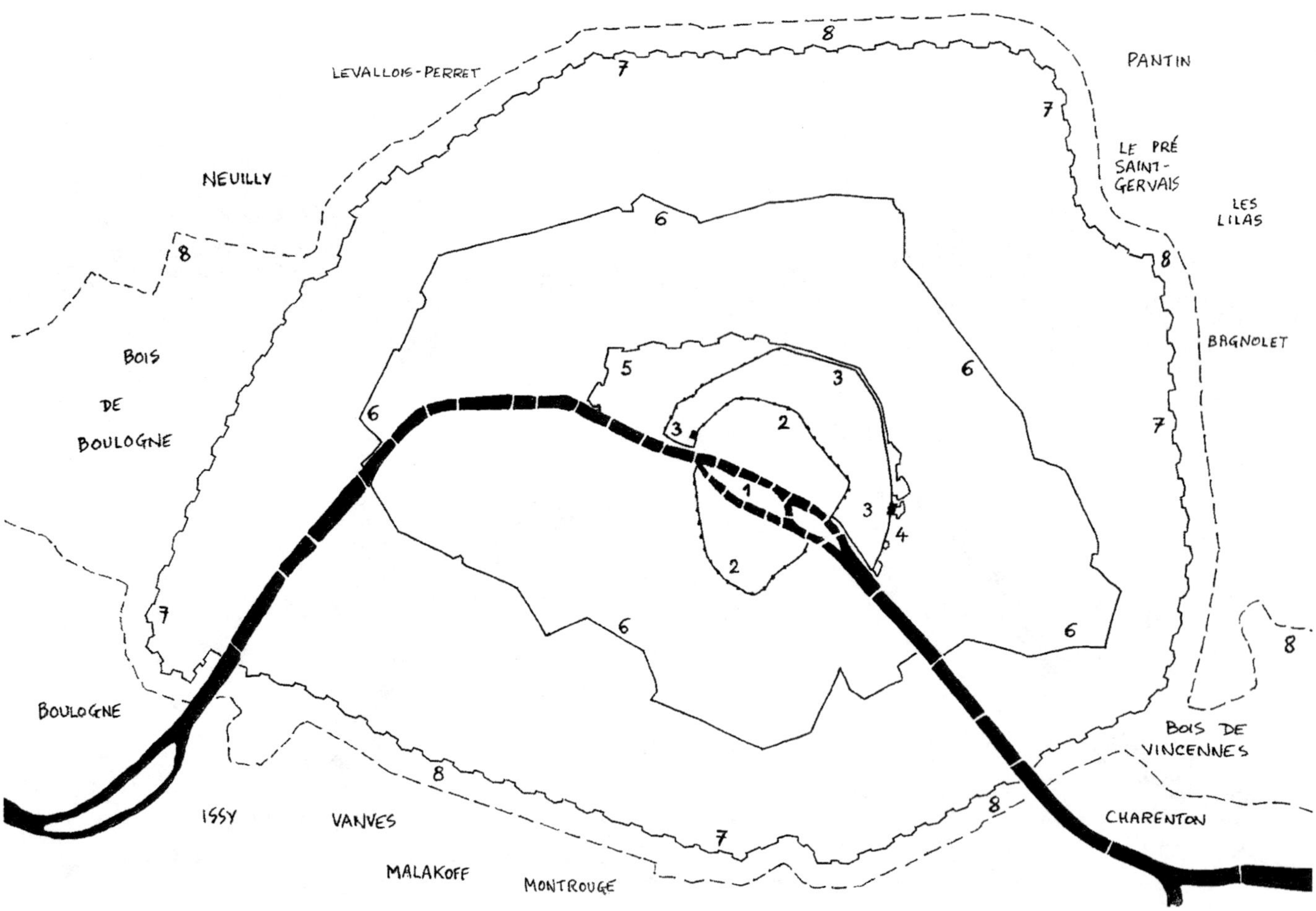

Map of the successive fortifications of Paris. 1. Gallic and Roman period 3rd century A.D. 2. Enceinte Philippe-Auguste 13th century. 3. Enceinte Charles V 14th century. 4. Bastions Henri II 16th century. 5. Fossés Jaunes end 16th century. 6. Enceinte Fermiers Généraux 18th century. 7. Enceinte Thiers 19th century. 8. Present-day administrative limits of Paris.

2

Gallic Time

The Celts

When it established itself on this site about 400 B.C., the Celtic tribe of the Parisii made a good choice. How did they come? As the area was very thinly populated and covered with thick forests, there were no roads or tracks. We may speculate that they came from the east by boat, that they halted and that they liked the place. Anyway, the tribe settled on the largest island in the middle of the river which they named *Sequana* (the present Seine), a term probably coming from the old Celtic *squan* meaning curved — an appropriate name indeed as it rightly described the numerous windings of the river.

The very name *Parisii* remains unexplained. We may set aside the highly legendary connection with the Egyptian goddess Isis and the link with the Trojan Greek hero Paris. An explanation could be that the term meant "efficient" in the ancient Celtic language. Efficient at what by the way? At war? At navigating? This point remains totally unclear.

The Parisii were one of the sixty Celtic tribes who populated what the Romans called Gallia or Gaul (today France). The Celts were people established in western Europe since the Iron Age, conventionally beginning about 800 B.C. They probably came from central Europe or farther east, from southern Russia, and moved slowly westward. All these people — then covering much of Europe — had the same lifestyle and no doubt the same beliefs and more or less the same language. Their civilization was essentially agrarian, and they continued the same kind of agriculture as the Bronze Age people before them. Archaeology has revealed that they were mainly traders and farmers, they were technically advanced, and they knew how to work with iron and could make good weapons and plows— which made it possible for them to farm heavier soils. They were a religious people; they worshipped natural divinities such as springs and trees under the direction of their priests (named druids), and they believed in the immortality of the soul.

Those established in what later would become France were *Gauls*, a name given to them by the Romans. Our knowledge of the Celtic world is rather slight. Much of what we know about them comes from Greek and particularly Roman sources, thus through the writings of enemies who considered Celts and Gauls barbarians. The Romans regarded the Celts as war mad, high spirited and quick for battle; they spoke fearfully of the Gauls and remembered the capture of Rome by one of their war leaders, Brennus, in ca. 390–383 B.C. The Greeks remembered the Celtic expedition to Macedonia and in Asia Minor about 279 B.C. So there are facts but also legends, tales of fantasy and hypotheses.

The Gauls were organized in tribes led by kings or warrior families forming oligarchies called by the Romans "knights" as they usually fought on horseback, while the free men of the common people fought on foot. Chiefs were chosen from each family or tribe, sometimes as the result of fighting matches between individuals and sometimes by election. Warriors would meet in assemblies which designated a chieftain, the *vergobret*. The Celts were considered barbaric by the Ancients; they were indeed terrible warriors thanks to their courage, their advanced weaponry and their savagery. Defeated enemies were either put to death or enslaved. Before and after a

Gallic warrior

victorious battle, human sacrifices were held to obtain the favor of the gods of war. The Gauls often carried the heads of their enemies on their belts, hung them around the neck of their horses or hung them at the door of their houses according to a ritual tradition; with the display of the enemy skull, one appropriated for oneself his strength and his courage. Their offensive weapons included swords, daggers, battle axes, spears and bows. Defensive equipment—probably only worn by the rich nobles—included shields, decorated bronze helmets, as well as curasses and corselets protecting the body.

Lucotecia

Today there are two islands in the heart of Paris (Ile de la Cité and Ile Saint Louis), but in Celtic times and until the late Middle Ages there was actually a kind of archipelago: in the West the Ilot de la Gourdaine, the Ile aux Vaches and the Ile aux Juifs were later joined to the Ile de la Cité proper. In the middle, another Ile aux Vaches (cow island) and the Ile Notre Dame were joined to form the Ile Saint Louis. The eastern Ile Louviers was joined to the right bank only in 1843. The river was wider than today, and its banks and those of the islands were extremely marshy. There were no dikes, and the low grounds in the vicinity of the river were often flooded by heavy rainfall, particularly in winter. The history of Paris was marked by countless floods, the most devastating being those of A.D. 584, 593, 1196, 1579, 1658 and 1910.

The human settlement on the Ile de la Cité presented many advantages. It was a convenient crossing point leading northwards to the Lendit plain, where each year an important ceremonial and trade gathering of Gallic people took place. On the left bank the road to the crossing followed the path of the present-day Rue (street) Saint Jacques, reaching the Seine between the mouth of the Bièvre to the east and a marshy plain to the west, then crossing it on the site of Petit Pont (bridge) and Pont Notre Dame. On the right bank it followed the path of Rue Saint Martin, the beginning of which was flanked by two sandy beaches. These were used as anchorage and harbor: the *Grève* (strand) to the east and the *Ecole* (from escale: port of call) Saint Germain to the West. The grounds on the right banks were low lying and marshy, from which the present *Marais* took its name.

The islands were the center of the Parisii and probably were populated by a few hundred of them. All around their "capital" several thousand other Parisii were scattered into numerous settlements in the surrounding forests. Trees were removed to make open spaces suited for agriculture and living. These clearings (named *oialos*) would later evolve the suffixes *-euil* and *–eil* which give their names to numerous suburbs (e.g. Auteuil, Montreuil, Argenteuil, Rueil, Créteil, Corbeil).

Fortifications of Lucotecia

If danger threatened, the Parisii could seek refuge on the main island, which constituted an easily defensi

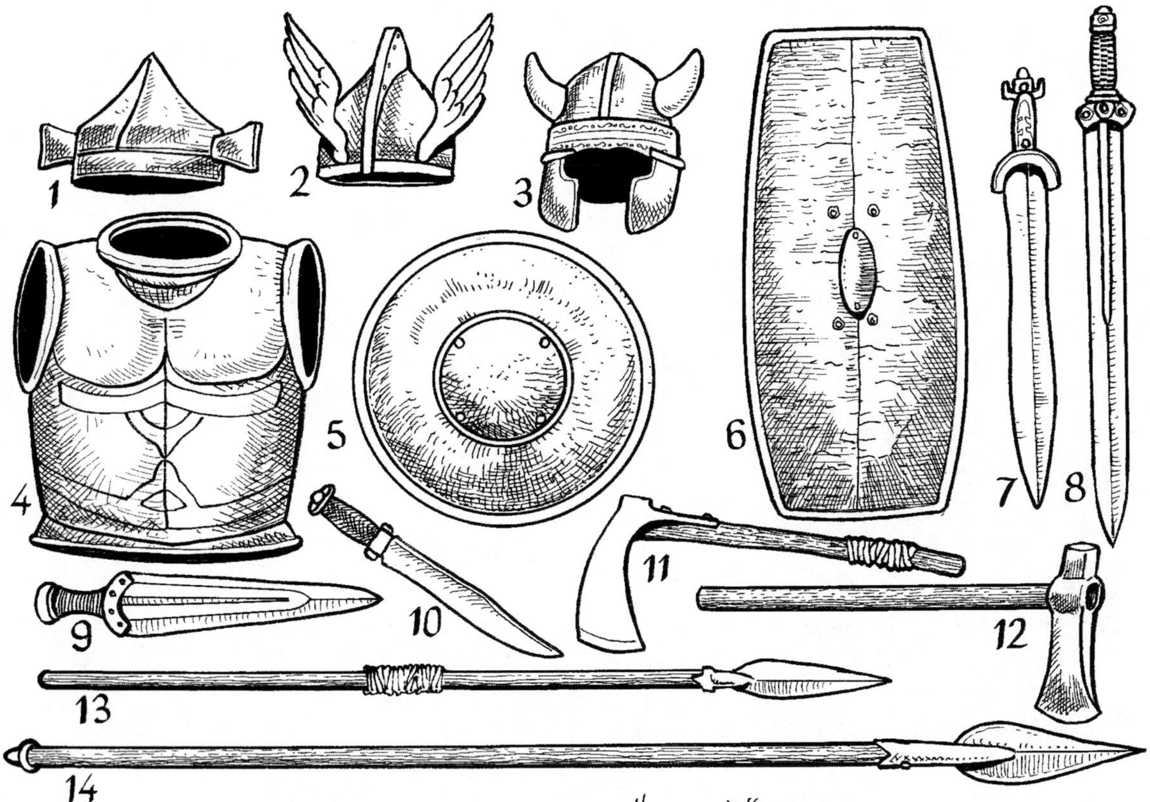

Top left: Celtic weapons. The bronze helmet (1, 2 and 3) was often reinforced with a crest and cheek-pieces and decorated with plume, horns or wings. The curasses (4) were generally short, molded to the figure, and decorated — sometimes in the Greek tradition, with a crude outline imitating the chief human muscles. The shield (5 and 6) was round or rectangular, made of wickerwork or of wood possibly reinforced with metal bars. The sword (7 and 8) — made of bronze, iron or steel — was about one meter long generally with a broad cutting blade. Daggers (9 and 10) and axes (11 and 12) were of various shapes and used both for domestic purposes and war. The throwing javelin (13) and the spear (14) were socketed and often displayed a sharp leaf-shaped metal head.

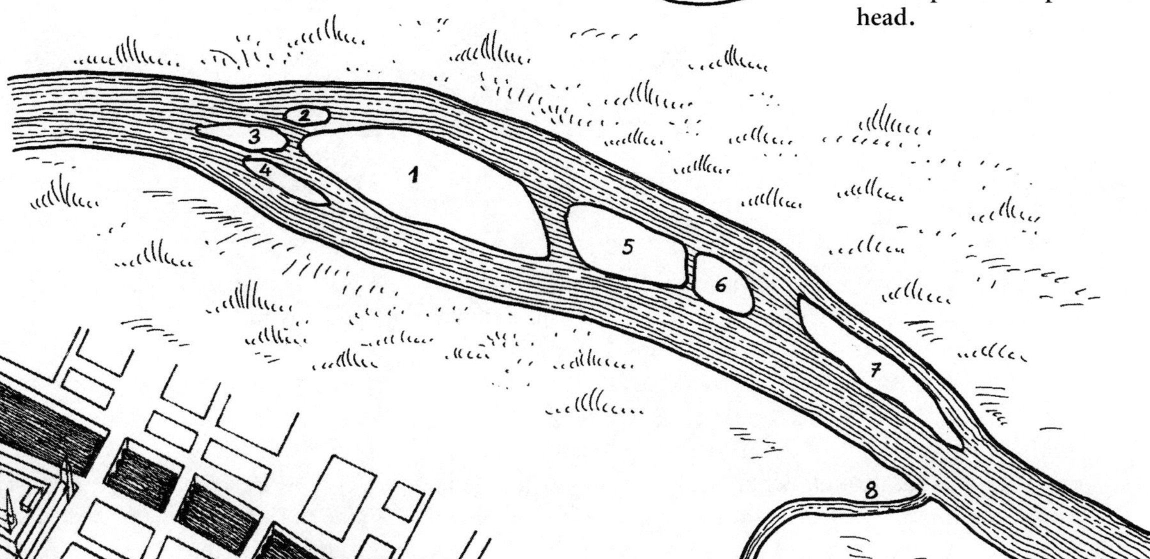

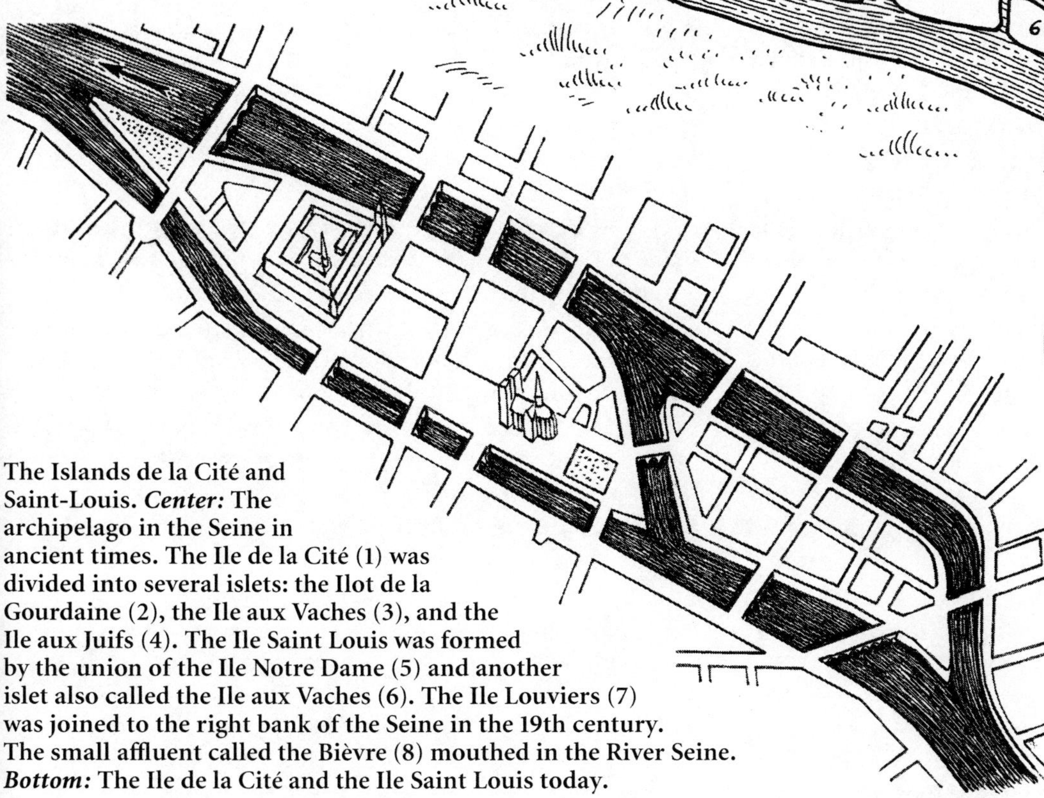

The Islands de la Cité and Saint-Louis. *Center:* The archipelago in the Seine in ancient times. The Ile de la Cité (1) was divided into several islets: the Ilot de la Gourdaine (2), the Ile aux Vaches (3), and the Ile aux Juifs (4). The Ile Saint Louis was formed by the union of the Ile Notre Dame (5) and another islet also called the Ile aux Vaches (6). The Ile Louviers (7) was joined to the right bank of the Seine in the 19th century. The small affluent called the Bièvre (8) mouthed in the River Seine. *Bottom:* The Ile de la Cité and the Ile Saint Louis today.

Murus gallicus: Cross section as described by Ceasar. 1. Wooden beams and earth. 2. Wallwalk. 3. Wooden palisade. 4. Stone wall. 5. Ditch.

ble position as both arms of the river with the strong current provided an impassible ditch. This natural defense was presumably reinforced with manmade fortifications. The island was a so-called *oppidum* (plural *oppida*) forming a fortified market place, a trading center, and a small town called Lucotecia probably meaning *marsh* in the old Celtic language, though other sources say that it would mean *dwelling in the middle of waters*— in either case an appropriate name.

The fortifications built by the Celts are known by the descriptions of Julius Ceasar in his book *De Bello Gallico* (Gallic Wars) Book VII, paragraph 23.

The *murus gallicus,* as Ceasar called it, was composed of a ditch and a wall; the wall was often but not always made of a stone revetment, a framework of wooden beams holding a mass of piled earth; the upper surface of the wall was arranged as a wallwalk and a wooden palisade forming a breastwork protected the combatants. This crude fortification protected the defenders from missiles thrown by the enemy and provided height from which to command the surrounding ground. It was fortuitously discovered that when the earth to construct the walls was taken from immediately in front of the wall, the resulting ditch formed a further obstacle to the approach of the enemy.

The precise outline and the surface of Lucotecia are not known, but we may presume that it was a small village enclosed by earth and wooden fortifications as described above. There may have been primitive towers and some form of gatehouses that defended the bridges linking the island to the banks.

The Parisii lived in simple square or round huts made of timber, wickerwork and clay walls, the roof being a dome of thatch according to the Greek traveler Strabo. There was probably a somewhat larger and more decorated house for the chief of the tribe and his family. The huts were undoubtedly placed along lanes, and the village might have had a pronounced countryside character with meadows and orchards mixing with the dwellings.

The oppidum of Lucotecia was the capital of the Parisii and the center of the *civitas parisiosum*— the land around their town that they controlled. The tribe earned its living by hunting, working the land and breeding animals (e.g. pigs, cows and horses). The Parisii would doubtless have fished in the river, and would also have levied tolls on those who wanted to cross the bridges they had built on the river. As the Gauls were skilled artisans inventing and producing numerous tools and weapons (scythes, plows, swords and lances), the Parisii were also traders. Trade across tribal borders was important for political and social contact between the Celts.

The Parisii had neighbors. In the north there was the tribe of the Silvanecti (around the oppidum of Senlis); to the east the civitas of the Meldi (oppidum of Meaux); in the southwest the civitas of the Carnutes with two major oppida, Chartres and Orléans; and in the southeast the civitas of the Senoni whose oppidum was Metlosedum (Melun). The relationships between these tribes was probably based on trade and exchange, and sometimes there would be conflicts which could degenerate into local wars. The tribes of Gaul had indeed no "national" feeling, they had a common civilization but they never formed a united empire; the people of Gaul lived in a state of political anarchy. They were bellicose, deeply divided, and often rivals. In about 80 B.C., there seems to have been a war between the Parisii and the Senoni with a Parisian victory and the breaking of the Senoni domination. The unstable political situation was to benefit powerful and better organized invaders coming from the South.

The Roman Conquest

After the Punic Wars against Carthage, which ended in the victory of Rome in 146 B.C., the Romans began a policy of conquest. They subjugated Spain and the southern part of Gaul including the southern Alps and the Mediterranean coasts. This was known as the *Narbonnaise* (today Provence and Languedoc) as the town of Narbonne was its main town. The Romans did not venture northwards for years until Ceasar was appointed proconsul.

Caius Julius Ceasar (101–44 B.C.) was an ambitious young man who wanted power. To achieve his goal, he had first to acquire military glory. Taking advantage of the rivalry and division of the Gallic tribes, Ceasar undertook the conquest of Gaul. In just a few years—between 58 and 51 B.C.—Ceasar succeeded in beating a coalition of Gallic tribes, putting down revolts (notably that of the Veneti in Britanny in 56 B.C. and that of the Gallic war leader Vercingetorix in 52 B.C.). He also crossed the English Channel in 54 B.C. and established Roman rule in southern England (Centium, now Kent). The disciplined legions of Rome had proved their efficacy in the face of the brave but divided Gauls.

As for the Parisii, they were defeated in 52 B.C. They were of so little significance that Ceasar did not bother to come personally. Instead he sent only four legions led by his lieutenant, Labenius. The Parisii had elected the old Camulogene as their chief. At first, they succeeded in resisting the invaders by containing them (probably) in the marshes near the mouth of the River Essonne. The Romans retreated to Melun and launched a second attack on the right bank of the Seine. In order to starve and stop them, Camulogene ordered the destruction of food stocks and the demolition of the bridges across the river, after which he concentrated his troops on the present Sainte Geneviève hill. But the cunning Romans managed to find boats; outflanked (possibly in the plain of Grenelle), the Parisii were defeated in a series of confused battles, about which little is known, as Ceasar's own report (*De Bello Gallico*, Book VII, paragraphs 57, 58, 59, 60, 61 and 62) is rather vague and lacks topographical precision. However the outcome was clear: Camulogene was killed and his warriors defeated.

The conquest of Paris was merely a small campaign in the Gallic Wars. Ceasar subjugated other tribes in northern Gaul and Belgium and established the border of the Roman world on the River Rhine between Gaul on one side and Germany on the other. By 51 B.C. the entire country had submitted and Caesar could proudly announce to the Senate in Rome that new, large and rich provinces had been conquered.

Ceasar's triumph marked the end of the Roman Republic and the imminent birth of the Empire in which a single man, the Emperor, would exercise almost total control over the huge territory conquered on the shores of the Mediterranean Sea. Lucotecia was henceforth submitted to Roman rule.

3

Roman Rule

Romanization and Urbanization

After Julius Ceasar's final victory, Gaul entered upon a long period of peace. Gaul—and therefore Paris—had become a part of this mighty Empire and belonged to an admirable mixed Gallo-Roman civilization. The war of conquest had been harsh but once they were victors, the Romans showed great mercy towards the vanquished—at least those who fully accepted their rule, and as long as the taxes came in regularly. On the whole the local traditions and customs were respected, the noblemen of Gaul retained their rights and thus aspired to Roman citizenship; there gradually were Gallic senators representing the country in Rome. They learned to think of *Romanitas*—the Roman heritage—as something to be proud of. To be Roman became gradually not to have been born in Italy, but to belong to a great civilization. The population and the leadership became totally loyal, a few troops garrisoned in the main towns were sufficient to maintain law and order in a Gaul that had been pacified. The Romans brought with them the skills of reading and writing, Latin was used as a universal language, Roman law took root in much of Gaul and the Roman culture was encouraged. The Roman way of life quickly spread; it was universally adopted as it became more a model than an oppression. Through marriage, links between Romans and Gauls were strengthened, giving rise to a Gallo-Roman society. This symbiosis was also evident in religion as the Romans venerated their own gods but also respected the Gallic divinities, and a veritable merger was achieved through a somewhat confused but workable Gallo-Roman religion.

Gaul and Paris enjoyed a long period of peace, growth and security referred to as *Pax Romana* (Roman Peace)—a term created by Plinus the Younger to characterize the Roman beneficent civilization. This "Roman peace" considerably favored population growth, the development of business and increasing wealth. The Romans gave their large empire swift communication; a network of roads allowed the rapid movement of troops but also greatly contributed to the development of trade and commerce as well as political and cultural unity.

The Roman culture remained alive long after the ancient civilization had died out. The achievement of Rome inspired admiration for centuries to come. What the Romans left behind in brick, stone and concrete was enormously impressive and long unrivalled in Western Europe. The most obvious characteristic of Roman civilization was its towns. One of the most lasting and important aspect of the romanization was the development of the existing Gallic oppida, and more particularly the creation of new modern towns which were the basis of Roman administration and civilization. Rome—like ancient Greece—was an urban civilization. Administratively, Gaul was divided into provinces with the capital established at Lugudunum (today Lyon). Paris was only one of the numerous cities in the province called Lugdunensis IV. The *civitas* continued to be the unit of territorial administration, and, most commonly, the former *oppida* of the Celtic tribes became the new Roman provincial and local capitals.

Lutetia

The Roman town of Lutetia—the new name of Lucotecia—increased in size, and in the 3rd century A.D., the town numbered some 6,000 inhabitants. As the right bank of the Seine was too marshy but there was no shortage of space on the left bank, Lutetia gradually grew between the highest point of the left bank which later became Montagne Sainte Geneviève and the River Seine. It spread on the gentle slope in grid layout with the *cardo* (main north-south axis, also known as *Via Superior*) corresponding to the present Rue Saint-Martin and Rue Saint-Jacques. As this street soon appeared not to be enough, another parallel axis was developed known as *Via Inferior* (the present Boulevard Saint-Michel and Boulevard Denfert-Rochereau). Perpendicular to both these main roads, several secondary streets were developed, notably the *decumanus* (main east-west axis) corresponding to the Rue Cujas, Rue Lhomond and Rue Mouffetard. Outside the city these streets were arranged as regional roads leading to Rouen (in the northwest direction), Senlis (to the north), Dreux (to the west), Melun (to the southeast) and Orléans (to the south).

The small city was fitted with monuments and facilities typical of the basic Roman town. The *forum*—created in the first century A.D.—was a wide square at the junction of the two main streets (today Rue Soufflot); it was the center of public, political, economical and religious life. Though the Gauls remained faithful to their original druidic form of worship, the forum was flanked by a temple and a basilica dedicated to the Roman upper god Jupiter. Lutetia possessed three sets of *thermes* (baths) where people could bath and relax but which were also places of art, leisure and social life. The ruined vaults of the most recent baths (3rd century A.D.) are still visible at the junction of the Boulevard Saint Germain and Boulevard Saint Michel.

Monuments decorated the town and triumphal arches recalled the victories of Rome as a discreet reminder that law and order had to be upheld. The town was supplied with water brought in by a 16-km-long aqueduct—a vault of which still exists today in Arcueil—from springs around Rungis and Chilly-Mazarin. The town had a small theater (situated in the foundation of the Saint Louis grammar school) and a large amphitheater for entertainment, horse racing and gladiators combat, indeed for all the games which the Romans considered to be as essential as bread. The latter, much restored and today known as the *Arènes de Lutèce*, can be seen in the quadrilateral formed by Rue Monge, Rue de Navarre, Rue des Arènes and square Capitan. As the Romans considered death impure, the dead were traditionally buried in a *necropole* (cemetery) outside the town, situated near the present-day Rue Pierre Nicole.

In the north, on the right bank of the Seine a small Gallic center continued to exist around the Grève harbor where trade depending on the river was established: butchery, tanning, dyeing and inland transport navigation.

With a population estimated between 6,000 (and soon 10,000), Lutetia was a town of middle importance. Apparently the Romans were not deeply interested in Paris, maybe they found it too "northernly" and cold. They lavished all their favors on Lyon and the southern cities such as Frejus, Aix-en-Provence, Valence and Nîmes. By comparison Paris cut a poor figure in Roman times. Strabo barely mentions the future capital of France in a list of the cities of the provinces of Lugdunensis and Belgica. In Paris there were only a few civil servants and tax collectors working for the Roman administration, as well as a few merchants and army veterans. As long as the Parisians paid taxes, the town was left with a great level of autonomy, allowed to have its own right of justice and manage its own finances and economy. The town enjoyed modest development; it attracted peasants, craftsmen and shopkeepers from the area. In this loose and tolerant frame, the ancient Gallic Parisians willingly romanized themselves. They adopted the Roman way of life, dressed in Roman fashion wearing the *toga* (cloak), and lived in stone houses. They must certainly have kept many of their original Gallic customs and their original language (at least in the lower classes of society), but gradually all of them spoke a bastardized form of Latin which became ancient French.

Around the city there were numerous hamlets, agricultural domains and farms which today remain in the toponymy of Parisian boroughs and suburbs. Passius's farm (Passiacum) is now Passy, Bercus's farm (Bercianum) has become Bercy, Nullus's domain (Nulliacum) Neuilly, Eburus's land (Eburiacum) Yvry, that of Gentillus (Gentiliacum) Gentilly, that of Victor (Victoriacum) Vitry, as well as Issy, Antony, Orly, Choisy, Champigny, Rosny, Noisy, Bondy, Clichy etc. These agricultural settlements encroached on the wide Celtic forests which also still exist today in the suburban toponymy, e.g. Aulnay (place where alder trees grow), Fresnes (ash tree), Chatenay (chestnut tree), Tremblay (aspen), and Herblay (maple tree).

Fortifications of the Ile de la Cité

The city on both banks of the Seine was not fortified because the *Pax Romana* made no need for defense. By employing a double policy of ruthless annihilation of dissidents and favorable treatment of friendly factions, the Romans guaranteed peace throughout their empire for 400 years. Therefore Roman city walls were symbols of municipal pride, rather than weapon systems of military

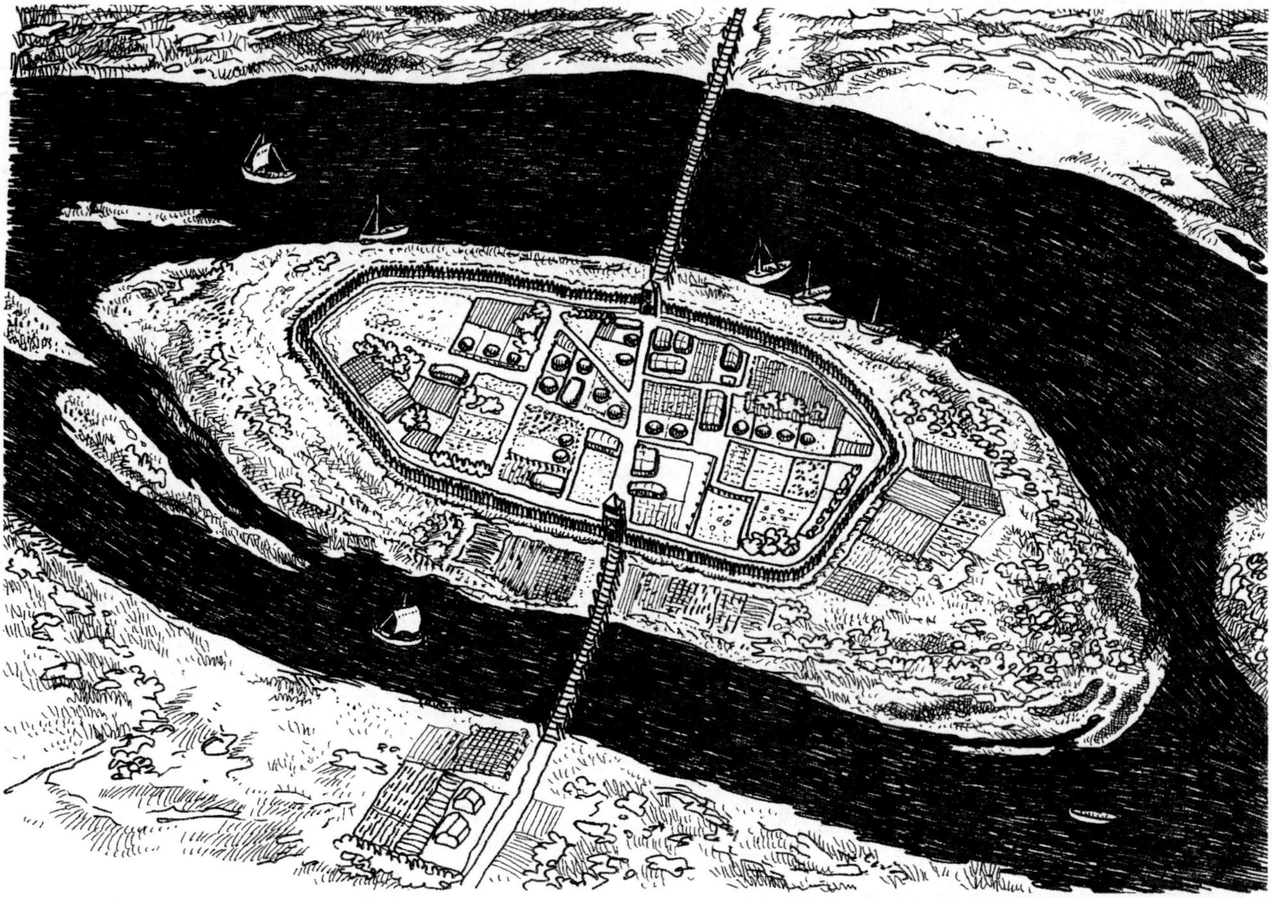

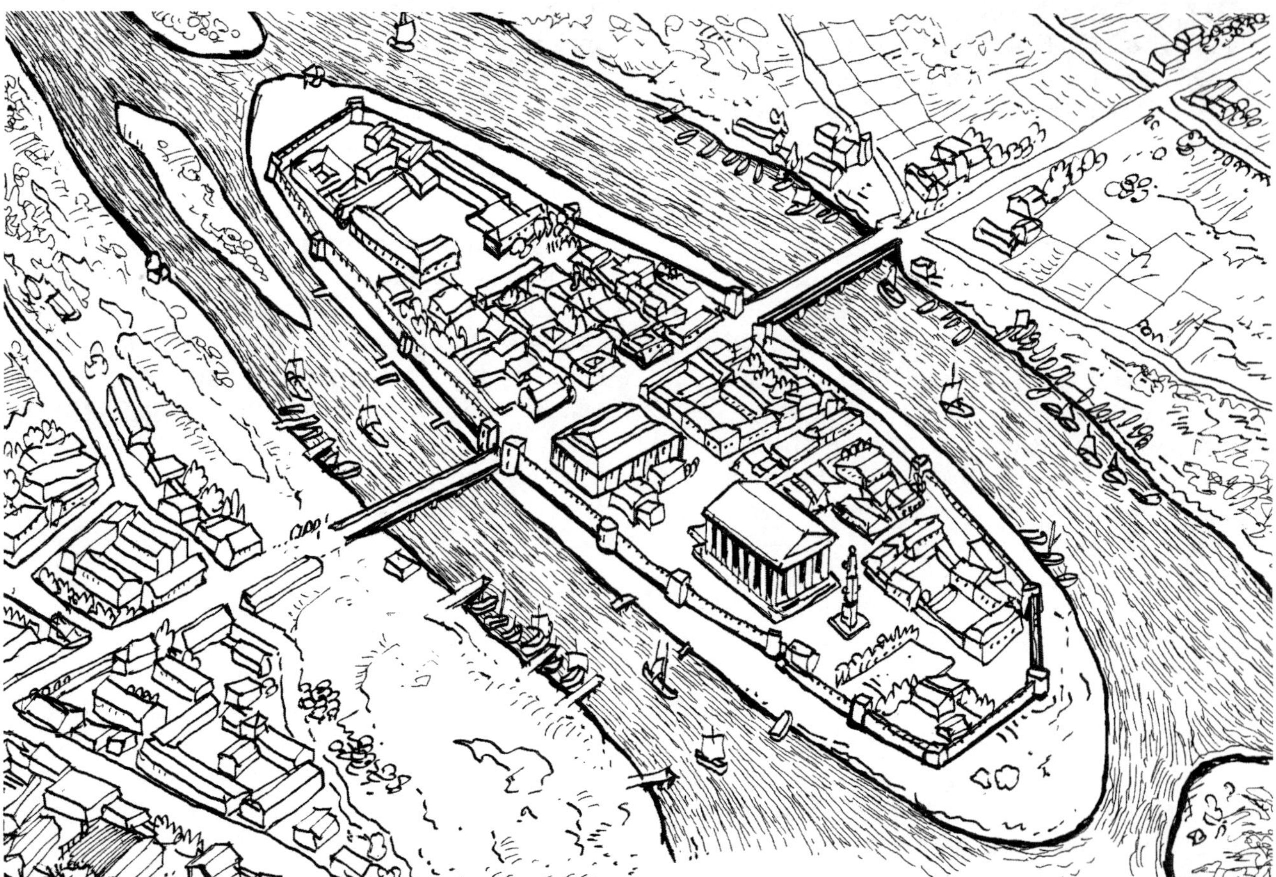

significance. Paris was difficult to fortify; it would have cost a lot to build fortifications and to maintain a garrison to man the walls. Moreover Lutetia was a city of middle significance, and Roman fortifications were only built around important Gallic towns e.g. Vienne, Nîmes, Autun, Lyon, Orange or Aix-en-Provence.

But Lutetia was an important crossroad which would have been unwise to leave totally undefended. So the only fortified part of Paris was the Ile de la Cité which merited the designation of *castrum*, or *arx*, a citadel defending the town, a safe place to which the population could retreat. The Ile de la Cité was the administrative and religious heart of the town. It contained temples, offices and other official buildings.

The island was fortified with a stone wall. It is difficult to say with precision when this was built, probably between A.D. 308 and 358. Surveys—made between 1834 and 1988—indicate various dimensions. The outline—of which only fragments are known—followed the banks of the island with a total length of about 1.2 km. On the average, the wall was between 2 m and 3 m thick at its base, and about 2.30 m and 3.22 m high (in some places possibly as high as 9 m); these modest dimensions may seem weak but it must be considered that peace reigned, and that both arms of the Seine and the river's strong current prevented the use of siege machines, such as assault towers, mines and battering rams.

The Roman method of constructing defensive walls was to build an inner and an outer casing with loose rock filling the intervening space. At the base of the wall, massive blocks of building stone were often keyed together with iron tie-rods and lead seals, as well as being set in mortar. The inner facing would have earth banked behind it, while the outer was fronted by a ditch. In the case of Paris, the ditch was the River Seine. The top of the wall was fitted with a *chemin-de-ronde* (wallwalk) and a man-high crenellated breastwork. This consisted of *crenels* (openings) which enabled the defenders to hurl missiles at the enemy and *pinnae* (solid standing parts) providing cover.

The great 19th century artist Hoffbauer made beautiful illustrations of Paris in Roman times which include towers and gatehouses. But it is not known with certainty whether the walls were reinforced with flanking towers and whether bridges linking the island to the banks were fortified.

Cross section of the Roman wall. 1. Outer facing. 2. Inner facing. 3. Loose rock in core. 4. Wallwalk. 5. Pinnae. 6. Crenel.

The island was well furnished with drinking water (wells and cisterns) but the people could eventually be subdued by starvation in a long siege. The defense wall also fulfilled an important practical function: it constituted a dam against the river overflowing.

Christianization

As the years went by, Middle Eastern churches gained a following in Gaul, and Christianity also spread through the country. The process of Christianization was, however, slow; it took more than three centuries for the Gauls to abandon their old tutelary gods, particularly in

Opposite: (Top) **Map of Gallo-Roman Lutetia.** ***(Bottom)*** **Ile de la Cité in Roman times (from Jean-Claude Golvin).**

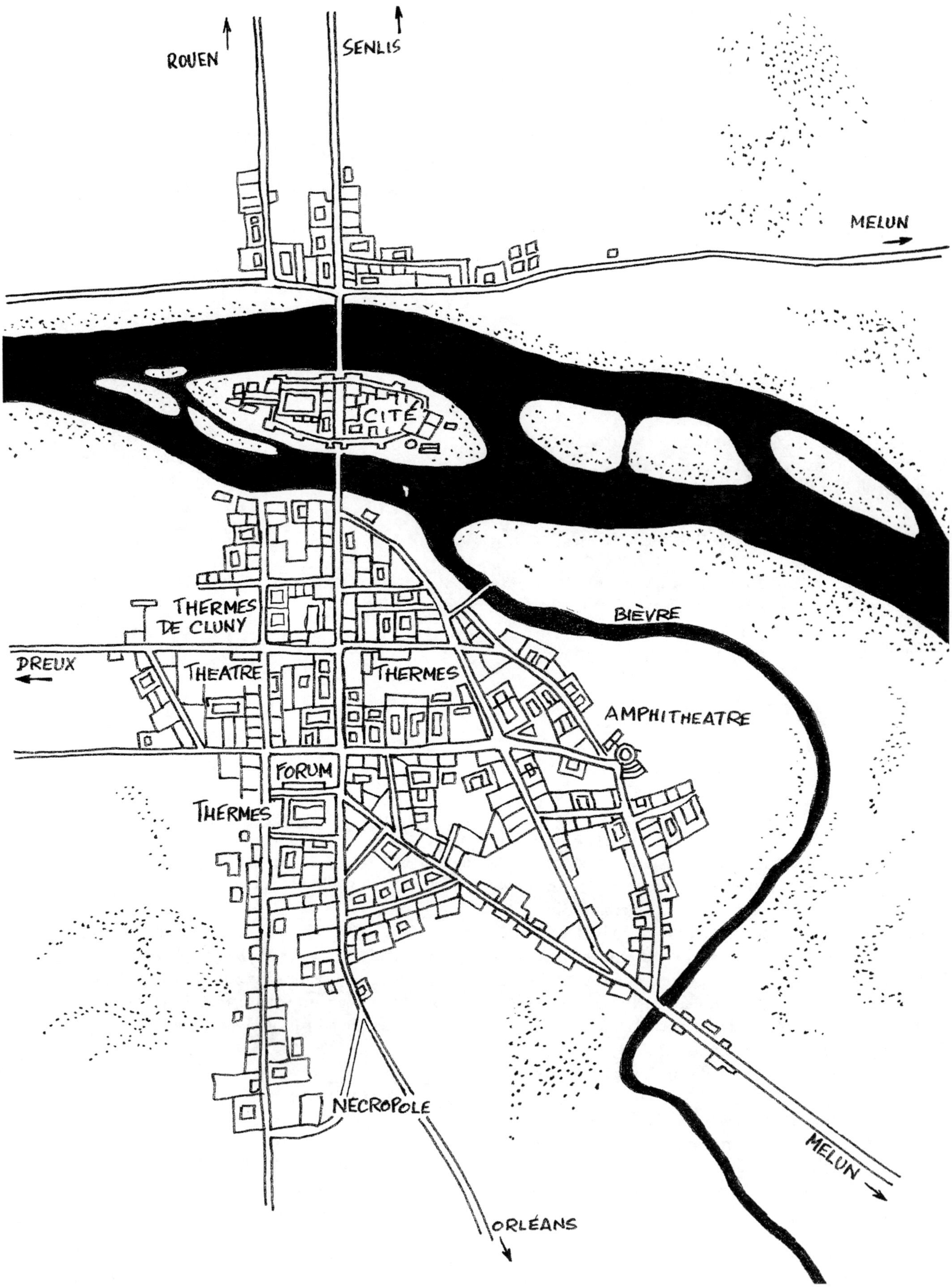
ROUEN
SENLIS
MELUN
CITÉ
THERMES DE CLUNY
BIÈVRE
DREUX
THEATRE
THERMES
AMPHITHEATRE
FORUM
THERMES
NECROPOLE
MELUN
ORLÉANS

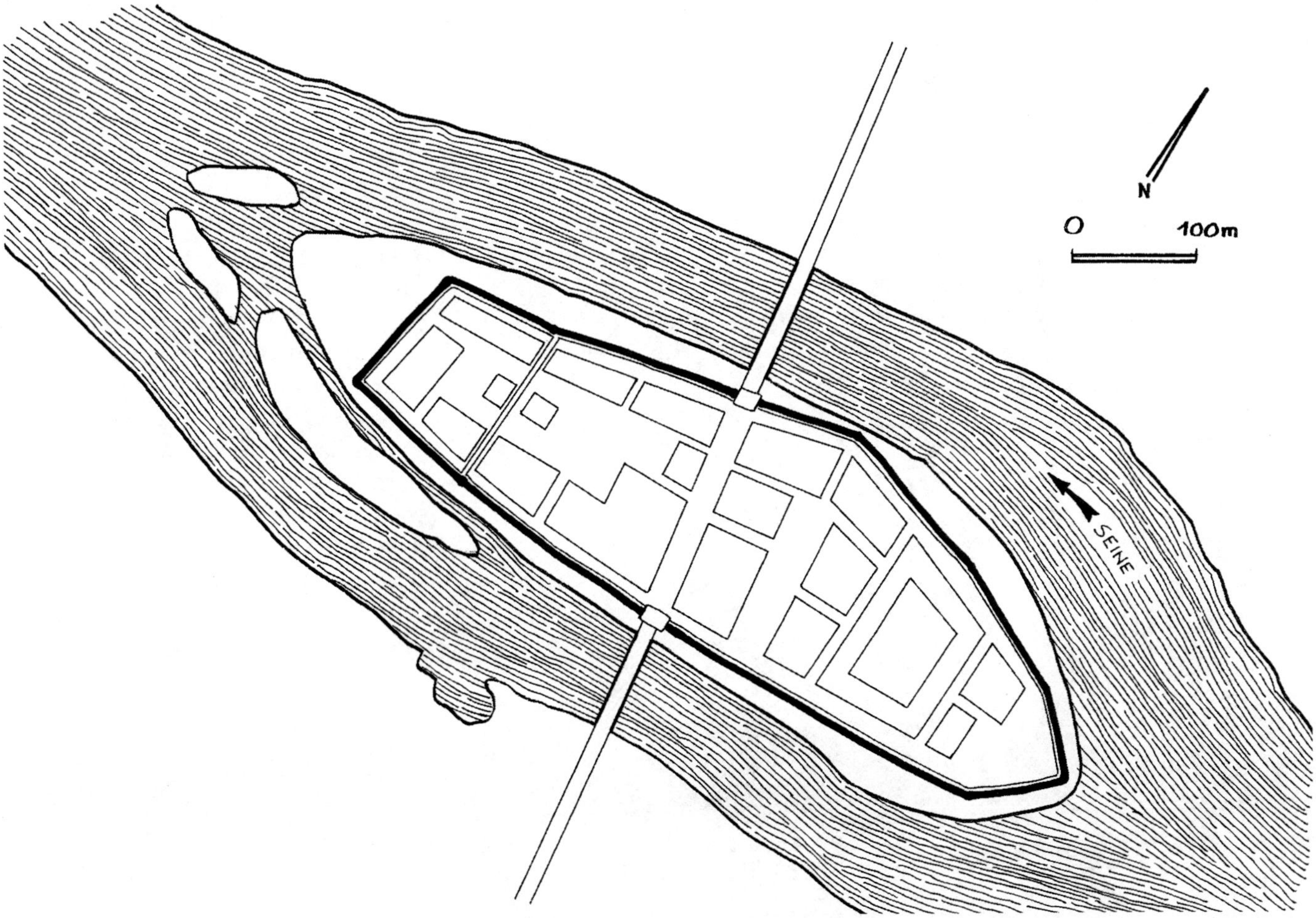

Map of the Roman wall in the Ile de la Cité (from F. Lagarde).

rural areas, which explains why *peasant* was synonymous with *pagan* (paganus in Latin).

Christianity made its first appearance in southern Gaul towards the end of the 1st century A.D. It was in Lyon that Christians were martyred in A.D. 177, among them Sainte Blandine. In Paris, Christianity seems to have been introduced by a certain Dionysius (Denis) who was martyred in A.D. 250, according to some sources, or A.D. 287, according to others. Tradition and legend assert that Denis was a nobleman from Athens (Greece), a direct disciple of Saint Paul, or an evangelist sent from Rome by Pope Clement. Whoever he was, he was regarded by the Romans as a rebel who endangered the security of the state; he was beheaded on Mount Mercury, today *Montmartre* (= the Mount of Martyrs). The legend says that instead of dying instantly, Denis picked up his head, cleaned the blood of the wound in a fountain, walked north holding his head in his hands and finally died in a small village, Catulliacum, which later was named after him: Saint Denis. This place (now a northern suburb of Paris) later became a Christian sanctuary, a place of pilgrimage and a basilica where the kings of France were buried.

Gradually Christianity was more or less tolerated, and a semi-clandestine Christian community developed in the southeast of Paris. Under the leadership of a bishop, the early adepts of the new monotheist religion discreetly established themselves aside on the left bank of the Seine near the road to Melun (today approximately the Saint Marcel and Gobelins boroughs); they lived in huts and probably had a primitive church and their own cemetery, and the small and shallow Bièvre brook provided a place for baptism. In 360 the Parisian Christian community must have been important, as an assembly of bishops met in Paris and condemned the so-called *Arianism*, a heretical doctrine developed by the theologue Arius from Alexandria (ca. 256–336), accepting Jesus Christ as only a messiah but not as the divine son of God.

After being the belief of a few minority groups of deviating Jews from the Middle East, Christianity became

Opposite: **Sketch map of Gallo-Roman Lutecia.**

an official religion and finally the only authorized religion in the Roman Empire in a.d. 391. Churches were built in place of the pagan temples, and monasticism — a Middle Eastern practice — began to be established. The first monastery in Gaul was founded at Liguge near Poitiers, followed by another at Marmoutier.

An administrative reform resulted in a new map of Gaul, showing divisions that were taken over by the Church in the form of bishoprics. The bishop sat in a town and ruled over the *pagus* (the land around it) within former provinces. The highest positions in society were spiritually held by bishops and administratively by *comes* (companions) later to become *counts* appointed by the emperor. The first Parisian bishop in the 4th century was a certain Marcel who gave his name to a suburb, a monastery and a cemetery in the southwest part of the town.

Saint Denis holding his head

4

The End of the Roman Empire

The Barbarian Invasions

In the 3rd century A.D., the Roman Empire entered into a slow but profound decline due to various and complex reasons. Under Roman rule, Gaul had become a rich, fertile land and, as such, attracted the envious attention of Germanic barbarian tribes from beyond the Rhine. Taking advantage of the Empire's increasing weakness, German tribes (Franks, Alemanni and Goths) from the northern side of the Rhine crossed the *limes* (the fortified frontier which separated them from the Roman Empire) and began to launch dreadful raids into Gaul. In 253 and in 275, Lutetia suffered barbarian incursions, and a long period of insecurity and decline began. At first the raids were on a rather small scale.

In about A.D. 355 the bloody confrontations between pretenders to the imperial throne further weakened the Empire, and Franks and other barbarians were again able to invade Gaul. The country was then the key element in resistance to invasion, and the emperors Julian (331–363) and Valentinian (321–375) established their headquarters in Lutetia. From there, they led a number of victorious campaigns, defeated the Franks and authorized them to settle on the left bank of the Rhine provided they would serve in the Roman army and help repulse other Germanic invaders. Soon the Franks occupied an increasingly large place in the Roman army and affairs of state.

The Huns

In 451 the Franks helped save Gaul from invasion from the ferocious Huns led by their leader Attila.

The Huns were an Asian nomadic people, living off the tribute money paid to them by terrified princes such as the emperor of the Orient. One cannot be really sure about the precise nature of the Hunnic invasion. It seems that Attila decided to obtain the same submission from the western world by attacking Gaul. The Huns, surpassing themselves in savagery, captured and sacked several towns including Metz.

Paris resisted the attacks of the Huns in 451, and it was a simple shepherdess from Nanterre, named Geneviève (about 422–502) who roused the panic-stricken inhabitants of Paris, restored their courage and prevented them from surrendering and abandoning their town. For this act of gallantry Geneviève was later canonized by the Church and became the patron of the city. Attila—who had so far met no obstacle in his path—abandoned his attempt to take Paris by siege and turned to Orléans. The Huns were finally defeated by a Roman general, Aetius, in June 451 between Troyes and Chalons-sur-Marne (probably near the village of Moircy). The hordes of the Huns retreated and left the country altogether. Paris and Gaul had been saved, but the ambitious Aetius—the last man to maintain Roman unity in Gaul—was assassinated by Emperor Valentinian III in A.D. 453.

From then on the fate of the Roman Empire was sealed. Nothing and no one could stop its collapse. In A.D. 476, Romulus Augustus—the last emperor ever—was overthrown by a barbarian king, Odoacre, who was elected king of Italy. This date traditionally marks the official end of the Roman Empire and the beginning of the Middle Ages. Gaul was divided among the Germanic invaders, and many small barbarian kingdoms were cre-

Frankish warriors

ated. The Germanic influence was to be a distinctive contribution for the making of Europe.

Lutetia During the Invasions

The gradual collapse of the Roman Empire affected urban life more profoundly than other aspects of society. Roman civilization had been distinguished by a high level of urban development, and the Germanic invasions, by disrupting commerce and overthrowing the governmental structures that had once provided coinage, undermined the most crucial supports that made urban life possible. Cities were depopulated, sometimes to the extent of complete abandonment.

Fortunately, Paris did not cease to exist, it remained in continuous occupation as an urban center, albeit in a decayed state. During this troubled period the once rich and prosperous Roman town on the left bank was depopulated and deserted; the population was estimated to be only 2,000. As a means of protection, the Parisians sought refuge by retreating to the Ile de la Cité, a somewhat cramped structure including the governor's palace, the bishop's church and a number of streets for tradesmen and craftsmen. To the best of their ability, the Gallo-Roman Parisians tried to defend themselves against the invaders. This period was to last a whole century. The Cité island became a fortress again. By that time, the fortifications of the island of the Roman period — which had been neglected and poorly maintained — were reinforced. The stone wall was about 3.50 m high, 2.50 m thick at the base and 2 m thick at the top. Its total length was about 1.620 m enclosing a surface of 10 ha. This wall formed a poor defense as it — probably — did not include towers but, as ever, the Seine acted as a large ditch. Most of the stones used to rebuild those fortifications came from buildings and monuments salvaged from the deserted Roman town on the right bank. The pulling apart of cities and fortresses stone by stone was simply part of a policy of recycling strategic raw materials, a practice which lasted for centuries. The fortified island was linked to both banks by two bridges: the present Petit Pont and the Pont Notre Dame. These bridges were probably fortified as they formed important bridge heads allowing the besieged to sally and attack the besiegers.

It is during this period, about 307, that the Roman name of Lutetia was abandoned, and the older designation of *Civitas Parisiorum* reappeared. As the original Latin grammar was bastardized, the name later deteriorated into *Civitas de Parisiis*, soon shortened to *Parisii*, and finally giving the city its current name: Paris.

How the Barbarians conquered Paris in the 5th century is not known. It seems that the Franks were already everywhere, notably in the Roman administration and particularly in the army as auxiliaries. To these movements of people into Roman territories we should also add another fact of great demographic importance: death via bubonic plague that depopulated large areas. There were apparently no large-scale battles, as there was no armed force to oppose the invaders, they just took command without a fight and their leaders created new realms. Few Gallo-Romans seemed to have been displaced by invading Franks who spread out thin as conquerors and settled on vacant lands. Thanks in part to plague and depopulation, a waste of underpopulated forest, marsh, and brush, there was ample room for the newcomers to settle without disturbing the existing population. One of the main results of barbarian migrations was to bring into many regions a new population that was eventually to make the lands they settled more productive than they had earlier been.

5

The Merovingian Period

Clovis

Clovis—the chief of the Franks who had settled in the north and northwest of Gaul—was a tough, energetic man. He vanquished Syagrius's Gallo-Roman troops at Soissons in 486 and proceeded to extend the kingdom of the Franks as far as the Loire River. He overthrew his brothers and cousins and annexed their lands. In 493 he married a Christian princess, Clotilde, and he and his warriors converted to Christianity after the "miraculous" victory of Tolbiac (Zulpich, southwest of Cologne, Germany) in 496. Then the Franks held almost all of Gaul except Provence in the south and Britanny in the west.

The baptism of Clovis was an event of major significance. It was a clever move and a turning point in the history of Gaul as Clovis secured the support of the bishops, the clergy and the population. This enabled him to lead a victorious campaign against the Visigoths who were defeated at the battle of Vouillé, near Poitiers in 507. The result was that the Franks now held sway over the entire southwest of France. The council of Orléans in 511 consecrated the alliance between the Catholic Church and the Frankish king.

Clovis is often regarded as the first king of France, wrongly though, as his kingdom was divided in the Germanic fashion between his four sons. Thierry was king of Reims, Clodomir was king of Orléans, Childebert was king of Paris and Clotaire was king of Soissons. The brothers soon quarreled among themselves. Though officially Christian, they were still thoroughly barbarous and did not hesitate to use assassination as a means of getting rid of a rival for power. The Merovingian dynasty's inheritance traditions—stipulating the division of the kingdom among all male descendants—caused the Frankish kingdom to be repeatedly divided and rarely reconstituted for the benefit of a single heir. Long wars ravaged Austrasia (northeastern Gaul) and Neustria (northwestern Gaul). This protracted struggle lasted throughout the later part of the 6th century, and Gaul suffered greatly from internal strife. King Dagobert (reign 629–639) succeeded in unifying Gaul once more under his rule. He protected the Church and promoted the growth of the economy by instituting the Lendit fair at Saint Denis. He gave generously to the abbey of Saint Denis and with the help of his minister Eloi, bishop of Noyon, succeeded in imposing the royal will upon the nobles.

After Dagobert, came an eclipse of the Frankish royalty, the Merovingian dynasty continued its progress downhill at an even faster rate. The kings were weak, short-lived and constantly subdividing their kingdoms, thus helping localism to triumph over royal centralism. The kingdom of the Franks entered a period of total confusion and, at the beginning of the 8th century, of complete anarchy. The very unity of the Frankish kingdom was in jeopardy as the southwestern region of Aquitaine won total independence. In Neustria, Austrasia and Burgundy, the Merovingian kings gradually lost control over parts of their realm. The noblemen spent much of the time squabbling among themselves, they shifted their support from one king or potentate to another causing wars which sapped the strength of the kingdom precisely when it was being threatened by grave danger.

Paris as the Capital

Clovis chose Paris as capital of his kingdom probably for two main reasons. First, the town was strategically placed in the northern part of his realm. Second, Clovis had a particular devotion to Saint Geneviève, so much that he had ordered to be buried next to her in a church (somewhere near the actual Pantheon). When he died in 511, he was buried on the highest point of the left bank, the Saint-Apotres church beside Saint Geneviève who gave her name to the "mountain."

Actually Paris was not the "capital" of France, as the early Merovingians kings were still nomadic in their way of life, but the city was their principal dwelling place. It should be noted that if the Visigoths had won, the capital of France would probably have been Toulouse or Narbonne. If the Burgunds had triumphed, no doubt Lyon would have become the capital of France. But Clovis won and the fortunes of battle assured the promotion of Paris.

Clovis's son, Childebert I (511–558), took the title of *roi de Paris* (king of Paris). The king was often absent, and the permanent religious and civilian power was exercised by a bishop, who possessed a house in the Ile de la Cité, and by a count representing the king. Because of the weakness of Clovis's successors, bishops and counts were progressively important rulers.

For the city, the privilege of being the royal residence was not illustrated by a regain of territorial growth. By that time, the surface of Paris was probably less than that of the late Roman Empire. The town shrank, the left bank emptied and activity became concentrated on Ile de la Cité and around Grève harbor on the right bank. In the eastern part of the Ile de la Cité, Childebert I had the Saint Etienne cathedral built and another church dedicated to the Holy Virgin Mary—the future Notre Dame cathedral. On the western part of the island, on the ancient Roman citadel, he started with the building of a royal palace.

Outside the city, monasteries were erected: Saint-Victor, Saint-Martin-des-Champs, Saint-Germain-des-Prés, Saint-Séverin, Sainte-Geneviève and Saint-Germain-l'Auxerrois. In the future, those suburban religious places of cult would form important cores for the religious, artistic and economic development of Paris. A few agricultural domains were developed outside Paris, composed of ancient Roman *villas*, giving certain suburbs their present names: e.g. Romainville, Villemomble, Villetaneuse, Sartrouville, Chaville, Joinville, Aubervilliers. Other farms were called *cohors* or *cour*, still existing today as other suburb names: e.g. Clignancourt, Billancourt, Roquencourt, La Courneuve.

On the whole, nothing remains of the achievements of the Merovingian dynasty in Paris. From the 6th to the 8th century Paris languished.

Nothing is known about fortifications from that period. If they existed, a fact we only may suppose according to the insecurity of the time, they were made of earth walls and wooden palisades in the Gallic style, but no archaeological evidence has ever been found.

6

The Carolingian Era

The Carolingian Dynasty

At the beginning of the 8th century, the Arabs, also named Saracens or Moors, had invaded Spain and launched deadly raids into southern Gaul. Meanwhile, the political power was in the hands of the *major domus*— a high ranking officer with large influence — named Charles. When the Saracens reached the province of Aquitaine in southern Gaul, Charles decided to fight them. He levied an army and defeated them in October 732 near Poitiers. The Christian cause triumphed, the Saracens withdrew from Gaul, and the successful outcome of Poitiers greatly enhanced the prestige and reputation of Charles who was given the nickname *Charles Martel* (the Hammer). When Charles died in 741, his son Pippin the Short came to power. The new ruler, who reigned from 751 to 768, removed his adversaries from the scene, and, having secured the support of the Church and the nobles, was elected king. The last Merovingian monarch was locked up in a monastery and Clovis's dynasty was over.

Pippin — elected by the nobles and consecrated by archbishop Boniface — enjoyed popularity and founded a new dynasty, the Carolingian. He allied with the Pope, defeated the Lombards in northern Italy, and subdued southeastern Gaul. After Pippin's death in 768, his two sons (named Charles and Carloman) came to power, but Carloman withdrew into a monastery in 771, leaving Charles as the sole king of the Franks.

Charlemagne

Charles (born in 742; reign 768–814) was a conqueror who spent the first thirty years of his reign fighting the Lombards in northern Italy, the Muslims in Spain and above all the Saxons— a pagan people from northern Germany. Charles was known as the Great (in Latin *Carolus Magnus*, whence Charlemagne) and ruled over a united Christian Europe. Charlemagne was also a good administrator, he divided his large domains into *comtés* (counties headed by counts), *duchés* (duchies headed by dukes) and *marches* (frontier areas headed by margraves). These high-placed dignitaries had great political and military power, but they governed their lands in coordination — and sometimes in competition — with the bishops. The whole administrative structure was checked by *missi dominici* (king's envoys) who inspected the counties, heard complaints and rendered justice. Charlemagne issued *Capitularies*, texts and instructions governing the administration of the various domains. He also established schools and saw to it that his officials were educated. He introduced a new script, and as a pious man reformed monastic life which had begun to suffer from a number of abuses. Economic prosperity and peace returned, and Europe lived a kind of *Renaissance* after the troubles of the Merovingian period. The Church was naturally grateful to Charlemagne for all he had done on its behalf. So as an expression of its thanks, Pope Leo III crowned him Emperor of the Franks on 25 December 800.

Between the years 800 and 806 Charlemagne succeeded in pacifying Saxony and concluding the war against the Avars— another pagan people of eastern Germany.

During the Carolingian period, Paris was relegated to a second rank role and underwent little development as Charlemagne had established his capital at Aix-la-Chapelle (today Achen in Germany). In 806 the emperor divided his large states between his three sons: Pippin, Charles and Louis. However as Pippin became a monk and as Charles died, Louis eventually inherited the empire after Charlemagne's death in January 814.

Louis—nicknamed the Pious—continued the work of his father, but he was certainly a far less resolute and capable character. His weakness was to give rise to serious unrest in the Carolingian empire. In 817 he divided Charlemagne's large realm between his three sons. A bloody struggle ensued during which the central authority was greatly weakened to the benefit of the nobles, dukes, counts, margraves and bishops who dissociated themselves from the central rule. In 843, Louis's sons signed the treaty of Verdun. Lothaire received a noncontiguous realm including the territories between the mouth of the river Escaut to the north down south to Italy; Charles received what was to become France; and Louis ruled over the eastern part which became Germany. The unity of Europe was broken forever at a time when a new threat appeared from the sea.

Viking Warrior

The Vikings

Towards the end of the 8th century, invaders from Denmark, Sweden and Norway, referred to as Vikings—but also known as *men from the North* whence Northmen and Normans—began to lay waste the coast of Gaul. Moving swiftly on boats with a figurehead of a dragon, they swept inland, up the rivers looting and killing in their path. During the period of dynastic fragility, the Normans began their attack on Gaul. The great French waterways such as the Loire and the Seine, gave the Vikings easy access to a rich countryside and wealthy Frankish cities. In 845 they came up the Seine and raided Paris. The Normans made another dreadly appearance in 869, and as they were pagans they had no compunction about attacking, plundering and setting fire to the abbey of Saint-Germain-des-Prés. The crown was too weak to organize any coordinated defense. The whole of France lived in a state of mounting insecurity.

When the Vikings laid again siege to Paris in November 885, King Charles the Fat (839–888) was away fighting in Italy, and it was the bishop, Gozlin, who roused the inhabitants to resist the invaders. Under the leadership of Gozlin and the count of Paris, Eudes (c. 860–898), the city wall built during the Late Roman Empire around the Ile de la Cité was strengthened. A dam across the northern

Viking Ship

arm of the River Seine was built, thus protecting the active part of the towns. On both banks of the Seine two large wooden towers were erected to defend the bridges; these towers would later become large stone gatehouses known as the *Grand Châtelet* (on the northern right bank of the river) and *Petit Châtelet* (on the southern left bank). Paris was defended only by a small garrison while the Vikings, it was said, had 700 ships and a troop of 30,000. The besiegers used catapults (torsion hurling machines) and attacked furiously for weeks while Paris put up heroic resistance. But the Vikings, firmly deployed on both banks of the Seine, were determined to lay siege to the town for a whole year, establishing camps and living off the surrounding countryside. By February 886, the Petit Châtelet to the south, already weakened by repeated assaults, was swept away by the pressure of high water in the Seine. This allowed the Vikings to break through and plunder the rich lands between the Seine and the Loire. They were careful, however, always to leave behind enough troops to maintain the siege of Paris. In the encircled town, conditions became appalling; plague and other diseases easily took their toll on the already weakened and starving inhabitants. By the end of 886, Charles arrived at last to lift the siege. But instead of fighting the Vikings, he shamefully decided to come to terms with them; he had them leave on payment of a large ransom and, moreover, allowed them to plunder the rich province of Burgundy. For his cowardice, Charles the Fat was deposed in 887.

The successful defense of Paris was only a local victory. Elsewhere, all attempts to stop the Vikings were in vain.

Because of a quarrel between incompetent kings and the Norman raids, the Carolingian dynasty became weaker and weaker, the local counts were consolidating their power, establishing quasi-independent territories and loyalty toward the central power greatly decreased.

At first the Vikings made raiding expeditions, seizing plunder and disappearing. Later, however, they took to conquest. They drove the Saracens from southern Italy and settled both there and in Sicily. They established themselves in the northern part of the British islands. As a result of repeated harrying of the French kingdom, the Vikings were eventually able to establish themselves in France too. The last Carolingian kings were powerless and had to grant land to the invaders; in 911 at Saint-Clair-sur-Epte, king Charles III the Simple (879–929) signed a treaty ceding a part of Neustria, the coastal Channel region around the mouth of the Seine to a Northman chief named Rollo. This required him to defend the territory entrusted to him and, by the same token, pay homage to the king of France. Rollo became the vassal of France. In this way Charles ensured a buffer between his vulnerable kingdom and the encroaching Scandinavian hordes. From being a landless marauder, Rollo became a landowner. He and his men were baptized, married local women, and mingled freely with the native Frankish inhabitants. The wild warriors turned from adventurers into farmers and laborers, and little by little Scandinavian and French societies blended together. The Northmen were not numerous, they were swallowed up by the local population, and after a few generations the Vikings spoke French, had adopted French customs and behaved like good Christians. The territory prospered, the fief was enlarged and soon developed into the dukedom of the Northmen, better known as *Normandy* with a political capital, Rouen, and a religious center, Bayeux. When the Normans invaded England in 1066, they were more French than Scandinavian.

7

The Capetians

Hugues Capet

The last Carolingian king in France, Louis V died childless in 987, and the house descending from the count of Paris was consolidating its power and decided to seize power. Hugues Capet — a direct descendant of Eudes, Count of Paris — had no difficulty getting himself elected king of France by the nobles assembled at Noyon with the aid of archbishop Adalberon. It was a turning point for the history of Paris as Hugues established his capital in Paris. Hugues Capet — the founder of the Capetian dynasty that would rule France until 1848 — was chosen because of his modesty rather than for his talent. The name *Capet* seems to come from the cape that Hugues wore, this — according to the legend — being the half of the cloak that Saint Martin once shared with a pauper, a relic which had been in the Capet family ever since.

If Paris was the new capital of the future realm of France, it was a pitiful city by the time of Hughes's election. Violence was rife; the population suffered raids launched by gangs of bandits that roamed the land. Famines, epidemics and diseases killed hundreds, business was ruined, fields were left to waste. It was a time of confusion and chaos which was ruled by the

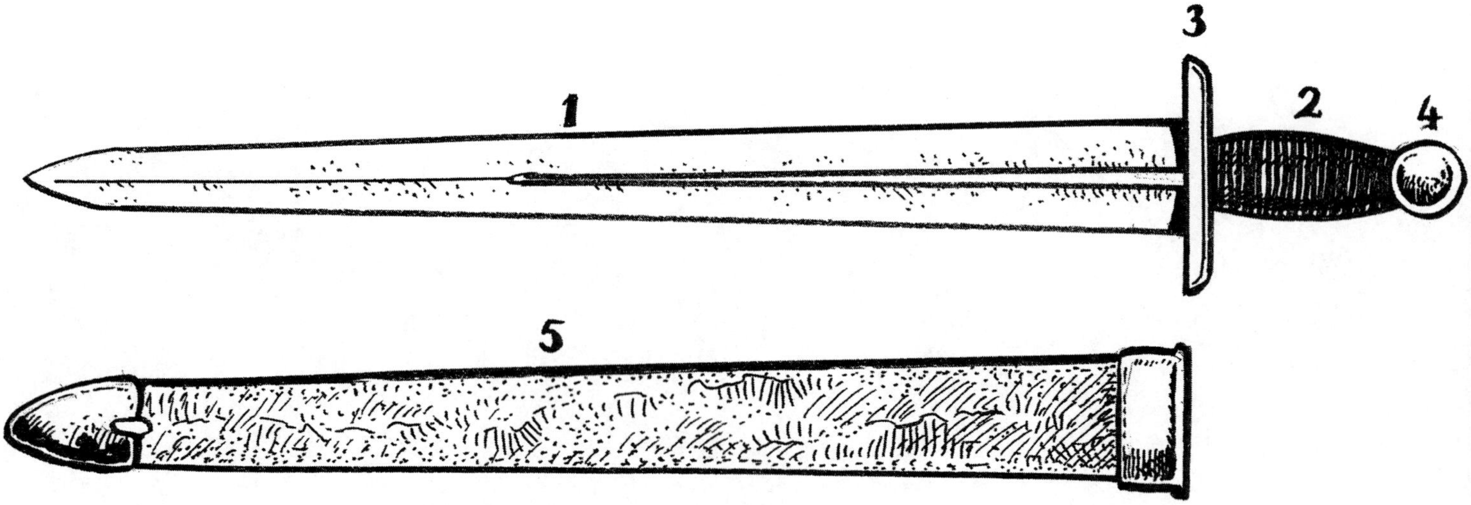

Sword. The sword was the knight's principal weapon for hand-to-hand fighting. It was composed of a sharp blade (1) for cutting, slashing and occasionally thrusting. It included a hilt or grip (2) protected by two guards called quillons (3). The pommel (4) was a knob helping to balance the weight of the blade. The sword was carried in a leather scabbard (5) held at the waistbelt.

Miles (knight). Using the stirrup and the large saddle, the mounted warrior had good balance and was one with his mount. Protected by a long pointed shield, a conical helmet, and body armor made of mail and armed with a long sharp spear, the mounted knight would gallop, charge and stab his enemy. The time of the infantrymen was over, and the day of the cavalryman had come.

principle "Might Is Right." Such was the pitiful end of the once powerful and glorious dynasty of Charlemagne. The collapse of central authority and the weakening of the power of the king led to the formation of the feudal system.

The Feudal System

The barbarian kings of the 6th and 7th centuries had brought an end to the political system of the late Roman Empire but not its social structure, which continued, though disintegrating, largely unchanged for another two centuries. The great change in the social order of western Europe took place in the 8th and 9th centuries. It came about as the cumulative result of the successive waves of invasion, raiding and settlement by the Vikings and the conquests of the Muslims. These finally destroyed the old social fabric of the Roman world and led to the creation of new institutions in its place. The so-called *feudal system* emanated from the weakness of the last of the Carolingian kings and was caused by the absence of any centralized power. It was characterized by special relations between the members of society and by the exchange of part of one's freedom for the promise of protection. For the sake of security against the Northmen, certain particularly powerful or energetic warriors seized power. Then having become overlords or *suzerains* (masters of an area), they received the *homage* (oath of loyalty and military help) from their *vassals* (subordinates). In return, the suzerain rewarded his faithful followers by granting them pieces of lands called *fiefs*. The vassals undertook to help the suzerain in certain cases and went to war with him for a given time. Insecurity was so widespread that non-nobles made a statement recognizing the sovereignty of the overlord, paid duties in the form of taxes and statutory labor, paid tolls for the upkeep of roads and bridges and had to use the common oven or mill; in exchange the rulers guaranteed to protect them.

Society was gradually divided into three unequal classes: the clergy who prayed, the upper noble class who fought and defended the community, and the common people who worked to feed the two other privileged classes. Each overlord was himself subordinate to another lord at a higher level. Europe as we know it in the Middle Ages began to take shape; tribal organization had disappeared, and equally important was the fact that Europe shared a common Christian civilization and culture. The great French provinces, then *seigneuries*, came into being including Champagne, Burgundy, Provence, Auvergne, Aquitaine, Anjou, Britanny, Normandy, Flanders, Hainaut and many others. The age of nations lay far in Europe's future, but already these areas were beginning to develop in such a way that they could form a French nation later on. The lords at the head of these seigneuries formed a hierarchy of dukes, counts, barons, earls and so on who gave homage to the king. The feudal system thus constituted a pyramid which reached from the humblest vassal up to the king.

It was at that time of insecurity and disorder that castles were built all over Europe. Castles were originally made of wooden palisades and earth walls surrounded by a ditch, called *motte-and-bailey castles*. By the end of the 9th century, the first stone dungeons made their appearance. Within their sturdy walls, the lords felt themselves to be secure, and castles tended to increase the power of the fighting upper class of warriors who alone, as large landowners, could afford the expense of their construction and maintenance, and the equipment needed for war. From then on warfare was dominated by the mounted armored *miles* (knight) who monopolized military power and tended to be drawn from the class of large landowners.

A Wall Around Paris in the 10th Century?

Though no archaeological evidence has ever been found, some historians (among them Fernand Bournon in 1886 and Anne Lombard-Jourdan in 1985 who both specialized in the history of Paris) believed and asserted that there was a wall on the right bank of the River Seine. The existence of a wall seems to be proved by writings in which King Charles the Bald had ordered the construction of fortification on towns situated on the River Seine (including Paris) to oppose the Vikings. The writings also made mention of gatehouses (Porte Baudoyer and Porte Saint-Merry). A portion of ditch was found in 1996 in the Rue du Temple, but an excavation does not imply the existence of a ditch and certainly not that of a wall with a military purpose. Anyway, if it existed — a fact that cannot be proved — the wall would have constituted the second enceinte of Paris. These defenses were probably built in the 10th century by the last Carolingian kings in order to resist the Vikings' incursions, and the first Capetian kings would have continued to maintain them in the 11th century.

After the Viking threat diminished and the great fear of the year 1000 when superstitions announced the end of the world, peace and hope in the future were gradually restored. Population increased, the Ile de la Cité became too small and new settlements were established on the right bank of the Seine. Businesses developed around the Place de Grève as the market center for such things as hay, wood, fish and meat; warehouses, houses and parish

Opposite: **Castle and knights. As a knight's armor, equipment and horse were very expensive, some means of paying for them had to be worked out. Instead of hiring and equipping ordinary soldiers, medieval kings, counts and dukes preferred to grant away part of their lands to their warriors. These men governed the estates for their overlords and supplied them with warriors whenever they needed them. This produced a new social system of landholding — the feudal system — and brought into being a new kind of man-of-war, the miles (knight). The landholders ruled their demesnes from a castle.**

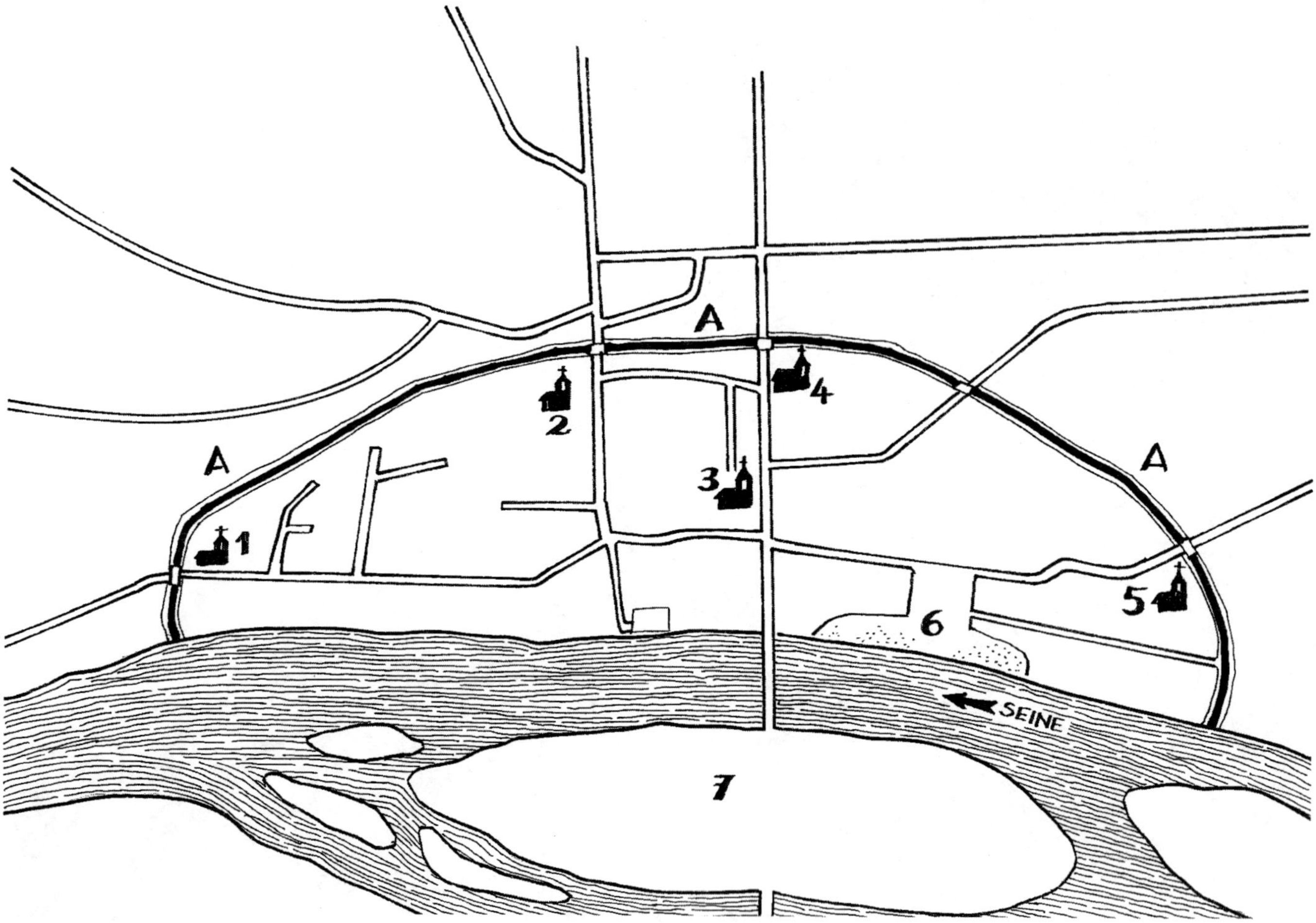

Probable tracé of the 10–11th century fortifications. 1. Saint Germain-l'Auxerrois church. 2. Saint Opportune church. 3. Saint Jacques church. 4. Saint Merry church. 5. Saint Gervais church. 6. Place de Grève (harbor). 7. Ile de la Cité. At the A A A are fortifications of the 10–11th centuries.

churches were built near the port. So it is reasonable to presume that this part of the city was fortified. This part of Paris, the right bank of the Seine, was called *Outre Grand Pont* (Beyond Great Bridge).

The fortifications, if they actually existed, probably had the shape of a crescent stretching from the church Saint-Gervais in the east to the Saint-Merry church in the north, to the church Saint-Germain-l'Auxerrois in the west. Nothing is known of these fortifications. Were they built according to Gallic tradition with a ditch, a wall made of piled earth with a wallwalk on top and a palisade breastwork? Were they built in stone in the Roman tradition? Were they a mix of stone, earth and wood? Were there towers and other refinements? No one can answer those questions unless new archaeological evidence is found to shed some light on this mystery.

PART II

Medieval Period (987–1512)

8

The Growth of France

The First Capetian Kings

The first Capetians were, however, not a very impressive lot. The realm of Hugues Capet covered about the size of two or three modern *départements*; it included Paris, the Ile-de-France (the territories surrounding the city) and a few territories reaching to Orléans to the south and Sens to the north. Hugues Capet made Paris the capital of his little kingdom and established his residence in the Ile de la Cité.

Although in the following centuries France was to be the most influential political and cultural area in Europe, during the early Capetian's rule it showed little political promise and did not share the trend toward political consolidation. Hugues Capet was respected but also regarded only as one equal suzerain — after all, the other great lords had *elected* him, and many of them were much more powerful than him. In practice, Hugues had full power as king of Paris, but as king of France, his position was symbolic. The land that lay between the Pyrenees, the Alps and the German kingdoms continued to be as disorganized, disunited and independent as it had been during the late 9th century. The powerful noble lords of the realm were thoroughly militarized, had at their disposal large resources, and thus could afford the expensive castles, soldiers and military equipment that permitted them to dominate large local districts; they did what they wanted in their own fiefs. The weak king of Paris was officially the undoubted feudal overlord of the nobility, but local rulers ignored him. Hugues's main trump was the support of the Church, his status of anointed king, consecrated to his office in a manner accorded to none of the provincial nobility. His prestigious position was recognized, but not obeyed, as far south as the Pyrenees.

Hugues had the sense to have his son Robert crowned king of France as early as 987 making the succession by *primogeniture* (heredity of the eldest son) virtually assured. When Hugues died in 996, Robert succeeded him with no trouble at all. The hereditary monarchy gave the French kings a clear superiority over the German dynasties who quarreled among themselves over the title of emperor, which remained elective. The fragile dynasty founded by the modest Hugues would rule France — with a short break between 1792 and 1815 — until 1848.

The precarious Capetian monarchy remained weak and could do little to prevent the private wars which occurred frequently throughout the 11th century. The great barons of the realm fought among themselves, seeking to expand their domains, as was the case with a certain Foulques Nerra (Fulk the Black), Count of Anjou. Meanwhile the common people suffered a lot, as private wars had a shattering effect on the rural economy and population. The disruption of rural economy had catastrophic consequences for Paris, and the period 1021 to 1035 was marked by terrible disasters; famines and epidemics depopulated Paris in 1021, 1027, 1028, 1029 and 1035. In addition a giant fire destroyed a part of the town in 1034.

The first Capetian kings after Hugues— Robert II the Pious (996–1031), Henri I (1031–1060) and Philippe I (1060–1108)— intervened in order to subdue the lords of neighboring territories, though they were not uniformly successful.

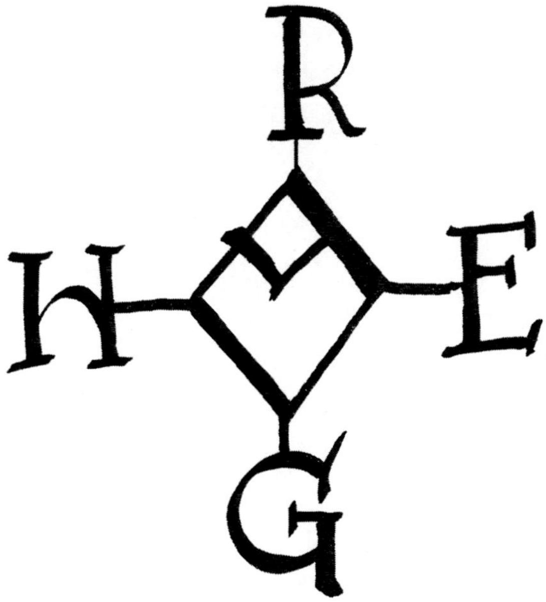

Monogram of Hugues Capet (king from 987 to 996).

By that time Guillaume (William), Duke of Normandy, landed in England and became master of the country after the battle of Hastings (October 1066). The resulting situation constituted an unusual paradox: William was king of England while, as duke of Normandy, he was a vassal of the king of France. The perils of such a state of affairs were the source of numerous wars between France and England for the centuries to come. Nonetheless the Capetian monarchy gradually obtained a fairly good standing, and it was from France that the first Crusade for the Holy Land set off late in the 11th century.

In 1076 Palestine and Jerusalem fell into the hands of the Seldjukides Turks, and Christianity could not simply sit by and do nothing. In response to Pope Urban II, thousands of men took up the cross, moved by an immense upsurge of faith and enthusiasm. A first Crusade of poor people assembled by a certain Pierre l'Ermite failed to complete the long journey, but

Crusader knight (12th century). At a time when the Church and the kings forbade private wars among the feudal lords, the Crusades enabled adventurers, knights and members of the ruling class to give vent to their warlike instincts while earning the remission of their sins. For hundreds of years the basic form of body armor consisted of the chain-mail shirt, called hauberk.

another better-organized expedition composed of warriors and knights led by Godefroy de Bouillon did reach Palestine and took Jerusalem on July 15, 1099. In keeping with feudal custom, the victorious barons divided up Palestine into kingdoms and principalities, creating the Frankish realm of *Outremer* (Oversea).

The Crusades were unmistakably an international movement, but the first Crusade was notable for the participation of French noblemen. King Philippe I had taken very little part in the first Crusade and his son Louis VI the Fat (1108–1137) prudently gave all his attention to domestic issues.

This troubled era saw the spread of the monastic movement, a start of great artistic creativity, and the rise of distinct forms of architecture; it was the time of French Romanesque art, characterized by solidity, massiveness, thickness and roundness, that was later to develop so gloriously into "Gothic" style.

Emancipation of Towns

Louis VI's most important work was to set his own domain in order so as to be master in his own house. He began his reign by restoring security as he put an end to the plunderous raids conducted by lords of the Ile-de-France and nearby areas. He also did much to promote the communal movement. France had long remained isolated from great trading regions, its economical life was local in character, matching the area's political fragmentation, but the situation gradually changed. Commerce increased along the Seine, and development of the French economy was spurred by the Crusades. Slowly at first and then swiftly, it joined in the economic growth. Trade and the number of trade fairs held in cities greatly increased. Towns, particularly those of northern France, became rich — notably by the textile trade. Gradually a new social class emerged comprised of the rich traders who resented having to bear the feudal yoke of lay or ecclesiastical overlords. Feudalism was oriented toward the economic exploitation of land and presupposed a fairly stationary peasant population. The feudal arrangement was incompatible with the needs of an urban community founded on trade and craft, which required a mobile population and a flexible labor market. The urban population revolted and, sometimes, won the right to administer themselves. In his royal domain, Louis VI severely punished the rebels yet granted many towns a communal *charter*, defining the duties and rights of the inhabitants. Indeed the king was quick to recognize the advantage of having a large and rich *bourgeoisie* as a source of taxation revenue and as a center for trade and manufacture. The term *bourgeois* had then no political or social class significance in the modern Marxist sense. In the Middle Ages it meant anyone of humble origin who lived, worked or traded in a town. Whoever lived one year and one day inside Paris was granted the status of free citizen who had rights (notably to be protected and placed under the justice of the king) but also duties (to pay taxes and join the municipal militia for military defense and police purposes). Medieval towns in northern France had no slaves, but rapidly there came into existence social classes divided into a few very rich, wealthy, and slenderly rich, and a large majority of people who were relatively poor, poor and very poor.

The pattern that emerged was one in which the town became a semi-independent structure granted certain freedoms from the usual constraints of the feudal system. The urban community was allowed some measure of self-government and authority to handle minor legal matters.

Because of the importance of Paris, the king kept the city's liberties on a short leash, allowing it rather less independence than was granted to many other towns in his demesne. In Paris, the principal overlord was the king himself, as the town had been a royal residence for centuries. Paris had no charter and, for most of the Middle Ages, it possessed only minimal institutions for self-government, although more independence was obtained during the course of the 13th century.

Anxious to make his sovereign weight felt throughout France and keep the rebellious barons under control, the king intervened everywhere. At the end of his long reign in 1137, Louis VI had greatly enhanced the royal domains, and Paris had enjoyed remarkable growth.

9

Growth of Paris

Since the election of Hugues Capet in 987, the fate of Paris was ineluctably linked with the destiny of the Capetian dynasty. In the 11th century, Paris was, however, still a little city among many others, well situated on a river axis, but no more. It was far from surpassing the other Capetian town, the one on the Loire river: Orléans, which, like Paris, was a trade center, but which, with its famous schools, was more of a cultural center than Paris. The early Capetian kings did not permanently dwell in Paris, but divided their residence among the town, palaces and castles they possessed in their small realm. Parisian ascendancy dates from the 12th century, for three main, related reasons: the development of Seine commerce connected with the rise of the Champagne trading fairs; the success of the professors, drawing crowds of students; and finally, the king's choice for Paris as favorite resort—for a variety of motives, but probably mostly because that town was the best situated with respect to hunting on uncultivated grounds and in virgin forests. Indeed, hunting wild animals was—for the kings and for the rich landowning ruling class at large—the most common of pleasures: it formed good training for war and furnished a valuable supplement to the food supply.

Henceforth, Paris experienced tremendous development and became a real capital to a kingdom that grew in importance. By the 13th century, Paris had become a leading political, religious, cultural and economic center and, arguably, the most important city in Europe north of the Alps.

Very little of medieval Paris survives after centuries of warfare, political turmoil, destruction and reconstruction, and economic development, but a rich body of documentary evidence allows a fairly detailed glimpse of Parisian life. In the early 12th century, the population numbered about 25,000, hardly impressive by modern standards but still larger than any other town in northern Europe. By the 14th century, the population had boomed to more than 120,000. However, one must keep in mind that the capital of France was a dilapidated, sadly primitive and old-fashioned city. The kings' quarters were in a gloomy Merovingian palace tower at the west end of the Cité island. Paris was a noisy, noxious, and disease-ridden place. It was a town full of contrasts, between rich merchants and penniless vagrants, wealthy houses and slums, Christians and Jews.

Jews were tolerated in Paris; they were, however, heavily taxed by the kings, and confined to their own streets (Rue de la Juiverie and Rue des Rosiers are today still the place of an important Jewish community). In time of difficulties, the Jews (regarded as "murderers of Christ") were used as scapegoats, accused of all crimes, molested, and murdered, their wealth seized. By the time of King Louis IX, they were obliged to wear a distinctive yellow rouelle, an odious discriminating practice later renewed by the Nazis in the form of a yellow star of David bearing the label *Jude* (Jew). The most highly placed medieval men had a nervous constitution appreciably different from ours, which made them more resistant to physical pain although less capable of curbing their emotional fears and imaginative impulses. Their helplessness before the unexplained and uncontrolled forces of nature might explain the rash of superstition, the worship of relics, the terrifying fear of hell, and ruthless anti–Semitism.

The growth of Paris was characterized by the division into three distinct parts: *La Cité* (island), *l'Université* (left bank) and *la Ville* (right bank).

The Cité Island

The Ile de la Cité in the middle of the Seine served an obvious military purpose since the water constituted a natural barrier to an attacking force. It had also always had a political and religious function.

In the western part of the island was the royal palace, which covered nearly a third of the island. It was reconstructed during the reign of King Robert II the Pious (996–1031). The palace was a large rectangle, 110 m wide and 135 long, ending in the west in a large triangular garden. The complex housed the kings' palace, a great hall with adjoining chambers, the royal chapel, gardens and various buildings serving both residential and administrative purposes, and lodgings for servants and guards. The entire complex was fortified with an encircling wall reinforced with towers and a keep, known as the *Grosse Tour*, 25 m high, built by King Louis VI to protect the royal treasure and jewels. The palace functioned as the seat of national government. But government in the Middle Ages followed the person of the ruler and the kings were rarely stationary, so Paris was one of the most important governmental seats in France, but not the only one. Even when the king was absent, the fortified palace was a symbolic reminder of his authority.

The middle of the island was an area of economic activity concentrated around the Rue de la Juiverie (Jewry, today's Rue de la Cité), with two small harbors (Saint Landry and Notre Dame), as well as a hospital (Hôtel Dieu), merchants' houses and shops. The east side of the island was the domain of the Church with several buildings including oratories, a monastery, a church — later the Notre Dame cathedral — the bishop of Paris's palace, a cloister and the canons' chapel.

As ever, the island was linked to both banks by two fortified bridges. To the north was the *Grand Pont* (Great Bridge) defended by a stronghold, called the *Grand Châtelet*; the money changers — the bankers of the day — were grouped on this bridge which was also called *Pont au Change* (Exchange Bridge). To the south the *Petit Pont* (Small Bridge) was protected by a fortified tower, named the *Petit Châtelet*.

The University

The left bank of the Seine, the ancient Roman town on the gentle slope of the Montagne Saint Geneviève, which for centuries had been abandoned and had returned into fields and vineyards, was gradually reconstructed and repopulated. The left bank developed much more slowly than the right one, but it underwent substantial growth during the course of the 13th century. It derived its impetus from religious and educational rather than commercial institutions.

A new neighborhood called *Outre Petit Pont* (Beyond Small Bridge) developed on each side of the main axis, the Rue Saint Jacques. This street had his name (St. Jacques is St. James in English and Santiago in Spanish) from the starting point of an important medieval pilgrimage. The Rue Saint Jacques was bordered with inns, hostels, churches and other facilities for travelers as it was the start of a long way leading to the famous pilgrimage of Saint James of Compostella in northwestern Spain.

In the late 12th century, the teachers in Paris acquired an international reputation, and the scholastic population boomed and expanded onto the left bank. By the 13th century and the beginning of the 14th century, this part of town became host to colleges — about thirty in all. The most important colleges were the Sorbonne founded in 1253, the college of Harcourt in 1280, that of Cardinal Lemoine in 1302, the college of Navarre in 1304, and that of Montaigu in 1314. This district became the center of knowledge and was known as the *Université* (University) and today it still referred to as *Quartier Latin* (Latin Quarter). The University of Paris became one of the most famous in the Middle Ages, attracting intellectuals, students, masters, theologists and teachers from all over Europe.

The Ville

The bulk of the Parisian population lived on the right bank of the Seine to the north of the Cité island. The right bank of the Seine was known as *Outre Grand Pont* (Beyond Great Bridge) or more commonly the *Ville*, which was populated by *burghers* or *bourgeois*.

The country folk needed local markets, and the merchants and tradesmen needed safe stopping places on their journeys: hence the development of Paris's borough of Beyond Great Bridge. The existing economic settlements rapidly developed around the Saint Germain l'Auxerrois church and the Grève and Ecole harbors. The Seine was the best available means of commercial transport, and Parisian trade depended heavily on it. The Seine was one of France's principal rivers, wide enough to carry a great deal of traffic. Upriver was a network of waterways connecting Paris to the rich agricultural lands that provided much of the city's grain and wine. Downriver were Normandy and the English Channel. Since the 11th century, the *Nautæ Parisiaci* (Parisian inlands boat transporters)

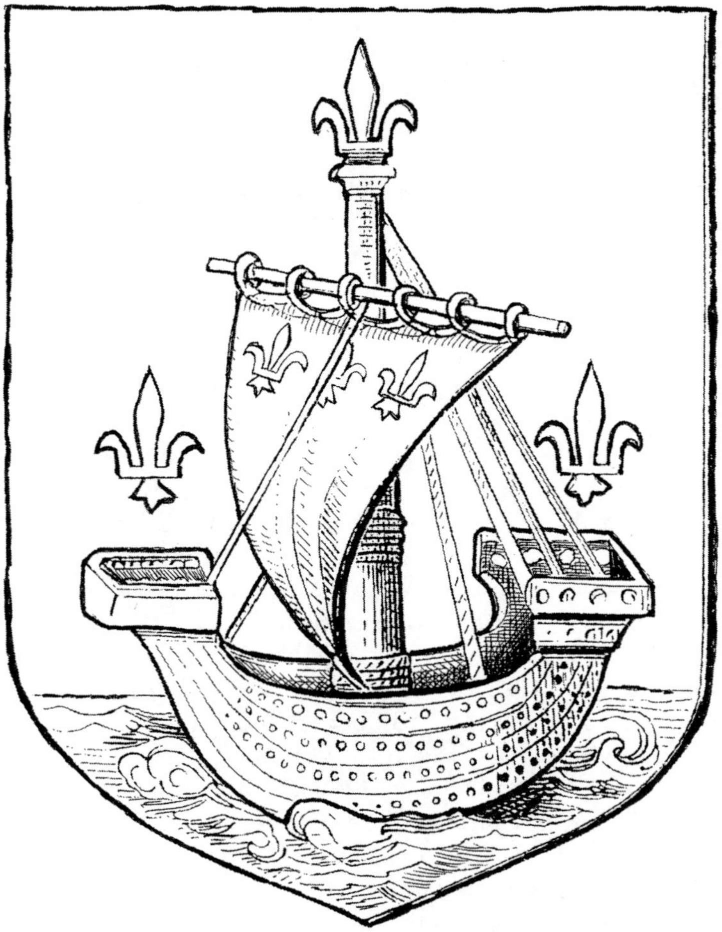

Left: **Emblem of Paris at the time of Philippe Auguste (1180–1223), In February 1190, king Philippe Auguste created a council of six aldermen (municipal magistrates) to represent Paris. At the same time he gave the city its emblem representing a sail boat with the motto: Fluctuat Nec Mergitur (Hit by Water but Never Sinking).** ***Right:*** **Emblem of Paris today.**

were a powerful economic group — and thus a significant political lobby — which gave Paris its emblem displaying a sail boat with the motto: *Fluctuat Nec Mergitur* (Hit by Water But Never Sinking) granted by king Philippe Auguste in 1190. Another important professional association was that of the butchers who were on the whole quite rich and had numerous aids armed with dangerous weapons at their command.

Farther to the north stretched the borough of Champeaux with craftsmen and traders; an important market for the sale of cloth, furs and small wares; and the Saint Innocents cemetery. The main axes were the Rue Saint Denis and Rue Saint Martin because Paris was also an important crossroad in France's land transportation system.

Paris was thus engaged in local trade; it offered commercial services for the hinterland, providing goods for rural buyers and receiving from them the agricultural produce needed to sustain its population. Paris was also a large craft center but one whose products were infinitely more diverse than those of the wool weaving town in Artois and Flanders; during the reign of Louis IX some 150 professional associations (guilds) were recorded. Paris was, in particular, a center for the art objects and luxury articles made in a multitude of workshops and not destined for local consumption. Indeed Paris was also involved in interurban commerce, exchanging commodities over longer distances with other French and foreign urban centers.

As already pointed out, the northern *Ville* seems to have been protected by a defensive wall build in the 10th century.

10

Capetians versus Plantagenets

Louis VII

Unlike his father Louis VI, whom he succeeded in 1137, Louis VII was not a very energetic character. In 1137, Louis VII (reign 1137–1180) married Eleanor of Aquitaine who brought to the French crown control over the splendid province which stretched all the way from Poitou to the Pyrenees. The new king was a pious and scrupulous man. Acting against the advice of his friend and councilor the abbot Suger, he decided to set off on the second Crusade which had been encouraged by Saint Bernard at Vezelay in 1147. Louis took his wife with him, but during the crusade, Elinor, brimming with vitality, discovered that she was married to a very boring man. Arguing that they were too closely related, she persuaded Louis to ask for the annulment of their marriage. The matrimonial dispensation on the ground of consanguinity was pronounced by a council of bishops in early 1152. As soon as she was repudiated, Elinor offered both her hand and her immense dowry to the Plantagenet Henry II.

The rise of the dynasty of Anjou began with Foulques V the Younger (1095–1143); by means of a series of successions and marriages, Foulques's son, Geoffroi Plantagenet (1113–1151), became count of Anjou, Touraine and Maine, duke of Normandy and pretender to the English throne. His son, Henry II (1133–1189), became king of England in 1154, and — with Elinor's dowry — the Anglo-Angevin empire was founded. In France it included the whole Atlantic shore, reaching from the northern province of Normandy to the southern Pyrenees. Its sheer size created an intolerable situation for the French Capetians, causing a long struggle which, including truces, was to last almost a hundred years.

By that time, the *opus francigenum* (French art, later called *Gothic art*) began to flourish. The use of the pointed arch and the flying buttress made it possible to build high church walls and light them abundantly with the daylight streaming through lavish stained glass windows. Statues became much more beautiful. The first stone of Notre Dame of Paris cathedral was laid by Bishop Maurice de Sully in 1162. The cathedral of Paris was built between 1163 and 1345. It was restored in 1841 and in 1864. A cathedral (Latin *cathedra* meaning chair) was the chief church of a diocese and contained the bishop's throne. Gothic art spread to the whole of western Christianity.

Philippe II Auguste

The reign of King Philippe II, from 1180 to 1223, got off to a good start. By marrying Isabelle de Hainaut he joined the rich northern province Artois to the royal demesne.

When Sultan Saladin captured Jerusalem in 1187, the Latin kingdom of Outremer in the Holy Land was in need of help. In July 1190, Philippe set off for the Third Crusade with king Richard the Lionhearted of England. The Crusade was, however, cut short. Both kings quarreled and Philippe quickly returned to France in 1191 and took advantage of the absence of Richard, who had been made prisoner on his return from the Holy Land by the emperor of Germany. Philippe undertook the conquest of the territories held by the Anglo Plantagenet. He captured the huge fortress of Château Gaillard in 1204 and regained the provinces of Berry, Normandy, Touraine and Anjou.

Meanwhile, in response to the appeal of the pope, the lords of northern France embarked on a crusade against the heretical Cathars in southern France.

The *Cathars* (also referred to as *Albigensians* because they were from the city of Albi) were members of a religious movement, a spiritual group trying to revert to the ideals of purity, poverty and austerity of the early Catholic teaching. Catharism also developed the concept of Manichaeism in which Good and Evil confronted each other in the world. The movement grew up from 1167 onwards in southern France around Toulouse, Foix, Albi and Carcassonne. The Cathar movement was condemned by the official Catholic Church, and Saint Dominic attempted to win over the heretics by means of persuasion. This method had little success and the conflict escalated from religious deviance into a political issue resulting in civil war, invasion and fanaticism. After several military expeditions and bloody massacres, the French monarchy succeeded in taking enormous advantage of the crisis by gradually integrating the southern territories into the king's estates. The southern part of France (then called *Occitania* and including Guienne, Languedoc, Toulouse and Provence) had remained distinct in many ways from the Capetian North; it had always been more Roman than German-Frankish and had evolved a civilization, a culture and a language of its own. Under the cover of religion, the whole Cathar affair was merely an excuse to open the Mediterranean Sea to the kings of France and the riches of the south to their subjects.

When Philippe II Auguste died in 1223, the royal demesne was greatly enlarged and the authority of the French sovereign was strengthened.

11

The Enceinte of Philippe II Auguste

The First Medieval Enceinte

Before leaving for the crusade in 1190, Philippe Auguste issued an edict to enhance the appearance and security of Paris by ordering the construction of a fortified wall.

Until Philippe II's reign, there had been no need—and probably not enough funds—to fortify Paris. Except for the Ile de la Cité, the capital of France was a defenseless open city largely spreading on both banks of the Seine with an estimated population of 50,000 inhabitants, making it one of the most important cities of Europe. By the end of the 12th century, the situation had changed. With the constant conflicts with the Anglo-Angevin-Plantagenets, it became a necessity to protect Paris.

The enceinte of Philippe Auguste served several purposes. Its primary function was military, but the wall was also an object of pride and prestige, a sign of independence, and a source of confidence and self-awareness for the crown. The fortifications showed the union of the king and his Parisian subjects; by defending the lives and wealth of his people, the king gained his rich bourgeois' respect and support, a precious trump for his struggle against his enemies. The newborn *bourgeoisie* and the Capetian monarchy had many common interests, e.g. the humbling of the powerful feudal vassals (including the Anglo-Plantagenet) and the establishment of peace and security for the development of a safe and fruitful business. The wall was certainly a stimulant to economic increase.

The enceinte also constituted a juridical border, it defined the urban space as distinct from the surrounding countryside and indicated the space to be populated. Fortifications were always very expensive but the Parisian wall was also an investment: it facilitated the collection of import and export taxes. Duties levied at the gates of Paris depended on the merchandise, but were typically 2 to 4 *deniers* (pence) for a wagonload, 1 to 2 *deniers* for a cartload and 1 *denier* for a horseload. The enceinte allowed to control entry and exit. It also worked as a dike against the dangerous floodings of the River Seine.

The fortifications were built around both the *Ville* in the north and the *Université* to the south. Thanks to archaeology and remnants, the outline is known perfectly.

On the northern right bank, the walls enclosed *Outre-Grand-Pont* with the boroughs of Marais, Beaubourg, Saint-Paul, les Halles and Saint-Germain-l'Auxerrois approximatively following the tracé of the actual Rue des Jardins-Saint-Paul, Rue Mahler, Rue des Francs-Bourgeois, Rue Barbette, Rue aux Ours, Rue de Tiquetone, Rue Montmartre, Rue du Louvre, and ended in the actual Cour Carrée in the Louvre Museum.

On the southern left bank of the Seine, the fortifications enclosed *Outre-Petit-Pont*, including the boroughs of Saint-Germain-des-Prés and Saint-Victor, and followed the actual Rue Mazarine, Rue de l'Ancienne Comédie, Rue Monsieur le Prince, Rue Soufflot, Rue de l'Estrapade, Rue du Cardinal Lemoine, Rue des Fossés-Saint-Bernard, and ended up by the Seine near the actual Sully bridge. Paris counted then eight boroughs: five in the Ville, two in the University and one in the Cité islands; these were divided into parishes, merging administrative and religious functions.

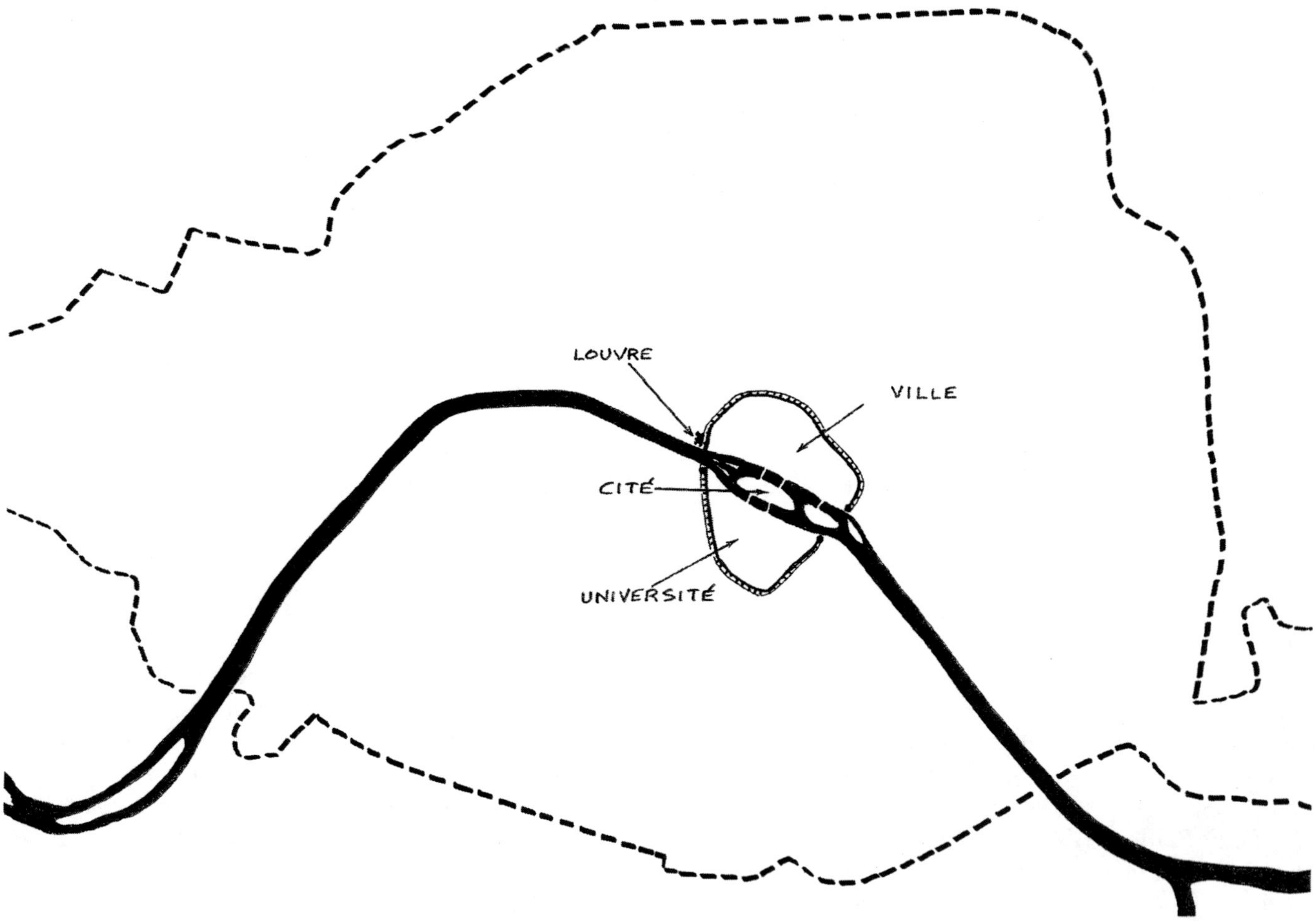

Philippe Auguste's city wall (1190–1210). The dotted line indicates the actual administrative limits of Paris.

The Enceinte: Too Large?

In all, the wall had a length of about 5,200 m (2,500 m on the right bank and 2,700 on the left bank), enclosing a surface of 250 hectares.

Compared to other French city walls, e.g. Avignon (4,300 m), Carcassone (1,672 m) or Aigues-Mortes (1,600 m), the enceinte of Philippe Auguste seemed immoderately large and possibly beyond measure. There were indeed large unoccupied areas, with scattered houses standing here and there amid farms, stables, barns, fields, vegetable gardens, vineyards, meadows, and fallow lands. The town produced a part of the food it needed and consumed every day—including milk and wine. But it was intended that the population would rapidly grow. And indeed, just about a century after the construction of Philippe's enceinte, the population reached 200,000 and all space was occupied.

Paris followed a typical pattern of settlement, characterized by a fairly compact urban area in close contact with agricultural land. A Parisian dweller was no more than a few minutes' walk from the farmer's fields.

The defenses of Paris were thus particularly magnificent for their age, reflecting the importance of the city and its royal overlord. The whole enceinte was amazingly quickly built given the poor technology of these days. The construction of the wall was begun in 1190 and completed in 1212. In general, lesser towns were much slower to build stone walls. Earthern ramparts and wooden palisades were still in use in many places during the 12th century and even later. Stone walls were principally a feature of larger cities since small towns lacked the resources for such major works projects.

Financing

The construction of Philippe Auguste's enceinte was a collective undertaking financed by both the king and the rich Parisian bourgeois. The fortifications on the right

Opposite: **Philippe Auguste's enceinte**

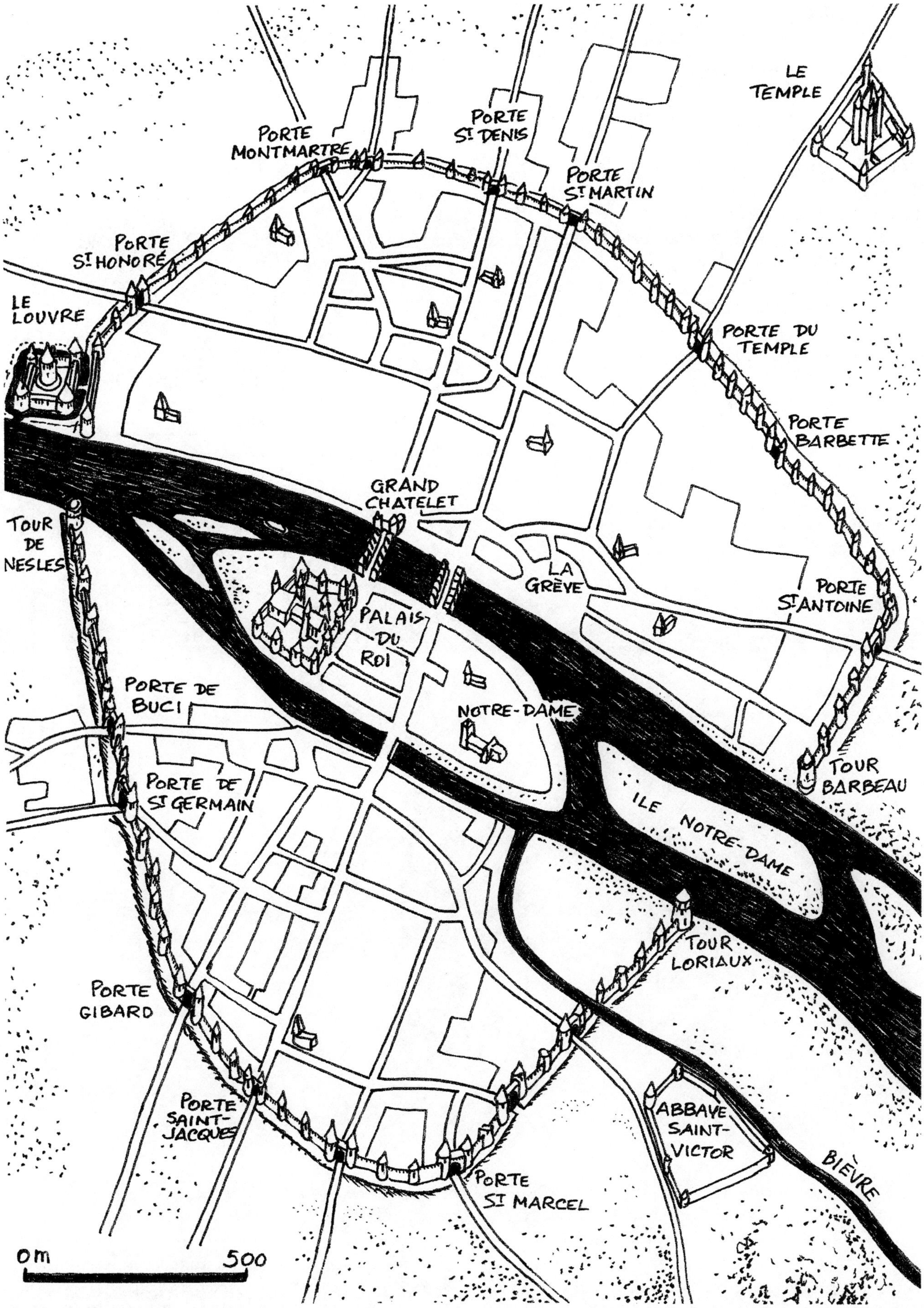

LE TEMPLE
PORTE St DENIS
PORTE MONTMARTRE
PORTE St MARTIN
PORTE St HONORÉ
LE LOUVRE
PORTE DU TEMPLE
PORTE BARBETTE
GRAND CHATELET
TOUR DE NESLES
LA GRÈVE
PORTE St ANTOINE
PALAIS DU ROI
PORTE DE BUCI
NOTRE-DAME
TOUR BARBEAU
PORTE DE St GERMAIN
ILE NOTRE-DAME
TOUR LORIAUX
PORTE GIBARD
PORTE SAINT-JACQUES
ABBAYE SAINT-VICTOR
PORTE St MARCEL
BIÈVRE
0m
500

bank were built at the expense of the citizenry of Paris; the cost of the defenses on left bank was covered by the king himself. From surviving royal accounts we know that the left bank wall was nearly a mile and a half long and cost 50 *sous* per yard, and that the gates cost 120 *livres* each; its total cost was over 7,000 *livres*, a fortune for the time.

In time of war, the walls and towers were manned by a few professional soldiers and by the *guet* (watch), a municipal militia drawn from the traders and craftsmen of Paris. This militia was organized in companies, and each unit, headed by a captain, was assigned to man a part of the ramparts. The *guet* was also used as a police force, patrolling the city at night during the *couvre-feu* (curfew) from dusk to dawn.

Cross section wall and tower in Philippe Auguste's enceinte.

Evolution of Urban Fortification

The evolution of urban military architecture was directly connected to castle fortification, and most elements used to protect castles were applied in the protection of towns—basically including ditches, walls, towers and gatehouses. Until the introduction of reliable firearms in the Renaissance, the concept of defense focused on two major ideas in order to counteract the main means of attack. Verticality was the key to opposing assault by ladder and allowed the defenders to benefit from a high position. Sturdiness and thickness of walls permitted them to resist the battering ram and underground mining.

The only difference was that a private castle housed a tiny group of combatants and their servants in a small space, while a town embraced a rather large number of noncombatant inhabitants whose lives and activities were spread over a relatively large surface. The configuration of a fortified town was the result of difficult compromises between the requirements of defense, which demanded inaccessibility, and living and working conditions, which tended on the contrary to establish the city near a commercial road, to develop the land and to provide many access points.

Little is known about the technical details of Philippe's enceinte. But owing to remnants built at the same time by Philippe elsewhere (e.g. La Ferté-Milon, Laon, Soissons, Bourges, Montreuil-sur-Mer, Mennetou-

Castle 14th century. Most features of castle military architecture were applied to fortify a medieval town. The main elements were as follows: 1. Donjon (keep), often the oldest part of the castle. 2. Wall (curtain) with crenellated breastwork and chemin-de-ronde (wallwalk). 3. Tower (cylindrical, square or U-shaped, open or covered with a roof). 4. Hoarding. 5. Gatehouse with draw-bridge. 6. Wet ditch (could be a river). 7. Barbican (added end of 15th century). 8. Breteche and postern (sally-port). 9. Palisade. 10. Dry ditch. 11. Artillery tower (added end of 15th century). 12. Bailey (yard) with service buildings, lodgings, well, chapel, stables, stores etc. In the background a village has developed under the protection of the castle.

sur-Cher, and Vierzon), we may deduce some common features.

Wall

The Parisian wall (called in the military jargon *courtine* or *curtain*) was constructed according to the traditional Roman method. This included an inner and an outer masoned stone revetment with loose rock, earth, gravel, sand and other material filling the intervening space. A fragment of Philippe Auguste's wall in the Rue Clovis displays this method of construction very well. The vertical courtine was between 2.60 m and 3.40 m thick at the base (to thwart undermining, sapping and ramming) and about 2.30 m thick at the top. Its average height was between 8 and 10 m — enough to oppose assault by scaling ladder. Each part of the wall between two towers was straight, rather than curved, in order to reduce *blind spots* (areas below and beyond which the ground cannot be seen and fired at by the defenders). The top of the wall was furnished with a man-high breastwork protecting a *chemin de ronde* (wallwalk). The breastwork (also called *parapet*) was crenellated, which means that it was composed of a succession of *crenels* (voids through which the defenders could shoot with cross-bow or bow, or throw javelins); these apertures alternated with standing parts, called *merlons*, behind which the defenders could seek cover. Staircases gave access from the terre-plein to the wall-walk.

Towers

The Parisian wall was reinforced with cylindrical stone towers which were often given a name, at least the

Above: **Loophole (arrow slit) seen from outside.** ***Right:*** **Pepper-pot turret.**

strongest of them. The number of towers varies with the historians, some say sixty, others seventy, and still others seventy-seven. Towers were placed at a distance of 60 to 70 m from one another, a distance calculated according to the range of bow and cross-bow (the effective range of a cross-bow was about 100 m). On average, their diameter was between 6 and 7 m, their wall was 1.30 to 2 m thick and their height was about 13 m. They rose higher than the wall itself, providing maximum visibility for the defenders, who normally used the towers as their principal bases for defense. The towers also provided shelter against the weather, an important consideration to keep the morale of the guards and because rain lessened the effectiveness of the defenders' bows. The base of the towers was strengthened by a thick sloping apron or a buttress providing stability and protection against ramming. Towers were strongholds arranged for active defense; the summit was either covered with a roof or arranged as an open crenellated terrace. The inside of the tower was divided into stories (generally three) arranged for various purpose e.g. supply store, shelter for the guards etc. The stories were linked up by staircases and ladders, and their walls probably furnished with narrow openings (called *arrow slits* or *loopholes*) through which guards could observe and shoot at enemies with bows. The towers projected from the wall in order to *flank* the curtains, that was shooting

Opposite: **Loophole seen from inside.**

an enfilade fire nearly parallel to the wall; a few cross-bowmen and archers placed inside or on top of the tower could thus observe and defend a whole length of courtine at both sides. *Pepper-pot towers* were also built; these were overhanging watch turrets resting on corbel on top of the wall; they had the same flanking combat function as normal towers, but they were much cheaper to build.

The top of the walls and that of the towers could be fitted with nonpermanent *hoard* (also called *hourd*, *brattice* or *propugnacla*). This was a temporary wooden gallery built on the outside of the breastwork when war threatened. The hoard rested on beams on which planks were laid, constituting a second parapet overhanging the wall. The purpose was to permit the foot of the wall or of the tower to be covered by the defenders from above, as holes were made in the flooring; through these apertures the defenders could shoot or drop various projectiles, e.g. arrows, javelins and stones on enemies attempting a sapping or mining operation. As Philippe Auguste's enceinte was never tested at war, it is not known with certainty whether the defenses of Paris were fully equipped with hoarding.

Curiously the enceinte of Philippe Auguste was not surrounded with a proper ditch, only a vague excavation intended to collect rain waters. This wide excavation running all around the fortification, at the foot of the walls, towers and gatehouses would have formed a serious obstacle to an attacker. It was only in 1356 that a dry ditch was dug all around the fortifications.

Gates

At the junction of the existing main streets and the new walls, *portes* (gates) were erected. On the left bank of the river

Archer. Bow and arrows had been used as a weapon of war for centuries. Archers played an important role as much on the battlefield as in siege warfare. The superior English longbow was developed in the time of King Edward III (1312–1377), and soon represented a serious threat to the supremacy of the armored mounted knight, as the heavy French cavalry discovered at the battle of Crécy in August 1346.

these were the Porte Saint-Bernard, Porte Saint-Victor, Porte Saint-Marcel, Porte Saint-Jacques, Porte Saint-Michel, Porte Saint-Germain, Porte d'Enfer, and Porte Gibard. On the right bank of the Seine were the Porte Saint-Honoré, Porte Montmartre, Porte Saint-Denis, Porte Saint-Martin, Porte Barbette near the temple and Porte Saint-Antoine. The portes formed weak points in the city's perimeter wall, since they were by definition points of access. Of course, they were heavily fortified by powerful gatehouses which had on the whole the same structure as a castle gatehouse. The gatehouse included a wide arched portal large enough to let a cart through. The

Postern

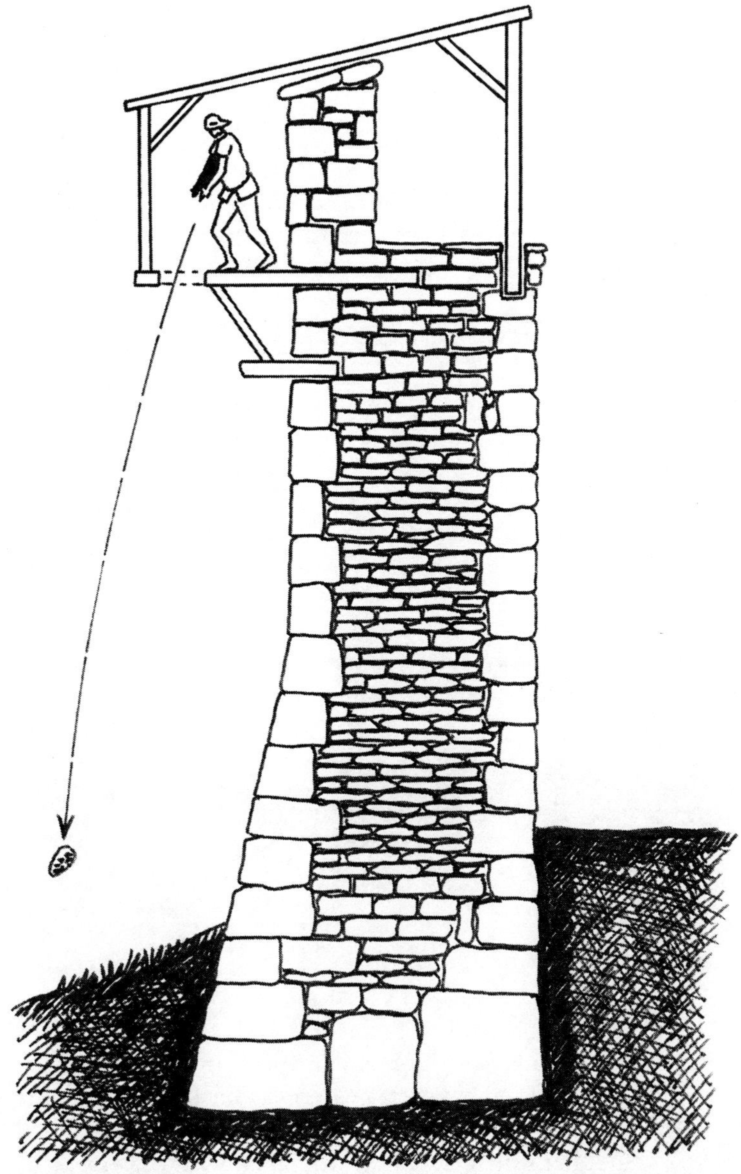

Cross section wall with hoarding

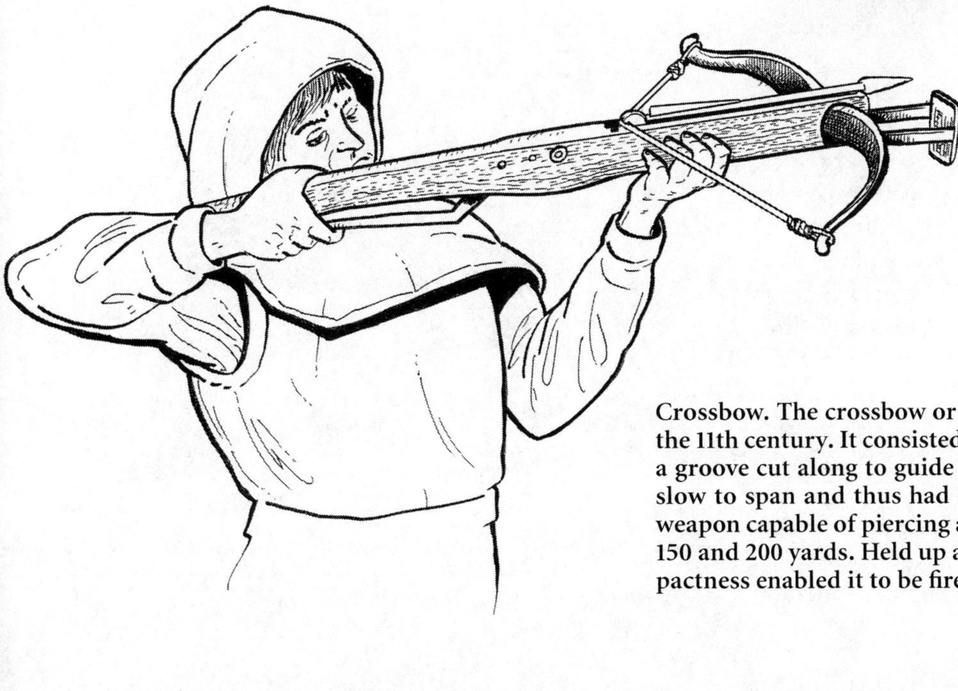

Crossbow. The crossbow or arbalest appeared as a weapon of war in the 11th century. It consisted of a short bow mounted on a stock, with a groove cut along to guide the quarrel or bolt (short arrow). It was slow to span and thus had a slow rate of fire but it was a powerful weapon capable of piercing a knight's body armor at a range between 150 and 200 yards. Held up and aimed very much like a rifle, its compactness enabled it to be fired easily from behind defensive walls.

Front view (left) and cross section (right) of a portcullis.

portal was arranged either into a rectangular building or a mural tower through which the entryway passed, or deeply recessed between a pair of strong flanking towers. Until 1356, there was no proper ditch, but we may presume that some gates were equipped with drawbridges; it probably was a simple roadway raised and lowered by chains or cables taken into the façade through sloping holes and wound upon a windlass for closed position. The portal included heavy wooden doors, which were reinforced with big nails. The gates also might have included a *portcullis* (also called *herse*)—a strong wooden barrier which could be vertically raised by a windlass placed on the first floor of the building and instantly lowered by its own weight. Active combat emplacements included battlements, crenellated turrets, and shooting-chambers equipped with loopholes, allowing bowmen to defend the entry against attack.

Besides military defensive elements, the city gatehouse also included a custom office where taxes and tolls were levied on all persons and all goods coming in or going out of the city. The gate taxes were one of the major forms of income for medieval cities. The gatehouse was obviously a highly guarded point and might also include

Draw-bridge

Gatehouse in Philippe Auguste's enceinte

Top: Saint Honoré Gatehouse. ***Bottom:*** Tour Hamelin (tour de Nesles). The tower was known for a scandal in 1315. The three princesses of Bourgogne, Marguerite, Jeanne and Blanche, received there their lovers. They were caught and imprisoned in the fortress of Château-Gaillard in Normandy.

Grand Châtelet

an arsenal for weapons and ammunition, apartments and lodgings for civil servants, tax collectors and guards. The city gatehouse also played a prestigious and symbolical role: its imposing defenses displayed the strength and power of the king of France and ornaments showed with ostentation to visitors and travelers the wealth and importance of its citizens. For security reasons access to Paris was as limited as possible, resulting on many occasions in annoying traffic jams, particularly on market days; therefore secondary accesses—called *posterns*—were arranged and opened in peace time. From dusk to dawn, gates and posterns were closed.

Defense by the Seine

The Seine bisected the enceinte, and thus formed an access for eventual invaders, as the Vikings had done before. The river was much too wide to construct water gates but special works were built to defend those weak areas in the defense. In the east on the right bank, there was a strong tower, named *tour Barbeau*; on the opposite side, another tower was erected named *tour Loriaux*; between both towers a long iron chain could be stretched to hinder navigation. On the left bank in the West, a large tower was built, named *tour Hamelin*; this tower was 10 m in diameter and 25 m high; in the 16th century the name was changed to *tour de Nesles*. Facing the tour Hamelin on the right bank, Philippe Auguste undertook the construction of a large fortress, the *Louvre*, which will be further described. There too, between the tour Hamelin and the Louvre, a strong chain could be stretched to forbid the navigation on the river in case of danger.

Grand Châtelet and Petit Châtelet

The *Grand Châtelet*, on the right bank, was originally a large wooden tower erected about 870 by king Charles the Simple to defend the Grand Pont, north of the Ile de la Cité. The tower was replaced by a stone building ordered by King Louis VI in 1130. Throughout the Middle Ages, it was constantly reshaped and enlarged to become a sort of castle. With the development of Paris and the construction of Philippe Auguste's enceinte, the fortress lost its defensive function. It became the head-

Petit Châtelet

quarters of the provost of Paris, an officer appointed by the crown to oversee the conduct of the various trades practiced in the city. The building also included a prison. The provost's men were also employed as a police force, the *guet* or *watch*. The Grand Châtelet was demolished in 1802 by order of Napoléon I. Today it is a large square with a fountain called Place du Châtelet and is bordered by theaters and restaurants.

The *Petit Châtelet*—originally built in 885—was placed on the southern right bank of the Seine. It was a fortified building intended to defend the bridge from the Rue Saint Jacques to the Cité Island. It included walls and turrets 16 m high and 2 m thick. Like its counterpart on the opposite bank, the Petit Châtelet lost a great part of its military function and became an administrative building. Both Châtelets also played a symbolic role; they were displays of royal strength and reminders of the king's authority.

Opposite: **The Louvre (after a 19th century engraving). The royal castle is seen here from the Seine.**

12

The Louvre

Additional security for Paris was provided by the royal castle known as the Louvre, constructed between 1200 and 1202 just outside the southern corner of the right bank wall. The origin of the term *louvre* (*lupera* or *louver*) is quite unknown, some historians believe it originated from a fortified camp or a hunting lodge built at the early Frankish time.

The Louvre seems to have been designed by the king's architect, Raymond du Temple. It was a powerful fortress dominated by a strong cylindrical keep, 31 m

SEINE

high, 18.5 m in diameter, with walls 4 m thick. Its top was crenellated and arranged as a combat and observation post, offering guards an unsurpassed view of the countryside, and allowing them ample advance warning of any approaching hostile forces. The keep, at the heart of the castle, was hemmed in by a square stone wall (about 100 x 100 m) composed of crenellated curtains, towers, and a 12.50 m broad ditch filled with waters provided by the Seine.

The castle had two accesses, one to the east, the other to the south, both furnished with strong gatehouses including defensive elements, portcullis and drawbridges. These accesses allowed the king to go in and come out of his castle without having to get inside Paris. Guards were always on duty at the gates, and prospective visitors were required to speak to them or report to their officer—called the *concierge* or *porter*—before gaining admission. Access to the Louvre was generally restricted to those having legitimate business within. To minimize intrusions into its grounds, many businesses were transacted in the gatehouse itself. The gatehouse was used as a residence for the porter; it was furnished with apartments to accommodate him and his household, as well as lodgings for the guards. The Louvre was thus completely independent from the Parisian system of defense; it may therefore be termed a *citadel*, an urban fortress that could be defended even if the city was taken. Its independence also made it a safe place for the king to retreat in case of a popular uprising.

The Louvre was a residence including large royal apartments, a hall for meetings, feasts and justice, a chapel with an attached sacristy, service buildings, stables, gardens, a menagerie with exotic animals, cellars and supply stores, and lodging for guards and servants. The fortress was also an arsenal and an armory where war machines, weapons and ammunition were stored, maintained and repaired. The keep was also a safe where the royal treasures, archives and jewels were stored, as well as the product of the collection of taxes. The Louvre had also a strong symbolic function, as clearly shown on the miniature painted by the brothers Pol, Hennequin and Hermann of Limburg (*October* from *Les Très Riches Heures du Duc de Berry*). The royal fortress was a place of decorated extravagance in which there was a happy amalgam of strength and beauty. The Louvre displayed the prestige, the authority and the strength of the king of France, with gleaming white walls, towers, turrets, chimneys, red tile roofs tipped with golden finials, pennants flying and other highly sophisticated appurtenances intended to create a fantastically bright and gay structure. Even from a distance, the castle was an outstanding presence in its surroundings, commanding the skyline for miles around.

The Louvre progressively lost its military function. The large central keep was demolished in 1529. During the following centuries, the building was partly demolished and reshaped, widely enlarged and totally transformed successively by François I, Henri II, Catherine de Medicis, Henri IV, Louis XIII, Louis XIV, Napoléon and Louis XVIII to become a magnificent palace. From King Philippe Auguste to President François Mitterand, 800 years of construction have made the Museum of Art we have today.

Opposite: **Louvre Castle in Paris (from a Musée Carnavalet document)**

13

The Temple

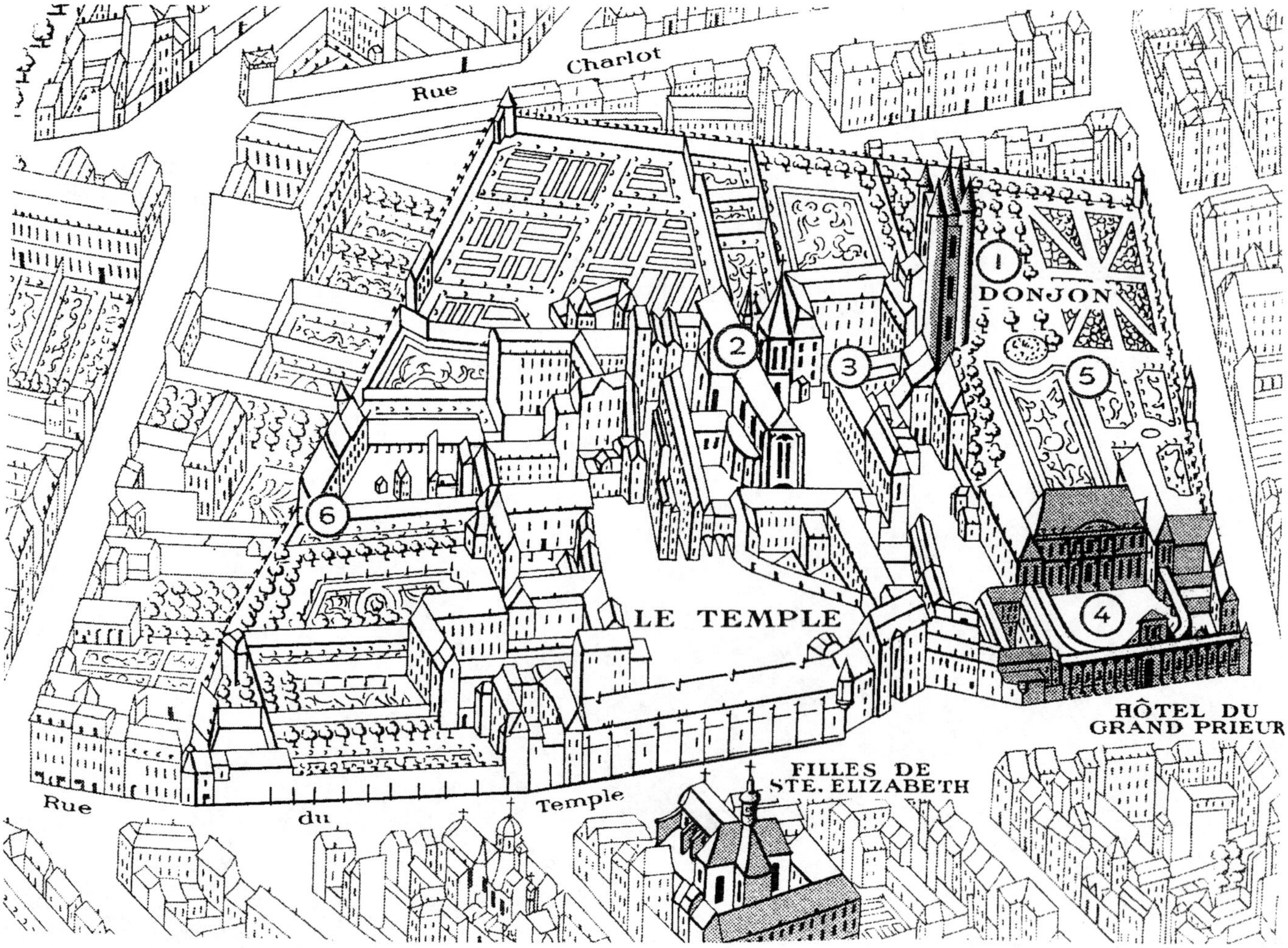

The Temple in 1734 (after Turgot). 1. Keep (Tour de César). 2. Church. 3. Conventual buildings. 4. Residence of the Grand Prior. 5. Garden. 6. Guest house.

Outside Philippe Auguste's wall was another fortress: the *Commanderie du Temple*.

In the 12th century the crusading zeal of the European aristocracy was joined with monastic asceticism and organization to create the military orders of Templars, Hospitallers of Saint John and Teutonics.

The Order of the Temple was created in 1118 near the Temple of Solomon in Jerusalem — whence its name. The knights Templar lived in communities under a monastic rule (including vows of poverty, chastity and obedience), but their primary purpose was warfare in the defense of the Christian states established by the Crusaders in the Holy Land. The monks/soldiers formed a military/police force to protect the Holy Land, to escort pilgrims and funds and to fight the "Turks." The popular Templars became extremely wealthy from gifts and donations, from the good management of their own properties, and from the profit made by their numerous estates. While a part of the Order resided and fought in Palestine, other brethren formed the administrative and logistical branch in Europe.

About 1140, the Templars had purchased a large piece of ground in the northeastern part of Paris and gradually built a fortified place for their monastic community, corresponding today with the quadrilateral formed by the actual Rue du Temple, Rue de Bretagne, Rue de Picardie and Rue Béranger. The domain — known as the *Enclos du Temple*— was fortified with the usual monastic facilities including gardens, a hospital and a guest house, chapels, a cloister, a cemetery, a conventual church, but also storehouses, stables, a palace for the prior, a hall, houses and lodging for about 4,000 people including knights, lay brothers, and chaplains of the Order, as well as craftsmen, peasants and traders working for them. The establishment was hemmed in by an 8 m-high crenellated wall and flanked with seventeen cylindrical towers, and its access was covered by a strong gatehouse with portal and drawbridge. The most impressive feature of the domain was the enormous keep called *Tour du Colombier* or *Tour de César*. Completed about 1305, the keep was a large square building with four turrets at each corner. It was 50 m high and its walls were 2.30 m thick.

It was not without reason that the Commanderie of the Temple was so strongly fortified. The establishment was the General Head-Quarters of the Templars in France. Other international "provinces" of the Order included Portugal, Castile and Leon, Aragon, Majorque, Germany, Italy, Apuly and Sicily, England and Ireland. Moreover, the Order had become an international banking structure, a trustworthy financier, a convenient capital holder, a flourishing commercial business, a naval power, the administrator in the care of European possessions and — as money opens all doors— a political lobby, a group of pressure, and a diplomat in international dealings. The Templar accountants assumed the function of financial counselor and creditor to the kings of France. As early as 1148, the Templars had lent money to king Louis VII of France to finance the Second Crusade. Before leaving for the Third Crusade in 1190, King Philippe Auguste entrusted them with the keeping and management of the treasury of the realm. In 1295, they lent important funds to finance Philippe IV's war against England.

After the fall of Acre in 1291, the last outpost of the Latin kingdom in Palestine had fallen and the Templars withdrew to their European estates, and the *Enclos du Temple* at Paris became their main base. The order — perceived to be dangerous, too wealthy and corrupt — became unpopular. Their untouchable wealth, their many privileges made them a law unto themselves in the countries of western Europe where they had lands— particularly in France. By 1304, there were rumors (probably false) about corruption, homosexuality, devil worship and irreligious and blasphemous acts committed by the Templars during their secret rites of initiation. In 1307, king of France Philippe le Bel (reign from 1285 to 1314) thought of a way to unlock them. Why Philippe sought to destroy the Templars remains unclear but it seemed that he saw an opportunity to seize the Order's wealth, being chronically short of money himself. The king and his chancellor, Guillaume de Nogaret, organized a cynical and squalid conspiracy. With forged evidence, they accused the Templars of various crimes and heresy. All Templars in France were arrested, some were tortured and confessed the alleged crimes. In 1317, after ten years of disparaging and false accusations, the damage done to their reputation was irreversible and Pope Clement V (himself a Frenchman elected with Philippe le Bel's support) reluctantly agreed to issue a papal bulle suppressing the Order in France, Germany and England. The leadership of the Templars— including the grand master Jacques de Moley — were burnt alive at the stake after refusing to confess to the charges of heresy and blasphemy, or for recanting confessions extracted under torture. The Templars' properties were officially handed over to the rival Hospitaller Order but most of the wealth went into the French king's coffers.

Until the French Revolution of 1789, the *enclos* and the huge keep were the property of the Hospitaller military order, whose headquarters was located in Malta since 1530. In 1791, all monastic orders were abolished in revolutionary France, and their possessions confiscated. The domain of the Hospitallers was proclaimed national possession, the knights-monks were expelled and the keep served as a state prison. The most famous prisoners were

Louis XVI and the royal family in August 1792. The king was executed on January 20, 1793, the queen in October. Their young son, who—if he had reigned—would have been Louis XVII, died in the Temple dungeon on June 8, 1795. The keep and the enceinte were demolished by order of Napoléon I in 1809 to avoid the formation of a monarchist place of pilgrimage. Today the Templar *commanderie* remains only in the Parisian toponymy. The once prestigious establishment has given several names to the neighborhood: the *Marché du Temple* (market), the *Square du Temple* (small public garden) and two streets, *rue du Temple* and *rue Vieille-du-Temple.*

Opposite: **Temple donjon. The Temple was originally protected by defenses including a ditch, a portal with drawbridge covered by a powerful gatehouse and two towers. The keep also called Ceasar's Tower was the core of the demesne.**

14

Paris at the Time of Saint Louis and Philippe the Fair

Louis VIII and Louis IX

The reign of Louis VIII The Lion (1223–1226), the son of Philippe Auguste was short but fruitful. The king took a particular interest in the Albigensian/Cathar affair and mounted another crusade against them in 1226. He took Avignon, Beaucaire and Carcassone, establishing his authority in the southern provinces. When Louis VIII died, his son, the heir to the throne, the future Saint Louis IX (1226–1270), was only twelve years old and his mother, the Spanish Blanche of Castile, governed the kingdom with a firm hand. She married the young Louis IX to Marguerite de Provence, a move that greatly enhanced the influence of the Capetians in the southeast of France.

When Louis IX was old enough to rule by himself, his first action was to put an end to the Albigensian affair by signing the Treaty of Meaux in 1229. Like Philippe Auguste, Louis IX was a chivalrous knight and a land collector. He acquired the whole of Languedoc, brought the duke of Brittany to his senses in 1234, and extended his rule in all directions. He defeated the English Plantagenet king Henry III at Taillebourg in 1246 and — preferring peace to a latent state of war — signed the Treaty of Paris in 1259. So came an end to the long and exhausting conflict between Capetian France and Angevine Plantagenet England.

Louis IX astonished his subjects by showing great virtues; he was authoritarian but not harsh, and generous without excess. He was a firm king who, for example, refused to intervene in the conflict opposing Emperor Frederick II of Germany and the papacy. Straight dealing won for Saint Louis a prestige hitherto unknown. He gained a reputation of fairness and impartiality, and from the four corners of Europe came requests for his arbitrage. Dukes and even kings asked him to settle quarrels, and, almost always, disputants bowed to his judgment.

He was also a pious man — a superstitious bigot who collected countless relics at high cost — and was inflexible and ruthless towards all heretics, particularly the Cathars, and Jews. In 1244 he took the cross to save the moribund Latin kingdom of Jerusalem. In 1249 he led the Seventh Crusade and won the battle of Damiette in Egypt but was taken prisoner and released after paying a huge ransom. In 1254 he returned to France and reformed the administration, lowered taxes and did a lot to promote trade. Yet he was constantly haunted by the need to defend the Holy Land and organized the Eighth Crusade. However, from sheer fatigue, the king died outside Tunis on August 15, 1270.

Louis IX's death was bitterly lamented by the French people. He had built such a reputation that he was the only French king to be elevated to the status of saint: he was canonized by the Church as Saint Louis.

French Predominance

The reign of Louis IX marked indeed the high point of the Middle Ages. It initiated a period of French predominance in Europe that was to endure for over five

Sainte Chapelle (Paris)

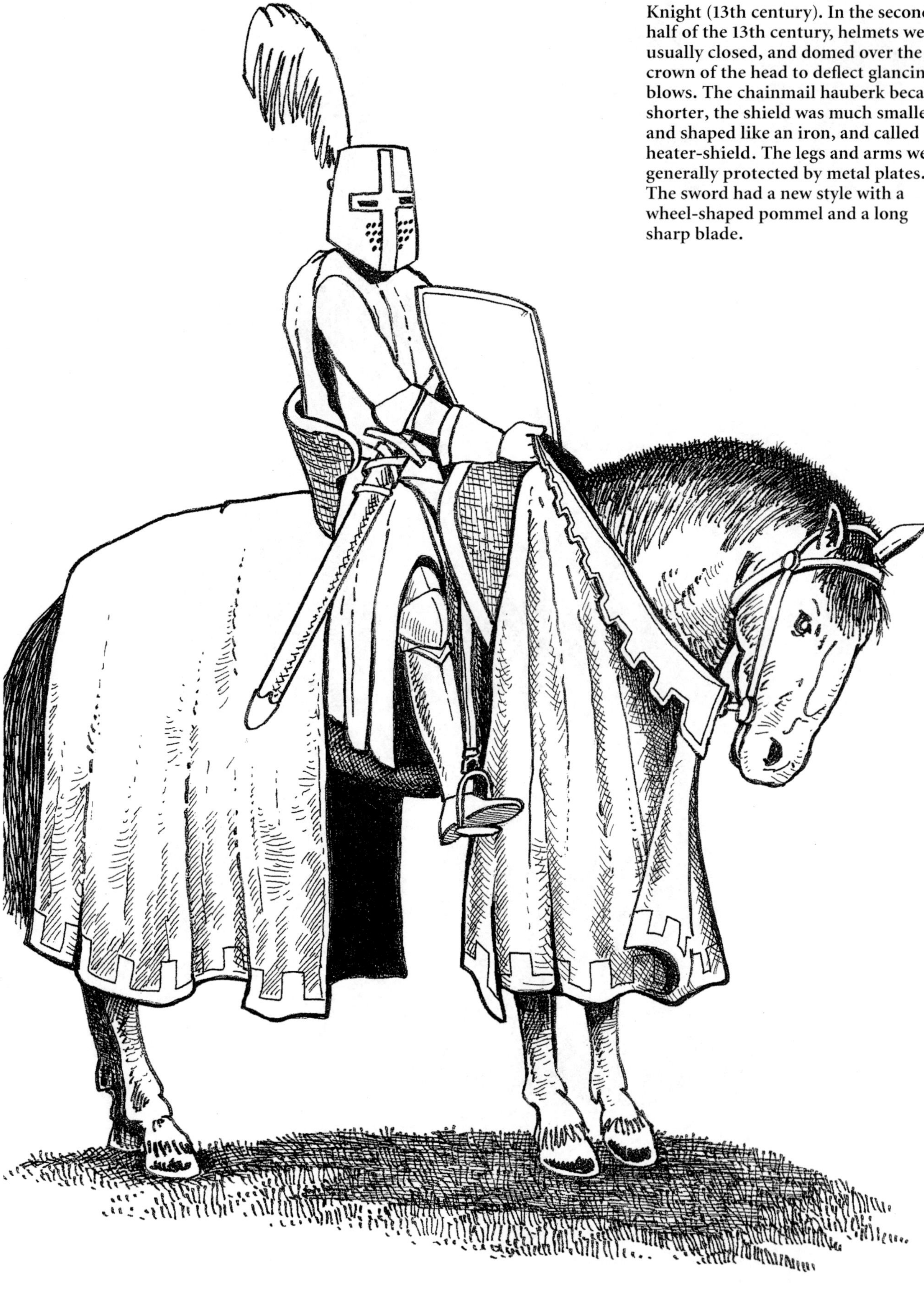

Knight (13th century). In the second half of the 13th century, helmets were usually closed, and domed over the crown of the head to deflect glancing blows. The chainmail hauberk became shorter, the shield was much smaller and shaped like an iron, and called heater-shield. The legs and arms were generally protected by metal plates. The sword had a new style with a wheel-shaped pommel and a long sharp blade.

Medieval cog. In the 12th and 13th centuries significant naval improvements had appeared: the stern rudder, deep-draught hull, better sailing techniques and rigging. The sturdy medieval one-masted cog (or Kogge) was a sea-worthy vessel, an effective compromise between warship and merchant. The cog was clinker-built, on average it was about 27 m in length and 7.2 m in width; the lone mast situated midship carried a large 185 square m rectangular sail. Well into the 15th century, the cog was the most prominent European ship.

centuries; his prestige enhanced the reputation of France, the credit of the Capetian dynasty, and the fortune of Paris. The town was then a true capital, a place of life, a center for the production and exchange of goods and services, a religious, cultural and administrative center, and the seat of political power. Henceforth any event, rebellion or revolution happening in Paris had direct consequences for the whole of France.

By the end of the 13th century, French culture radiated over all Europe. The French language evolved from the dialect spoken in and around Paris. Called *francien*, this language derived from Latin appealed to an ever-increasing number of people. It was the language of culture, big business, top politics, chivalry — in fact the language of the European élite. By this time the University of Paris had become fully organized, received its statutes from the pope, and was recognized as an autonomous body by Louis IX in 1231. The University of Paris enjoyed an extraordinary reputation; it became an unrivalled seat of learning, attracting the greatest thinkers of the age: Albertus Magnus from Germany, Bonaventura of Tuscany, and the greatest metaphysical genius Saint Thomas Aquinas.

Gothic art was then really at its height, as shown at the magnificent Sainte Chapelle in Paris; built between 1243 and 1248, the chapel of the kings of France was designed as one tall room with, except for a low dado-zone, walls entirely of glass. The Royal Palace of the Isle of Cité and the Sainte Chapelle are vividly depicted in the month of June in the book *Les Très Riches Heures du Duc de Berry*.

Philippe IV the Fair

Philippe III the Bold (1270–1285) lacked the qualities of his father Saint Louis, but his son and successor Philippe IV le Bel — the Fair — (1285–1314) was quite a different sort of person. He was a "modern" and unscrupulous king who surrounded himself with legists, lawyers

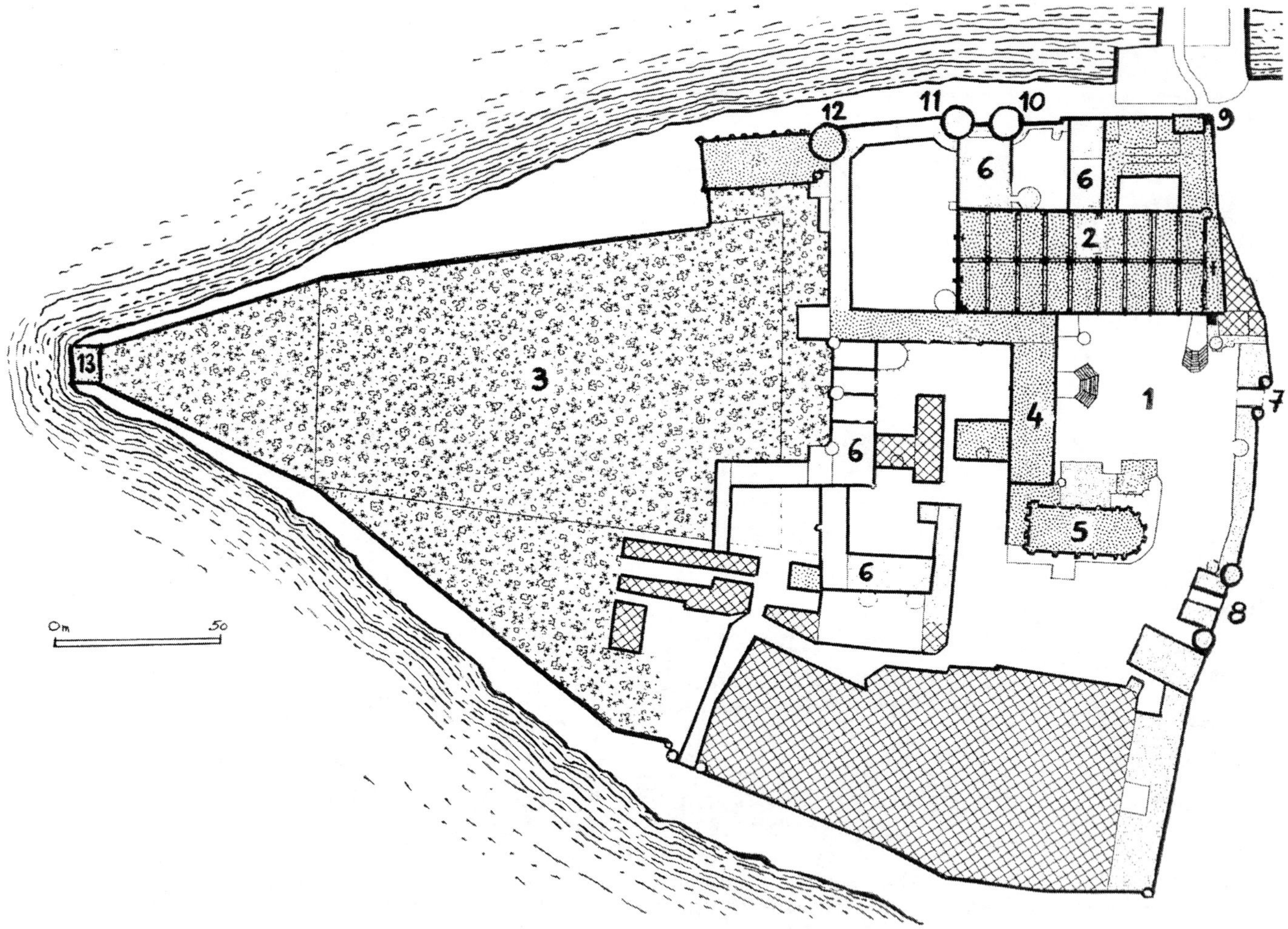

The Royal Palace in the Isle de la Cité about 1425 (after Jean Guérout). The ground plan shows the palace situated at the western point of the Cité Island. 1. Great Yard. 2. Conciergerie. 3. Gardens. 4. Saint Chapelle (built by Philippe Auguste). 5. King's House. 6. Service buildings. 7. Main Gate. 8. Saint Michel Gate. 9. Tour de l'Horloge. 10. Tour de César. 11. Tour d'Argent. 12. Tour Bonbec. 13. Point Tower.

and advisers who assisted his government and provided justifications for his frequently arbitrary acts. In his eyes, the *raison d'état* (interest of the state) was supreme, and he did not hesitate to seize the English fortresses in the southwest or wage war vigorously against the Flemish towns and rout them at Mons-en-Peleve in 1304. He added to the royal domain the provinces of Champagne and Navarre as well as the important city of Lyon. Being always short of money, he imposed new taxes, lowered the value of the state currency, expelled the Jews from France (and appropriated their goods), and accused the wealthy Templars of every conceivable kind of wrongdoing. In 1308 — as previously mentioned — the leadership of the Order was arrested; after a long trial, confessions extracted by torture, and recantations, the grand master, Jacques de Molay and the dignitaries of the Order were condemned to death and burnt alive in Paris in 1314. The Templar military order was abolished, and the king of France seized most of their huge properties.

The unpopular Philippe IV le Bel died several months later, and his three sons reigned successively: Louis X the Headstrong from 1314 to 1316 (his son, Jean I the Posthumous, only lived seven days in 1316 and thus did not reign), Philippe V the Long from 1316 to 1322 and Charles IV the Fair from 1322 to 1328.

The period 1314–1328 was a time of renewed conflict with England and with the Flemish, an era in which the French, groaning under a burden of taxation and a prey to unrest, sorely missed the good old days of Saint Louis.

Opposite: **The Conciergerie. Today the Conciergerie is a part of the Palace of Justice. The illustration shows the northern façade of the building at Quai de l'Horloge, including from left to right: the square Horloge Tower, the Ceasar Tower, the Argent Tower, and the Bonbec Tower. The awkward neo–Gothic façades with counterforts were built in the 19th century.**

The Royal Palace and the Conciergerie

During the reign of Philippe the Fair, the royal palace situated in the west of the Ile de la Cité was reshaped. A part of the severe and imposing fortress is known today as the *Conciergerie*. Its name derives from *concierge* (literally caretaker, porter or keeper), the title of the royal governor who was in charge of the building. Today it constitutes a wing of the Palace of Justice. In the Middle Ages it was a part of the royal palace, which is open to the public today. The visitor can admire the vaulted *Salles des Gardes* (Guards' Quarters) and the Gothic *Salles des Gens d'Armes* (king's dining-hall), which is no less than 224 feet long, 88 feet wide and 26 feet high. From the nearby large *cuisine* (kitchen) cooks of the royal house could prepare meals for about 1,000 guests. The charming miniatures of the book *Les Très Riches Heures du Duc de Berry* shows in the month of May the Palais of the Cité with the towers of the Conciergerie and the high tower de l'Horloge. From the 16th century on, the Conciergerie served as a state prison, and during the Revolution its cells were occupied by thousands of citizens (including Louis XVI's wife, queen Marie-Antoinette) who lived out their last hours here before climbing the steps to the scaffold and the guillotine in October 1793.

15

The First Part of the Hundred Years' War (1337–1414)

Main Cause of the War

The treaty of Paris signed by Saint Louis in 1259 had not extinguished all grievances between France and England. When King Charles IV died in 1328, he had no male heir and Edward III of England claimed the throne of France (his mother Isabelle was the sister of the deceased king). Edward was rejected and the French barons and lawmen chose Philippe de Valois, the brother of Philippe the Fair who became king of France under the name Philippe VI the Bold (1328–1350).

In October 1337 Edward III openly challenged Philippe VI and declared his intentions to uphold his rights to the crown of France by force of arms. A long conflict — popularly known as the Hundred Years' War — was begun.

The early stage of the war went wrong for France. The French intended to invade England, but their fleet was destroyed at Sluis in Belgium in June 1340; Edward routed French chivalry at the ill-fated battle of Crécy in August 1346; and he laid siege to Calais, which surrendered in August 1347.

The situation of France became increasingly desperate as a terrible disease had broken out in 1347. The Black Plague was rampant among the population; it was the greatest demographic catastrophe to strike medieval Europe. It caused great loss of life, 25 to 50 million European in a few years, representing about a quarter to a third of the total population.

Jean II Le Bon

Philippe VI died in 1350, and his son Jean II Le Bon (the Righteous) reigned from 1350 to 1364. Jean II was in grave difficulties. The Black Prince — the son of Edward III — landed in Aquitaine and headed north. Jean rushed south to meet him, the two armies collided near Poitiers on 19 September 1356.

Once again the heavily armored French knights were defeated by the English foot soldiers armed with long bows. Jean II was taken prisoner by the English. His son (called the *Dauphin* or regent — the future king Charles V), was then beset with the most extreme difficulties. While the Black Prince proceeded with the conquest of Poitou and neighboring provinces, the king of France's son was confronted with internal revolts, this time in Paris.

In February 1358, exploiting the Dauphin's weak position, some 3,000 rioters led by Etienne Marcel, provost of the merchants, forced the gates of the royal palace, and in the Dauphin's own chamber and in his presence, murdered two of his counselors, Robert of Artois, marshal of Normandy, and Jean de Conflans, marshal of Champagne.

It was the first serious clash between the Parisian bourgeoisie and the Capetian monarchy. Moreover it was an attempt at revolution as Marcel was a reformer who dreamed of a constitutional monarchy with the dominant part played by the burghers of Paris. With guile, the king — who was actually held prisoner — succeeded in fleeing from the town, and Marcel set up a virtual dictatorship over Paris. In July 1358 the burghers of Paris began to find Marcel's dictatorship unbearable and killed him.

In August 1358, the Dauphin entered Paris, acclaimed by the people; he spoke of reconciliation and proclaimed a general pardon.

On 8 May 1360, Charles and Edward III signed the treaty of Bretigny. Peace was restored, King Jean II was released with a huge ransom, but France had lost a lot of territories in the southwest: Poitou, Aunis, Saintonge, Quercy, Rouergue and Agenais. Jean II Le Bon died in 1364, and the *Dauphin* officially became king under the name of Charles V.

Charles V

The new king — who reigned until his death in 1380 — was a wise and clever monarch. France lay in ruins and devastation; companies of uncontrolled mercenaries roamed the countryside at will, looting as they went. The king managed to get rid of them, restoring the financial, economic and military situation. He allowed the Jews to come back in the realm. He reorganized the French army and gradually resumed the war against the English. With the competent military assistance of his constable, Bertrand du Guesclin, and using a type of guerilla tactics, he obliged them to withdraw. When Charles V died in September 1380, France had made an astonishing recovery. Large parts of the realm occupied by the English had been reconquered, prosperity had returned, and it seemed like the war was over.

16

The Enceinte of Charles V

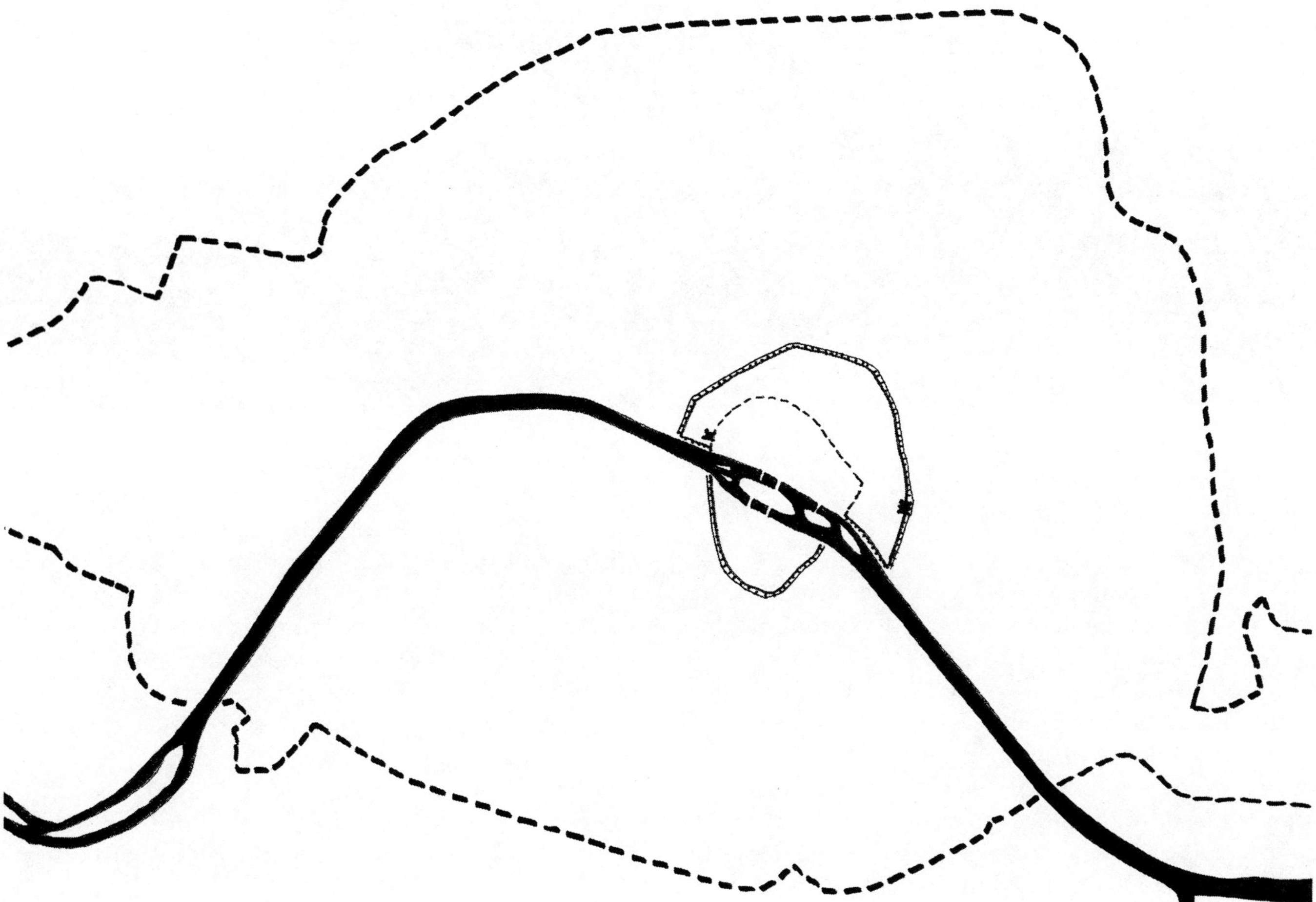

Charles V's wall. The new enceinte protected the northern part of the town. The dotted line indicates the actual administrative limits of Paris.

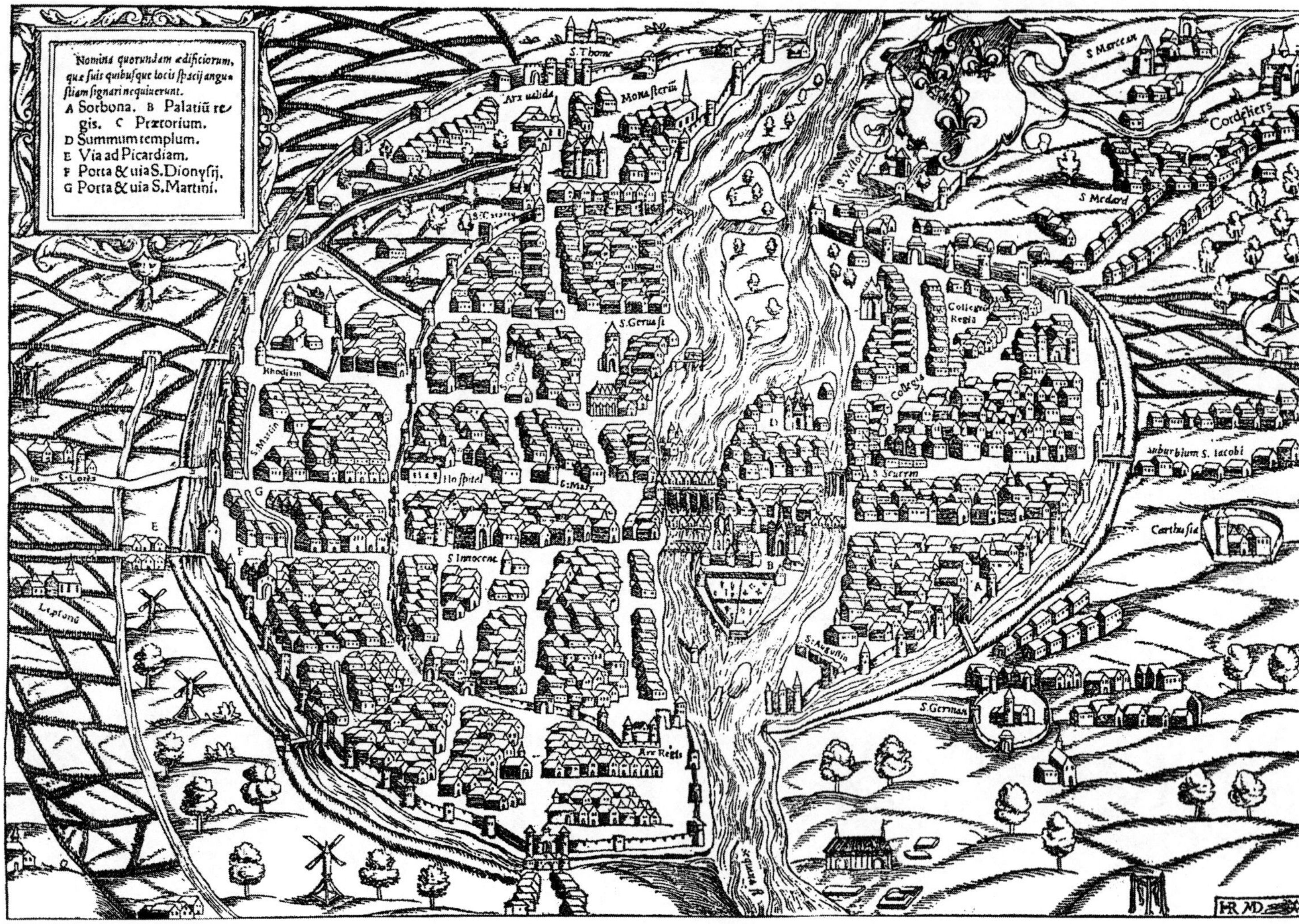

Paris in the 15th century (after an engraving by Sebastien Munster).

The Second Medieval Enceinte

In the 13th century, Paris—particularly the northern *Ville* on the right bank of the Seine—had continued to grow. Although the first part of the Hundred Years' War had badly disturbed business, and in spite of the Black Plague which had partly depopulated the town, the intensity of economic activity was quickly reactivated and even increased. New public market and living spaces were required, and this could be found only outside the walls completed by Philippe Auguste in 1212. It was officially forbidden to establish buildings outside Paris, but the authorities could not prevent the development of illegal settlements. Clusters of economic activity and new settlements had mushroomed outside the Parisian fortifications, and these new business and living locations were known as *faubourgs* (suburbs). The faubourgs were often grouped around religious establishments that had been founded outside the city in earlier centuries, such as Saint-Germain-des-Prés, Saint-Victor, Saint-Martin-des-Champs, Saint-Pol, and Saint-Honoré. These suburbs were small towns of their own, but as Paris grew, they were drawn into its orbit. Even farther beyond the walls and faubourgs were other villages that fell within Paris's sphere of influence. These agricultural settlements, called *banlieue*, ensured that the town had control over its short-term food supplies.

The economic pressure of the faubourgs and the growing population resulted in the construction of a new and larger wall in the second half of the 14th century.

As often happens, it was military defeat and fear that urged the construction of new fortifications. In September 1356, the French troops were defeated at the battle of Poitiers, and temporary defenses were built in the emergency. Hastily begun in late 1356 by order of the provost of merchants, Etienne Marcel, they were composed of a ditch, an earthwall and a palisade breastwork enclosing

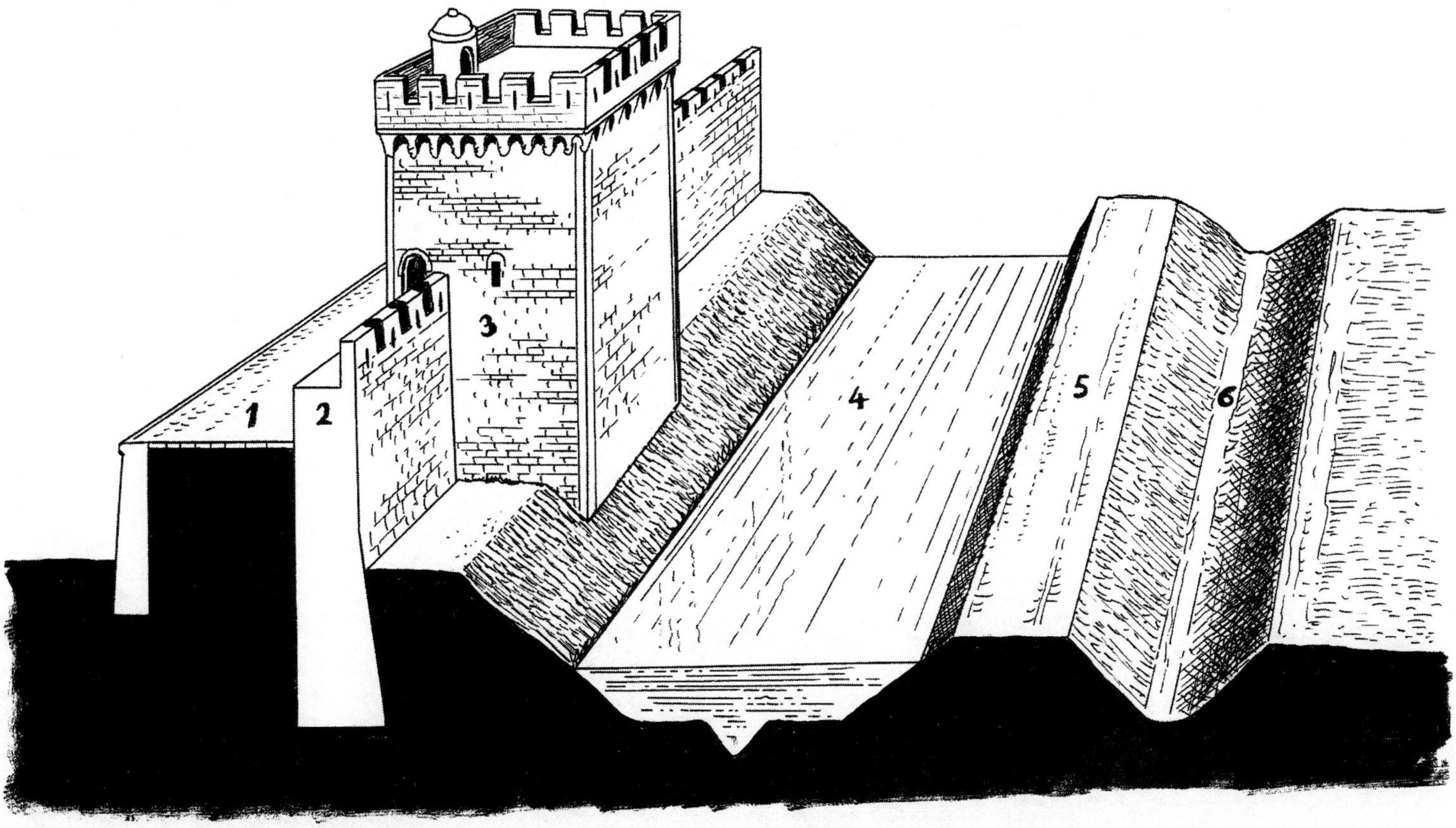

Cross section of wall and ditches of Charles V's enceinte. 1. Chemin de ronde. 2. Wall. 3. Square tower. 4. Main wet ditch. 5. Braie or dos d'âne. 6. Outer dry ditch.

the northern Ville on the right bank of the Seine. After the death of Marcel in 1358, works stopped.

Meanwhile, King Charles V ordered the reinforcement of the fortifications of the royal palace in the island de la Cité. As already described above, several strong stone towers were built to strengthen the Conciergerie including the 47-m high *tour de l'Horloge*, the *tour des Cuisines (Bonbec)*, the *tour de César* and the *tour d'Argent*.

In 1365, as war with England dragged on, Charles V gave the order to rebuild Etienne Marcel's temporary earth defense with a permanent stone wall.

The so-called *enceinte of Charles V* was a gigantic task, and work lasted for more than thirty years. Under the leadership of Hugues Aubriot, who was prevost of merchants from 1364 to 1381, it was completed in about 1420 under the reign of Charles VI. It is said that the huge costs were covered by a special tax levied on drinks. The new wall was only built around the economic center, the northern part of Paris. As for the southern side of the town, the University, it continued to be covered by the wall built by Philippe Auguste at the end of the 12th century. The old southern wall was, however, improved by the digging of a ditch, the reinforcement of the gatehouses fitted with drawbridges, and other minor adjustments.

Tracé of Charles V's Enceinte

The tracé of the new fortifications on the northern bank formed a large curve approximatively corresponding with today's *Grands Boulevards.* In the northwest, the wall began near the actual Place du Carrousel, along the Louvre fortress, across the actual Place des Victoires, followed the Rue d'Aboukir and Rue du Mail, coincided in the eastern direction with the actual Boulevard Saint-Denis, Boulevard Saint-Martin, Boulevard du Temple, Boulevard des Filles-du-Calcaire, Boulevard Beaumarchais, Boulevard Bourdon, and reached the Seine in the east near the actual Quai des Célestins.

The new wall was about 6 km long. It added 166 hectares to the surface of Paris and intentionally enclosed the Louvre, the Temple, and the abbey of Saint Martin.

With the construction of the new wall, the northern part of the enceinte of Philippe Auguste had become militarily useless. It was gradually swallowed up in the urban landscape. Parts of it were demolished, parts were used as stone quarry. Parts of it were phagocyted and integrated into other constructions. Some towers were demolished; others were sold, reshaped, or rearranged to be adapted as living or business space. For centuries, until

Defense of Saint Louis Island

the reign of Louis XIV in the 17th century, there were quarrels and endless suing between the crown and the municipality. Both the Parisian authorities and the kings of France claimed that they were owner of the fortifications.

Walls, Towers and Ditches

Basically, the new enceinte of Charles V was composed of the same elements as Philippe Auguste's wall. However, it included several refinements and improvements such as machicolation, ditches, and powerful gatehouses.

The new *curtains* were between 7 and 10 to 13 m high. The thickness was 3 to 6 m but some portions were thicker as earth was set against the masoned walls; the top of the wall was arranged with a *chemin de ronde* (wallwalk) covered by a crenellated man-high breastwork. The *crenels* (voids) could be provided with wooden *huchettes* (shutters), hanging upon swivels, which in open position allowed archers to fire their weapons and gave additional protection in closed position. The *merlons* (solid portions) could also be pierced with *loopholes* or observation slits.

The walls were flanked by pepper-pot turrets and by 67 major towers, most of them square shaped, some fitted with an open crenellated top, some covered with a pointed roof. Stories—linked by staircases—were furnished with combat emplacements including loopholes. These narrow openings were later widened to adapt to firearms. Some of the towers were crowned with *échauguettes* (sentry boxes), small round roofed turrets protecting guards from bad weather and—in combat—from enemy projectiles.

Walls and towers were surrounded by a double ditch, which formed considerable obstacles to enemies. The inner moat was about 8 m deep, "wet" (filled with water), and about twenty m wide. The outer ditch was smaller in dimension, it was V-shaped and "dry" (not filled with water). Between both ditches there was a circulation path for patrol called *braie* or *dos d'âne* (donkey's back).

Across the eastern small unpopulated Saint Louis island in the middle of the Seine, a wet ditch was dug, defended by a wall and a tower. If needed, chains were stretched across the river to hinder navigation.

Rear view of an échauguette

Cross section machicolation. Spaces were left open between corbels for the downward discharge of offensive materials.

Gatehouses

The main gates were the Porte Saint-Honoré, Porte Montmartre, Porte Saint-Denis, Porte Saint-Martin, Porte du Temple, Porte du Marais and Porte Saint-Antoine. Access to Paris was thus limited to a few gates, but for convenient communication several secondary *posterns* were built. There were also a few *sally-ports* set at the foot of the wall. These were concealed doors allowing raiding parties to leave, strike and regain the town.

Obviously the gates were defended by strongly fortified gatehouses. These had gained in importance, and had become the dominant feature of the city defense. They were imposing structures, several storey-high buildings projecting in the ditch for flanking purposes; they were extremely well-defended units fitted with judiciously placed combat emplacements, shooting chambers and loopholes.

Towers and gatehouses were fitted with a new defensive element called *machicolation*. This disposition retained the principle of the hoarding, but instead of temporary vulnerable wooden galleries, machicolation was a series of permanent spaced stone buttresses, known as *corbels*, supporting the projecting parapet, the spaces between them being open to the *chemin-de-ronde* (wall-walk), and thus permitting the downward discharge of projectiles and missiles. Machicolated and crenellated parapets, proudly crowning towers, curtains, and gatehouses, also had a decorative and — if possible — a deterrent function.

The portal included heavy stout wooden folding doors reinforced with nails and metal parts, a *portcullis* (a vertical wooden grill or a grating of iron instantly moving up and down to close an entrance passage) and *murder-holes*, apertures in the ceiling through which projectiles and offensive materials could be dropped upon the heads of intruders who had penetrated thus far.

The gate gave access to a small and narrow courtyard to hold up an assault in a confined space where the defenders could deal with assailants at short range.

Across both ditches there was a bridge leading to the portal. Its last section was a drawbridge; this was raised or lowered at will by counterweights moving chains hung from a pair of rainures or gaffs — timber beams received back into long chases or slots placed in the façade. In closed position the vertically raised driveway formed an additional thick barrier.

The gatehouse included a *guichet* or *wicket*, a pedestrian entrance, independent from the main

Saint Denis Gatehouse

Temple Gatehouse

portal and fitted with its own narrow drawbridge; this allowed the passage of pedestrians without having to open the main door.

As ever, the gatehouse also included a custom office where taxes and tolls were levied on exported and imported goods. As ever, fortifications—and more particularly gatehouses—were designed to be pleasing to the eye. Display of strength and various ornaments bespoke Paris's pride, wealth and importance.

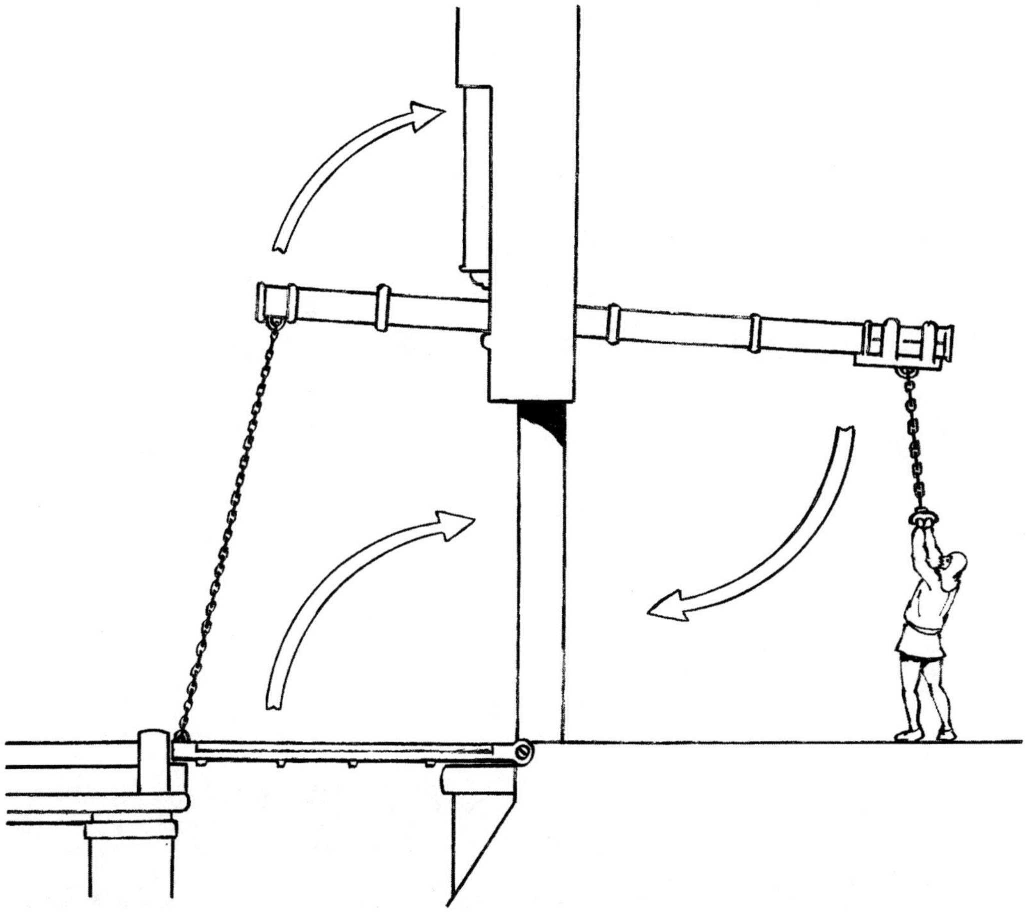

Counterweight drawbridge. The schematic cross section shows how the bridge was operated.

Barbican

The gatehouses were preceded by a detached forework with various names: *barbacane*, *barbican*, *chastel* or *bastille*. This was a large round or U-shaped outer tower or a strong rectangular building, with towers and turrets, erected on the far side of the ditch, at the end of the bridge leading to the city gate; it concealed the entrance, worked as a filter, and provided a powerful external line of defense as it was fitted with sophisticated combat emplacements, its own ditch and an additional drawbridge.

In 1369, the Petit Châtelet (on the right bank) was reshaped once again, and king Charles V and the Parisian municipality made some efforts to improve hygiene (by organizing a trash collection service) and communication within the city (by the construction of new bridges and the consolidation of the banks of the river); but Paris—like most medieval cities all over Europe—would remain for centuries a filthy town with dirty narrow sinuous streets, poor facilities, bad communication and unhealthy houses deprived of comfort and vulnerable to fire.

Opposite: **Montmartre Gate. The gatehouse included a well-defended building and a barbican.**

17

The Castle of Vincennes

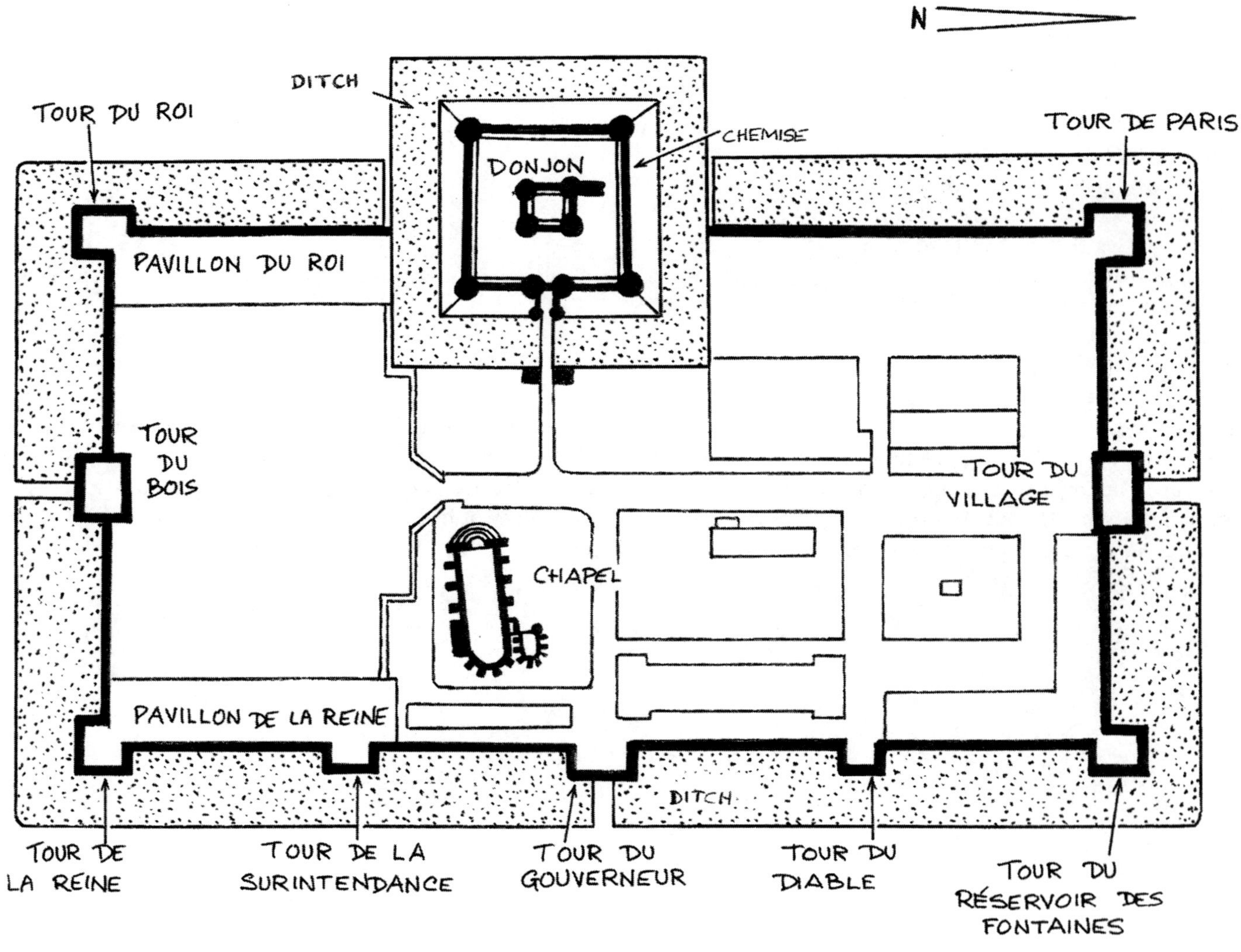

Ground plan of Vincennes

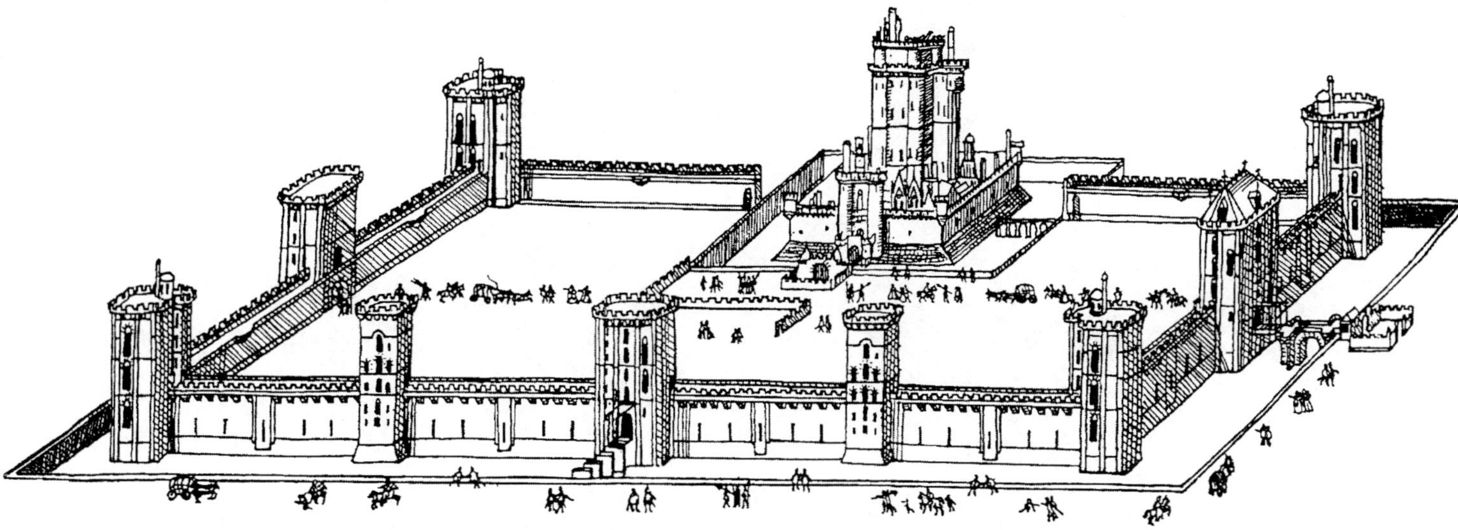

Vincennes castle (from an engraving by Du Cerceau)

A New Royal Residence

The development of Paris, which had begun under Philippe Auguste's reign, was partly interrupted by the Hundred Years' War. This long conflict marked by military defeats, civil wars, insurrections and uprising, epidemics and famines created an unfavorable climate of insecurity. In this context, the kings of France decided to create a new castle, a safe place of refuge in the east of Paris, in the forest near the village of Vincennes. The forest had been purchased by the crown in the 11th century, it was thus royal private property where kings went hunting, and for this purpose, a forest lodge had been built at the time of Saint Louis.

The construction of the castle of Vincennes was begun by King Philippe VI in 1337, the keep was built in the 1360s by Jean II le Bon, and the fortress was completed under Charles V's reign about 1373.

Manifestly, Vincennes was a residence, but it was also a military stronghold. The castle still exists today and though reshaped on several occasions still gives a vivid view of a 14th century fortress. We are fortunate in the survival of the Duc de Berry's *Très Riches Heures* to have a miniature depicting the castle of Vincennes in December with a number of seemingly isolated towers rising above the thick wood; the effect is extraordinarily like the tower blocks of a 20th century city, all white and shining, and set against a sky of ineffable blue.

Hard reality must have presented a rather different kind of picture: the stench of stagnant water in the ditch half filled with decaying refuse, the discomfort of the cold and drafty rooms, window slits boarded up, the harsh clank of iron on stone, and the dark windowless dungeon.

The Enceinte

Vincennes Castle is a vast rectangle, 175 m wide and 334 m long. The enceinte is composed of a crenellated 15 m high wall and of a 24 m wide, 12 m deep ditch. The curtain is flanked by seven strong square towers, 42 m high with 3 m thick walls. There are two main gates, one in the northern part of the wall, the other in the south, both arranged in a large square tower-gatehouse, both fitted with heavy doors, portcullis, drawbridges and defense emplacements. The vast inner yard, called the *bailey*, has a surface of 6 hectares and contained various lodging and service buildings, a hall and a chapel.

The Keep

The most impressive feature of Vincennes castle is the powerful keep, set up astride the middle of the western front. The keep forms an independent fortress within the castle. It has its own ditch (22 m wide and 14 m deep) and is composed of two parts: an enceinte (called *chemise* or *mantle*) and a large tower. The chemise is rectangular, and its base is fitted with a *talus*, a thick sloping reinforcement of heavy masonry that makes it more resistant to mining, sapping and ramming. The top is arranged as a crenellated wallwalk, covered with a tile roof and fitted with machicolations. At each corner, the chemise has flanking pepper-pot towers; finally its access was defended by a detached *Châtelet*, a gatehouse formed with two cylindrical towers which included the usual medieval elements: drawbridge, portcullis and combat emplacement fitted with loopholes.

The tower keep is noticeable by its monumental

Opposite: Cross section of the dungeon of Vincennes. ***Above:*** View of the dungeon of Vincennes Castle

dimensions. It is a square building, each side 16 m long, and its height is 52 m; its walls are 3 m thick, and reinforced at each corner by semicylindrical towers; the foot of the tower includes an inner ditch which may be crossed by a drawbridge. In the Middle Ages, the tower was divided into six large vaulted stories including (from bottom to top) kitchen and services, ceremonial hall, king's chamber, royal children's apartments, king's officers' quarters, and weapon store. The top of the tower was arranged as an open combat terrace including crenellations and machicolation. The premises were decorated, heated by fireplaces, lighted by small windows, and furnished with latrines placed in the northwestern turret. Drinking water was supplied by a 19-m deep inner well.

Vincennes Castle through Today

By the time of the Renaissance, the castle had lost its military function, and the ill-suited keep its residential role. King Louis XI ordered the construction of a royal house in the bailey. In the 17th century, by order of the governor of Vincennes/minister, Jules Mazarin, two residential buildings were built in classical style by architect LeVau: the *pavillon de la Reine* for the queen and the *pavillon du Roi* for the king Louis XIV. The southern front was then demolished and replaced by an elegant portico with columns.

In the beginning of the 18th century, the tower keep was used as a state prison. In 1738 a part of the castle housed a porcelain factory; this was transferred to Sèvres in 1756. Until the reign of Napoléon I, the castle was a prison, and one of the most illustrious prisoners was Honoré Gabriel Riqueti, count of Mirabeau. The building was, however, neglected, partly abandoned and there were thoughts of demolishing it. Napoléon I gave it to the army and the castle became an arsenal, returning to the castle of Vincennes some military value. The towers were lowered to the level of the walls, machicolations and crenellations were replaced by artillery emplacements; flanking casemates were built in the ditch and a wide glacis was established around the fortress. These poor defenses were used for symbolical and "heroic" purposes in 1814, 1815 and 1830 by the governor of the castle, Baron Pierre "Wooden Leg" Daumesnil (1776–1832). In the second half of the 19th century, the castle remained a military establishment, until the medieval-minded Napoléon III ordered his architect Viollet-Le-Duc to restore it. In 1939–1940, the castle was used by General Gamelin as Grand Headquarters. During the German occupation of 1940–1944, Vincennes Castle was used by the Nazis as a storehouse and prison. Before withdrawing in August 1944, they shot twenty-six hostages and exploded mines making a large breech in the northwestern wall and damaging the royal *pavilions*. Today Vincennes has been restored. The keep and a part of the castle are open to the public; another part remains army property and houses the archives of the French ground forces.

18

The Bastille

Chastel Saint Antoine. The Bastille is seen here from the outside of Paris.

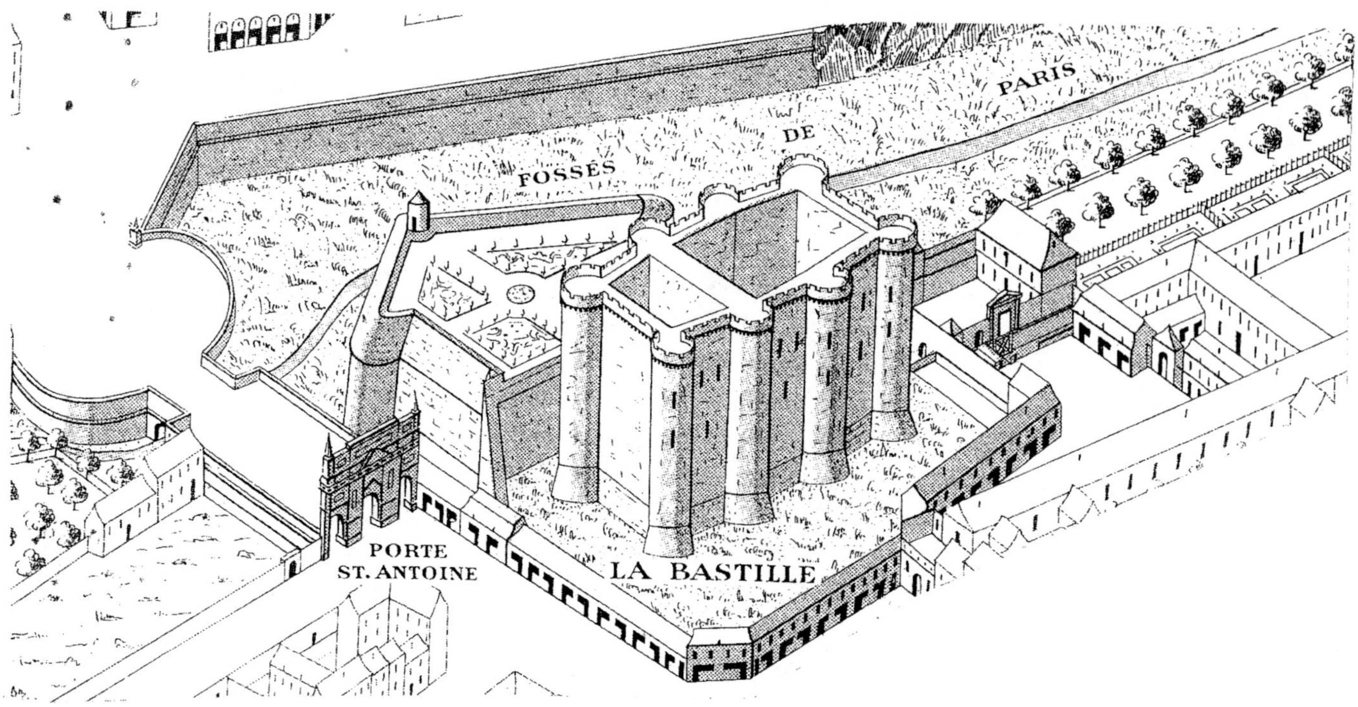

View of the Bastille about 1734 (after Turgot). The Bastille is seen here from inside Paris.

Hôtel Saint Pol and Palace of Tournelles

The bloody insurrection of 1358, led by Etienne Marcel, prevost of merchants, marked the first important conflict between the Parisian bourgeoisie and the Capetian monarchy. One of its consequences was the displacement of the residence of the French king since the monarch's security was no longer guaranteed in the building in the Cité Island. The *Dauphin*, who became king Charles V in 1364, left the royal palace of the Cité island, of which he had such bad memories, and established his residence in the east in the Marais borough on the right bank of the Seine in the *Hôtel Saint Pol*, which he had built from 1361 to 1365. This was much larger and more beautiful than the ancient and gloomy Louvre. The Hôtel included 10 hectares, with a stone enclosure protecting a hall, airy living quarters, numerous service buildings, chapels and a cloister, several yards, a large garden, and a menagerie with exotic animals. Placed near the town's fortifications and the Bastille, the residence allowed the French kings to escape from popular uprisings. The Hôtel was abandoned after 1516 and part of the buildings were hired out, sold or destroyed to make room for other buildings. It corresponds to the present quadrilateral formed by the actual Rue Saint Paul, Quai des Célestins, Rue du Petit Musc, and Rue Saint Antoine.

During the two following centuries, Charles V's successors— notably Charles VII and Louis XI —would reside in the *Hôtel des Tournelles* on the site of the northern side of the present Place des Vosges. The royal removal was followed by the establishment of aristocratic dwellings in this part of Paris. Near that of their royal lord, princes, courtesans, senior ranking civil servants and other important administrators built aristocratic *hôtels* in the Marais.

A Gatehouse Becomes a Castle

Another consequence of Etienne Marcel's uprising of 1358 was the construction of a new fortress inside which the kings of France could seek refuge in case of popular rebellion: the imposing *chastel Saint-Antoine* better known as the *Bastille.*

As already said, the terms *châtelet*, *chastel* and *bastille* were used in the Middle Ages to designate a detached strongly fortified work generally placed in front of a bridge or a gatehouse. The very proper name *Bastille* for the castle was in use from the 16th century onward. Before then, it was called *chastel Saint-Antoine.* The need for a new royal chastel was advocated by the loyal prevost of merchants Hugues Aubriot.

The construction of the Bastille, from 1370 to 1382, was realized in several successive phases. Originally there were two large cylindrical towers (*tour de la Chapelle* and *tour du Trésor*), which were simply part of the Saint Antoine gate in the enceinte of Charles V. In 1370, this gatehouse was reinforced at the side of Paris with walls and two other towers *(tour de la Liberté* and *tour de la Bertaudière*), with portal, ditch and drawbridge. This passage was then transformed into an independent castle by the adjunction of four other towers linked by walls: these were in the north the *tour du Coin* and *tour du Puits*, and in the south the *tour de la Comté* and *tour de la Bazinière*. At the same time, the castle was hemmed in by a wide and deep ditch filled with water provided by the Seine.

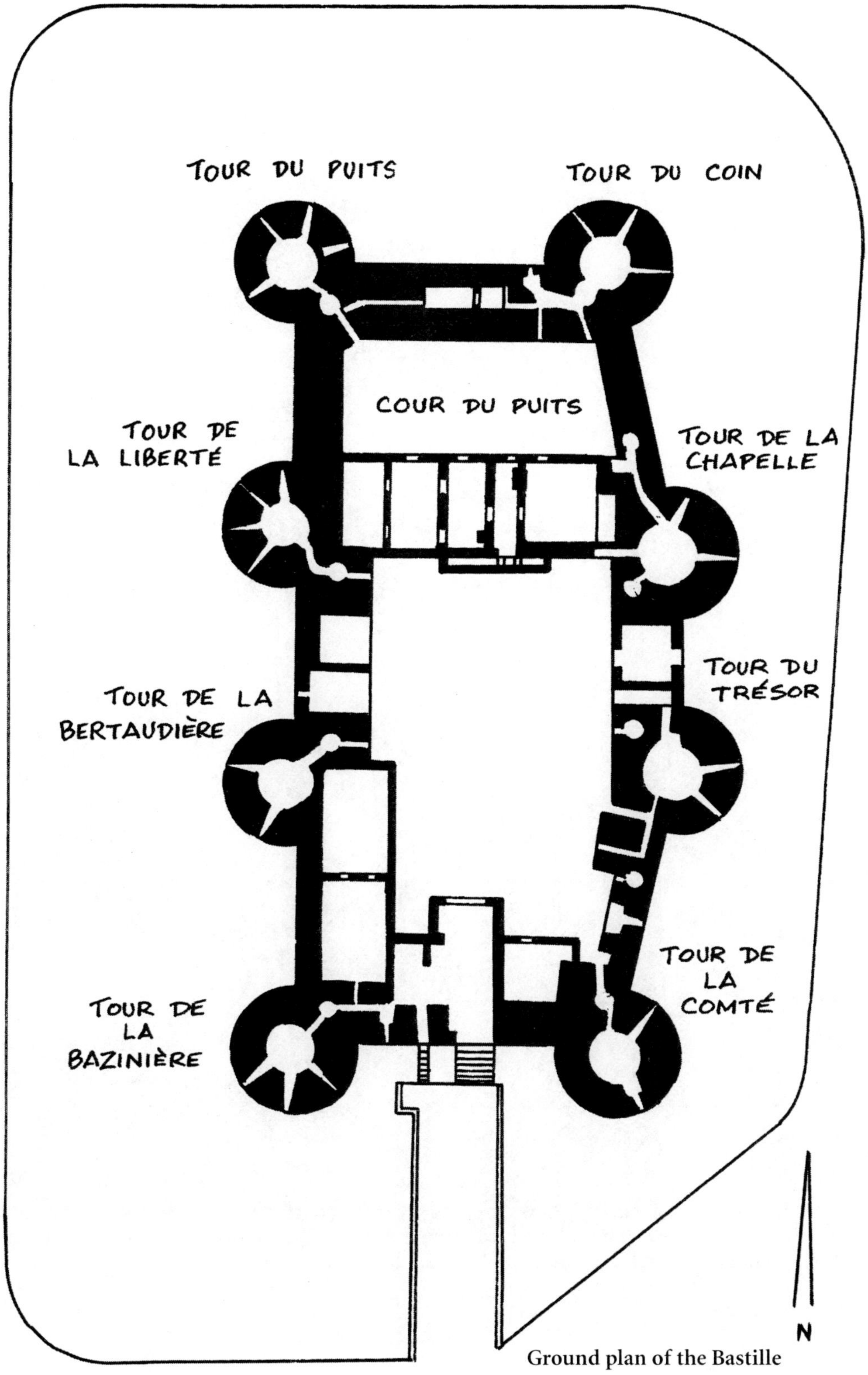

Ground plan of the Bastille

Description of the Bastille

As the gate had become an autonomous fortress, another *Porte Saint Antoine* was created north of the Bastille. The fortress had one entrance opening onto the Rue Saint Antoine, in order to be easily accessible by the king from his nearby Hôtel Saint Pol.

The *Chastel Saint Antoine* was completed in 1382. It was composed of eight 20-m-high towers, linked by 2-m-thick walls. The walls and the towers were fitted with a sloping *talus* at their base, a thick strengthening mass of masonry for better stability and resistance to the battering ram. The most noteworthy feature was that walls and towers were constructed at the same level, creating a massive core and a large combat summit terrace; this enabled easy communication and allowed defenders to deploy their hurling machines (and later firearms). This innovation in military architecture — typical of the late 14th century — was called *block-castle*. The top of the walls and that of the towers were crenellated and fitted with machicolation. Inside the towers there were staircases linking tiers of vaulted *casemates* (firing chambers) fitted with narrow openings for shooting with bows and crossbows; later these *loopholes* were widened into *embrasures* for operating firearms. The narrow space enclosed was divided into two small *baileys,* yards inside which various buildings were erected: an apartment for the king, a house for the governor of the fortress, a barrack for the garrison, and several other service buildings.

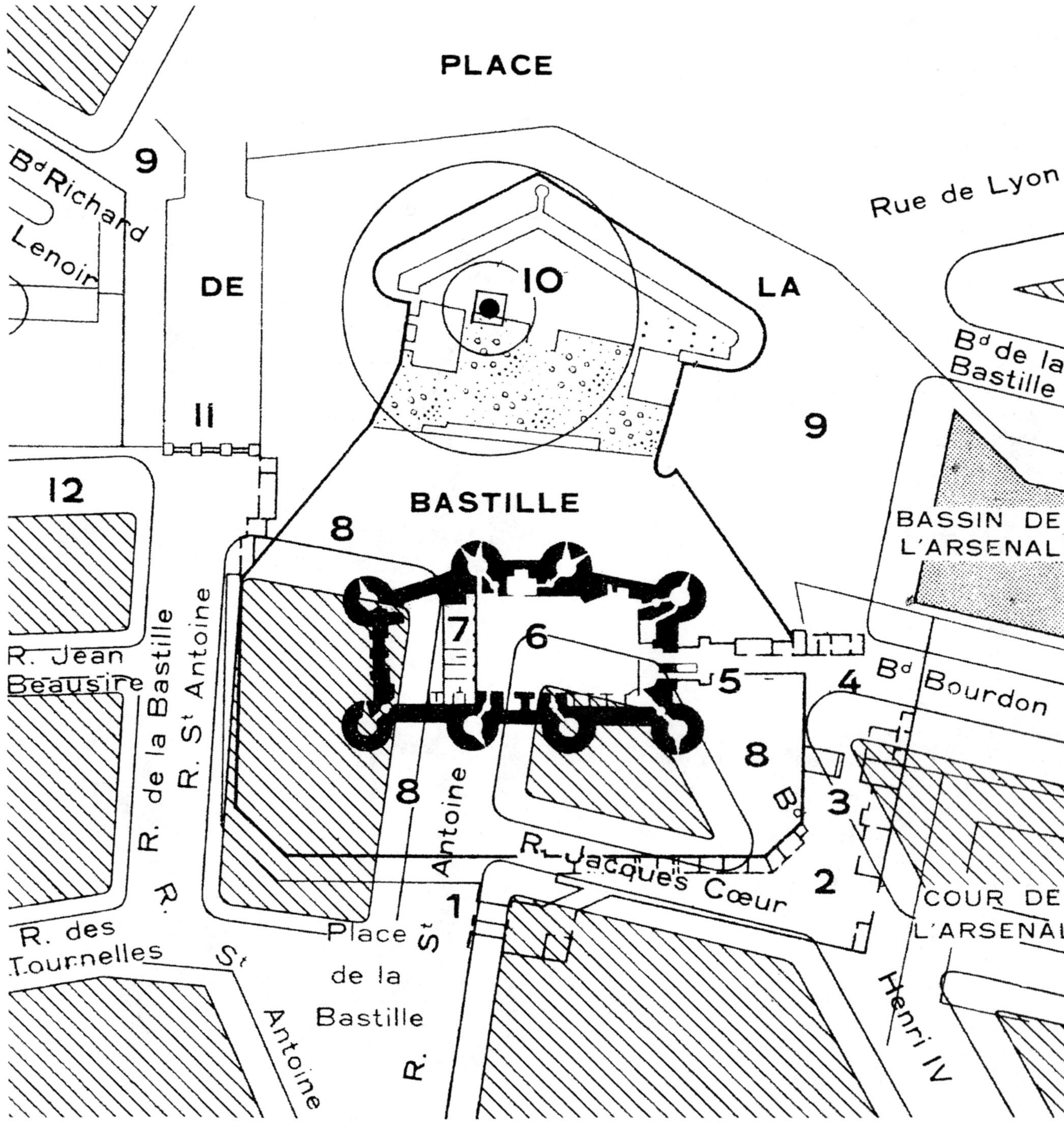

Situation of the Bastille. Superimposed on the present Place de la Bastille, the ground plan shows where the Castle stood. 1. Entrance to the castle. 2. First yard. 3. First drawbridge. 4. Governor's yard. 5. Main entrance with drawbridge. 6. Inner yard. 7. Garrison's barracks. 8. Ditch of the Bastille. 9. Ditch of the enceinte of Paris. 10. Italian style bastion built in 1566 (the circle represents the present-day Colonne de Juillet). 11. Saint Antoine gatehouse. 12. Enceinte of Paris. The hachured areas represent present-day buildings.

State Prison

The role of the Chastel Saint Antoine in Paris's military history is not particularly glorious. The fortress was besieged seven times— always during rebellions and civil wars— and surrendered six times. It was an important stronghold during the second part of the Hundred Years' War, notably during the civil war opposing the rival Bourguignon and Armagnac factions.

The fortress was occupied by the English in 1420 to control the Parisians. Its powerful artillery repulsed the troops of the duke of Burgundy, Charles le Téméraire, in

1464. In 1552 a bastion was established ahead of the Bastille; intended as an artillery platform, it was used in peacetime as a garden for the governor. From Chastel Saint Antoine, Governor Dubourg-Lespinasse vainly opposed by arms the entrance of King Henri IV in 1594.

In 1652, the Bastille and the Faubourg Saint Antoine were the scenes of a violent fratricide combat pitting the rebels of the *Fronde* against King Louis XIV.

However, in the 17th century, the military role of the Bastille decreased, the fortress became a state prison, and the artillery casemates were transformed into cells. The Bastille was especially intended for the incarceration of criminal, rebellious or simply annoying members of the nobility. By simple *lettre de cachet* (arbitrary royal decision) and without a trial, noble people could be jailed for an undetermined length of time — in the worst cases, for life. A special verb was created, *embastiller,* which meant "put in prison in the Bastille."

Among the most famous prisoners are the plotter Jacques of Armagnac, duke of Nemours in 1476, the marshal of Biron, the very mysterious Man with the Iron Mask, the superintendent of finance Nicolas Fouquet, viscount of Vaux, the chevalier de Rohan, and the poisoner Lady Catherine Deshayes-La Voisin.

Conditions in the prison were various, scaling from harsh to luxurious. Though it was not always the rule, some of the (rich) prisoners could enjoy a rather pleasant detention; in certain cases, and at their own expense, they could have their cells decorated and their own furnishings brought and — served by their own servants— they could hold banquets with relatives and friends.

In the 18th century, disturbing writers, intellectuals and philosophers were imprisoned in the Bastille. Among the most notorious prisoners were François-Marie Arouet, better known as Voltaire, who completed his book "Œdipe" in his cell in 1726; the disgraced ex-governor of India Thomas Arthur Lally, count of Tollendal between 1766 and 1770; as well as the scandalous pornographer Donatien Alphonse François, Marquis de Sade.

In 1784, the prison was practically empty and nearly disused. King Louis XVI considered demolishing the Bastille, as the maintenance costs were much too high.

July 14, 1789

History decided otherwise, and the hated prison was besieged by 600 rioters supported by the Parisian populace on July 14, 1789, marking the start of the French Revolution. On that day, the Bastille was defended by Governor Bernard Jordan, Marquis De Launay commanding 32 Swiss guards and 82 *invalides* (disabled soldiers), armed with a few muskets and 15 canons without ammunition. It is rather difficult to know precisely what happened. Some historians assert that the Bastille surrendered without a fight. Other historians assert that the garrison of the Bastille put up a strong resistance and that, after having forced the gate, the attackers made no significant progress and suffered 83 dead and 74 wounded. What is certain is that at about 5 o'clock PM, De Launay was informed that no relief would come and agreed to surrender. In the confusion he and several guards were murdered by the populace, while the mere seven prisoners detained in the Bastille (four forgers, two madmen, and one count) were liberated. Although it had always served to imprison noblemen (and exceptionally members of the common), the Bastille had become the symbol of despotism and oppression at large, the epitome of the hated *Ancien Régime*— roughly speaking, the period 1589 to 1792, ruled by the absolute Bourbon kings from Henri IV to Louis XVI.

Immediately, the revolutionaries decided to destroy this symbol of tyranny. Between July 1789 and May 1790 the Bastille was demolished by a contractor named Palloy leading a crew of 800 workers and the spontaneous help of the people of Paris. The stones were sold one by one by Palloy who made a fortune, and a part of these materials were used to construct the Bridge of the Concorde.

Where the fortress had stood, new houses and streets were built, and a wide circular square was arranged, named *Place de la Bastille.* This was reshaped in 1803 by order of Napoléon and decorated with a fountain in the form of a large elephant. In 1831 the square was rearranged and ornamented with a large 52-m-high column named *Colonne de Juillet;* topped by a gilded statue representing Mercury and called the Genius of Liberty, the column was erected to the memories of the Parisians who had been killed during the revolution of July 1830. Today the outline of the former Bastille fortress is represented on the ground south of the square by white paving.

19

Private Medieval Fortifications

Paris: An Unhealthy and Unsafe City

Like most medieval European cities, Paris developed without any clear urban plan. The crown, noblemen, religious communities, landowners and rich bourgeois jealously guarded their territorial possessions. Insistence on private property rights defeated any attempts at regulation or application of measures aiming at improving municipal facilities; the result was an irregular layout, making Paris a labyrinth of lanes, streets, alleys and backstreets. The city, with its accumulation of houses made of flammable material, was extremely vulnerable to fire.

The streets were tortuous, dark, narrow, muddy, filthy and encumbered with domestic animals—particularly stray pigs, which ate trash. About 1200, Philippe Auguste had, vainly, ordered the paving of the streets. In 1370, Hugues Aubriot, prefect of Paris, ordered garbage to be carted to dumps outside the walls, but these measures had mixed results. The River Seine was the main sewer and remained so until 1850 when the prefect of Paris Baron Georges Hausmann and engineer Eugène Belgrand provided the city with a large and effective network of underground sewers and clean water distribution.

Paris was also a dangerous town. At night it was deserted and dark. Due to the misery of large parts of the population, the absence of public lighting, the shortage and inadequacy of the police force (nightwatch or guet), insecurity reigned. At night Paris was the domain of brigands and robbers. There were a dozen nests of criminals where even the armed guet dared not go. Today there is still a street in the 4th Arrondissement called *Rue de la Grande Truanderie* (Street of Great Criminality). One of the most famous lairs was the so-called *Cour des Miracles* (Yard of Miracles) where daytime blind and crippled beggars "miraculously" became cured at night to become robbers. Today this place corresponds to a quadrilateral formed by the present Rue du Nil, Rue du Caire, Rue Dussoubs and Rue Réaumur. Described by Victor Hugo in his novel *Notre Dame de Paris*, the Cour des Miracles was a dirty square bordered with slums, miserable houses and shady inns where robbers, beggars, murderers, prostitutes, pimps and thugs met; this scum of the populace elected a king, operated following a special "code of behavior," and developed a secret language named *argot* (slang). One of the most notorious and romantic Parisian bandits was François Villon (ca. 1431–1463) who was at the same time a student, a talented poet, a pimp and a thief. The Cour des Miracles continued to be a dangerous and formidable haunt of bandits until 1667. There was another "Cour des Miracles" in the Rue Saint Sauveur.

Prostitution was officially forbidden but in practice it was tolerated. By the time of Philippe Auguste, it was organized into a corporation with its own status, privileges, rights, taxes and duties and a patroness: Saint Magdalena. Prostitutes were called *ribaudes*, *putes*, *putains* (whores), *femmes amoureuses* (women in love) or *filles folles* (mad girls). They operated in *étuves* (public baths) and in streets specialized in their business: the *Rue de Pute y Muse* (literally "street where whores walk around") has become the present Rue du Petit Musc, and the *Rue du Poil au Cul* (literally "street of the hairy behind") has modestly been renamed Rue du Pelican.

Hôtel de Clisson

The Hôtel de Sens

Private Fortifications

In this context of risk and insecurity, relationships between rich and poor were always tense, and therefore rich merchants and wealthy bourgeois, patrician families and noblemen resided in private fortified stone houses, urban manors and fortified hôtels. The Church too was concerned with protecting persons and property. We have already seen how strong the establishment of the Templars was. Other clergy residences and monasteries—within or right outside the city walls—were places of culture, learning and spirituality; these were wealthy feudal landowners too, which meant that they were significant centers of economic and temporal power. They were therefore fortified as well. Private fortifications could not of course resist a siege by an organized army, but they could hold at bay brigands and robbers. In the case of monasteries, walls also marked the limit between the profane world and the religious establishment.

Hôtel de Clisson

The remnants of an aristocratic dwelling can be seen today at 58 Rue des Archives in the 3rd Arrondissement: two corbelled pepper-pot turrets defending the entrance of the *Hôtel de Clisson*. This fortified residence was built about 1375 by Constable Olivier de Clisson, a companion of Bertrand du Guesclin. In 1553, the manor was acquired and later enlarged by the Guise family; a private demesne was constituted by the purchase of lands located in the present quadrilateral formed by the Rue des Francs-

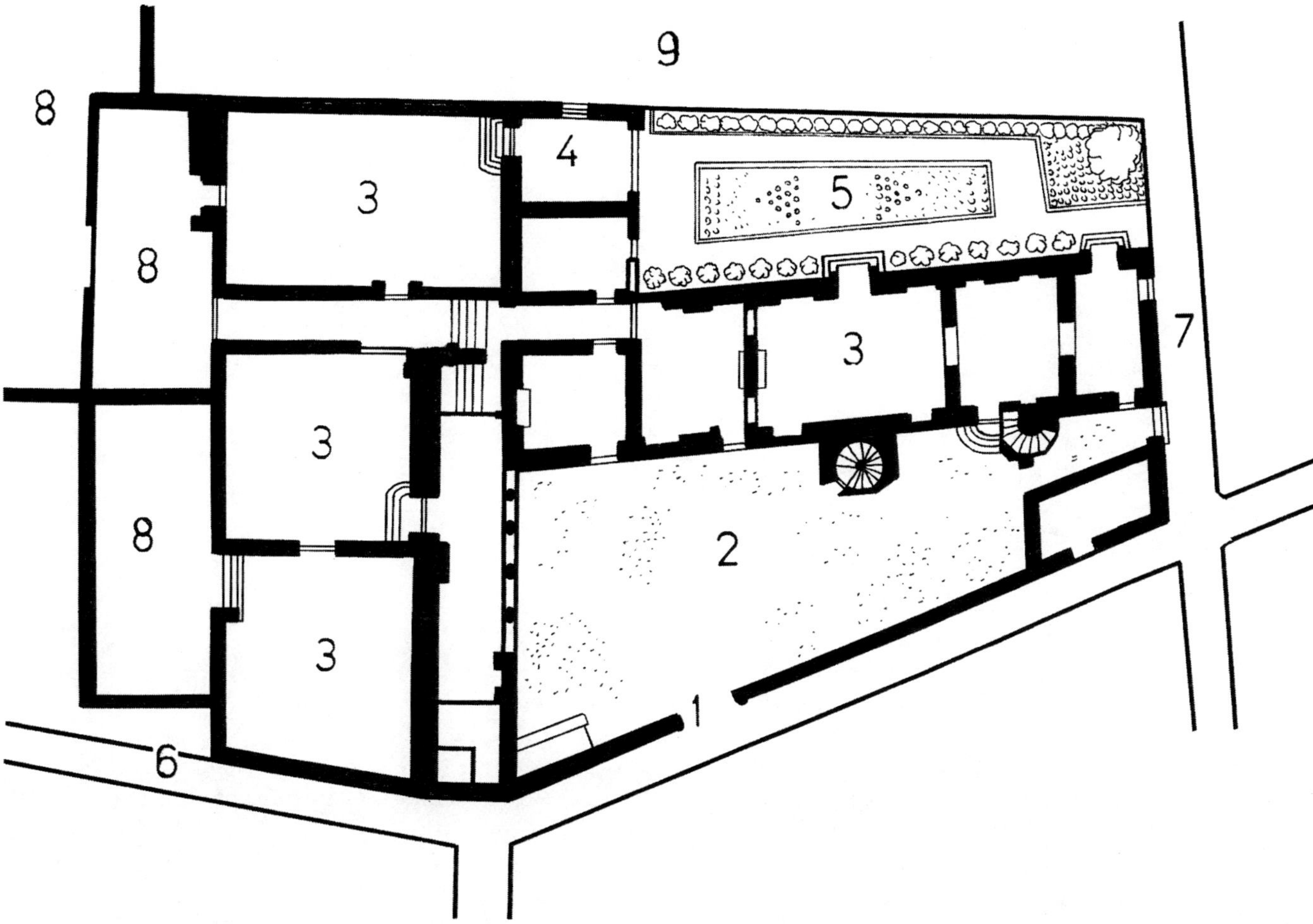

Ground plan Hôtel de Cluny. 1. Entrance. 2. Courtyard. 3. Lodgings and service buildings (now exhibition rooms). 4. Chapel. 5. Garden "The Meadow". 6. Rue du Sommerard. 7. Rue de Cluny. 8. Ruins of Roman bath. 9. Museum gardens.

Bourgeois, Rue des Archives, Rue des Quatre Fils and Rue Vieille du Temple. The Guise family played an important role during the Wars of Religions; deeply involved on the Catholic side, the Guise plotted the Saint Bartholomew's Day Massacre in their hôtel in August 1672 when thousands of Protestants were murdered. Since 1808, by order of Napoléon, the domain, its gardens and its numerous sumptuous buildings (including Hôtel de Guise, Hôtel de Rohan-Strasbourg, Hôtel de Boisgelin, and Hôtel de Soubise) have housed the French National Archives and the Museum of French History.

Hôtel de Sens

Until 1662, the bishopric of Paris depended of the archdiocese of Sens. The archbishops had a residence—called the *Hôtel de Sens*—built between 1475 and 1507 in the present Rue de l'Hôtel de Ville. In 1760 the Hôtel de Sens was purchased by a coach company and became the starting point of a transport line linking Paris to Lyon. In 1912, the Hôtel was bought by the municipality of Paris and now houses the Center of Documentation and Information of Parisian Crafts.

Hôtel de Cluny

Standing next to the ruins of the Roman baths from the end of the 2nd century AD, along the left bank of the Seine, the *Hotel of the Abbots of Cluny* was built about 1330 by Pierre de Chalus, abbot of the powerful Benedictine abbey of Cluny in Burgundy. The residence—located in the present-day Rue du Sommerard—was surrounded by a wall and was intended to house the abbots when they were visiting Paris. Between 1485 and 1498, the Hôtel was enlarged and beautified by Abbot Jacques d'Amboise (1484–1510). The U-shaped building enclosing an inner courtyard was surrounded by a defensive stone wall and overlooked a garden on the north side. From 1600 to 1681, the luxurious Hôtel de Cluny served as residence for the *papal noncios* (Ambassadors of the

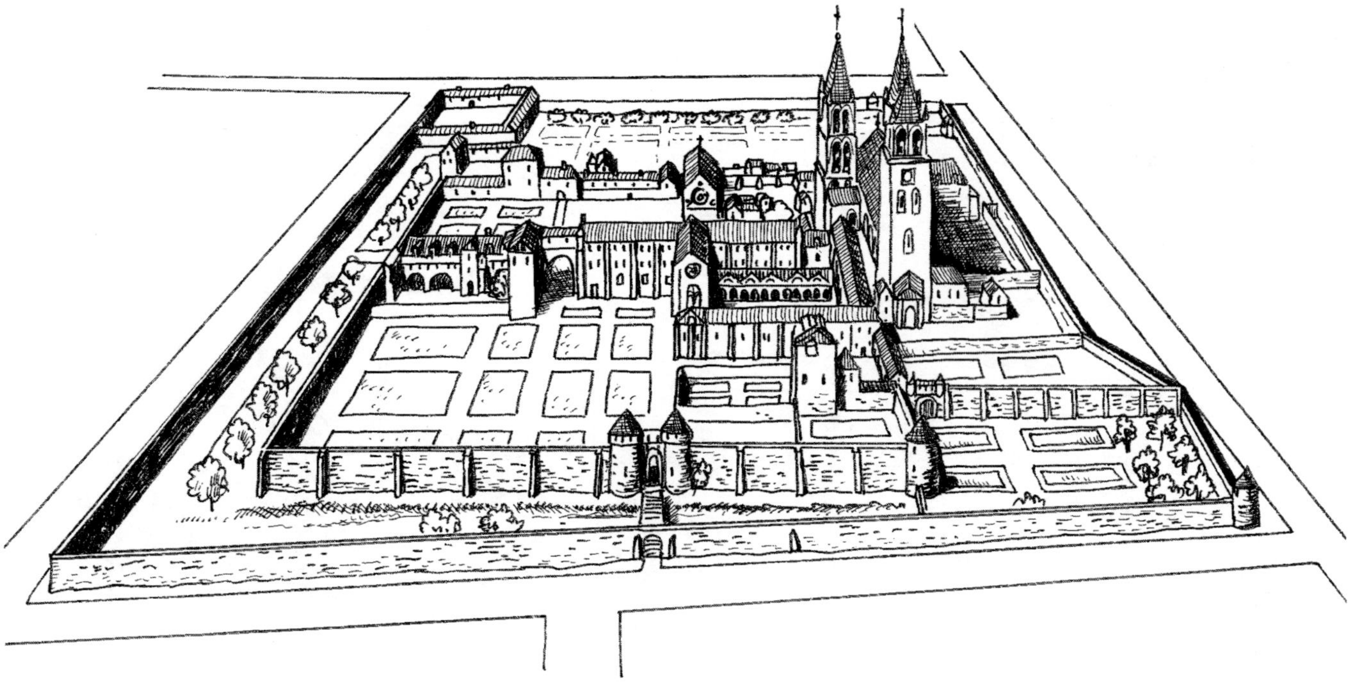

Saint-Germain-des-Prés Abbey

Vatican in foreign countries). During the French Revolution of 1789, the Hôtel was seized by the state, sold and successively occupied by several private owners. In 1833, a rich medieval and Renaissance art collector named Alexandre du Sommerard purchased the building. When he died in 1842, his son Edmond gave the building and collections to the municipality with the provision that they be open to the public. The French Museum of the Middle Ages was founded and still exists today in the former Roman baths and luxurious abbeys of Cluny's Hôtel. Enriched over the years by the acquisition of many remarkable masterpieces—tapestries (notably the *Lady and the Unicorn* hanging from the 15th century), embroideries, ivories, altar pieces, sculptures, stained glasses, paintings, books, and precious metal works—the present collection allows the full extent of medieval artistic activity to be discovered and constitutes a valuable testimony of medieval society in Europe.

Saint Geneviève Abbey

The *Abbey of Saint Geneviève* was founded by the Frankish king Clovis I in 510 AD, in gratitude for his victory of Vouillé against the Visigoths. Its location—near the present Panthéon—corresponds to the actual Lycée Henri IV. The abbey was enclosed by a wall and dedicated to the patroness of Paris, Geneviève. Throughout the Middle Ages, it was an important theological study center led by the regular canons of Saint Augustine. In 1758, lands belonging to the old Saint Geneviève abbey were used to build the Saint Geneviève church (the present-day Panthéon) built between 1758 and 1789 after a design by architect Soufflot. In 1796, what remained of the monastery was transformed into a secondary school named Lycée Henri IV, today still one of the most prestigious Parisian grammar schools.

Saint Antoine Abbey

The *Abbey of Saint Antoine* was founded in 1198 by a certain Foulques, priest of the parish of Neuilly-sur-Marne, and instigator of the Fourth Crusade. The establishment, located in the present-day Rue du Faubourg Saint Antoine, was fortified by a wall and a wet ditch, whose waters were brought from the Seine by means of a canal. Around the monastery developed a suburb, named the Faubourg Saint Antoine (stretching from the actual Place de la Bastille to the Place de la Nation). This borough was populated by craftsmen specializing mostly in cabinetry and furnishings, a specialty that continues to this day.

Convent of Celestins

The *convent of Celestins*, located in the triangle formed by the present-day Boulevard Henri IV, Rue Morland and Rue de l'Arsenal, was founded in 1352 by a branch of the Benedictine Order, the *Hermits of Saint*

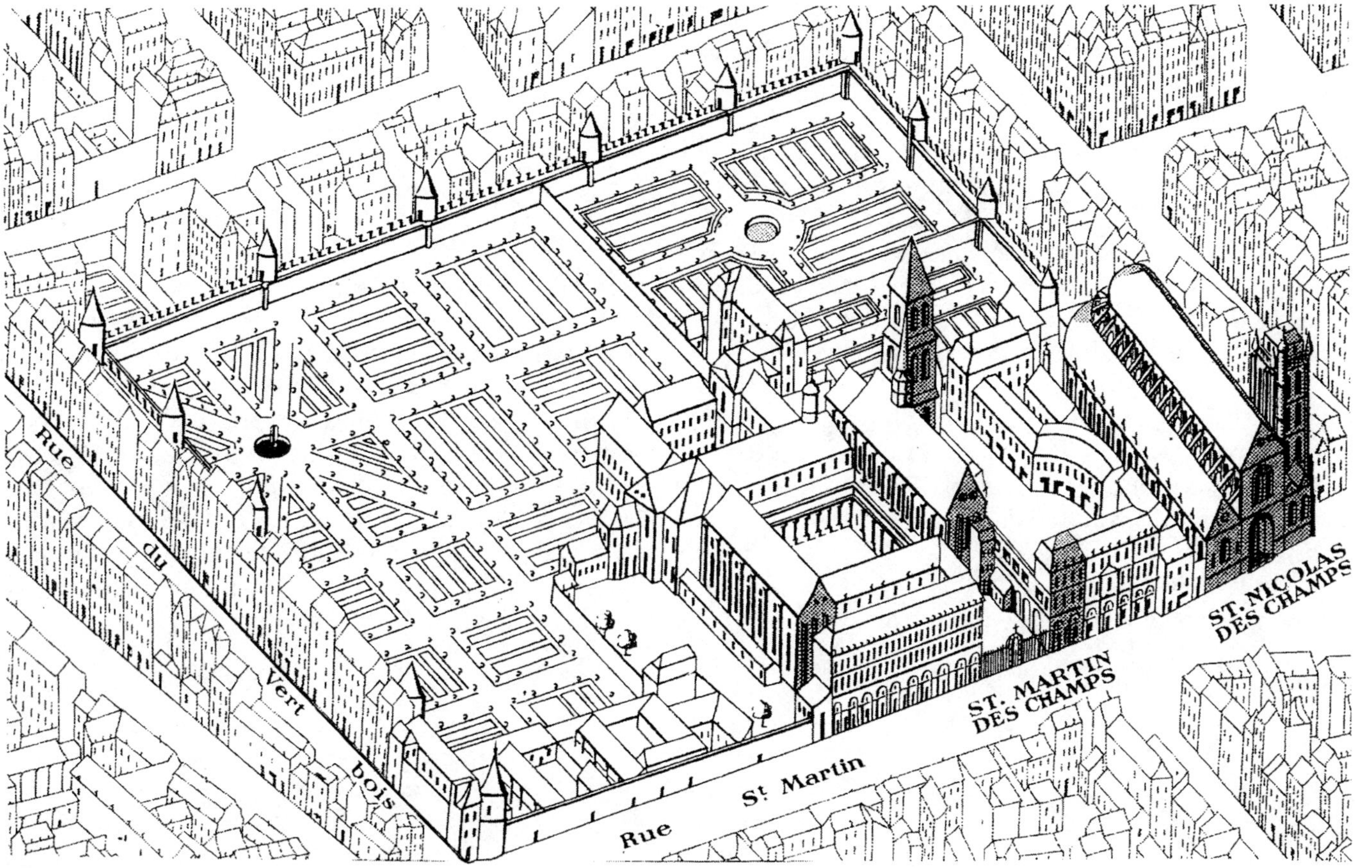

Priory of Saint-Martin-des-Champs in 1734 (from Turgot)

Damien or *Celestins*, as they were created by pope Celestine V. After the construction of Charles V's wall, the convent was well protected and judiciously placed near the royal residences—Hôtel Saint Pol and Hôtel des Tournelles—a favorable position which greatly benefited the monks; the convent became a rich establishment with numerous pieces of priceless art. In 1512, the municipality of Paris arbitrarily annexed a stretch of land (between the present Boulevard Morland and the Seine) which belonged to the Celestins. There an *Arsenal* was built, intended to produce artillery pieces and gunpowder. In 1785, the Church and the French Crown decided to reform the too wealthy and too relaxed Order of Saint Damien. As the Celestins monks strongly opposed the humbling of their privileges, the Order was abolished; their wealth and their large art collections were seized and set to decorate various royal buildings (Louvre Palace, Saint Denis Church and Versailles Castle).

Abbey of Saint-Germain-des-Prés

After a successful expedition against the Saracens in Spain in 542 AD, King Childebert—son of Clovis—brought back several holy relics, one of which was said to be the cloak of Saint Vincent who had been martyred at Saragossa in 204 AD. The bishop of Paris, Germain, encouraged the king to create a Benedictine abbey to house the precious relics, and the *abbey of Saint Vincent* was founded in 558 AD. Bishop Germain was buried in the abbey, which became a place of pilgrimage for the Parisians. Many "miracles" and unexpected healings occurred at the tomb of the bishop, and he was canonized the name of the abbey was changed into *abbey of Saint-Germain-des-Prés*, as it was then located in meadows outside Paris.

The abbey enjoyed prodigious development starting in the 8th century, but it was also pillaged four times by the Viking raiders.

The abbatial church was built between 990 and 1021; restored in the 12th, 17th and 19th centuries, it still exists today. In the 12th century, the abbey was defended by a wall and six towers.

Throughout the Middle Ages, Saint-Germain-des-Prés was an important spiritual and cultural center; around the abbey a new suburb mushroomed called the Faubourg Saint-Germain.

In the Renaissance, however, the discipline of the

monks was greatly relaxed, the abbots— appointed by the kings of France — lived in scandalous luxury and were corrupt.

The establishment was reformed in 1631 by the austere Benedictine congregation of Saint Maur. In 1636 the former medieval fortifications were reshaped with a new wall, towers and wet ditches filled by waters from the Seine. These fortifications were destroyed at the end of the 17th century. The French Revolution of 1789 abolished all monastic orders, the abbey was sold in 1794, and its buildings and gardens were swallowed up in the town. The abbatial church was secularized and used as a *salpétrière* (a gunpowder factory) and soon was badly damaged by fire. Neglected and abandoned, demolition was considered when, in 1822, it was restored and embellished by architect Hyppolite Flandrin. The abbatial church of Saint-Germain-des-Prés— after centuries of changes— is one of the oldest vestiges of French Romanesque architecture still existing today.

Saint-Martin-des-Champs Priory

In the 4th century AD a chapel was built in honor of Saint Martin, bishop of Tours. Around this chapel, many "miracles" occurred, the place became holy, a religious center developed, and in the 11th century a Benedictine priory was created — today corresponding to the quadrilateral formed by Rue au Maire, Rue Volta, Rue du Vert Bois, and Rue Saint Martin. In 1273, an enclosing wall with turrets, corner towers and a gatehouse was built around the priory. With the abolition of the monastic orders during the French Revolution, the Priory Saint Martin was seized by the state, and the premises have been used since 1799 to house the *Conservatoire National des Arts et Métiers* (National Conservatory for Arts and Crafts). Today, large parts of the old priory have been preserved, including the Saint Martin chapel, the Saint Nicolas church, various conventual buildings, and the remains of the 13th century fortifications.

20

The Second Part of the Hundred Years' War (1415–1453)

Civil and Foreign Wars

The impressive fortifications of Paris, the enceinte of Charles V, the castle of Vincennes, and the Bastille did not prevent Paris from being involved in another period of calamity. War with England, which everybody thought to have come to an end, raged again with particular violence at the beginning of the 15th century.

When Charles V died, his son the new king Charles VI the Madman (1380–1422) was only twelve years of age, and France was governed by the king's uncles who were primarily concerned with their own interests. When Charles VI assumed control of his realm he became suddenly mad and the uncles took power once again. They were soon at loggerheads among themselves, the rivalry became particularly intense and degenerated into a civil war with two opposing camps: the Armagnacs versus the Bourguignons. This was the moment which the king of England, Henry V, chose to resume his plans for the conquest of France.

Again the war began disastrously for the French. The battle of Agincourt on October 25, 1415 was another crushing defeat for the French cavalry, showing that they had learned nothing from their previous setbacks. The years that followed were among the darkest in French history. Again the control of Paris was at stake, torn apart between civil conflict and foreign war. The Bourguignons held Paris at first, then the city passed under Armagnac control and in 1417 the duke of Burgundy took control again while the king of England ruled over large parts of France. Yet France was not entirely occupied. The Loire valley had held out and parts of the center of the land had remained loyal to the new king Charles VII (1422–1461) who had established his capital in Bourges.

Jeanne d'Arc

Charles VII — the king of Bourges as his enemies called him with contempt — was powerless and discouraged. He was shaken from his apathy by a simple peasant girl, *Jeanne d'Arc* who— she believed — had heard divine voices ordering her to drive the English out of France. With a small escort she liberated Orleans, which was besieged by the English in May 1429. She won the battle of Patay and took the king to Reims where he was officially and solemnly crowned in September 1429. Jeanne was to continue her heroic struggle until her capture near Compiegne. After a shameful trial she was accused to be a witch and burned at the stake in Rouen in May 1431.

Along Rue de Rivoli in Paris, almost at the level of the Louvre's Pavillon de Marsan, is a small, rectangular square called Place des Pyramides with porticoes on three sides. In the center of the square is an equestrian statue of Jeanne d Arc, a work done by the sculptor Fremiet in 1874, which attracts pilgrimages every year.

The End of the War

The main achievement of Jeanne was that she shook Charles VII out of his torpor. The king soon reconciled with the powerful duke of Burgundy and began a series of military campaigns for which he got the nickname "The Victorious." At last, the French army was totally reorganized and well equipped with modern firearms and permanent battle-ready troops. As a result, the English were driven out of Paris, and Charles was able to make a triumphal entry into his capital in 1436. In the meantime many cities had risen in opposition to the occupiers and Charles defeated them in a series of victorious battles. By 1452, the English — who were divided in their turn by a civil war (the so-called War of the Roses) — were totally driven back to their island.

The Hundred Years' War was over but France — after so many years of foreign and civil wars — was truly a shambles.

Armor 15th century. In the 15th century many (rich) knights were clanking into battle and jousts encased in a complete armored suit. Articulated joints in the plate armor allowed for considerable maneuverability. In the course of the century, however, at the very time that the design of armor was nearing perfection, warfare was being transformed by cannons and handguns, whose explosive power would gradually turn the medieval ironclad knight into an antique curiosity.

21

Firearms

Gunpowder

The end of the Hundred Years' War, the wars between France and Burgundy, and the Italian Wars marked the end of the Middle Ages. The *Renaissance* saw the appearance of effective firearms and a change in the art of warfare.

The use of gunpowder as an explosive charge to provide the power to fire missiles was the most influential innovation in the history of warfare, but it is still not known who invented this substance. Though no certainty exists, the invention of gunpowder has been credited to the Chinese. The secret would have been known to the Arabs in the early 13th century and brought by them to Europe. Anyway the first convincing report of its manufacture was by the Franciscan friar Roger Bacon in the middle of the 13th century giving the formula of the mixture: salpeter, charcoal and sulfur in the proportion of 75 percent, 15 percent and 10 percent.

Early Guns

Who built the first cannon still remains a mystery. The first positive record of a gun was in 1326 at Florence (Italy), and the first known illustration occurs in the same year in an illuminated manuscript written by Walter de Milemete in honor of King Edward III of England. It showed a knight putting a red hot iron to the touch-hole of a pot-bellied, vase-shaped cannon from whose mouth an arrow is being fired. This early picture actually shows what artillery is all about and what a gun is: a tube closed at one end (breech) in which a charge of powder is burned to blow a projectile (shot) out of the other end (muzzle).

Primitive guns seem to have been used at Cambray in 1338, at Le Quesnoy in 1339, and at the siege of Algesiras in 1342. In 1346 it is known that King Edward of England used a number of guns in his victory over the French at the battle of Crécy. In March 1375 an order was received at Caen from Jehan le Mercier, one of the chancellors of the king of France, for the manufacture of a great iron gun, and Bernard de Montferrat was instructed to superintend the operation.

Inventive minds turned their attention to the novel machines and produced a proliferation of shapes and sizes. Ill manufactured, more dangerous for the user than for the enemy, cumbersome, slow to move and to load, shooting heavy stone balls at a very short range, these novelties in warfare were at first regarded as curiosities that did not seem to produce great effects on the battlefield.

One of the myths of history is that the twin inventions of gunpowder and cannons dominated the battlefields over night. This is untrue. Early guns made perhaps a fearful show but certainly proved to be of very little practical use. The unknown innovators, gun makers and early artillerists had little comprehension of the magnitude of the forces they were dealing with. The ineffectiveness of early guns was so common that many considered them dangerous toys which accomplished nothing except to frighten the horses. The appearance of artillery was a slow, dangerous and empirical process— not a sudden revolution. It took years and countless deadly failures before cannons were recognized as the weapons of the

Bombard Mons Meg. The huge muzzle-loading bombard Mons Meg, dating from about 1470, is now on exhibit at Edinburgh Castle (Great Britain). It weighs 5 tons, is 4 m (13 feet) in length, and its bore is about 50 cm (20 inches). It could fire a 136 kg (300 lb) stone shot over one mile.

future. From the battle of Crécy in 1346 (when primitive guns were used) to the campaign of Charles VIII in Italy in 1498 (when guns at last proved their worth), there is a period of 152 years. Together with technical difficulties, the development of fire weapons was thwarted by the invisible but powerful force of custom. Men of war were tolerably satisfied with their weapons on the whole, and they had good reasons for opposing a change which a later age was to consider a landmark of progress. Monarchs were reluctant to increase their military expenditures and were generally appalled at the cost of new weapons. The chivalric tradition held that it was ignoble to kill a man from a distance. The writer Cervantes put this sentiment in the mouth of his hero Don Quixote: "Blessed be those happy ages, that were stranger to the dreadful fury of these devilish instruments of artillery, whose inventor, I am satisfied, is now in hell, receiving the reward of his cursed invention!"

In spite of opposing forces, slow advances were made, imperfections were removed and improvements introduced. Progressively, artillery brought a change in the art of war. Early cannons were difficult — if not impossible — to move with the speed needed to keep up with the flow of battle, a cavalry charge or an infantry assault usually passed artillery in the field. But the most noteworthy impact of fire weapons would be soon felt in siege warfare.

Siege Artillery

In siege actions early guns were simply put down at a convenient point close to the selected point of breach, and that was it. The use of cannon against castles and fortified city walls led to the construction of monster guns. Their dimensions and the statistics of their firepower and capacities were formidable as was the terrifying effect they had on defenders. The most spectacular use of siege artillery so far witnessed came in 1453 when the Ottoman sultan Mehmet II attacked Constantinople. Cannons of considerably large size were used against the Byzantine capital; one of them was a 19-ton monster, eight m in length, able to fire a 680-kilogram stone ball for distances as far as one km. The Turkish artillery made wide breaches in the walls and allowed the Turks to capture the town and cause the collapse of the Eastern Christian Empire, a conquest that stupefied the Catholic Western world. An early monster cannon may still be seen today at the Edinburgh Castle; this famous gun, named *Mons Meg,* was probably built in Flanders about 1470. But giant guns, whatever their potential destructiveness, had severe limitations. They were extremely costly to produce, difficult to transport, and dangerous to operate, and had a poor rate of fire. They were thus useless on a battlefield and could only be employed in siege warfare.

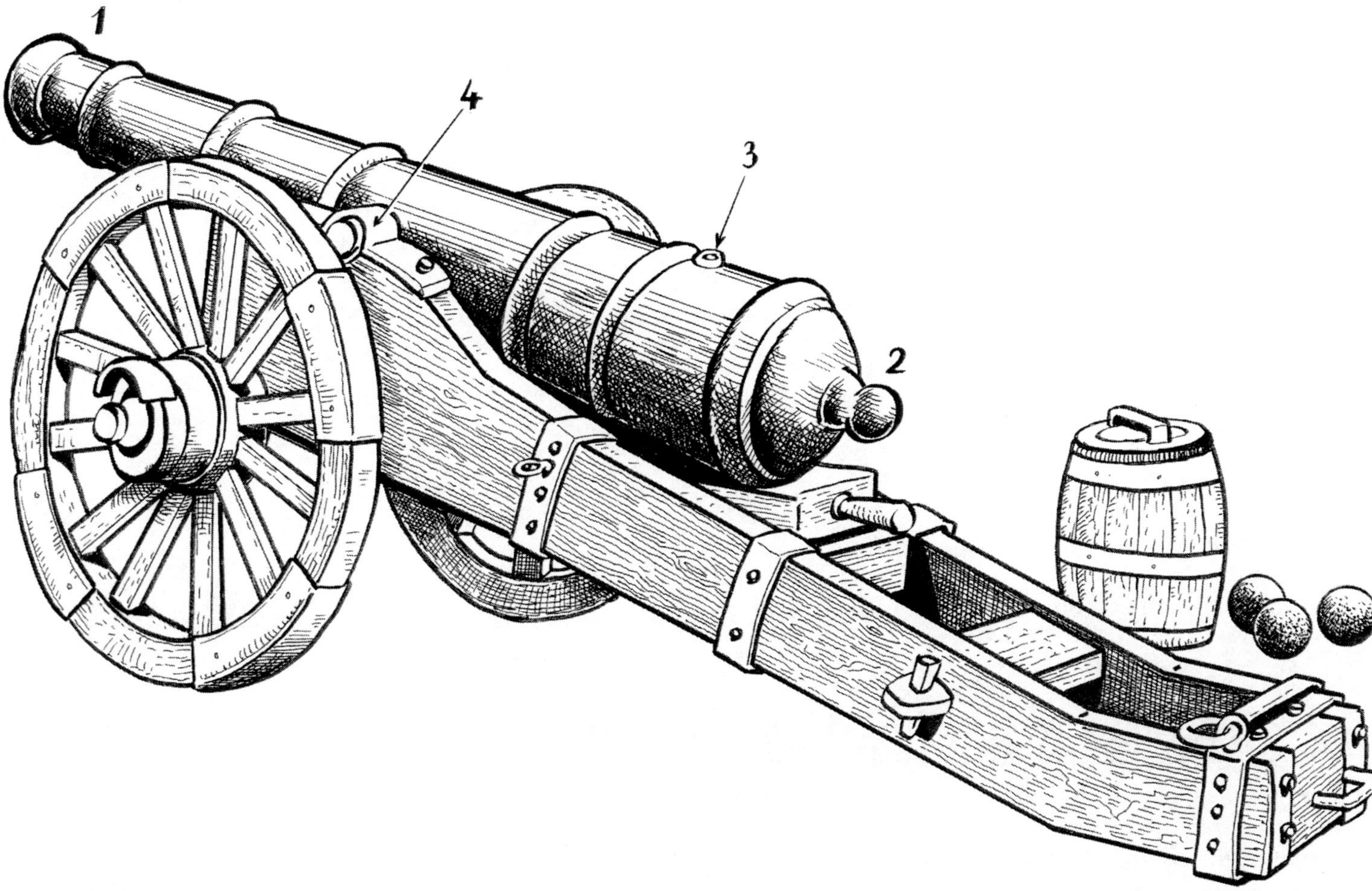

View of a gun. A cannon is composed of two main parts: gun and carriage. The gun is a tube open at the muzzle (1) and closed at the breech (2). The vent (3) is a small hole intended to ignite the propelling charge. The gun is fitted with trunnions (4) allowing it to be fixed firmly on a strong timber wheeled carriage.

Mine

Gunpowder also allowed a new siege method. Since ancient times, one of the standard techniques of breaching a fortress was to dig a tunnel under its wall and remove the foundations, shoring up the space with timbers which were then set on fire; when they collapsed so did the wall. Now kegs of gunpowder, or *mine*, could be detonated at the end of the tunnel to let the explosion blast away the solid foundations instead of excavating them by hand. This was however a double-edged sword, for the defenders could dig a *counter-mine* tunnel under or alongside the attacker's work and explode a countermine, thus entombing the attackers.

Improvement of Artillery

In the second half of the 15th century, several improvements made artillery effective weapons of war. The first nation to reverse the general trend towards larger and larger artillery were the French, who soon discovered that several small easily movable guns that could be fired at relatively short intervals were in fact much more effective than a single lumbering monster. It was during the reign of Louis XI that the first important advances were made. The king had created the charge of Grand Master of the Artillery and appointed two competent officers (the brothers Jean and Gaspar Bureau) to carry out the development of his artillery park.

The early large and heavy stone ball was gradually replaced by a small solid iron shot which had great effect against masonry and stone walls. Soon *grapeshot* or *langridge* (small metal balls, nails or miscellaneous hardware) was used, killing and maiming unprotected foot soldiers and mounted knights.

The art of manufacturing effective gunpowder was slowly acquired. The mixture was improved by developing a technique known as *corning* in which the three ingredients were mixed wet, dried into a cake and then crumbled and sieved to produce a granular *corned powder* giving rapid combustion and more powerful results. It became possible to safely stockpile and transport it and to charge stronger guns with more active propellant; the consequence was that projectiles had increased velocity and greater destructive power.

The technique of construction of cannons was gradually mastered. Barrels were greatly improved and bronze guns were cast and increased in strength. Their mobility was improved by the introduction of a *gun carriage* provided with trails and wheels, so that horses could be attached directly to the piece itself without the necessity for any independent means for transport. *Trunnions*—solid cylindrical projecting appendages—were placed at each side of the barrel, at the point where the gun received almost the entire impulse of the *recoil* (strong backward movement occurring when shooting), and they conveyed it to the trail of the carriage; this arrangement deprived the recoil of all that strength which had caused injury to the gunners. Various systems were invented for elevating and depressing the barrel, so that aiming was greatly improved.

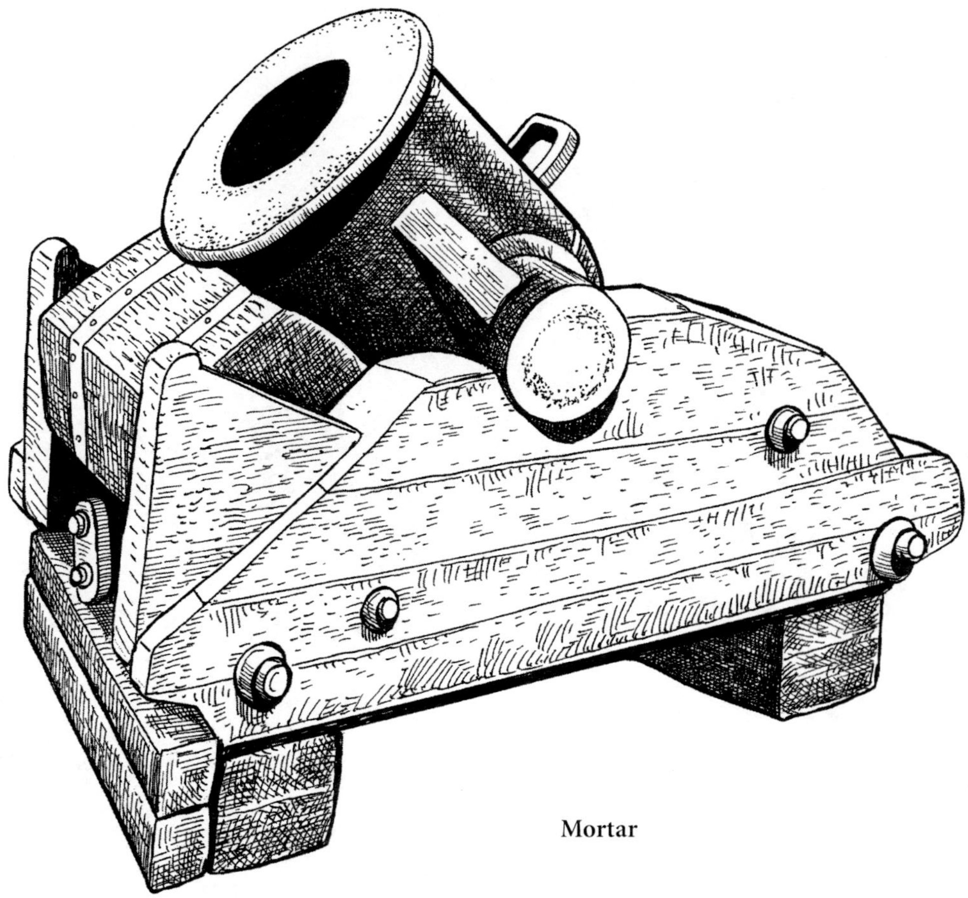

Mortar

Another significant development was the introduction at the end of the 15th century of the *mortar*. This was a short and massive gun, which fired its projectiles up into the air in a high trajectory (called *plunging fire*) so as to lob and drop them over walls and other defenses,

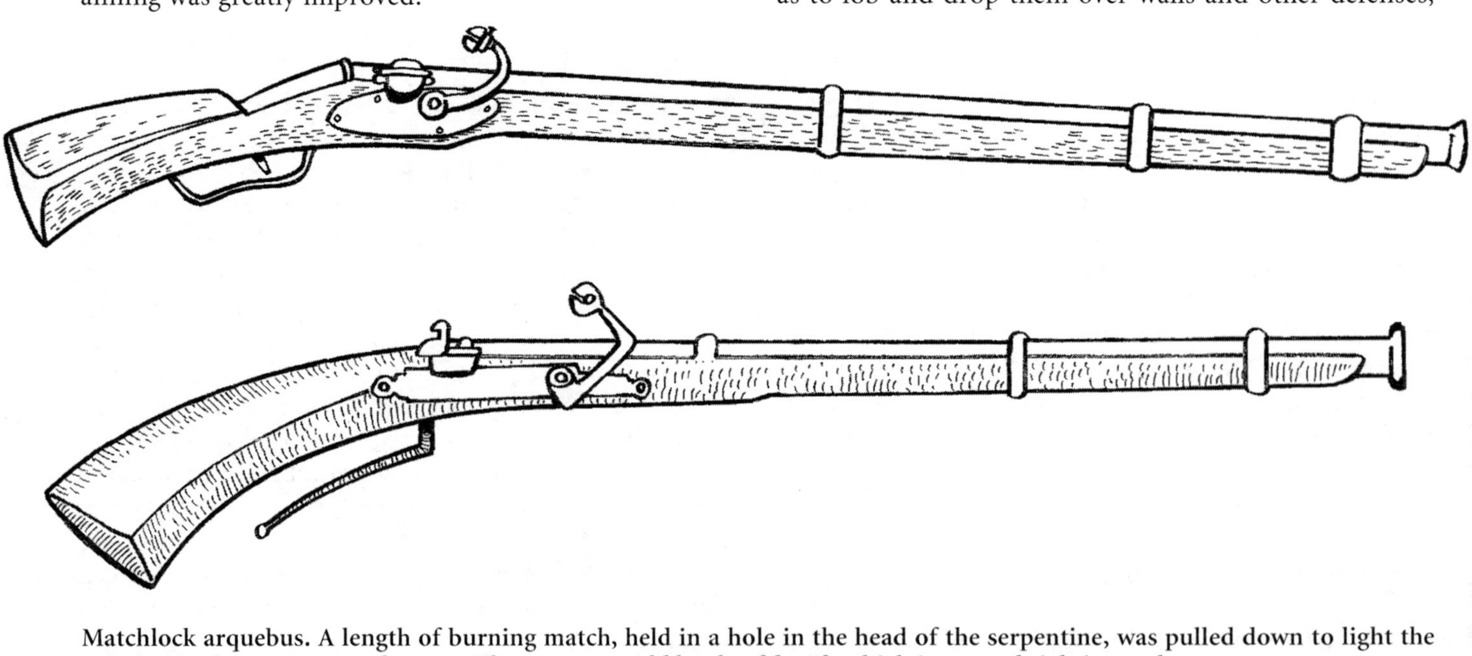

Matchlock arquebus. A length of burning match, held in a hole in the head of the serpentine, was pulled down to light the priming in the pan next to the vent. The weapon could be shouldered, which improved sighting and accuracy.

Early handgun man (15th century). The first handguns were in fact no more than muzzle-loading cannons in miniature. This one-man "firestick" was cradled under one arm, while the touch-hole was lit with the other hand holding a slow-burning match.

Principally used in siege warfare, it made no place in a fortress safe from plunging fire as it produced a veritable hailstorm of projectiles striking terror into the enemy and causing great danger and confusion. Instead of wheeled carriages, flat-based beds were used for supporting the mortar, which was transported on a wagon.

In the 18th century appeared a new piece of artillery, called *howitzer*; halfway between conventional gun and mortar, this short cannon mounted on wheels fired with a high angle of elevation in the *middle register* (between 10 and 45 degrees).

Handguns

Once the cannon had been recognized and established as a destructive machine of war, the next step was to arm the foot soldier with a smaller version of this device—a hand gun that could be carried easily and used in a flexible situation. As early as 1364, inventive minds developed a simple iron tube with a touch-hole; as the tube became too hot to hold after a few shots had been fired, it was fitted with a wooden handle or tiller. Early portable handguns were a strange and varied collection of motley cross-bred dangerous weapons. They were often clumsy, needed to be supported on the ground, and often required two soldiers to operate: one holding and aiming the weapon, the other applying fire (by means of a slow match) to the touch-hole. The *match* was a slow-burning fuse of rope in a treated gunpowder mixture, which smoldered continuously. Despite its imperfections, the handgun proved its worth rapidly as it could penetrate the knight's armor. There were many stages in the development of handguns. Soon one-man firing tubes were created fixed on crude wooden stocks. Barrels were lengthened to obtain greater accuracy and various mechanisms were invented for firing, each of which added to the weapon's reliability and effectiveness.

Decisive improvements were the introduction of the shoulder-stock to support the barrel and keep the butt steady, and a system simultaneously allowing the igniting of the powder charge while leaving the gunner free to

which the flat trajectory of the cannon could not reach. Cannons fire in what is termed the *lower register*, or *grazing fire*, below 45 degrees. Mortars fire in the *upper register*, that is over 45 degrees. The short and rather wide barrel of the mortar enabled a charge of shot to be spread over a broader area. The mortar was thus intended to hit an enemy hidden behind a cover, a parapet or in a trench. Shooting with small stones and later with large explosive and incendiary bombs (fused to explode after a set time), the mortar was originally haphazard, aimed in the general direction of the target and relying on trial and error.

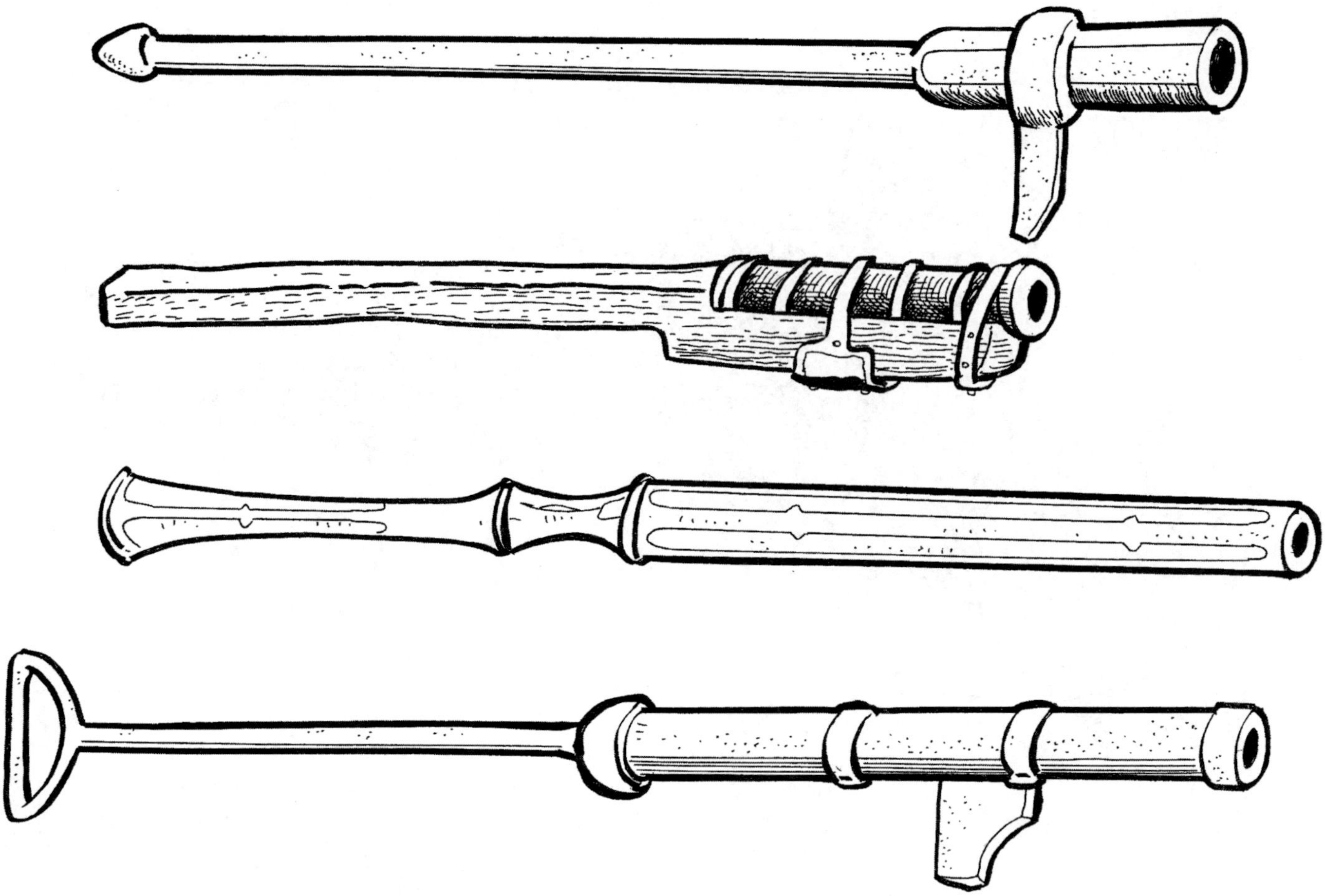

Early handguns. Early handguns were unreliable, complicated to fire and aim. The handgun became a useful and satisfactory weapon only when it developed into the arquebus.

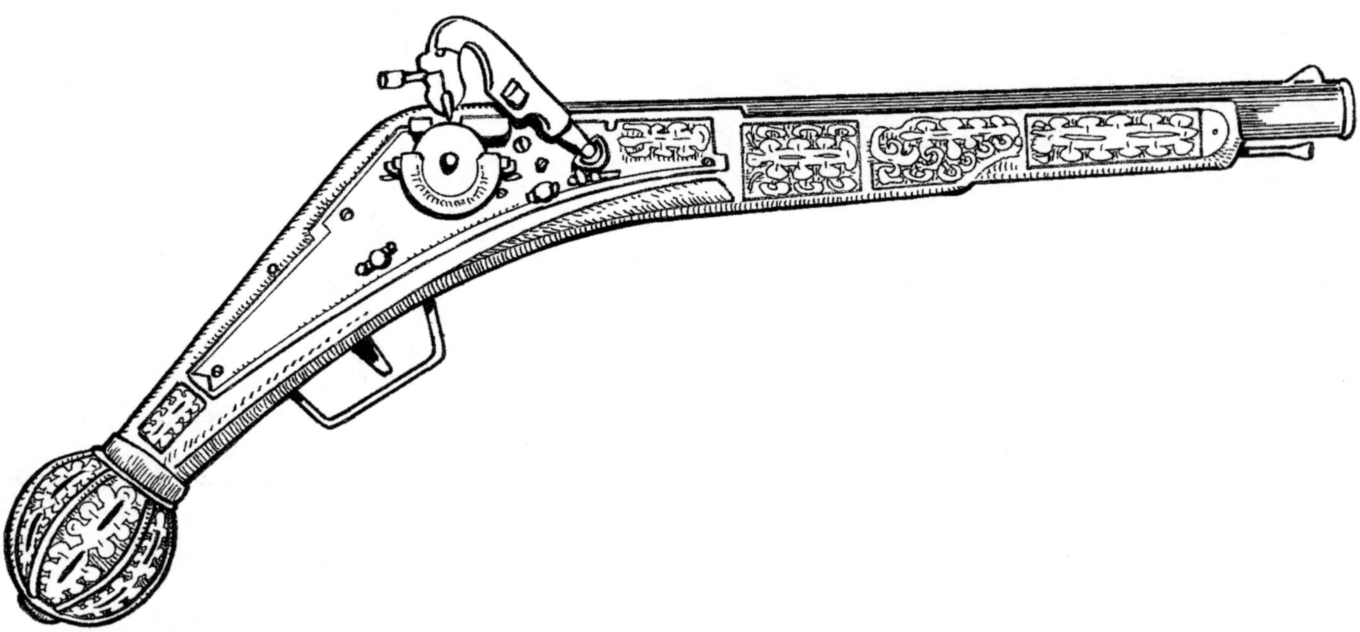

Wheel lock pistol. The first practical pistols were wheel lock, basically working on the principle of a cigarette lighter. The wheel protruding through the bottom of the pan, was wound up on a spring. Pulling the trigger let the wheel spin and brought a piece of iron pyrite down to strike a spark. Wheel lock pistols were eagerly adopted by the cavalry in Europe in the late 15th century.

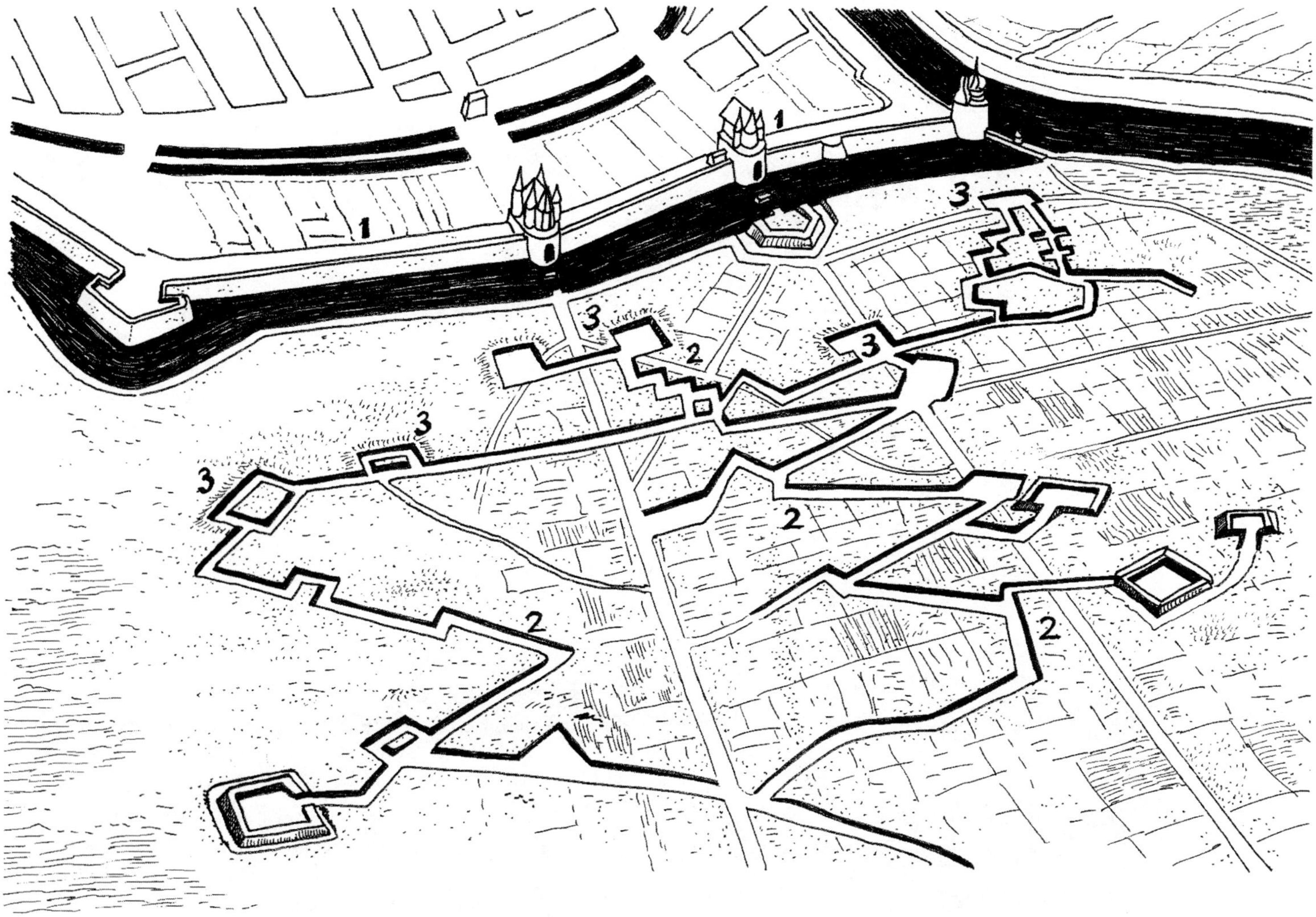

Siege with firearms. Firearms obliged the assailing party to develop techniques of screening siege-fortifications made of earth. The first phase of the siege was an artillery duel. The useful range of siege cannons being about fifty m, attacking methods consisted of bringing artillery as close as possible to the defensive walls (1) by digging a network of trenches (2) in zigzag patterns to avoid enfilade fire. Besiegers placed their guns in batteries (3) and bombarded the defenders deployed on towers and on walls.

steady his weapon and take aim. This was provided in the 1480s by the introduction of an S-shaped piece of metal fixed to the side of the weapon. The slow burning match was held in one side of the device and brought down on the touch-hole when the lower end of the S—the trigger—was pulled. Complex and efficient sophistications were added to this simple principle, giving birth to the *arquebus* and later the *matchlock musket*, gradually transforming the medieval soldier into an infantryman with lethal firepower.

At the same time a smaller version of the portable handgun was developed by Italian designers, known as a *pistol*, which could be fired with one hand, a suitable weapon for cavalrymen.

In the early 16th century, handguns were still heavy weapons (the arquebus weighed about 25 pounds) and took rather long to load; range was poor, but they could fire a one-ounce ball that could penetrate conventional armor with little difficulty.

Small fire-weapons did possess another advantage: they required little training for use. Unlike the archer, who had to develop a strong forearm in order to draw the bowstring effectively, an arquebusier could learn how to load and fire his weapon after only a few days' instruction.

Warfare with Fire Weapons

These new inventions were not found to be completely successful on a large scale until Charles VIII of France crossed the Alps and marched into Italy with a view to conquering the kingdom of Naples in 1498. The campaign failed, but the formidable French artillery made a profound impression on warfare.

Fortress gun. This small caliber cannon, dating from the end of the 14th century was carried on a primitive form of pivot mounting as a defensive weapon for the fortress.

Of the many consequences of the introduction of firearms was the abandonment of medieval armor and the supremacy of paid foot soldiers armed with long pikes and muskets, who rendered the medieval horse-mounted knight obsolete. The first convincing demonstration that handguns could determine the outcome of a battle was the 1503 clash at Cerignola, where charging French cavalry were mowed down by the massed fire of Spanish arquebusiers. Deadly as they quickly proved themselves to be, the first arquebusiers were little more than auxiliaries employed to create a protective fringe for the massive squares of traditional foot soldiers who—armed with shock weapons (usually very long pikes)—carried the main burden of battle. But the Spanish victory at Pavia in 1525 convinced the Spaniards that firearms were now an essential feature of modern warfare, and their infantry, organized after 1534 into 3,000-strong regiments known as *tercios*, included a substantial complement of shot. Other countries were soon to follow the Spanish example, and the ratio of pikemen and arquebusiers was gradually altered.

Gunpowder, cannons and handguns also represented a severe challenge to the traditional code of medieval chivalry that considered personal combat and duel between warriors to be an indispensable test of knightly valor. To many contemporary observers, firearms, with their belching flames, their sulfurous stench and their unprecedented destructive power, were tools of the devil. But the introduction of the new weapons could not be stopped. Even the Church argued that those who were fighting for a just cause—in defense of Christendom against the infidels, for example—deserved to be at least as well armed as were their enemies. To remove any doubt about where it stood on the matter, the Church provided gunners with their own patron saint: Barbara.Warfare with firearms and permanent armies composed of mercenaries cost huge sums of money. Only kings, emperors and great princes could afford to maintain a modern army, and to do so they had to levy new taxes on their population and to arrange for loans from bankers. War could no longer be a private business, it became the privileged undertaking of the State.

22

Transitional Fortification

A Gradual Problem

The introduction of fire weapons also had consequences on fortifications. Once again it must be pointed out that cannons did not render medieval castles and city walls obsolete overnight. Adaptation of fortification was as slow as the progressive evolution of firearms. Early cannons were heavy and cumbersome; and even fitted with wheels, they often had to be manhandled across difficult terrain, across rivers, through marshes, even up

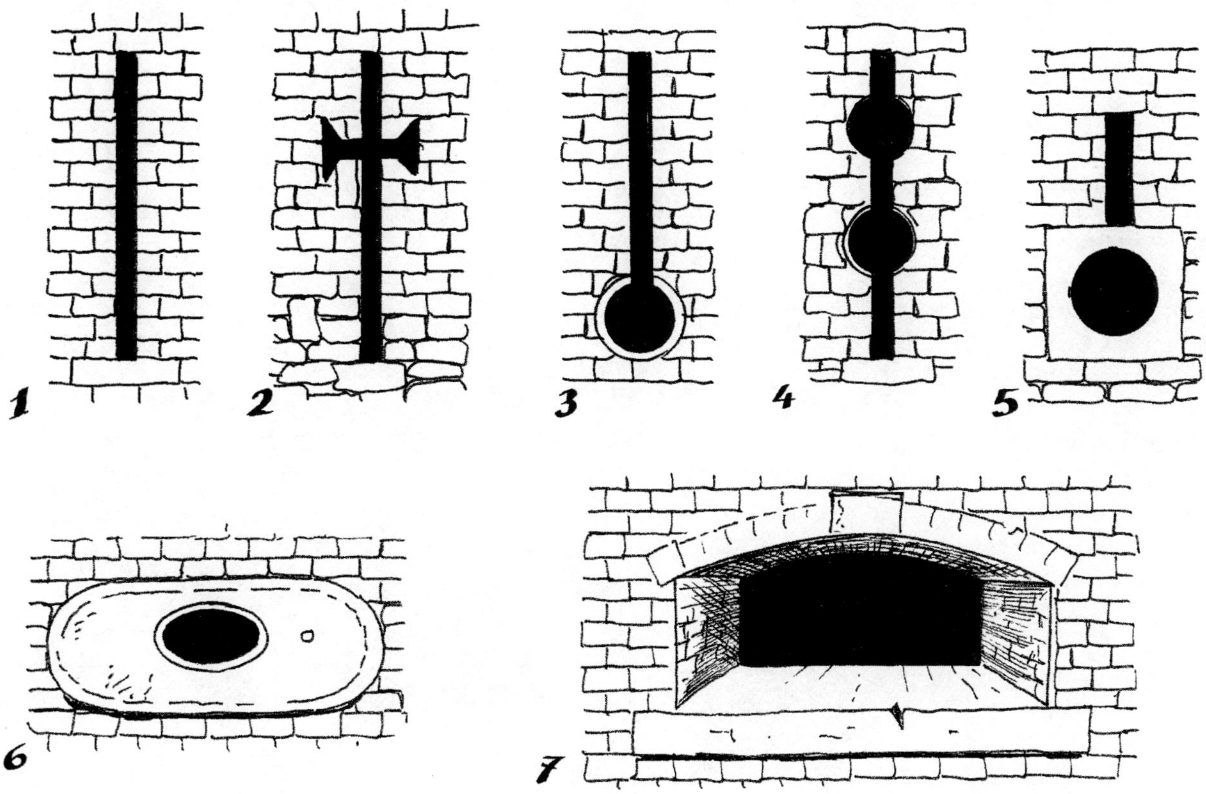

Combat apertures. 1. Medieval arrow slit for shooting with bows. 2. Medieval arrow slit for shooting with crossbows. 3, 4, 5 and 6. Adaptation for fire weapons. 7. Gun port.

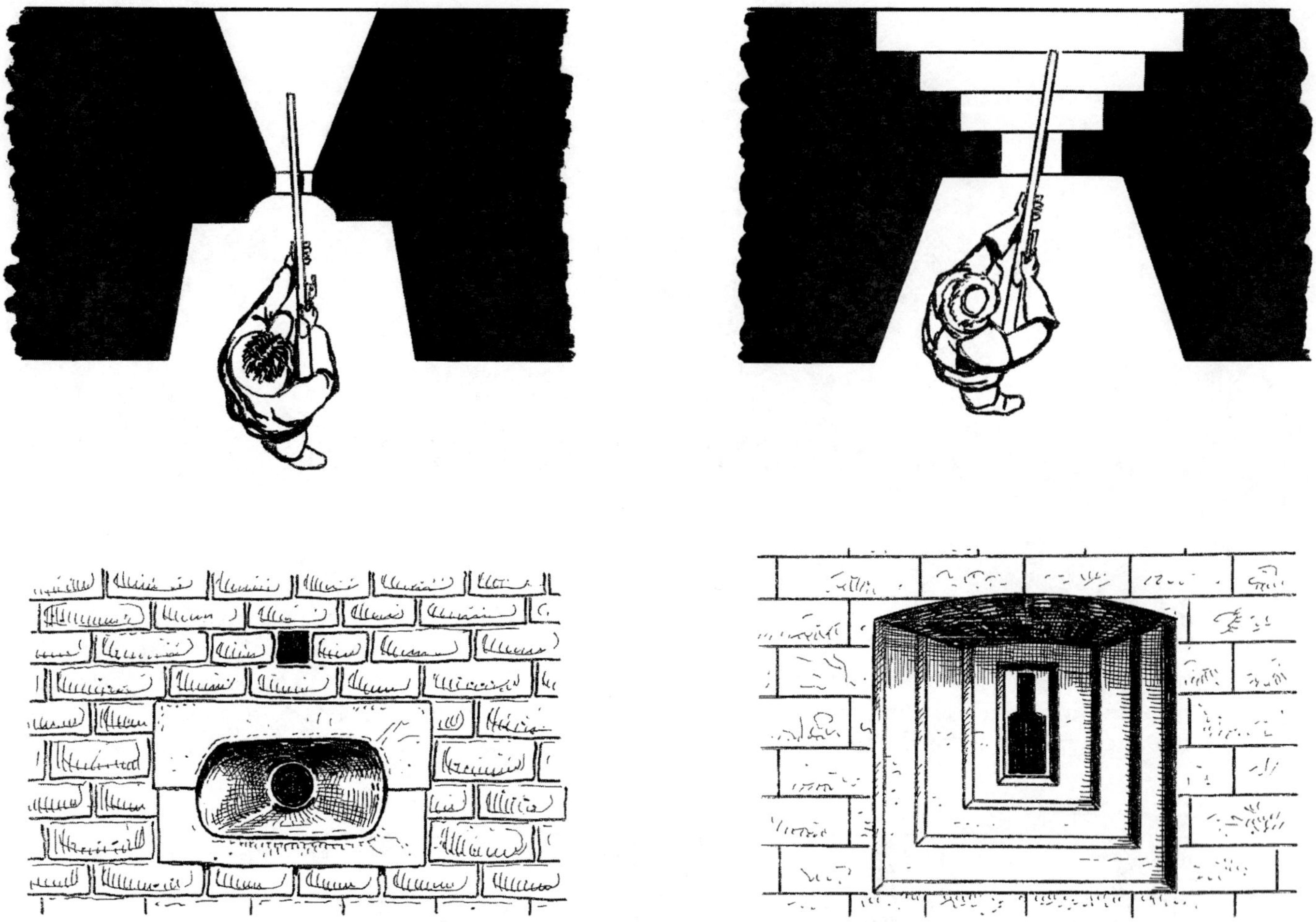

Embrasures for small firearms. ***Left (top and bottom):*** plan and front view of the so-called embrasure "à la française" about 1470. ***Right (top and bottom):*** plan and front view of an embrasure "à trémie"—with the aperture arranged as a kind of staircase in order to protect against ricocheting splinters and projectiles.

cliffs to be engaged against a castle or a city. A suitably situated fortress, well protected by natural defenses, could stay out of range.

Military commanders and engineers were quick to realize that the guns which so effectively attacked and reduced medieval strongholds and walled cities could equally well be used for defense. Obviously medieval fortifications were not suitable for mounting cannons. Gradually the problem of fortification versus firearms appeared to be twofold: how to protect oneself against enemy fire and how to use guns from a fortified position.

Gun port (embrasure)

Transitional fortification adapted to firearms (end of 15th century. Existing medieval fortresses were adapted to the operating of fire weapons by means of the following elements. 1. Combat aperture for small arms. 2. Embrasure for cannons in casemates. 3. Bulwark. 4. Tower lowered at the level of the wallwalk. 5. Ramparted wall transformed into a gun platform. 6. Fausse-braie. 7. Moineau or caponier.

Rampart

In order to protect existing fortresses against enemy artillery fire, several solutions were found. Elevated towers and high walls with crenellations and machicolation had become exposed targets; in reaction, the defenders gradually abandoned the benefit of height and reduced the size of their walls and towers. The tendency was to lower the works but at the same time to increase the thickness of the masonry. This quickly proved extremely expensive and of dubious efficiency. A cheaper and more effective method was introduced: the *rampart*, composed of a front and a rear masoned wall holding a large and thick mass of earth, absorbing the shock of cannonballs just like a pillow.

Embrasure

Making, or trying to make, fortifications resistant to artillery was only half the battle — the other half was integrating guns into defensive arrangements. The first step was to adapt existing elements. The long vertical and narrow loopholes, placed in medieval towers, gatehouses and barbicans, intended for shooting bows and crossbows were enlarged and widened. They became full-scale *embrasures* or *portholes*, permitting the discharge of firearms. Blocked with shutters when not in use, they were of various sizes depending on the weapons used: small for handguns and large for cannons.

Artillery Emplacements

The medieval wall was generally too narrow to allow the use of large guns, and the defenders could not easily move their artillery from one place to another in a hurry such as up and down stairs and from one tower to another. So new artillery emplacements had to be created. A solution was to place the guns on top of towers; these were lowered, arranged as a roofless firing platform, and fitted with thick parapets. Inside the tower, *casemates*

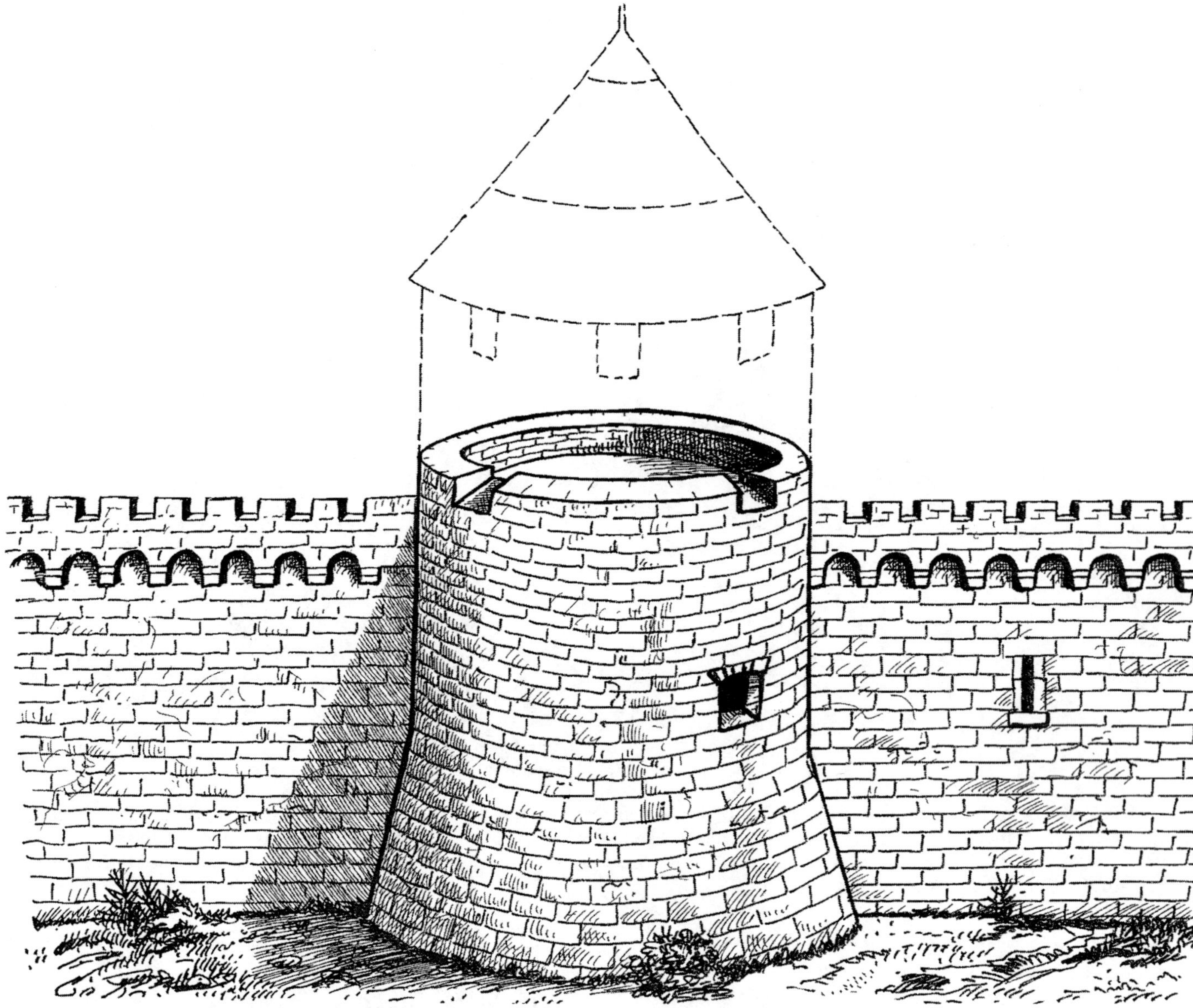

Artillery tower. In an attempt to adapt to firearms, medieval towers were lowered to the level of the wall. The top crenellation was replaced by a few gun embrasures, and the story was arranged as a casemate.

(firing chambers fitted with an embrasure) could be built in the stories; they protected gun and crew, but their arc of fire was considerably limited, and after a few shots the vaulted chamber was full of choking fumes.

Another solution was the creation of a *bulwark*, an open projecting ramparted terrace allowing placement, supply, firing, recoil and the clearing of smoke.

A similar arrangements was the *fausse-braie*, a low projecting ramparted gun terrace parallel to the main wall.

The 15th century saw the appearance of the *moineau*, also called *caponier*, a small, low-profiled work projecting across the ditch for short-range flanking defense; this closed vaulted casemate was fitted with firing holes through which musketry fire could be delivered against the enemy in the ditch.

Bulwarks, fausse-braies and artillery towers were projected ahead of the earlier medieval defenses to shield them from enemy fire.

Makeshifts

The addition of these structures—built in various dimensions, forms and amounts of solidity specifically for use with cannon to existing fortifications—were nonetheless only makeshift.

The so-called transitional fortification was merely

an improvised and hastened attempt to answer the crisis caused by the introduction of firearms; in essence it remained predominantly vertical and in the medieval spirit. Though difficult to breach and to undermine, it remained an ill-suited method of defense when the characteristic effects of artillery fire became more clearly understood.

Examples of transitional fortification are still numerous in Europe: the forts of Deal, Saint-Mawes and Southsea on the southern coast of England, the fort of Salses near Perpignan (southern France), Bellver castle in Palma de Majorca (Spain), Michelangelo castle in Civitavecchia (Italy), and the city of Rhodes on the island of the same name (Greece), just to name a few.

The improvement and the increasing costs involved in the construction of fortification signaled a move away from the private civilian castle to the state military fortress. Very few feudal lords could afford the cost of both guns and artillery-adapted fortresses. Warfare became the prerogative of kings, emperors and states, rather than a matter of petty quarrels among rival local barons.

Since the 12th century, feudalism was declining, and artillery brought a definitive end to the Middle Ages.

23

Paris After the Hundred Years' War

Louis XI

Louis XI (1461–1483) was active, authoritarian, clever and ruthless. Under his reign, France gradually recovered from the terrible ordeal of the Hundred Years' War. The new king reorganized finances, administration and justice, but his financial measures caused rumblings of discontent among the majority of the nobles who formed a common front against him, in what came to be known under the curious name of the *Guerre du Bien Public* (War of the Public Good). Louis XI defeated the rebels in July 1465, but during the civil war the king was concerned

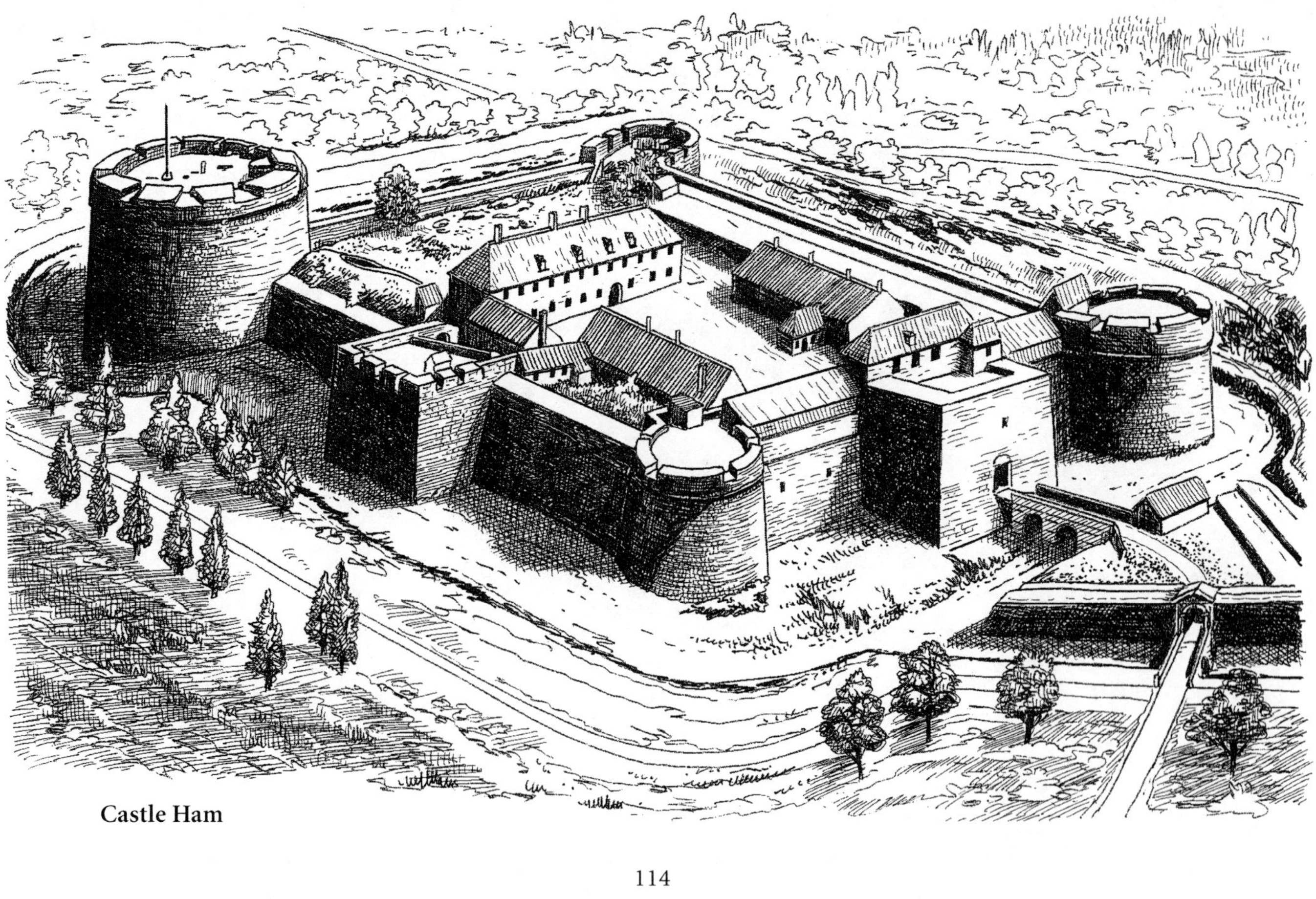

Castle Ham

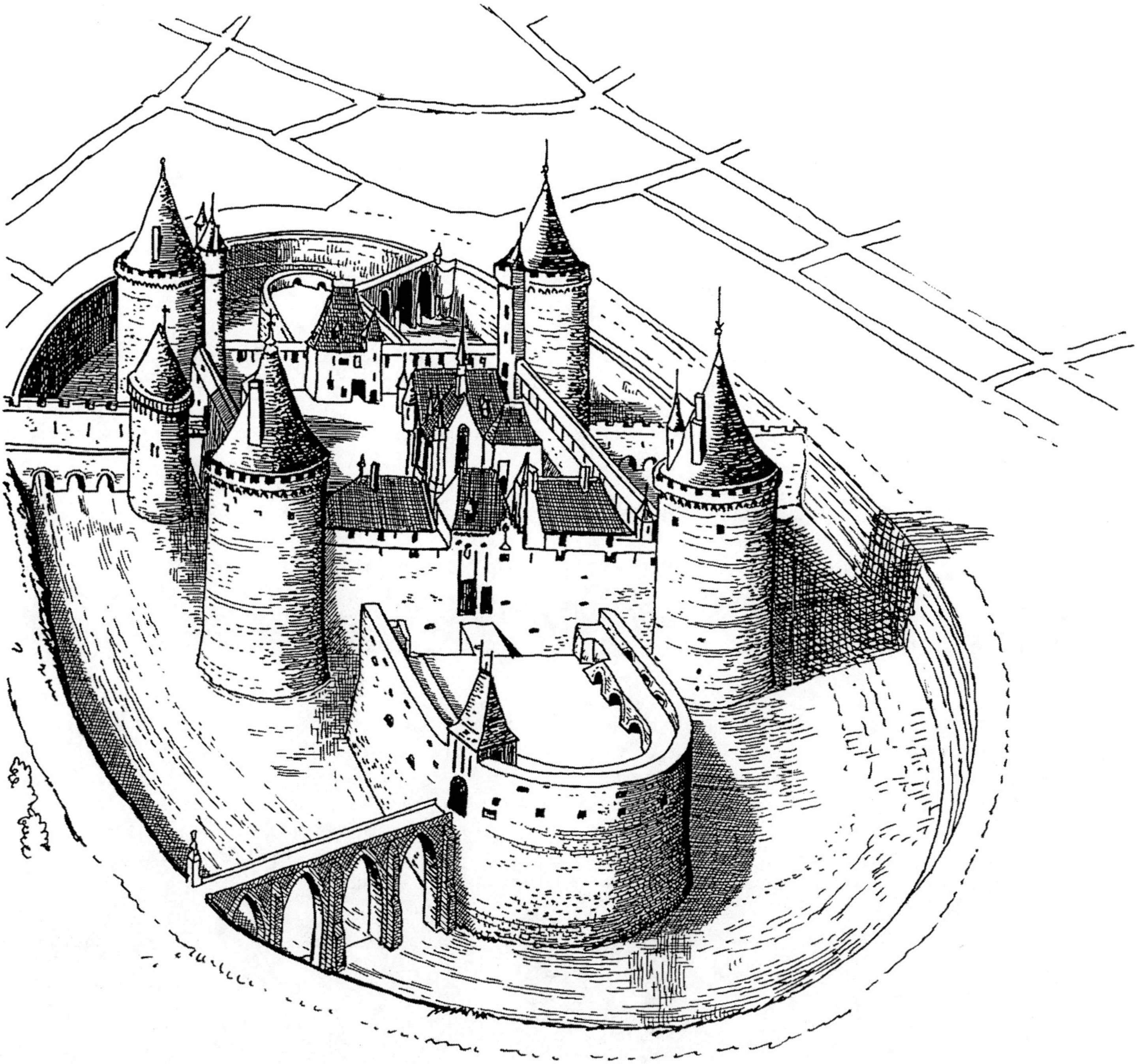

Citadel of Dijon (Burgundy)

with the defenses of Paris and had improvements made to the fortification of the capital.

Throughout his reign, Louis XI also worked tirelessly for the enlargement of France. One of his main concerns was to secure the towns in the Somme region — Arras and Peronne — as a protection for the vulnerable northeastern frontier. At the time, these towns were in the hands of Charles Le Téméraire (the Bold), the powerful duke of Burgundy, whose ambition was to create his own kingdom between France and Germany. After a bitter struggle, the kingdom of France swelled considerably as Louis XI seized Burgundy after the death of Charles the Bold in 1477. Louis XI added to the royal possessions not only the rich duchy of Burgundy but also Anjou and Provence in 1480.

In spite of his bad reputation, Louis XI was a rather good monarch. He restored monuments, revived agriculture, encouraged the first industrial enterprises and mines, had the road network repaired and established the first postal service.

Citadels and Forts

Militarily, the reign of Louis XI marked the appearance of important innovations: the introduction of efficient artillery (as discussed above) and new kind of fortification: citadels and forts.

In the capital of Burgundy, Dijon, and in the important cities of Beaune and Auxonne, Louis XI ordered the construction of *citadels*. This was a typical fortress built inside a fortified town. It had its own garrison, accommodations and supply house to resist a siege. It could be used as a final fall-back position, a safe place to withdraw if the rest of the town was conquered. The citadel was also a military, fiscal and administrative center intended to control and awe the newly conquered population. The citadel of Dijon—completed in 1512 under Louis XII's reign—was a huge square with four high circular corner towers and two large barbicans covering the gatehouses: the Boulevard de la Ville facing the town and the Boulevard Louis XII turned towards the countryside. The fortress—though fitted with machicolations and crenellations reflecting the strength of medieval tradition—was fully adapted to the use of fire weapons with thick stone walls, artillery emplacements, embrasures and casemates. It was dismantled in 1890.

The royal authority also manifested itself at the borders and on the coasts of the realm by the creation of forts. A *fort* was quite different from a traditional medieval castle; it was a stronghold built by the state to defend a strategic point and only manned by a professional military garrison. For example, the Castle Ham situated near Péronnes in the Somme was completed by 1480 as an advanced defense placed on the road north of Paris. Fully adapted to firearms, the fort was a regular rectangle surrounded by a deep ditch; it had low and thick walls, massive casemated artillery towers and a huge donjon called the Tour du Connétable with walls 11 m thick. Fort Ham was still in military use in the 17th century and became a state prison in the 19th century. The most famous prisoner was prince Louis-Napoléon Bonaparte (future Emperor Napoléon III), who managed to escape in 1846. Fort Ham was destroyed by the Germans during World War I in 1917.

Transitional Fortifications in Paris

In Paris, during the Guerre du Bien Public and during the conflict against the duke of Burgundy, Louis XI ordered the improvement of the defense. The fortifications completed in 1420 under Charles V's reign were partly adapted to the use of firearms. Details of these local improvements are little known, but archaeological excavations made in 1989–1990 near the Carrousel square and the Louvre museum seem to indicate the construction of low U-shaped artillery towers, earthen bulwarks and the widening of the ditch. At the same time, the Louvre castle, the Palais of the Cité island, the Bastille, as well as both Châtelets lost their military and residential functions; they were used as prisons, arsenals and administrative buildings.

Paris began gradually to grow again after the calamity of the Hundred Years' War. The city remained the capital of France but the kings preferred other places to dwell, notably the Loire valley. Charles VII resided in the provinces of Touraine and Poitou, while Louis XI liked to govern from his own castle Plessis-lès-Tours. The kings of France had forgotten neither Etienne Marcel's uprising nor the equivocal pro–English attitude of the rich citizens. Henceforth they eyed the Parisian bourgeoisie distrustfully.

24

The End of the Middle Ages

Wars in Italy

The successor of Louis XI was his son, Charles VIII the Affable (1483–1498), but being only thirteen, his elder sister, Anne de Beaujeu, was made regent. A lively and clever woman, Anne obtained the annexation of Brittany, the large western province with Celtic background which had always been virtually independent from France. From his great uncle, King René of Anjou, Charles VIII had inherited rights to the kingdom of Naples (Italy). In 1498, he set about the conquest, which turned out to be a fairly easy matter owing to his modern army and his efficient artillery.

The victorious conquest of Naples was however short lived as almost all the Italian princes and cities united against the king of France and ousted him. The only positive aspect of this ill-advised war was the introduction of works of art and Italian artists bringing to France the first achievements of the Italian Renaissance.

When Charles VIII died in the end of 1498, he left no male heir for the throne of France. The crown went to his brother-in-law and cousin, Louis of Valois-Orleans, the son of the poet Charles de Valois; Louis became king Louis XII the Father of the People (1498–1515).

Louis XII revived Charles VIII's Italian ambitions. On the pretext that his grandmother, Valentine Visconti, held certain right over the duchy of Milan, Louis XII foolishly embarked on another Italian adventure. In 1499, he took Genoa, Milan and Naples. In 1501, Pope Julian II formed a Holy Alliance of Italian princes and free cities; soon all conquests were lost and the French driven out of Italy. When Louis XII died in 1515, he left no male heir and the crown of France passed to his son-in-law and cousin, François d'Angoulême who reigned from 1515 to 1547 as François I. In a resolute attempt to recover the duchy of Milan, François I—once again—crossed the Alps and defeated the pope's Holy Alliance. But soon France was confronted by a new and powerful enemy. Charles V of Spain (also known as *Carlos Quinto* or *Charles Quint*)—a great-grandson of Duke Charles the Bold of Burgundy—was not only king of Spain, duke of Austria, master of Flanders and of almost the whole of Italy, he was also elected Emperor of Germany in 1519; Charles was also the ruler of huge territories in South America. In Europe, his states encircled France. A long struggle with intermittent truces began between France and Spain, only to end in 1659. Wars raged continuously with various outcomes, but the king of France fought tenaciously against Carlos Quinto. He managed, with difficulty, to maintain his position and in the end triumphed over him. François I was also a patron of the arts. He seldom resided in Paris but preferred to sojourn in the many castles—which were more palaces for pleasure than military fortresses—that he had built in the new elegant and light Renaissance style: Chambord, Blois, Fontainbleau and Rambouillet, where he died in 1547.

The Renaissance

The *Renaissance* (French for rebirth) of the 15th century originated in Italy, especially in Florence, but gradually it spread all over western Europe. It marked the decay of medieval certainties, a new era in thought and feeling, and the appearance of a new and constructive attitude toward the whole world, as well as a new conception of man himself. By that time there arose the sense of man's tremendous powers and the conception of "modern" and "ancient" times. There was a resurgence of interest in Greek and Roman Antiquity, and certain perceptible changes heralded the approach of a new age: the great discoveries of unsuspected worlds such as America increased the quest for new lands, the printing press made books more widely available, and gunpowder and firearms changed the way war was waged. To the upper classes of society, the new attitude changed both taste and way of life. It praised a proper enjoyment of wealth, glorified the activities of man, and put the emphasis on individualism and outstanding attainments. This was masterfully reflected in the area of culture, particularly in new forms of painting, sculpture and architecture.

The organization of society remained basically the same. The king was still the supreme sovereign, but he was advised by a council and a parliament. Medieval serfdom was definitely on the way out; despite the great demands which were still made on them by means of taxes, the material situation of the peasants was improving.

The towns, since the 12th century, had greatly expanded, and the *bourgeoisie*—the urban middle class—assumed more and more importance. International trade and industrial enterprises (mines and quarries) began to make their appearance. Universities were developed which were attended by thousands of students who became educated men, high functionaries, civil servants, administrators, officers, and royal counselors.

Once its war wounds had heeled, Paris welcomed in Renaissance art, although none too hurriedly. The Hôtel de Sens (as previously described) was still considerably Gothic in style. In 1532, the construction of the Saint Eustache church was begun, a brilliant reflection of the transition from Gothic to the new-born art form. The Hôtel de Ville (town hall) was rebuilt in 1533 by Pierre de Chambiges to plans drawn up by a Tuscan architect named Buccador. The Louvre was considerably changed in Renaissance form from 1546 onwards. François I commissioned the work to architect Pierre Lescot who built the southern half-wing on the west side, while Jean Goujon made the elegant sculptures.

The end of the 15th century also saw the appearance of new methods of fortification.

PART III

Bastioned Fortifications (1512–1874)

25

Italian Bastioned Fortifications

Early Italian Theorists

The kings of France's pointless expeditions in Italy in the Renaissance—where artillery had been so important and decisive—had clearly shown the weakness of medieval fortification based on verticality. The Renaissance had made military engineers well aware of mathematics and geometry and all the other sciences necessary for their trade. Niccolo Tartaglia, a mathematician from Brescia (Italy), produced in 1537 his *Nova Scienta* (New Science), the first important treatise on the scientific application of gunnery and the first attempt to evaluate *ballistics* (science of the trajectory of projectiles). Before him, great artists and architects such as Albrecht Dürer, Leonardo da Vinci, Michelangelo and Giorgio Martini, who also made a living with military designs, gave this problem some thought—some of it

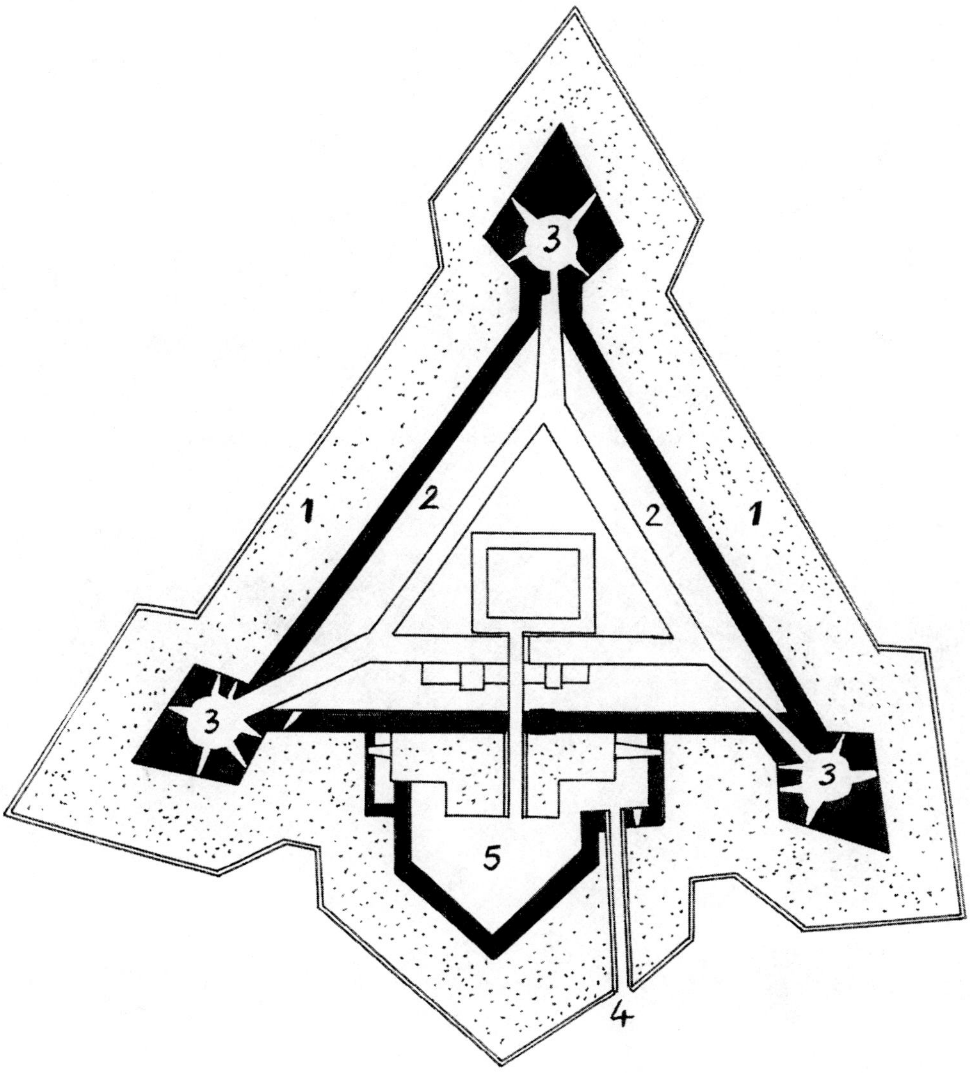

Theoretical design of a fort by Francesco di Georgio Martini (about 1490). Martini's design included a ditch (1) enclosing a triangular enceinte (2) defended by pentagonal towers (3) placed at the angles. The entrance (4) was protected by an early form of ravelin (5).

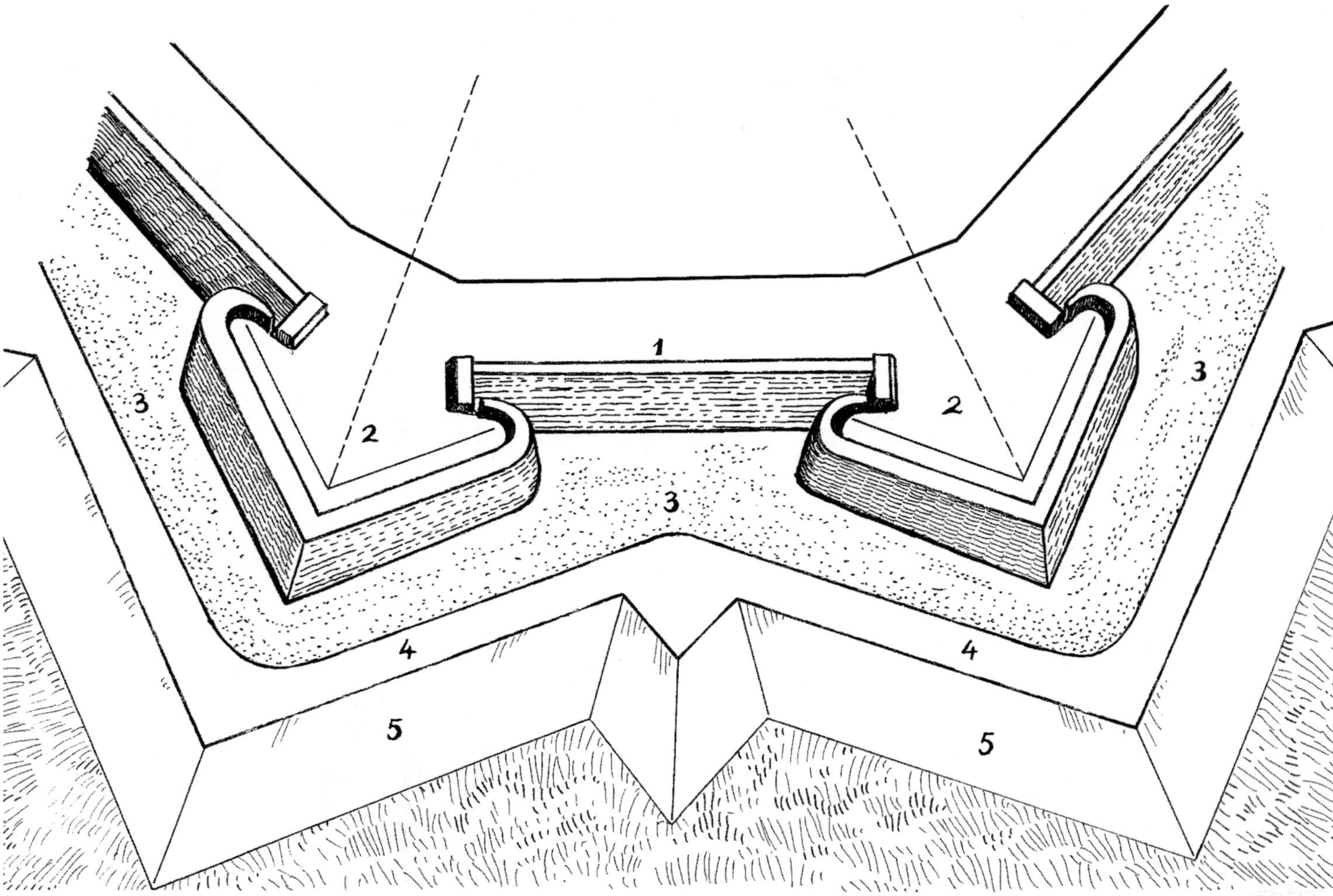

Italian bastioned front. The ground plan shows the basic elements of a typical Italian bastioned fortification including: 1. Curtain. 2. Bastion with orillon. 3. Ditch. 4. Covered way. 5. Glacis.

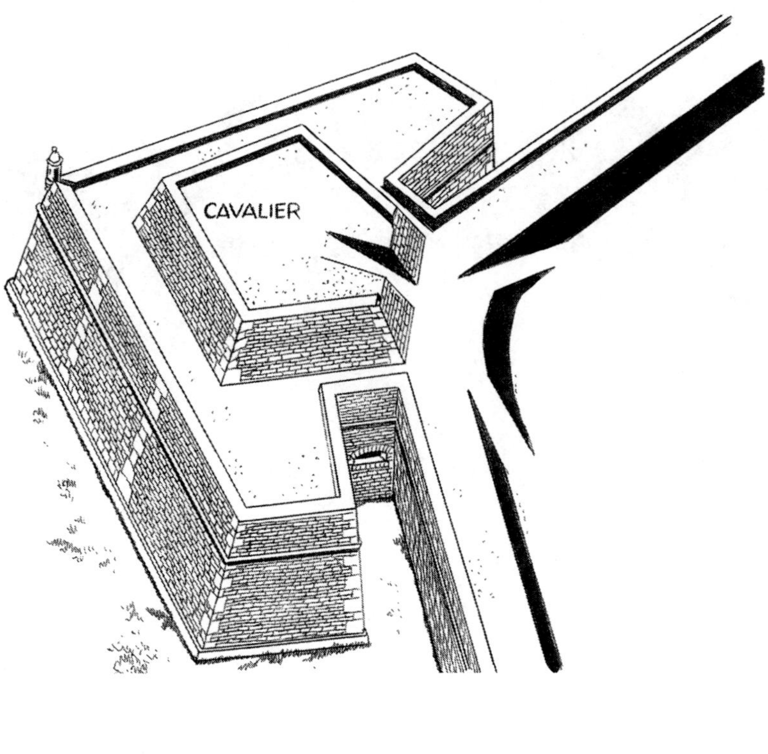

Left: **Bastion with "cavalier"**

extravagant and some quite useful — paving the way for further developments. Approaching the matter rather more as a theoretical exercise in architecture design than with any appreciation of tactics with firearms, the early theorists, however, produced a number of speculations, resulting in the introduction of a new method of fortification based on deep ditches, thick ramparts, artillery towers and casemated works with interlocking fields of fire.

Italian Bastioned Front

Indeed, it was noted that a shot fired across an enemy line (called *enfilade* or *flanking fire*) was far more effective than a direct frontal barrage. It was also advocated that digging down for defense was more effective than building up; fortifications should be low with the walls sunk into a deep ditch. The research of these early theorists gave birth to a consistent mode of military architecture that came to be known as *fronte bastionato*, or *tracé à l'italienne* or *Italian bastioned system*.

Exactly who invented the *bastion* is not known, but it is clear that the idea originated in Italy. Perhaps the first work built according to bastioned principles was the citadel of Civita Castellana, built about 1494 by Antonio da San Gallo the Elder. Fort Sarzanello, erected between 1493 and 1502 by Francesco Giambetti near Carrare in Tuscany, also displayed features of bastioned fortification. One of the oldest known bastioned works is that of Fort Nettuno, ascribed to engineer San Gallo the Elder in 1501. Other early bastioned fortifications were built at Verona by the Italian engineer Michele San Michele about 1523.

It did not take long for engineers, architects, generals and draftsmen to figure out that bastioned fortifications were the most effective. The great merit of the Italian system was its flexibility, ease of construction and adaptability to suit varying conditions—important characteristics which quickly led to its adoption as an international method of defense. Its only disadvantage was the very high cost involved.

The bastioned tracé gave a fortress not only the necessary solidity to withstand enemy bombardment but also the ability to bring as much fire power as possible to bear on the attackers, combining the destructive power of artillery itself with an aggressive form of mutually flanking defenses.

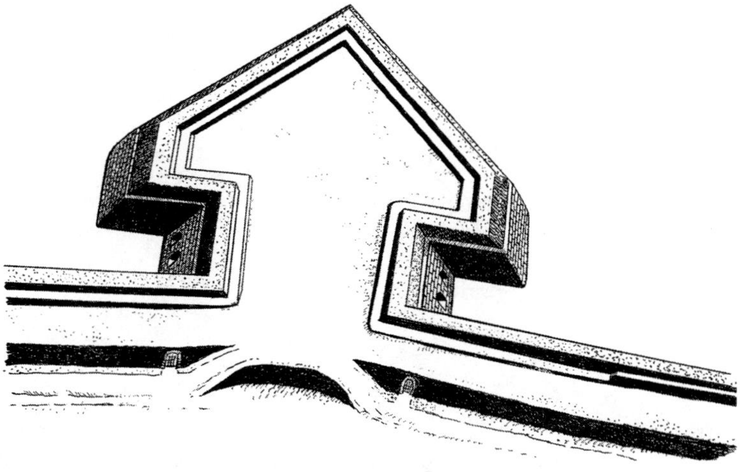

Bastion with "ears"

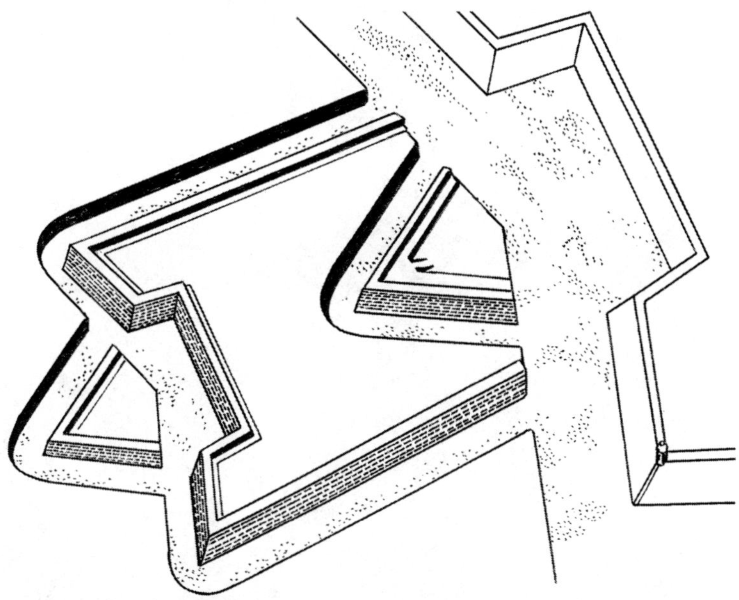

Hornwork

Description of the Italian Bastioned Fortification

Although countless bastioned systems were designed, the basic elements were the following.

A bastioned enceinte was composed of low and massive walls (named *curtains* or *courtines*) and equally sunk and strong *bastions* (projecting pentagonal-shaped combat emplacements replacing towers).

The *bastioned front* was an ensemble of elements related by rules and geometric ratios; it was a unit, composed of one curtain and two half-bastions, which could be repeated at will with various salient angles to enclose a city or outline a fort. The practice of constructing massive masonry walls as a defense against battering by artillery was recognized by the logical Italians as being a waste of time, money and materials; instead both curtains and bastions were *ramparted*—that is strengthened by masoned revetments holding a thick packing of earth and rubble. Counterforts were buttresses built inward from the stone wall into the earth rampart; they strengthened the wall and made breaches more difficult. Curtains and bastions were fitted with a thick *parapet* (breastwork). They were built at the same low level, forming wide passageways along which artillery, munitions carts and troops could be rapidly deployed and brought to bear on any part of the enceinte, thus leaving no dead ground to be exploited by the attacker.

The basic dimensions varied a lot, but the interval between two bastions (thus the length of the curtain) was generally dictated by the firing range of the contemporary arquebus and musket, so that the works lay within easy musket shot of each other; this made it possible to cover all areas in front of the fortification.

Towering *cavaliers* (rising gun platforms built on top of the bastions) dominated the surrounding ground.

Well-protected gun batteries, concealed behind *orillons* (projecting *ears* placed in the recessed flanks of

Covered way. Placed on the counterscarp, the covered way was a continuous broad lane protected by a breastwork.

bastions), provided deadly enfilading fire in the wide and deep ditch. Systematically a triangular outer work (called *ravelin* or *demi-lune*) was placed in the ditch to protect the curtains and the entrance to the bastioned fortress.

Bastions, cavaliers and demi-lunes were so designed and positioned that cannons mounted on each of them could provide cover not only to the full length of the rampart walls and ditches but to the neighboring works and surroundings. The full area could be swept by flanking cross fire, leaving no blind spots and denying attackers any cover. The overall effect of this search for flanking and cross fire zones was to give bastioned fortifications a distinctive "star" shape.

A *covered way* (continuous broad lane fitted with a breastwork) was established on top of the *counterscarp* (the outer side of the ditch); at the angles formed by the covered way, *places of arms* were established; the covered way and places of arms were protected outer spaces where the defenders could rush under cover to any threatened point, patrol, assemble for a sortie, and position themselves to fight a first delaying combat outside the actual defenses.

All around the fortress a wide, bare and gently sloping *glacis* was established, preventing an attacker from obtaining any cover from the defender's fire.

Later additional works were created and widely used

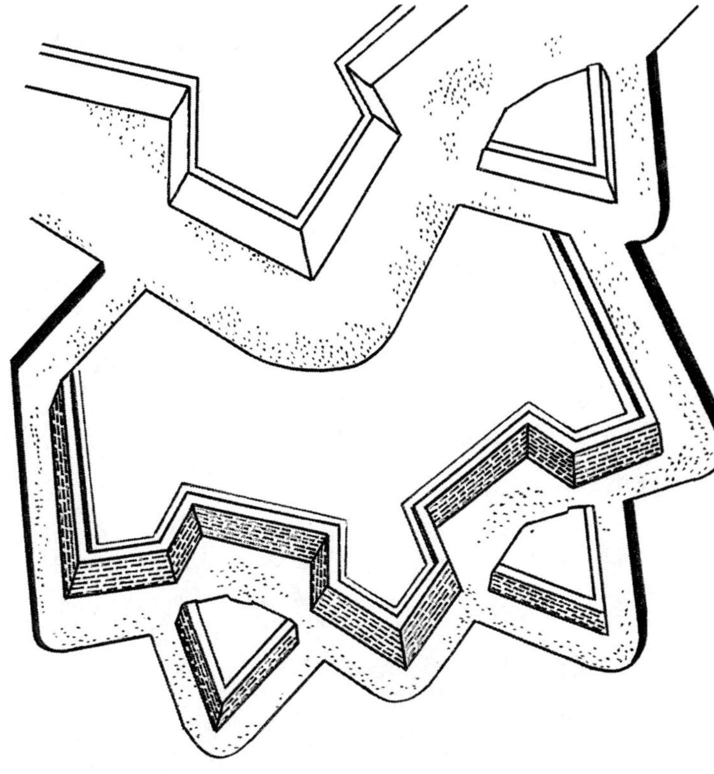

Crownwork

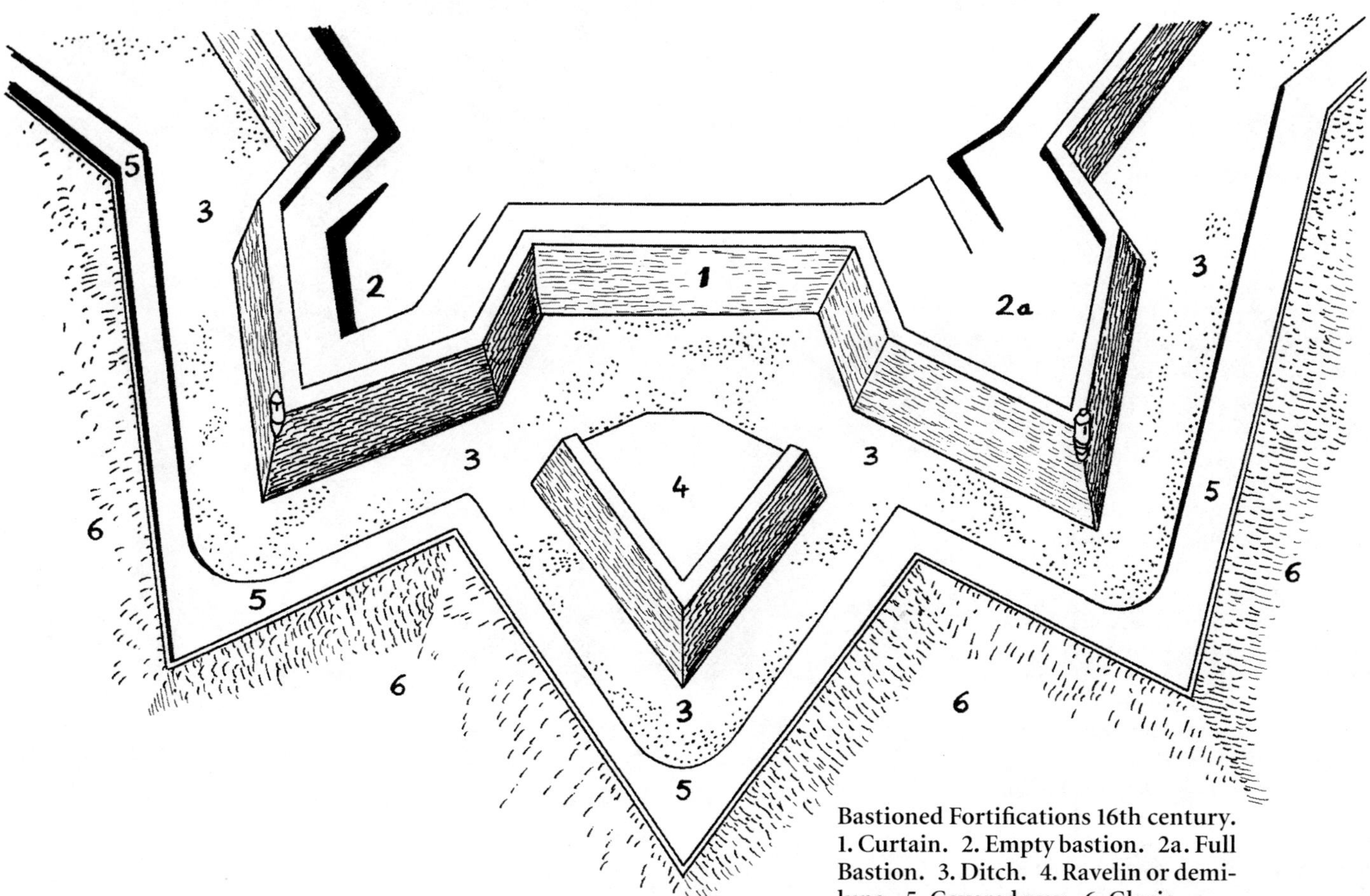

Bastioned Fortifications 16th century. 1. Curtain. 2. Empty bastion. 2a. Full Bastion. 3. Ditch. 4. Ravelin or demi-lune. 5. Covered way. 6. Glacis.

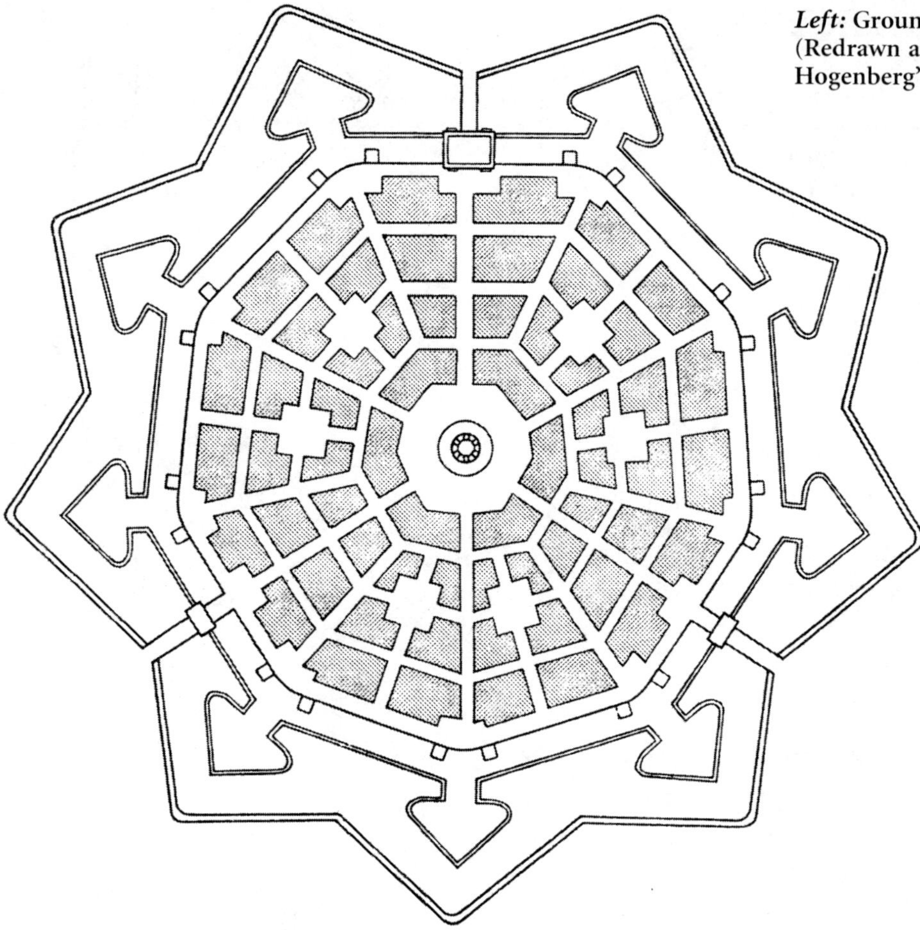

Left: Ground plan of the ideal city of Palma Nuova (Italy). (Redrawn and simplified from an engraving in Braun and Hogenberg's Civitates Orbis Terrarum from 1599).

Right: Ground plan Rocroi. Situated near Mézières in the Ardennes, the military city of Rocroi was created in 1554 by the king of France Henri II to defend the border facing the Spanish place of Charlemont and control the road between Charleroi and Mézières. Rocroi was directly influenced by Italian style with a radio-concentrical ground plan, a pentagonal outline and five bastions. In May 1643, Rocroi was besieged by Spanish troops commanded by Francisco de Melo; the young Louis II, prince of Condé and duke of Enghien, aged twenty-two, came to rescue the besieged city and won an important battle, saving Paris from invasion. In 1676, Vauban incorporated Rocroi in the second Pré Carré line and strengthened the old-fashioned fortifications by outworks and a traversed covered way. Today Rocroi's defenses are well preserved. 1. Bastion of Nevers. 2. Bastion of Dauphin. 3. King's bastion. 4. Bastion of Petit Fort. 5. Bastion of Montmorency (with cavalier).

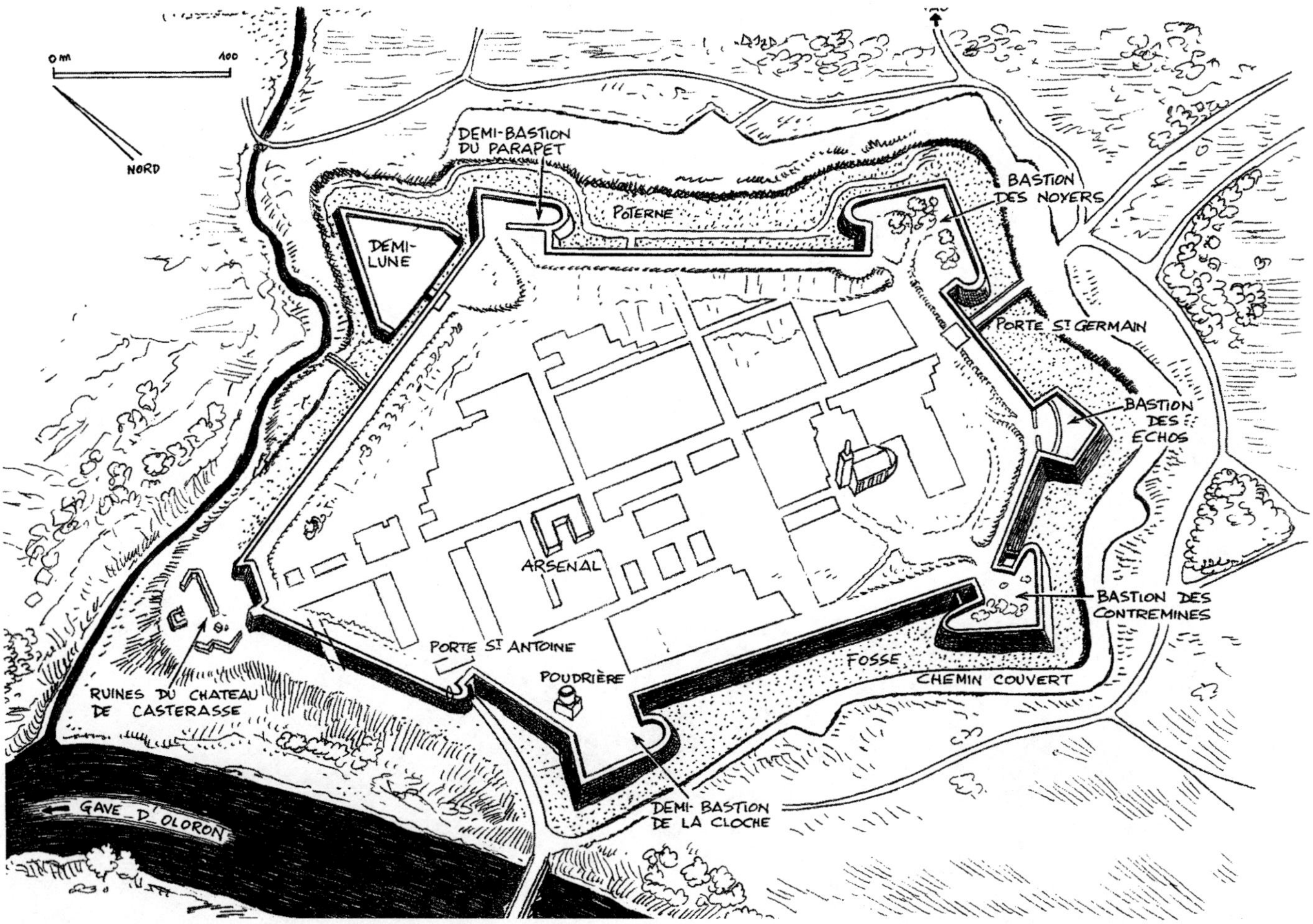

Navarrenx. Navarrenx in the French Pyrénées-Atlantiques was originally a bastide created in 1316. The small fortified city was modernized in Italian fashion by Fabricio Siciliano between 1538 and 1549. Perfectly preserved today, Navarrenx is a unique witness to the early Italian bastioned fortifications in France.

to multiply the obstacles and the defenses before the enemy. The most noteworthy were the following.

The *tenaille* was a low outer work placed between two bastions to cover the curtain. The *counterguard* was an outer work with two faces forming a salient angle; it was placed opposite the bastion or ravelin to prevent the opposite flanks from being fired from the covered way.

The *hornwork* was a projecting advanced structure placed in the glacis, composed of two half-bastions and a curtain; it was joined to the major work by two long sides, paralleling the faces of ravelins or bastions. The *crownwork* was the reunion of two hornworks, comprising a bastion between two curtains terminated by two half-bastions; it was connected to the major work by two sides.

Italian Predominance

Throughout the 16th century, Italian military engineers wrote countless technical treatises on the subject of bastioned fortification in which numerous variations were designed; these books were widespread as a result of the development of printing, and Italian theorists were translated, copied, and critiqued. Italian engineers were also to be found in person all over Europe disseminating and, of course, selling at a high price their new method of fortification. The following few examples clearly indicate how the Italian style of defense dominated European military architecture.

In The Netherlands, the castle of Breda was reshaped with bastioned defenses in 1536 by the Italian architect Thomas Vincidor. Utrecht was fortified by engineer Donato Boni di Pellezuolli in 1540. The same Pellezuolli designed Fort Rammekens in 1547. The bastioned citadel of Antwerp in Belgium was completed in 1569 by Francesco Pacciotto from Urbino. The capital of Austria, Vienna, was fortified in 1544 by engineer Francesco de Pozzo from Milan. The brothers Giulo and Ottavio Baldigara designed the fortress of Nove Zamsky near Budapest (Hungary) between 1578 and 1588. In Germany

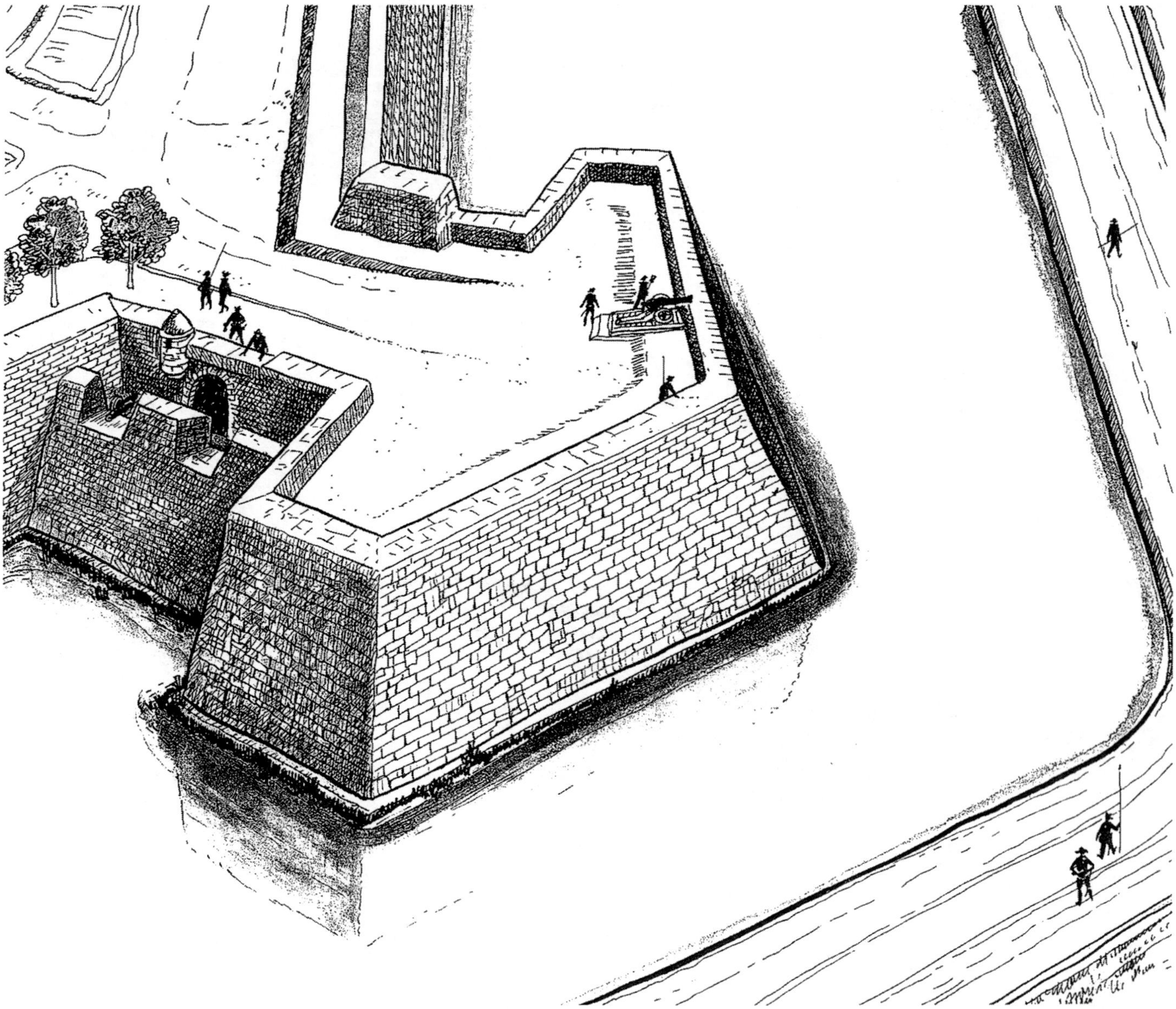

Early Italian bastion. This early Italian-styled bastion was built at Utrecht (The Netherlands) in 1540 by engineer Donato Boni di Pellezuolli.

the citadel of Spandau in Berlin was constructed between 1560 and 1578 by Rocco Guerrini from Florence. In England the fortifications of the frontier town of Berwick-upon-Tweed were completed in 1564 after a design by Giovanni Portinari from Florence and Jaccopo Aconcio from Milan. Between 1597 and 1599, engineer Federico Giannibelli reinforced the castle of Carisbrooke on the Isle of Wight.

In France, the port of LeHavre was created by King François I and fortified by engineer Girolamo Bellamarto. Between 1525 and 1535, Bordeaux was fortified by engineer Anchise from Bologna. The Italian Girolamo Martini was appointed General Commissaire of Fortifications of Champagne and created the city of Vitry-le-François in 1545 and Rocroi in the Ardennes in 1554. The Atlantic port of Brouage was founded in 1555 and fortified in bastioned style by Francesco Orologio. A new suburb, Nancy, and a bastioned citadel were created and fortified between 1588 and 1620 after a design by military architect Girolamo Citoni and engineer Stabili. On the island of Malta, held by the Knights Hospitaller, the new capital, Valetta, was created in 1566 and fortified by engineer Francesco Laparelli.

Among Italian engineers arose also the desire to create ideal cities, not focused on a cathedral or appended to a castle but offering an environment for civic life protected by bastioned fortifications. Hypothetical designs were proposed and some in fact were implemented. Palma

Fort Mont Alban (France). Situated on Mont Boron dominating Nice in southern France, the fort Mont Alban was designed in 1557 by the Italian engineer Domenico Ponsello.

Nuova—founded in 1593 in the state of Venice (Italy)—was surrounded by fortifications. The street pattern was arranged around a central square approached by three highways leading from entrances in the walls. The remaining streets were designed in a radio-concentric plan with subsidiary squares.

In the second half of the 16th century, however, the Italian domination began to decrease. The expensive Italian mercenary engineers were gradually replaced by national fortification builders who had mastered the technique.

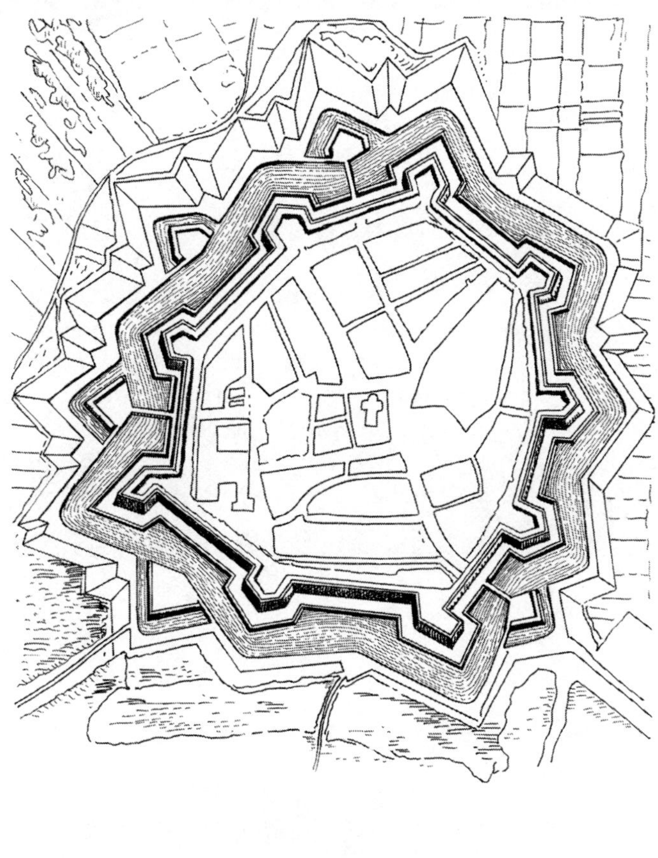

Right: **Ground plan Hulst (The Netherlands). Strategically situated at the mouth of River Scheldt in the southern Netherlands, the city of Hulst was fortified between 1506 and 1518 by engineers Domien de Waghenmakere and Rombout Keldermans. In 1591 Hulst was conquered by stadhouder Maurice of Nassau, and the fortifications were reshaped according to the so-called Old Dutch System including bastions, walls and ravelins made of earth, a fausse-braie, a wide wet ditch and a covered way.**

Fort Bourtange (The Netherlands). Fort Bourtange was intended to control and defend a pass in the marshes between The Netherlands and Germany in the northern province of Groningen. In 1645, the fort was strengthened by the addition of a crownwork, two hornworks, and a broad wet ditch.

Old Dutch and French Bastioned Systems

During the long war of independence against the Spaniards from 1468 to 1648, the Dutch evolved their own bastioned style, fully adapted to the peculiar conditions of their low and marshy land. The Dutch method, developed by mathematician Simon Stevin and engineer Adrian Anthonisz, was characterized by large flooding, broad wet ditches and bastions and curtains totally made of earth; it often featured a *fausse-braie*, a continuous low breastwork built at the foot of bastions and curtains. The *Old Dutch System*, as it was called, was largely exported into Scandinavia and northern Germany.

In France engineers such as Jean de Beyns, Raymond de Bonnefons, Jean Errard, Antoine de Ville and Blaise de Pagan came to prominence; they developed a typical French style which was to culminate with the immense work of Vauban during the reign of Louis XIV.

26

The Religious Wars

The Crisis of the Catholic Church

The *Renaissance* affected only the upper classes of society and — to a lesser extent — the urban bourgeoisie, while its effect on the mass of the common people was virtually nil. The *Reformation*, on the other hand, was to disturb the whole of European society profoundly and durably.

From the 14th century, the Catholic Church was passing through a grave crisis, marked by the Great Western Schism between 1378 and 1417 with open conflict between rival popes. The prelates of the Renaissance were certainly no models of piety. Popes, abbots and bishops neglected their flocks; their way of life was shameful; and their wealth, arrogance and corruption were in total opposition with Christ's purity. Because of the lack of a moral attitude, the Christian faith had declined, giving rise to widespread anxiety. Reform was badly needed. In Germany, a monk named Martin Luther had broken away from the Catholic Church. In France a young cleric, Jean Calvin, imitated him. They preached a return to the purity of the early Church and the abandonment of certain forms of worship and challenged various basic dogmas. The Protestant preaching and doctrine met with a favorable response and quickly won new disciples not only among the common people but also among some European courts. In France the reformers were called *Protestants* or *Huguenots*; the latter term coming from the German *eidgenossen* (oath fellow), which was simplified to *eignot*. The Catholic Church counter attacked and sought ways to reform by means of the Council of Trent. Though originally a religious dispute, the Reformation became a political and social issue which degenerated in widespread and implacable civil and foreign wars.

From Henri II to Henri IV

In France the so-called Religious Wars lasted for about thirty years. King of France Henri II (1547–1559) was encouraged by the ardent and ambitious Duke François de Guise to eradicate the Huguenot rebels while there was a renewed outbreak of war against England and Spain ending with the treaty of Cateau-Cambresis in 1559. During Henri II's reign, the Reformation had been moving steadily ahead and could now claim many supporters among the French nobility and even princes such as Antoine de Bourbon, king of Navarre. Henri II died in a tournament in June 1559, and his son François II succeeded him for a short while from 1559 to 1560. Henri II's second son became King Charles IX (1560–1574), but being only 10 years old, his mother Catherine de Medici became regent. She tried vainly to keep some kind of balance between Catholics and Huguenots, but the murder of François de Guise at Wassy sparked off a new period of extreme violence until peace was signed by both sides in 1563.

In 1567 the fratricidal fighting started again. Henri de Guise *le Balafré* (Scarface) at the head of a Catholic army defeated the Huguenots at Jarnac and Moncontour in 1569. Another truce was signed in 1570, but another war broke out after the ugly slaughter of thousands of Protestants in Paris on August 24, 1572 (the Saint Bartholomew's Day Massacre) ordered by Catherine de Medici.

When Charles IX died, his brother became king as Henri III (1574–1589). The new king could not decide on a policy for handling the grave situation, and fighting went on between the two rival factions. The financial situation of France was deplorable, and the civil conflict quickly became a war marked with foreign intervention, the Spaniards assisting the Catholic party and the Lutheran German princes helping the Huguenots. On May 12, 1588, the Parisians rebelled against Henri III; they erected barricades and appointed a new leader in the person of the duke of Mayenne. On August 1, 1589, Henri III was murdered by a monk paid by the Catholic party, and the confusion was total. France was more severely divided than ever, foreign troops and mercenaries roamed the lands, anarchy was rife, and — to make matter worse — Henri III had no male heir.

The legal heir to the throne of France was Henri of Bourbon, king of Navarre (the royal branch of the Bourbon family descended from Robert, son of Saint Louis), but Henri de Navarre was, ironically, the leader of the Protestant faction. He became Henri IV (1589–1610), but he was a king without a crown, as the kingdom had yet to be conquered. Henri defeated the Catholic League in a series of battle at Arques, Ivry, Chartres and Noyon and tried in vain to capture Paris. An experienced and good man-of-war, Henri de Navarre was also an amiable, intelligent easy-going man devoted to the ideals of peace and tolerance. Realizing that the situation was intolerable and that he would never conquer France by force of arms, and understanding that the French people (who was in majority Catholic) would always deny their support to a Huguenot king, Henri renounced Protestantism in July 1593 and was at last able to enter triumphantly in Paris.

Henri IV fought the Spaniards, defeated them and signed the peace of Cambrai in 1597. The entire kingdom recognized him as legal king of France, and Henri signed the famous *Edict of Nantes* (April 30, 1598), establishing freedom of conscience and of worship and marking the triumph of the spirit of tolerance.

The atrocious Religious Wars were over, but France had to be rebuilt, and the French had to be reconciled. It was a long, difficult and huge task. Henri IV — helped by his minister, Maximilian de Béthune duke of Sully — reduced expenditures, recreated a network of roads, increased or created indirect taxation, and reorganized farming, trading and industry. Henri's foreign policies were realistic in trying to hamper the relations between the Hapsburgs of Spain and those of Austria. Henri IV, today still the most popular of the kings of France, was, unfortunately, murdered on May 14, 1610.

Paris had suffered a lot during the civil and foreign wars. It was partly reconstructed and embellished with superb features such as the Place Dauphine and the Place Royale (today Place des Vosges) while work proceeded on the construction of the Louvre, the Palace of the Tuileries and the castle of Fontainebleau, all in architecture combining classical sobriety and elegance.

Another building erected under the reign of Henri IV — and worthy of mention as we deal here with the military history of Paris— was the *Arsenal,* situated along the present Boulevard Morland. As early as 1512, the municipality of Paris had seized a piece of ground possessed by the convent of the Celestines. There, a workshop was built to manufacture gunpowder. By the reign of Henri II (1547–1559), the small factory was enlarged to become the Arsenal Royal, producing artillery pieces and ammunition.

In 1563, an accident occurred and the factory was totally destroyed by a gigantic explosion. Henri IV had the arsenal rebuilt with a large lane (the present Boulevard Morland). Minister Sully, appointed Grand Master of Artillery, lived there as well. In the 18th century, the Arsenal became a research institute where distinguished scientists worked e.g. the chemist Antoine Laurent de Lavoisier (1743–1794). Today the ancient gun foundry and gunpowder factory houses the *Bibliothèque de l'Arsenal* (Arsenal Library), created in 1757 by a rich ambassador fond of art, Paulmy d'Argençon.

27

Modernization of the Parisian Fortifications (1512–1562)

A Chaotic Development

Unlike the earlier Capetian kings who permanently lived in Paris, the French kings of the Renaissance led a semi-nomadic life. François I and Henri II's courts traveled from one palace to another with a clear preference for the castles of the Loire valley, such as Azay-le-Rideau, Amboise, Blois and Chambord, but also Fontainebleau and Saint-Germain-en-Laye near Paris.

At the beginning of the 16th century, the Parisian fortifications were completely obsolete. At a time when the potential of artillery was fully recognized, the northern part of the city on the right bank of the Seine was still defended by the medieval enceinte of Charles V and a few artillery works erected by Louis XI about 1465. The southern part of the city of the left bank was poorly covered by Philippe Auguste's enceinte from 1212. New suburbs had mushroomed outside the walled city: the faubourgs Saint Marceau, Saint Michel, Saint Jacques, Saint Germain, Saint Honoré, Montmartre, Saint Denis, and Saint Antoine were the most important.

During the conflicts against Charles Quint and the Religious Wars, it was then clear that something had to be done, but modernization of the Parisian fortification in the 16th century went in the most chaotic and haphazardous way.

As early as 1503, the Saint Honoré Gate was completed and adapted to firearms. In 1513, Paris was threatened by the troops of King Henry VIII of England, and the ancient enceinte of Charles V was hastily refurbished, the ditches widened and deepened. Between 1516 and 1518, a part of the ditches were deepened and filled with

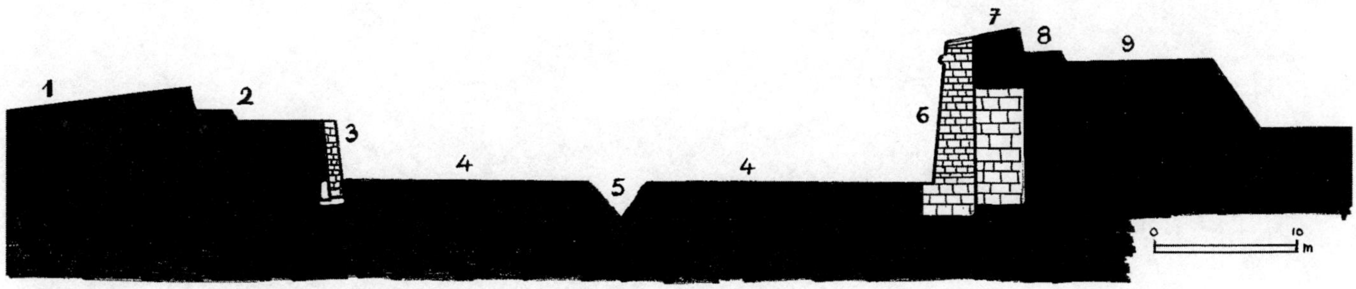

Cross section of the Fossés Jaunes. The cross section shows from left to right: 1. Glacis. 2. Covered way. 3. Masoned counterscarp. 4. Moat. 5. Cunet (a V-shaped excavation intended to collect rain water). 6. Masoned scarp. 7. Breastwork. 8. Firestep. 9. Wallwalk.

BASTION DES ARQUEBUSIERS
BASTION SAINT-ANTOINE
FAUBOURG SAINT ANTOINE
RUE SAINT-ANTOINE
LA BASTILLE
ARSENAL
ILE LOUVAIN
BIEVRE
SEINE

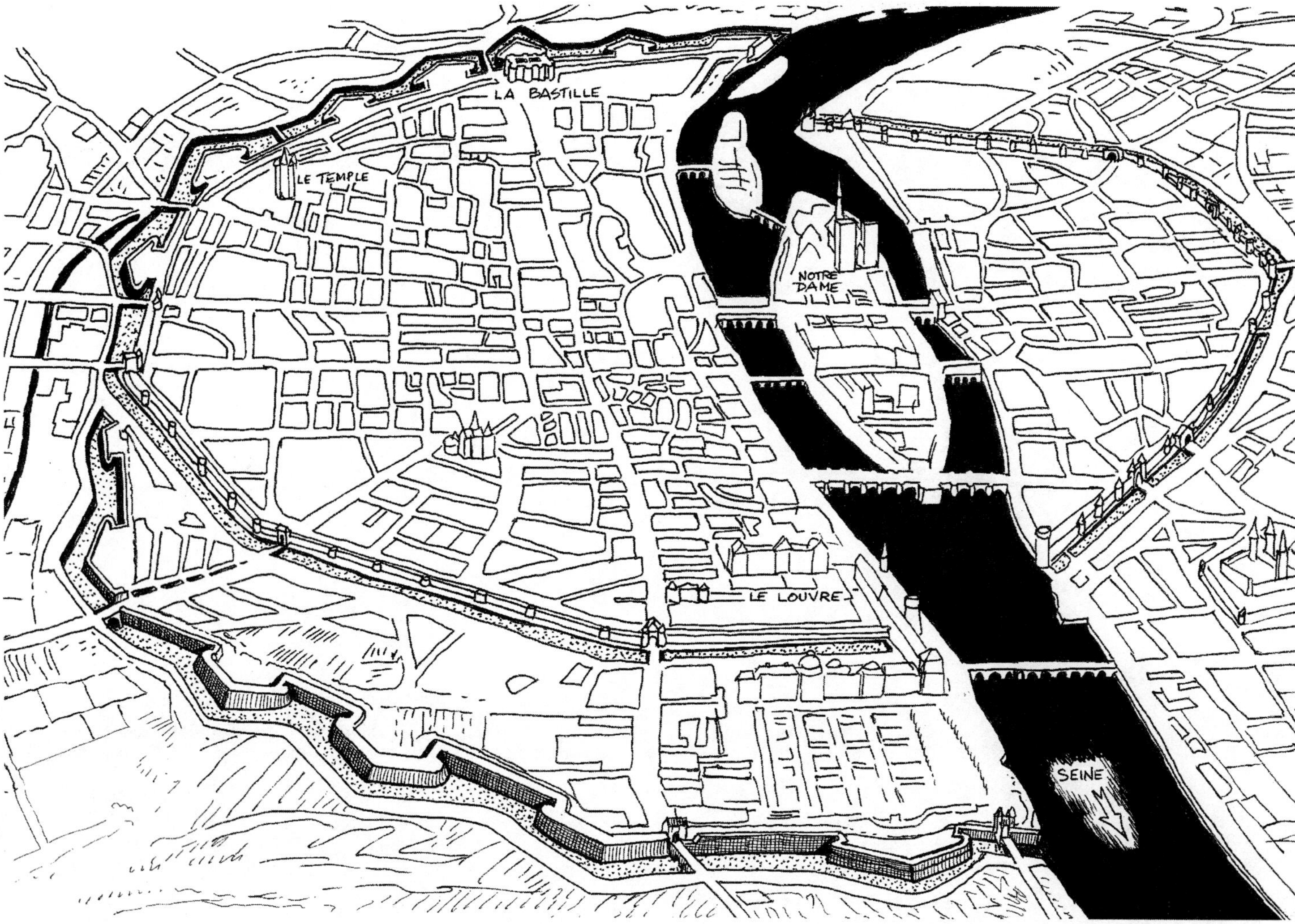

View of Paris about 1630 (from Melchior Tavernier)

water from the Seine. In 1523, artillery bulwarks and larger ditches were established by prisoners forced to work in the north and the west of the wall. Due to lack of funds, the works could not be completed. In 1536, Charles Quint's Spanish forces conquered Corbie (only 150 km from Paris) and works were hastily resumed. A year later, the governor of Paris, François de Montmorency, charged the Italian engineer Girolamo Bellemarto with designing new modern bastioned fortifications. With the Spanish threat gone, the municipality refused to further invest funds, and the project was cancelled after four months of work. In 1550, Henri II ordered the implementation of Bellamarto's design in the northeastern part of the city, principally to cover the Arsenal, and protect Saint Antoine Gate. The king emphasized that Paris was the most beautiful city of the kingdom and that it should also be the strongest. Works began in 1553 and would last until 1566 with underbreaking in 1560. Two Italian-styled bastions were built along the wall north of Saint Antoine Gate, one opposite the Bastille fortress, as well as two bastions, and a projecting casemated flanking *moineau* (small caponier) on the courtine between the Bastille and the River Seine. This front was built by rounded up jobless persons placed under the supervision of Italian military engineers named Baptista Porcello, Augustino Michoni, and Rocco Guerrini, who—it seemed—had a stormy relationship with the municipal authorities about their wages. The total cost was 120,000 livres, reluctantly paid by the Parisians.

In 1557, king of Spain Philip II (Charles Quint's successor), with an army of 50,000 soldiers, invaded the north of France and defeated Henri II's French force at the battle of Saint Quentin. In Paris—again threatened by invasion—defense works were refurbished, again in

Opposite: **Bastioned wall built in the period 1553–1566 by Henri II. The bastions were erected in the eastern part of Paris.**

Musketeer (ca. 1640). The Mousquetaires du Roy — popularized by Alexandre Dumas's novel *The Three Musketeers*— were the French kings' own bodyguards.

great haste; cunningly the king profited from the panic to have the Parisian bourgeois pay for the works. Fortunately for France, the Spaniards did not exploit their victory, they did not march toward the capital but retreated to Belgium. The duke of Guise, the commander of the French army, captured the harbor of Calais, the last stronghold occupied by the English since the end of the Hundred Years' War.

The "Fossés Jaunes" Bastioned Enceinte (1566–1633)

In July 1559 King Henri II gave a luxurious party in his palace of Tournelles in honor of the marriage of his daughter Elisabeth to King Philip II of Spain. A spectacular act of the party was a joust opposing the king himself against Captain Montgomery, leader of his private Scottish bodyguards. The joust was a chivalrous duel between two mounted armored challengers armed with lances charging and attempting to unseat each other. The feast ended tragically as Montgomery unintentionally — but seriously — wounded the king of France in the head. After a few days, on July 10, 1559, King Henri II died as a result of the fatal wound. As for Montgomery he flew to England and became a Protestant; he later participated in the French Religious Wars and, captured, was beheaded in 1574.

After the tragic feast of July 1559, Henri's widow, Catherine of Medici refused to live any longer in the Tournelles Palace where she had such sad memories. She moved to the Louvre Palace, and after a while decided to have her own palace built. She chose a site located 500 m west of the Louvre, called the *Tuileries* (literally tile works), outside the fortified wall. The construction of the Royal Palace of Tuileries with its garden was begun by architect Philibert Delorme in 1563. When Catherine died in 1589, the building was far from completion. In fact work soon stopped; they were resumed in 1594, and the palace was ultimately completed during the reign of Louis XIV. The Tuileries Palace was intentionally destroyed by fire during the Commune of Paris in 1871. Today only the elegant French-styled garden of the Tuileries remains, situated between the Louvre Museum and the Place de la Concorde.

In 1536, it was decided to fortify the northwestern part of Paris, but nothing happened — again because of lack of funds. In 1566, the project was relaunched and modified as Catherine de Medici's Tuileries Palace was to be included in the plan as well. A wide arc of bastioned fronts with ditches was planned; this extension, spread-

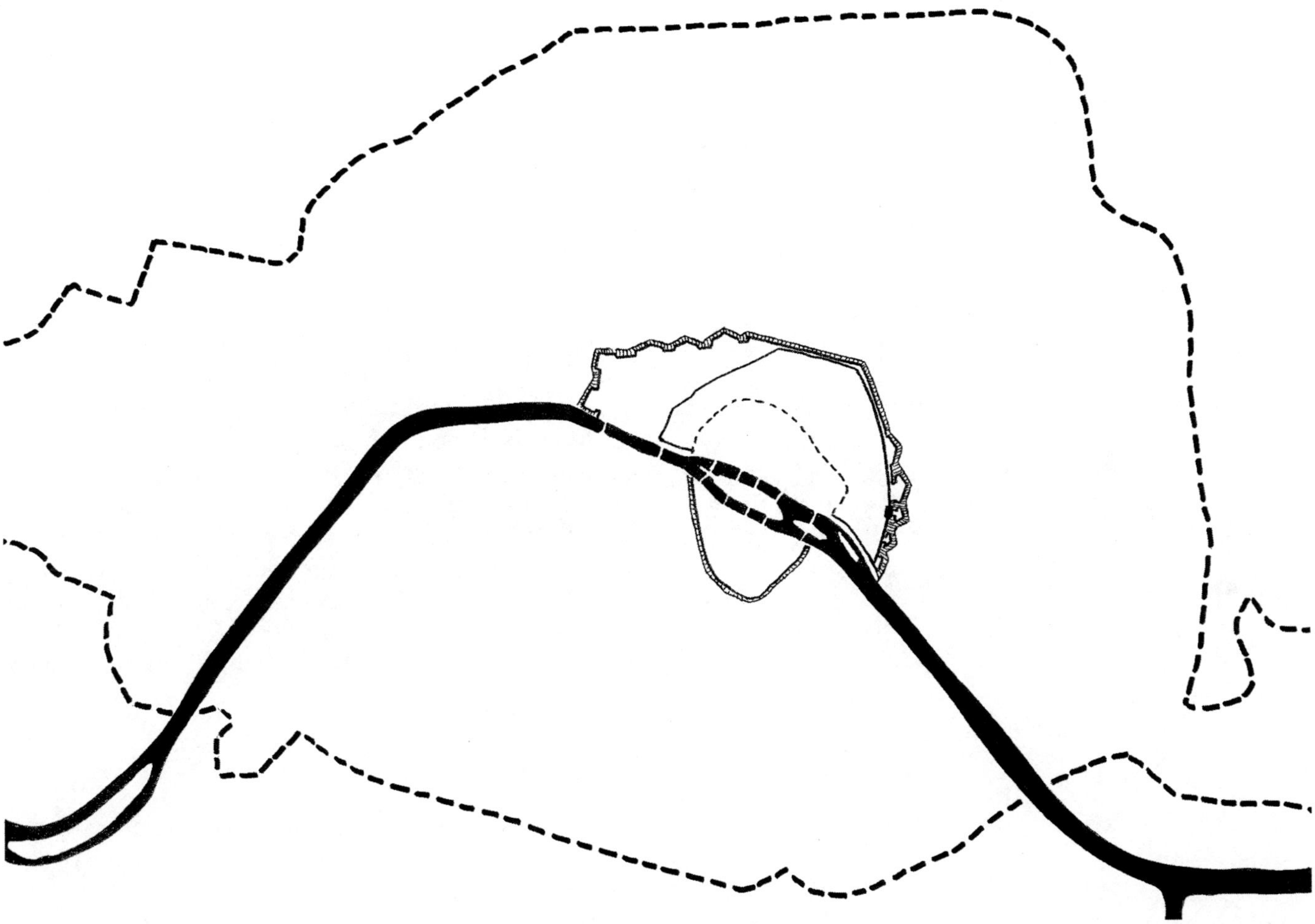

Map of Parisian fortifications. Shown are the works constructed between 1550 and 1633, including the Fossés Jaunes. The dotted line indicates the present administrative limits of Paris.

ing from the garden of the Tuileries to the Saint Denis Gate, was curiously called *Fossés Jaunes* (Yellow Moats). This odd designation has two possible origins; according to the historian Michel Le Moël it may have come from the yellowish color of the earth on the site; according to the historian Guy Le Hallé it may have been because engineers drew the planned works on their maps in yellow. Anyway, as one may expect the construction went very slowly in a background of civil religious war and quarrels between Crown and Municipality, both reluctant to pay the huge costs. In the 1580s, only two nonrevetted earthen bastions were completed opposite the present Tuileries garden. Construction was resumed only in 1608 during Henri IV's reign and completed at last in 1633 under Louis XIII's reign.

When one carefully observes the map of Paris drawn in 1630 by architect Melchior Tavernier, one may actually see poor defenses. The *Fossés Jaunes* enceinte was composed of flat-angled, Italian-style bastions with *ears*. Bastions and curtains had a total length of 6,200 m, they were only about six m high; they were made of brick and quarry stone with clampings made of freestone. The whole enceinte was bordered by a wet ditch. The curtains and the entrances were not covered by outer works such as the usual *ravelin*. The bastioned wall included six main entrances: the Conférence gate, Saint Honoré Gate, Gaillon Gate, Richelieu Gate, Montmartre Gate and Poissonerie Gate. The gatehouses were beautifully ornamented, but poorly defensible as they had no drawbridge or combat emplacements. The *covered way* was not fitted with *place-of-arms* and resembled a strolling path more than a combat emplacement. The *glacis*, particularly near the Saint Antoine Gate, the Temple Gate and the Faubourg Montmartre Gate were encumbered with structures, buildings, gardens, meadows, and vegetation. The ancient medieval towers and walls were still present but looked badly neglected. After a whole century of work, huge costs and many quarrels, the Parisian fortifications displayed a poor military capacity. To this we must add that only the northern right bank of Paris was covered by bastioned fortifications. The southern left bank was practically defenseless.

Louis XIII

Henri IV's son, who became king as Louis XIII the Just (1610–1643), was only nine years old and the regency was conferred upon his mother, Marie de Medici. Unintelligent and obstinate, Marie surrounded herself with Italian adventurers, Concini and his wife Elenora Galigai, who made a nuisance of themselves until Louis XIII took power and had them executed in 1617. Louis could now at last reign. An intelligent, active—and secretive—king, Louis found a great minister to help him in the person of the Cardinal Jean du Plessis de Richelieu. Although he was a greedy, ambitious and proud man, Richelieu proved inflexible, rigorous and to have only the greatness of France in mind. He remained in charge of the affairs of the realm for nearly twenty years. The domestic policy was marked by the reinforcement of the king's power. Richelieu engaged the struggle against the Protestants, who had become a state within the state, enabling them to endanger the security of France. The king and the cardinal, regarding this as unacceptable, defeated them after a campaign in southern France and the siege and the capture of their main stronghold La Rochelle in 1628. Freedom of worship was maintained, but the Protestants' privileges were restricted. The same firm hand was applied to the nobles. Dueling—a murderous noble pastime—was prohibited and repressed by the cardinal's police.

On order of Richelieu, many medieval castles were destroyed so that their owners would not use them for resistance centers against the royal sovereignty. New offices were created, such as that of *intendants* who were appointed in territorial subdivisions throughout the country and were instructed to develop industry and trade and to ensure that the royal edicts were complied with. Richelieu took a particular interest in the colonies abroad; he developed a powerful navy and encouraged the foundation of trading companies for the colonization of Africa, Canada and India. To fight the Houses of Austria and Spain, the very Catholic Cardinal Richelieu allied with the Protestant German princes, Sweden and Denmark during the atrocious, pointless and forgotten Thirty Years' War, which ravaged and depopulated Germany from 1618 to 1648. In 1635 the Spanish threatened Paris, but Richelieu and Louis XIII managed to repulse them. Richelieu died in December 1642 and Louis XIII a year after him.

28

Louis XIV's Reign (1661–1715)

The Fronde Revolt

The new king, Louis XIV (born in 1638), was only five when his father Louis XIII died. The regency was entrusted to his mother Anne of Austria. The queen-regent was helped by minister Cardinal Jules Mazarin (1602–1661), a sophisticated, competent and clever man who had worked under Richelieu. War with Austria was ended by the treaty of Westphalia, signed at Munster (Germany) in 1648, but the conflict against Spain continued for another eleven years.

The youth of Louis XIV was marked with a large-scale revolt. The years of war had cost a lot of money, and the magistrates of the Parliament of Paris voiced loud opposition against the increase of taxation in 1648. This led to a protest movement called *Fronde* (sling) in which the magistrates sought to extend their prerogatives and limit the power of the king. Once again, Paris bristled with barricades and full-scale riots raged. The faithful General Condé laid siege to Paris, which eventually yielded a year later. The principal opposing figures were arrested, but disorder and rebellion continued to occur, notably at Bordeaux which surrendered after a two-month siege. The *Fronde* started again when Gaston d'Orleans (Louis XIII's brother) and his daughter La Grande Demoiselle, led a group of princes seeking to wrest power from the hated minister Mazarin. In January 1649, riots raged again in Paris, and Queen Anne and her children were obliged to flee from Paris and seek refuge in the castle of Saint-Germain-en-Laye, a chilling trip which Louis XIV was never to forget or forgive. The king's dislike for Paris and its inhabitants dated from that day. Meanwhile the princely insurgents had obtained the military assistance of France's enemy, Spain, and the rebellion took the form of a civil war. The young Louis XIV and a few faithful troops defeated them at the battle of Angers in February 1652 and marched on Paris, which again was in a state of rebellion. After a bloody skirmish in the neighborhood of the Bastille and the suburb Saint Antoine, the king made a triumphant entry into Paris which brought the *Fronde* to an end. The absurd struggle had exhausted the realm and caused enormous, pointless destruction.

The Sun King

After the civil war, Louis XIV was absolutely determined to impose his authority on the princes and the nobility. The whole episode of the *Fronde* resulted in the establishment of the *absolute monarchy*, an authoritarian system based on the almighty, unquestionable and unique power of the king. The repeated rebellious attitude of the Parisians had convinced the king that it was absolutely necessary to establish the seat of his government away from the capital. This is why Louis XIV ordered the construction of the Versailles palace, a luxurious residence and his own center of power.

The war against Spain, which started during the reign of François I in 1519, dragged on until peace was restored by the signing of the Treaty of Pyrenees in November 1659.

When Cardinal Mazarin died in March 1661, Louis XIV announced his firm intention to rule his kingdom on his own.

Porte Saint Denis. The gate was built in 1672 to commemorate Louis XIV's victories in the campaign of Holland.

A hardworking and devoted man, Louis XIV was keenly aware of his importance and passionately fond of his kingly function, and he performed it with strict *etiquette* (ceremonies and rituals) which he himself devised. As symbol of his majesty, he had chosen the Sun as emblem. In his mind the greatness of France and his own glory were one and the same illustrious thing.

During Louis XIV's long reign, France was involved in several wars, all connected to and even caused by the Sun-King's ambition, pride and lust for power. The first conflicts, the War of Devolution (from 1667 to 1668) and the War of Holland (from 1672 to 1679) were rather successful, France acquired territorial expansion, and Louis XIV's reign was at its apex. The last armed conflicts, the War of the Augsburg League (from 1688 to 1697) and the War of Spanish Succession (from 1701 to 1713), on the contrary, were marked by a few brilliant victories but also by several setbacks. A total disaster was avoided by the victorious battle of Denain in 1712. This was followed by peace negotiations and the signing of the Treaty of Utrecht on 1713, which deprived France of most of her earlier conquests.

To back up of his aggressive policy, the *Sun King* had appointed as ministers ordinary members of the upper bourgeoisie and lower nobility, men chosen for their talent and competence, in whom he had full confidence, whom he showered with honors, but whom were nothing without his support.

Jean-Baptiste Colbert (1619–1683), the son of a draper, was an extremely hardworking man who restored order in the state's finances by introducing new indirect taxes, promoting industry and manufacturing enterprises, facilitating trade, and imposing a protectionist policy. Colbert developed the French navy by making Brest, Rochefort and Toulon into major military harbors. Lastly he set up new trading companies and encouraged settlement in the colonies—notably *Louisiana* (named after Louis XIV), a huge territory in the United States of America from the Great Lakes to *Nouvelle Orléans* (New Orleans); the Mississippi was then known as *Colbert River*.

Michel Le Tellier Lord of Chaville (1603–1685) and his son, Michel Le Tellier jr. marquis of Louvois (1639–1691) were successively appointed Secretary of State for War and set about reorganizing the French army, which they subjected totally to the service of the king. They compelled the officers (all of them noble) to concern themselves with their regiments. They restored discipline and promoted recruitment while—gradually—uniforms were adopted. Both father and son created stockpiles of foodstuffs and weapons and tried to develop ambulances for the wounded.

Lastly Vauban revolutionized military engineering, siege warfare and military architecture.

Paris at the Time of Louis XIV

In 1675, Paris, counting 550,000 inhabitants, was the most important French city: Lyon had 120,000, Marseille and Bordeaux 100,000. While still preferring to spend his time in his court at Versailles, Louis XIV decided to

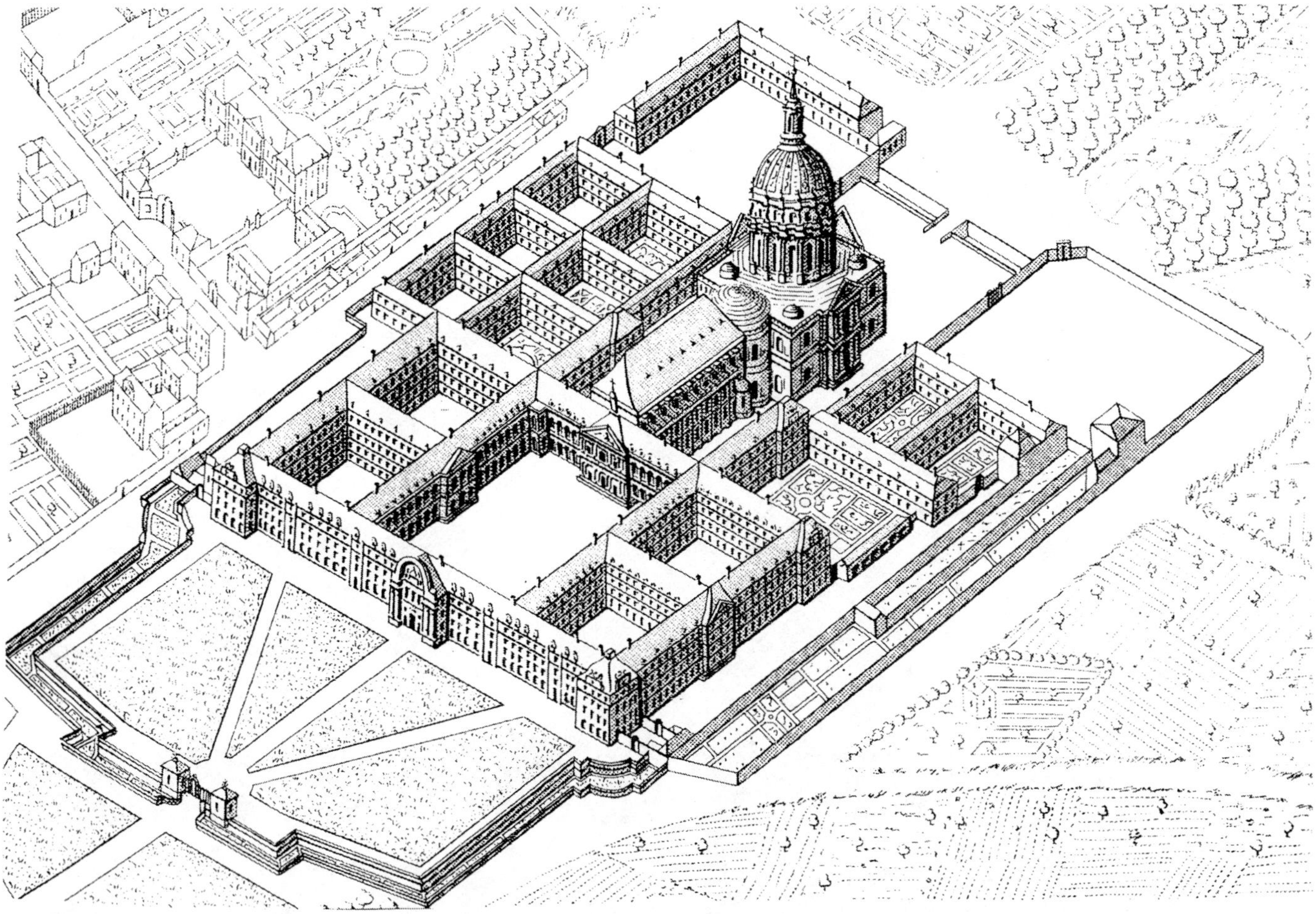

View of the Hôtel des Invalides about 1734 (from Turgot)

beautify the capital. Paris is indeed a particularly good example of the influence of the "grand manner" on urban building, since the king felt obliged to put his stamp on its townscape. His desire to show his affluence and splendor, the urge to produce a visual expression of worldly power and grandeur resulted in several magnificent monuments.

But first of all, for political and security reasons, the king ordered the demolition of the bastioned fortifications (including the *Fossés Jaunes*) built in the previous period, as he did not wish the Parisian citizens to revolt against him again.

The demolition began in 1670; the bastions and curtains were razed, ditches were filled, and grounds were equalized and leveled. In their places, the king ordered the construction of what is still called today the *Grands Boulevards*, wide lanes and promenades lined with trees, an operation which would continue until 1715. In the long run, the removal of fortifications permitted the development of accessibility. Today, the *Boulevards*— a stretch of about 3 km between the Madeleine Church and the Square of the Bastille — include the Boulevard de la Madeleine, Boulevard des Capucines, Boulevard des Italiens, Boulevard Montmartre, Boulevard Poisonnière, Boulevard de Bonne Nouvelle, Boulevard Saint Denis, Boulevard Saint Martin, Place de la République, Boulevard du Temple, Boulevard des Filles-du-Calvaire, Boulevard Beaumarchais and end up at the Place de la Bastille. At that time, the neglected walls, towers and gatehouses on the southern left bank of the Seine, which had been built at the time of Philip Auguste, were also demolished.

Meanwhile, the gates of Paris were renovated. Totally losing their defense function, they were triumphal arches in classical style celebrating the Sun King's military glory. The Porte Saint Antoine was refurbished by architect Blondel in 1671, the Porte Saint Bernard rebuilt in 1674, the Porte Saint Denis was erected in 1672 to celebrate Louis XIV's victories in Holland, and Porte Saint Martin in 1674 to commemorate the annexation of the province of Franche Comté. That same year, work started on a triumphal arch in the middle of what is today Place de la Nation. Louis XIV ordered the continuation of works at the Louvre Palace; the Cour Carrée and colonnade were completed in 1670 by architect Claude Perrault. In the

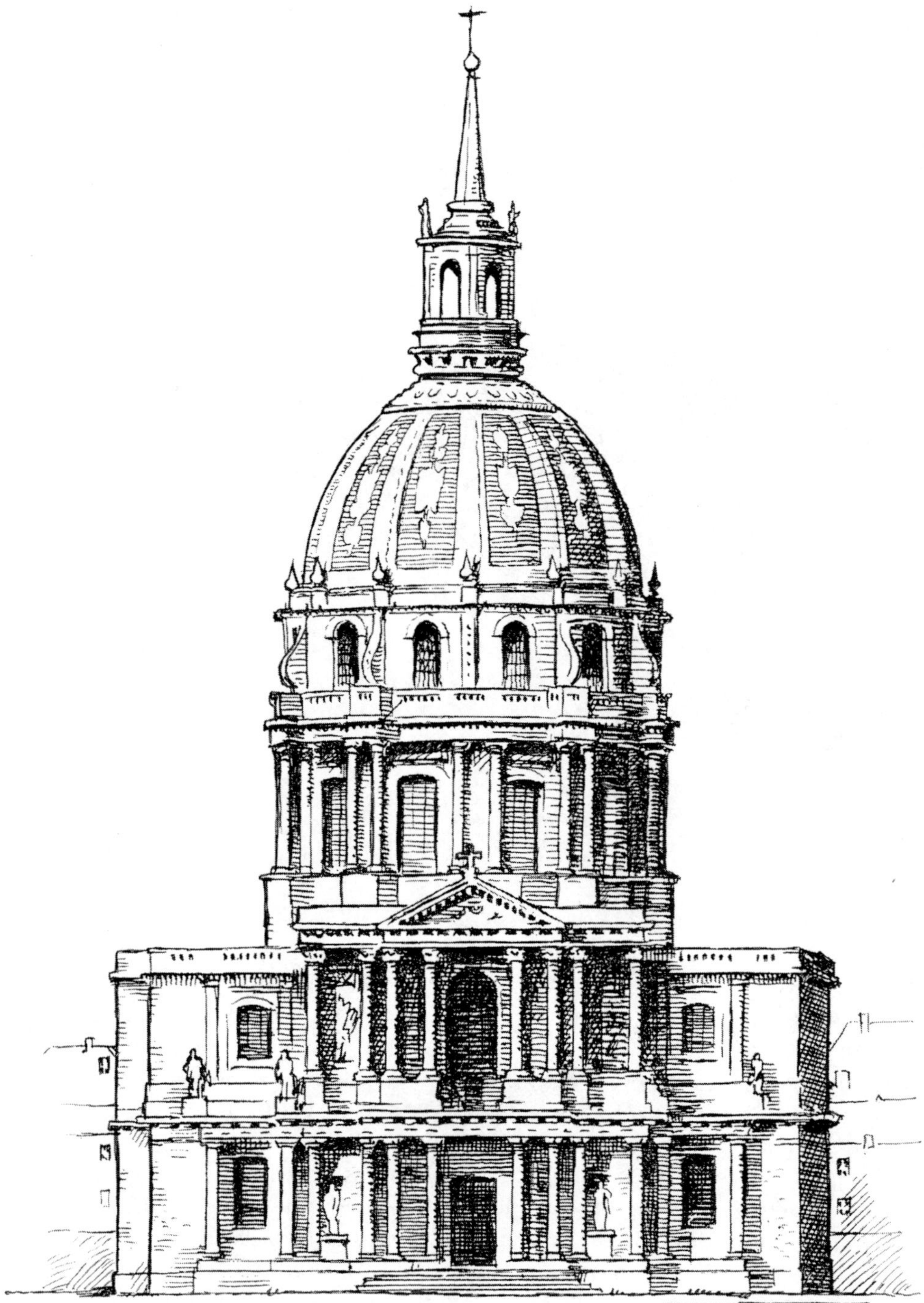

Front view of the Church of Saint Louis in the Hospital of Invalids

bank of the Seine, in the Faubourg Saint Honoré.

The Hôtel des Invalides

The *Hôtel des Invalides* was built in the plain of Grenelle. It is a vast complex ordered by Louis XIV at the request of Louvois and Vauban. The purpose of the hospital was to create a home for old and invalid soldiers. For centuries, nothing was done regarding invalid soldiers and veterans. Crippled and old combatants were abandoned to their unfortunate fates. The luckiest among them might be assisted by charitable Christian institutions, a few privileged veterans would be exceptionally granted a retirement pension, but most of these poor souls miserably survived as beggars or thieves. A small effort was made though under Henri IV's reign in 1596 by the foundation of the *Maison de la Charité Chrétienne* (Home of Christian Charity) to comfort, house, dress and feed veterans. On Vauban's request, Louvois convinced Louis XIV to follow his grandfather's example by building a home for veterans. The *Hôtel des Invalides* was designed in 1671 by architect Liberal Bruant and completed in 1676 by Jules Hardouin-Mansart. The latter also added and designed the Church of Saint Louis (also called Church of the Soldiers) and its huge dome, built between 1679 and 1706, in pure elegant symmetrical forms and classical sober style reflecting the glory of Louis XIV. The hospital could house about 7,000 maimed, disabled, sick and old veterans. Vauban and Louvois divided disabled soldiers into three groups. The so-called *invalides parfaits* (total invalids) and *invalides imparfaits* (nontotal invalids) who could no longer serve at all; these two categories included the blind, the legless, and others who were maimed who were housed in the Hôtel des Invalides. Their life in the military home, which at the time was like a miniature town, was governed according to a military and religious system; supervised by their officers and chaplains, the men were organized into companies and

west of Paris, between 1668 and 1709, architect Le Notre designed gardens and a wide lane, today called the *Champs Elysées.* Place des Victoires was laid out between 1684 and 1686, on the initiative of Marshal de la Feuillade and to designs by architect Mansart and later by Hardouin-Mansart. In the southwestern Faubourg Saint Germain, the great servants of the State took up residence and prestigious dwellings were built. The same movement of rich construction developed on the northwestern right

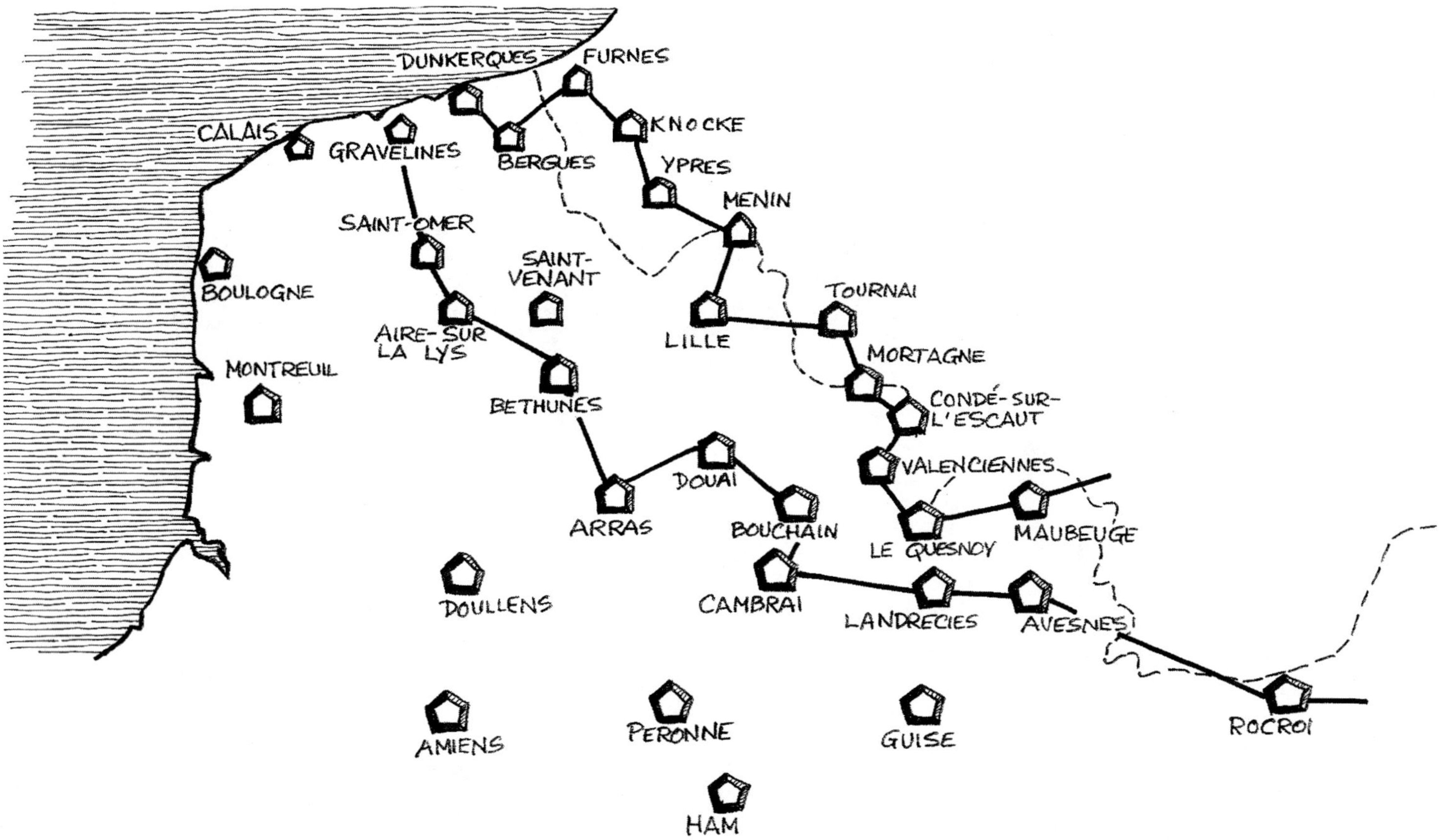

Vauban's Pré Carré

ran shoe-mending, tapestry and illumination workshops. The third category were *invalides de service* (duty invalids), the least disabled who were regrouped into special companies. Taking into account their handicaps, these men were employed to do minor auxiliary service such as maintenance or peace-time fortress-garrison.

Between the building and the Seine (to the present-day Bridge Alexander III), a wide *esplanade* bordered with trees was arranged from 1704 to 1720 by architect Robert de Cotte.

In 1840, the decision was made to transfer Napoléon's body from the island of Saint Helena to Paris. The Church of the Dome was chosen to house the tomb, and since at that time a crypt contained the coffin and the body of Emperor Napoléon I, his son, Napoléon II, rests beneath the Emperor's statue.

From October 1896 until today, the complex of Invalides is still a hospital in its own right and continues to provide the very service for which the foundation was initially created: it houses a few veterans of the French army. But the largest part of the building is arranged as the National Museum of the French Army, one of the most important military collections in the world including uniforms, weapons, armor, equipment, and flags.

Vauban's "Pré Carré"

If Louis XIV purposely left the capital of France totally defenseless, his intention was to fortify the frontiers of the realm. This gigantic task was entrusted to a team of military engineers under the leadership of Vauban.

Sébastien Le Prestre, marquis of Vauban (1633–1707) originated from the low gentry of Morvan (northern Burgundy). At the age of sixteen he entered the rebellious army of the *Fronde*. Pardoned by Mazarin, he then served Louis XIV with total loyalty until his last breath. Originally a cavalry officer, Vauban was also interested in military architecture. Commissioned for several projects, he was so successful that Louis XIV appointed him *Commissaire Général des Fortifications* in 1676 and elevated him to the dignity of Marshal of France in 1703.

The term *Pré Carré* (literally "Square Meadow" to be understood as "enclosed property") designated the double line of fortresses that Vauban set up at the vulnerable northeastern frontier, along the provinces of Flanders and Hainaut. The organization of this military network, which may be considered as a forerunner of the 20th century Maginot Line, had two purposes. It was a

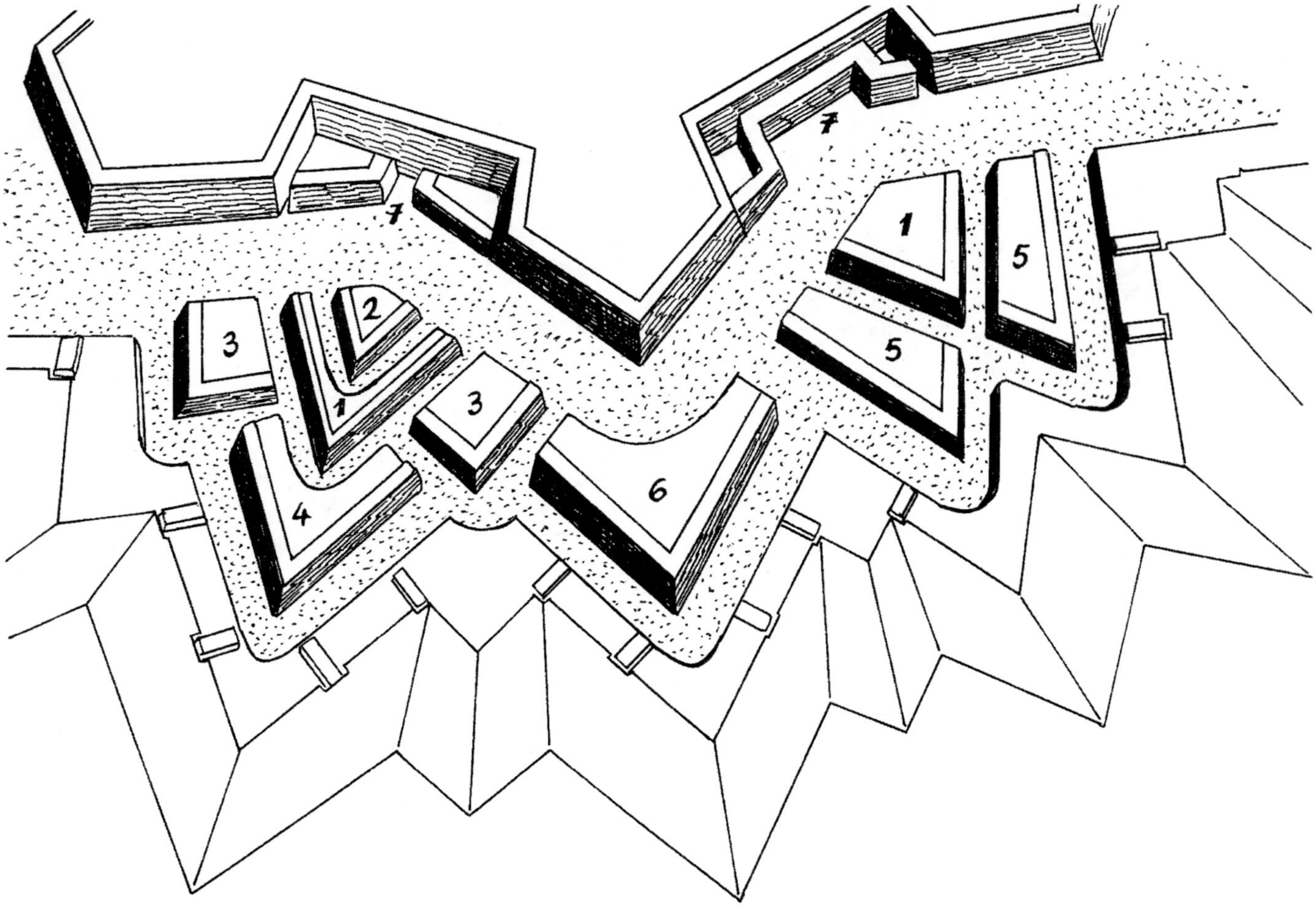

Outworks developed by Vauban. The demi-lune (1) could comprise a reduit (2) and additional structures known as lunet (3) and bonnet (4). It could also be flanked with tenaillons (5). The counterguard (6) was generally placed in front of the salient of a bastion. The tenaille (7) was a low breastwork protecting the curtain. Outworks were placed in the ditch and formed a sort of labyrinth; each of them could cover its neighbor. Each outwork necessitated a siege or at least an assault to be taken.

deterrent and defensive line intended to avoid the invasion of France and the capture of Paris; it also served as an offensive base to launch operations to the Spanish Lowlands (present-day Belgium) and the Republic of the United Provinces (the present kingdom of The Netherlands).

The *Pré Carré* was composed of two lines of fortified cities. The first line, at the front, included thirteen towns and two forts: Dunkerques (Dunkirk), Bergues, Furnes, Fort Knocke, Ypres, Ménin, Lille, Tournai, Fort de la Mortagne, Condé-sur-Escaut, Valencienne, Le Quesnoy, Maubeuge, Philippeville and Dinant. This first line could be reinforced by vast flooding. The second line, at the back, included thirteen fortresses: Gravelines, Saint-Omer, Aire-sur-la-Lys, Béthune (later Saint Venant), Arras, Douai, Bouchain, Cambrai, Landrecies, Avesnes, Marienbourg, Rocroi and Mézières.

Some of these fortresses already existed and were reshaped by Vauban; others (e.g. Lille and Maubeuge) were entirely new creations designed by Vauban. Behind those two lines there were other fortified cities, fortresses, castles and forts where French troops could withdraw and regroup in case of invasion. These included Calais, Boulogne, Montreuil, Lucheux, Doullens, Picquigny, Amiens, Péronne, Ham, Guise and Laon. Vauban's *Pré Carré*— intended to protect Paris— perfectly fulfilled its role until the invasions of 1814 and 1815.

Vauban's Project for Paris

Vauban also wanted to furnish Paris with new fortifications. In 1689, he wrote a report *Mémoire sur l'importance dont Paris est à la France* (Dissertation on the Importance of Paris for France) in which he proposed a very ambitious and costly design (24 millions *livres*). This included a large enceinte enclosing the commanding hills around the city: Chaillot in the west, Montmartre in the

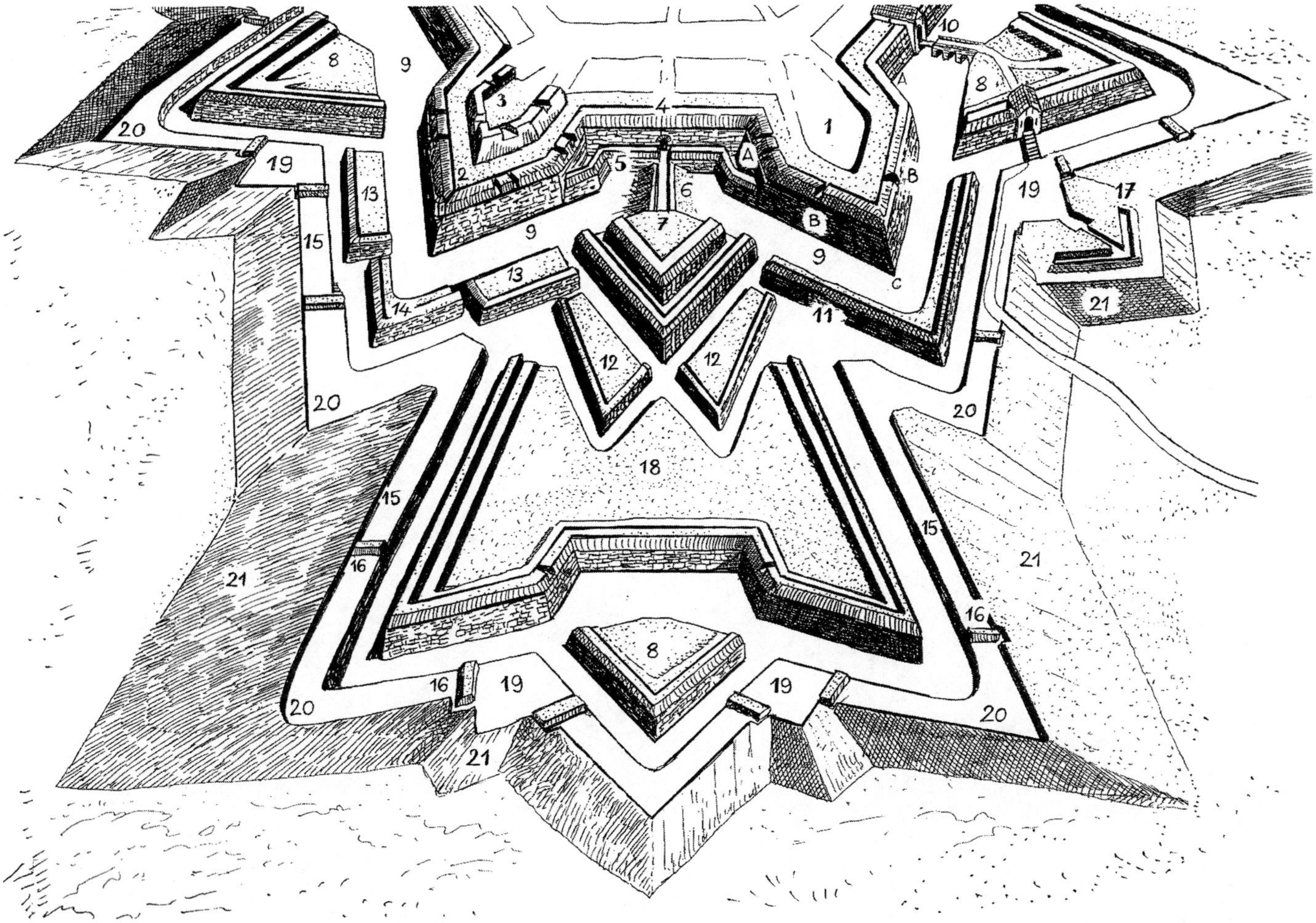

Vauban's bastioned defenses. 1 and 2. Bastion (A. flank; B. face; C. salient). 3. Cavalier. 4. Curtain. 5. Tenaille. 6. Caponier. 7. Demi-lune with redoubt. 8. Demi-lune. 9. Main ditch. 10. Gatehouse with drawbridge. 11. Counterguard. 12. Tenaillon. 13. Lunet. 14. Bonnet. 15. Covered way. 16. Traverse. 17. Flèche or arrow. 18. Hornwork. 19. Re-entering place of arms. 20. Salient place of arms. 21. Glacis.

north and Belleville in the east; it would be composed of 350-m-long bastioned fronts with 12-m-high scarps. The bastions proposed by Vauban would have been of the *tour bastionnée* (bastioned towers) type used in Besançon and Belfort. Gatehouses would have been furnished with portcullis and drawbridges. A ditch, 7 m deep and 21 m broad would be dug all around. The garrison would have counted between 25,000 and 30,000 royal soldiers, and 10,000 militiamen raised among the Parisians. Vauban advocated the creation of an arsenal to store 400 cannons and 60,000 muskets with gunpowder and ammunition. In the event of a siege, large food stores would also have to be founded in order to feed for three months the garrison, population and refugees, a grand total of 800,000 persons. Two strong self-contained bastioned citadels were to be built as advanced protection and, if need be, to control and repress the boisterous Parisians. The first one would be erected on the top of Mont Valérien hill in the west and the other at Charenton or Alfortville on the heights dominating the junction of the rivers Seine and Marne in the east. Vauban also integrated social measures: the creation of royal food stores where grains would be distributed or sold for a cheap price to the Parisian population in times of need, to avoid riots and revolts. He also argued that the fortifications he planned would give work to the jobless.

Vauban's report was presented to the king, but Louis XIV, remembering the *Ligue* against his grandfather and the *Fronde* revolt against himself, refused to have Paris fortified for political reasons.

French Border Fortifications

The long range defense of Paris was not Vauban's only concern. Louis XIV ordered the strengthening of all the borders of France, including the Mediterranean, Atlantic and Channel coasts. Vauban's work was colossal

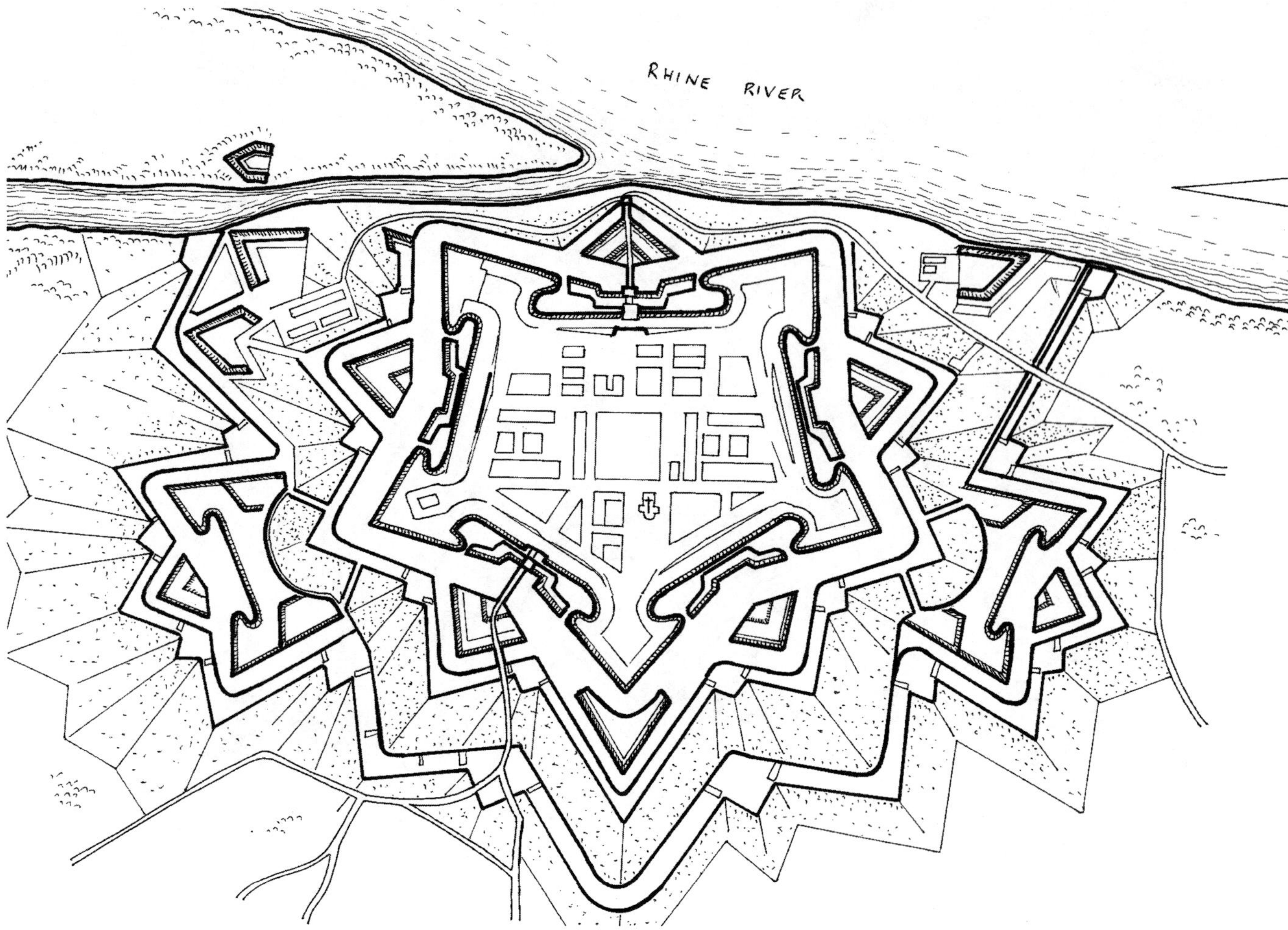

Huningen. Situated near Basel, Huningen is a strategic crossroad in southern Alsace between France, Germany and Switzerland. In spite of Swiss protestations, Louvois ordered Vauban to construct a fortress on the passage. Huningen's beautifully well-ordered fortifications were erected from 1679 to 1682 and included five bastions with oreillon, outworks, two covered ways, two hornworks advanced in a wide glacis and a bridge-head on the opposite Rhine bank; they were a fine example of Vauban's "first system." The surface of the fortifications represented seven times those of the city which made Huningen more a large fort than a fortified town. Huningen played a dissuasive role and acted as a support position for Marshall Villars during the battle of Friedlingen in 1702. After the second treaty of Paris in 1815, the Swiss at last obtained the complete dismantling of the menacing French fortifications.

and, for the first time in its history, France had a comprehensive, unified and efficient system of protection.

Vauban created and reshaped new fortified places in Lorraine (Sedan, Montmédy, Longwy, Bitche), in Alsace (Fort Louis, Strasburg, Neuf-Brisach), and in the Jura (Belfort, Besançon). In the Alps, the main passes were defended by new or modernized fortresses (Briançon, Mont Dauphin, Colmars-les-Alpes, Seyne, Sisteron). The Mediterranean French navy harbors were strengthened with coastal forts and batteries (Nice, Antibes, Toulon, Marseilles). At the eastern border with Spain in the Pyrenees, Vauban established new fortifications (Collioure, Bellegarde, Villefranche-de-Conflent, Mont Louis). The same was done in the western Pyrenees (Socoa, Bayonne).

The important Atlantic navy harbors of Rochefort and La Rochelle were covered by coastal fortifications established on the islands of Ré, Aix and Oléron.

In Brittany Vauban made designs and modernized the fortification of the islands of Houat, Hoëdic and Belle Isle, as well as the ports of Concarneau, Camaret, Brest, Carantec and Saint Malo.

In Normandy the Channel harbor of Cherbourg — facing England — was strengthened by coastal defenses added at Tatihou, Saint-Vaast-La-Hougue and Port-en-Bessin.

Vauban's Legacy

The work of Vauban was so immense that even today his name is inseparably connected with bastioned forti-

Musketeer at the beginning of Louis XIV's reign

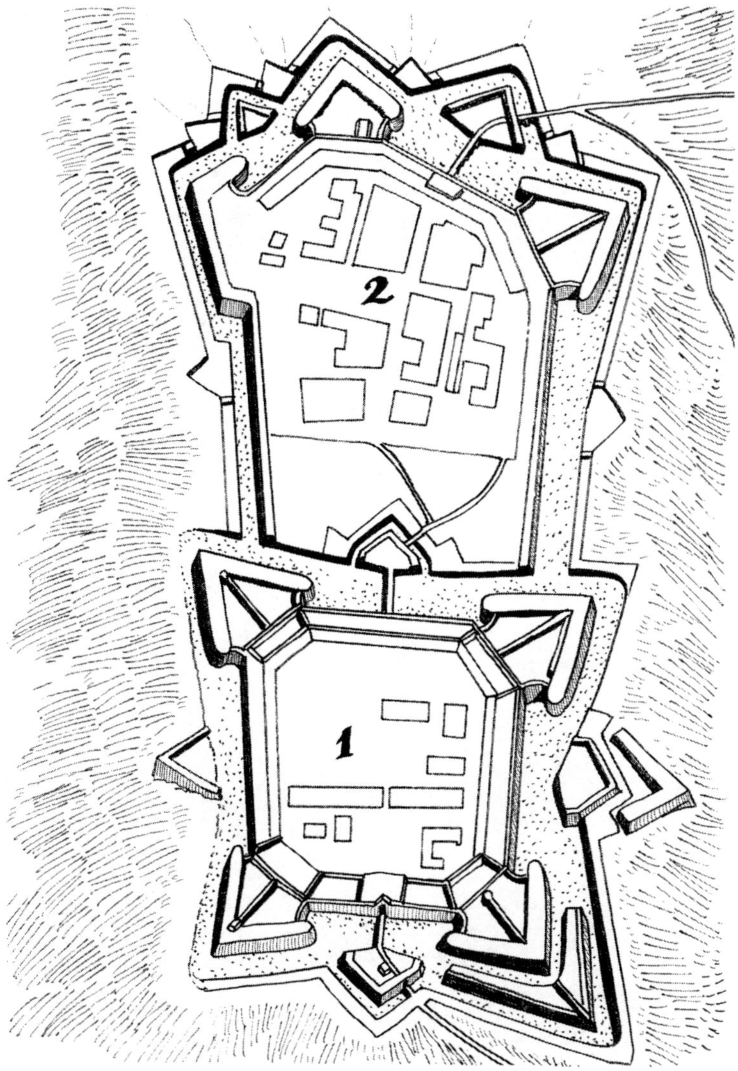

Montlouis. The fortress of Montlouis is situated east of Prades in the department of Pyrenées-Atlantiques. The treaty of Pyrenées in 1659 divided the Cerdagne region: Spain kept the Sègre valley with the city of Puycerda and France obtained the upper Têt valley. To protect this new acquisition, Louis XIV charged Vauban with creating a new fortress. In 1679, Vauban inspected the region, selected several possible places and finally chose a steep rocky ridge (altitude 1,600 m), dominating the river Têt and La Perche pass. The fortress, baptized Montlouis in Louis XIV's honor, was conceived ex nihilo and rapidly realized. Montlouis is a testimony to Vauban's fantastic capacity to adapt to natural conditions. Due to a step decline, the fortress was composed of a square fort (1) with four bastions with ears, three demi-lunes and a dry moat. The stronghold dominated a small village (2) surrounded by an enceinte reinforced with three bastions and two demi-lunes. Today Montlouis, perfectly maintained and preserved, is still occupied by the French Army as a commando training place.

fication. As we have seen, Vauban did not invent bastioned fortification. With talent he brought together the various features and theories which had been invented in the previous hundred years and welded them into a coherent and effective system. However, Vauban's designs were largely governed by geometry, and they were not always completely sound; in his hands permanent fortification grew to be treated somewhat as a geometrical puzzle, a species of maze, and complicated labyrinths which on the whole were little more successful in keeping out the enemy. But he had acquired such a reputation that — after him — any French military engineer who dared criticize his work was considered an iconoclast heretic. Vauban's authority on the art of fortification became military gospel, an unfortunate honor which paralyzed French military thoughts on the subject during the 18th

Above: **Dragoon at the time of Louis XIV (armed with a pistol)**

Opposite: **Fusilier at the end of Louis XIV's reign.**

and 19th centuries. Even today Marshal Vauban remains such a legendary figure in France that anything remotely resembling a bastioned work is immediately ascribed to him.

Vauban also participated and assisted Louvois in the reorganization of the French army. He created a new military professional branch, the *Génie Militaire* (engineering corps). One of his major contributions was the design of a new tactic of siege warfare. Vauban had a regard for the life of his soldiers; he knew that most casualties incurred in attacking a stronghold were from the use of frontal assault. He insisted on methodical digging to approach a fortification. He brought some order to the business of siege by codifying and organizing a rational method of attack under cover, characterized by the digging of parallel and zigzagging trenches that afforded protection for assault troops; his properly sited siege batteries were aligned to fire down the length of the angled fortifications in order to destroy guns and gunners on top of the bastions. He also advocated the rational use of mines to explode the enemy's walls. Thanks to Vauban's success, it became an honored military tradition to abandon a stronghold or to surrender if the defenders believed they could no longer hold it. The art of defending strong places became a subtle practice of fighting with gallantry and surrendering with honor after conventional formalities.

By the end of Louis XIV's reign, the heavy musket was replaced by a new lighter weapon — soon fitted with a bayonet; the introduction of the bayonet was an important step in warfare: the pike-man and musketeer of former periods gradually disappeared and were replaced by a single soldier, the *fusilier* (rifleman). It is said that it was Vauban who introduced the socket bayonet. By that time a new soldier also made its appearance, the *grenadier*, an elite infantryman armed with grenades, small bombs thrown by hand.

Vauban was above all a competent soldier, but also an intellectual, an intelligent technical-minded humanist who wrote numerous books about extremely varying subjects e.g. fair taxation, inland boat transport, development of colonies in North America, agriculture, and religion.

The End of the Sun King

The megalomaniac Louis XIV died at the age of 77, on September 1, 1715. During his later years, he was a lonesome and sick man; all his children were dead. All that was left to him was a great-grandson, a five-year-old child, the future Louis XV. The Sun King's popularity declined markedly as a result of military defeats, loss of colonies, successive devaluations of the currency, heavy taxation and various shortages that heavily burdened the French people. For his aggressive policy in foreign affairs, Louis XIV had brought war, destruction and misery to a large part of Europe. He was hated by all. His reign had lasted much too long.

29

Paris at the Time of Louis XV (1715–1774)

As Louis XV was too young to reign, a government of regency was led by Philippe d'Orléans (Louis XIV's nephew). The nobility felt liberated from Louis XIV's bigoted yoke, the palace of Versailles was left unattended, and the royal court re-established itself in Paris. The Regency was a time of unbridled pleasures, of debauchery and depravity, while France was exhausted by Louis XIV's last disastrous wars.

The new king was handsome, elegant and intensely devoted to the ideal of peace, but he was also timid, skeptical and became bored very quickly. Lacking willpower, Louis XV could only govern with reliable advice provided by talented ministers Fleury, Choisel and his mistress Jeanne-Antoinette Poisson, marquise de Pompadour. During the first part of Louis XV's reign, France was drawn into two major wars: the War of Polish Succession (1733–1738) and the War of Austrian Succession (1740–1748). Both wars were costly in terms of men and money and unfruitful for France.

Most noteworthy, the era of Louis XV was a period of great intellectual ferment, called *Siècle des Lumières* (Age of Enlightenment). With biting irony and lucid style, philosophers and liberal thinkers such as Montesquieu, Voltaire, Diderot, d'Alembert, and Rousseau did much to change the thinking of their age. They attacked all forms of tyranny and injustice, undermined the very foundations of the monarchy, challenged traditional beliefs, and advocated more liberal systems of trade, institution and education. The French philosophers played a significant role in the history of people's struggle for freedom. They were the initiators of the American Declaration of Independence of 1776, they announced the

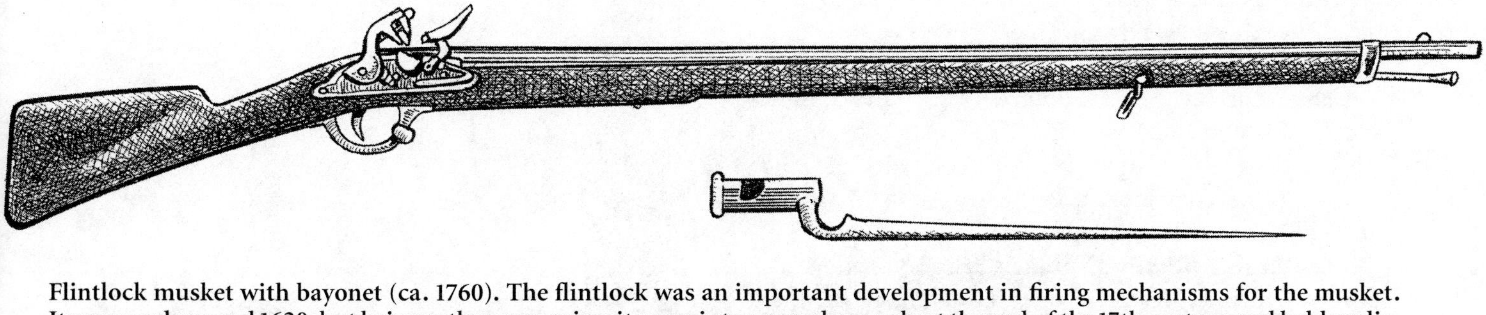

Flintlock musket with bayonet (ca. 1760). The flintlock was an important development in firing mechanisms for the musket. It appeared around 1620, but being rather expensive, it came into general use only at the end of the 17th century and held undisputed sway for nearly 200 years. It could be carried preloaded, was reliable even in wet weather, and was lighter than the matchlock musket, but accuracy, rate of fire and range remained relatively unchanged. Nevertheless, fitted with a socket bayonet, the flintlock was a major step in infantry warfare.

French Revolution of 1789, and they were the precursors of Romanticism.

In both India and North America, skirmishing went on constantly between France and England. Several wars broke out in 1756. Without adequate resources and a navy, France was unable to help its colonies. By the end of Louis XV's long reign, all French territorial possessions in Canada and India were lost, making the path free for English colonial domination.

In 1768, France purchased the Mediterranean island of Corsica from Genoa, where a certain Napoléon Bonaparte was born a year later.

The end of the *Ancient Regime* (the pre–Revolutionary absolute monarchy) in France is the story of an impossible search for financial stability hampered by the selfish hostility of the aristocratic "elite," which utterly failed to face its responsibility. The frivolous and incompetent Louis XV died, unlamented, in 1774 at the age of 64.

In Paris Louis XV continued the prestigious architectural policy of the Sun King with the emphasis on open spaces, wide vistas to show off monuments and churches.

The Louis XV Square (today Place de la Concorde) was established between 1755 and 1775 by architect Gabriel. The massive square formed part of a considerable extension of the city to exalt Louis XV. In 1792, the large square was renamed Place de la Révolution; here, public executions were carried out with the *guillotine*, a machine for beheading invented by Professor Joseph Ignace Guillotin. The most spectacular public execution was without doubt that of King Louis XVI on Sunday, January 21, 1793 at 10:30 a.m. Since 1833, the center of the square has been ornamented with the 24-m-high, 200-ton monolithical *Obelisk of Luxor*, a four-sided tapering pillar with a pyramidal top from Ancient Egypt.

The prestigious *Hôtel d'Evreux* was built between 1718 and 1720; today the residence is called *Elysée Palace*, and it is used as a dwelling for the French Republic presidents.

The impressive *Palais Bourbon* was built between 1722 and 1728; in 1807 the palace was further beautified in neoclassical Greek style by order of Napoléon I. Since 1843 and until today it has been the seat of the *Assemblée Nationale* (French Parliament).

The *Ecole Militaire* (Military School) was erected between 1751 and 1773 after a design by architect Jacques-Ange Gabriel. This building, which stands at the south end of the Champs-de-Mars, was constructed as a result of the initiative of the financer Paris-Duverney and of Madame de Pompadour, both of whom wanted young men of the poorer classes to be able to take up military

Infantryman about 1744

careers. The neighboring *Champs-de-Mars*, (Mars' Fields) is a wide esplanade, which was originally intended for the cadets' marches and maneuvers.

From 1770 to 1776, the Avenue of Champs-Elysées was extended to the present Etoile knoll.

In 1744, Louis XV fell seriously ill and promised—if he was healed—to build a church. It happened, and at the place of the old Saint Geneviève abbey, the cured king had the Saint Geneviève church (today's *Panthéon*) built between 1758 and 1789 after a design by architect Soufflot.

Today the Panthéon is a necropolis where significant and great Frenchmen are buried e.g. Rousseau, Voltaire, Soufflot, Carnot, Victor Hugo, Emile Zola, Jean Jaurès, and Felix Eboué to name just a few.

At Versailles, Louis XV ordered the construction of the Petit Trianon, the Saint Louis cathedral and the Opéra.

Echoing the Age of Enlightenment, there was also a concern for public health. The hospitals of Saint Antoine, Cochin and Beaujon were built between 1767 and 1784 within the grounds of religious communities. Through a concern for hygiene, food markets were established such as those of Saint Catherine in the Marais, Aligre in Faubourg Saint Antoine, and the wheat market—today the *Bourse du Commerce* (Trade Exchange)—in the rue du Louvre.

30

Cormontaigne and Montalembert

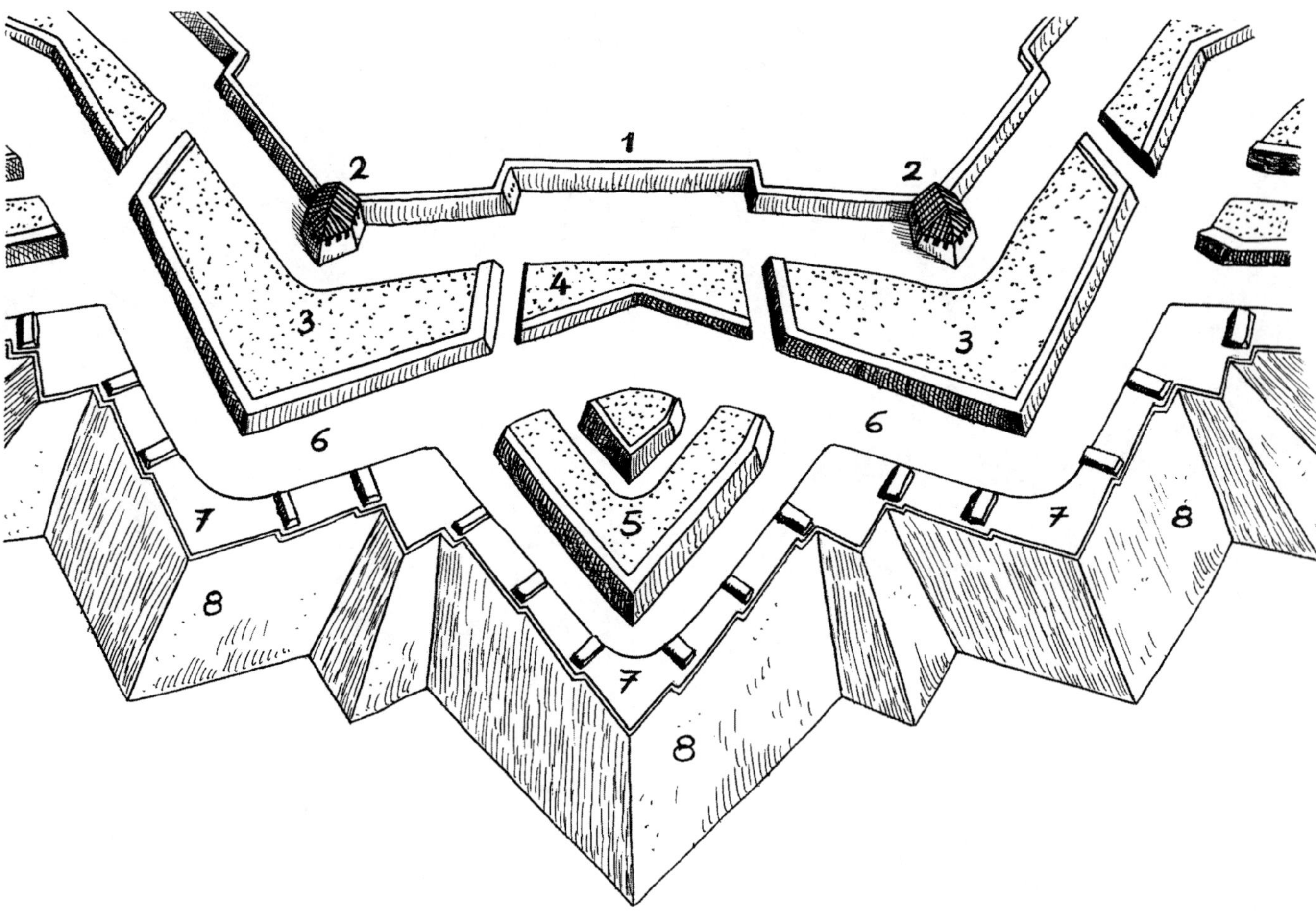

Vauban's "third system." Designed and employed only at Neuf-Brisach (southern Alsace) by Vauban, this bastioned front was made a "system" by fellow engineers after the marshall's death. It was composed of the following elements: 1. Bastioned curtain. 2. Bastioned tower. 3. Counterguard. 4. Tenaille. 5. Demi-lune with redoubt. 6. Main ditch. 7. Covered way with traverses and places of arms. 8. Glacis.

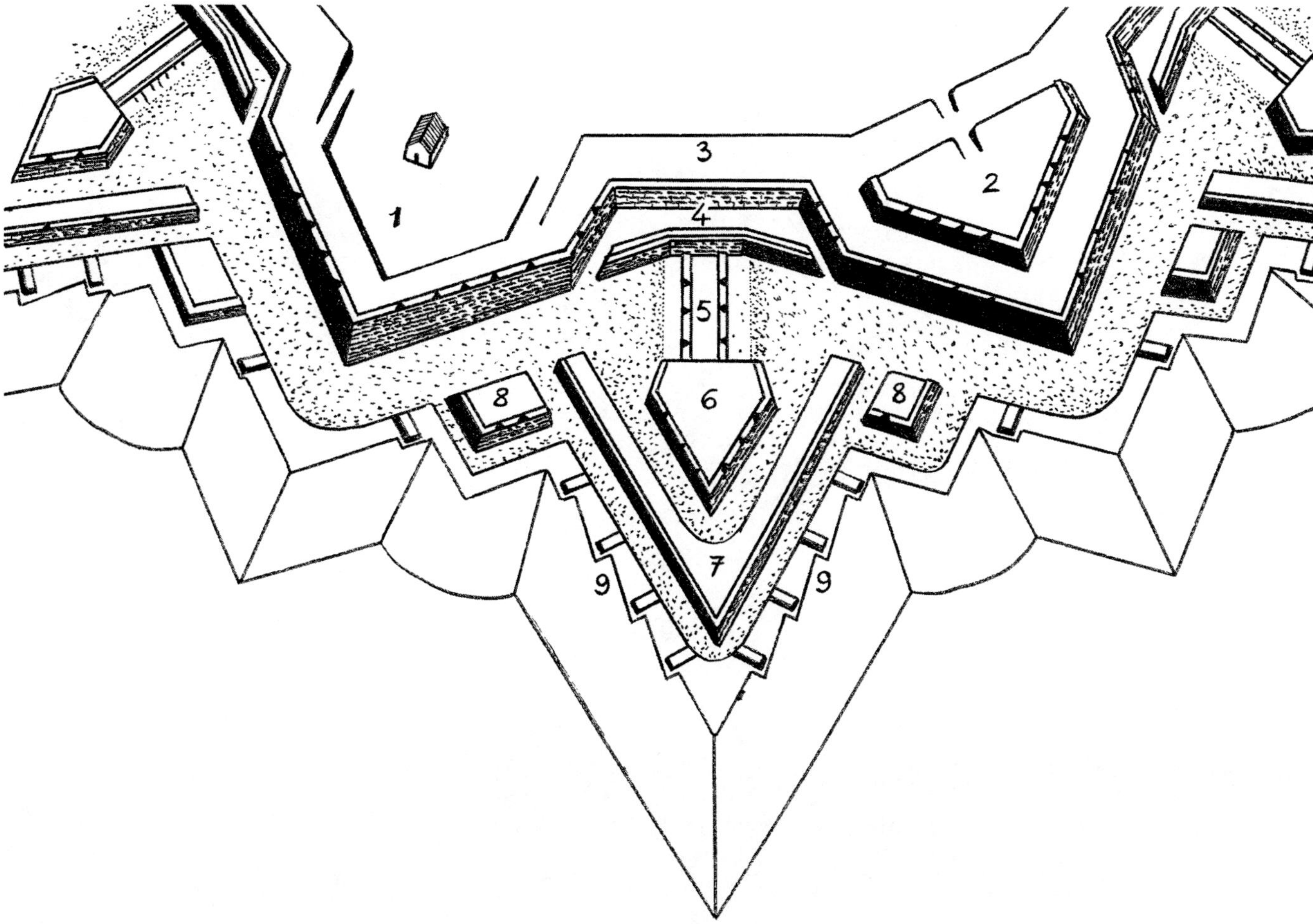

Cormontaigne's Improved System. 1. Bastion (with powder house). 2. Cavalier. 3. Curtain. 4. Tenaille. 5. Caponier across the ditch leading to demi-lune. 6. Demi-lune. 7. Counterguard. 8. Detached re-entering place-of-arms. 9. Covered way "en crémaillère" with traverses.

Cormontaigne

During the 18th century, Vauban's successors could not be so liberal with money, men and materials. In any case, Vauban and his contemporaries had built so much and so well, while muzzle-loading solid-shotted guns had reached the limit of development. Moreover the frontiers of France had become more or less settled, so there was hardly any need to design new types of military architecture. Marshal Vauban was and remained "The Master," and it was heresy to suggest improvements on his work. Vauban's reputation made it impossible to promote any totally new system of fortification, and the only safe course was to make a well-argued amendment to his "system." The marshall, although a prolific author, had never published on the theory of fortification. After his death his works were widely analyzed, critiqued and sorted out into three theoretical "systems." There was no lack of military engineers, though, willing to try to create new system of fortifications, if only on paper. In 1729, Bernard Forest de Belidor, professor of Mathematics at the French Artillery School, designed a "system" based on turning bastions into detached and fragmented units; Belidor's method was quite sound on paper but highly unlikely to be acceptable in practice. A successor to Vauban at the post of General-Commissaire of Fortification was Louis de Cormontaigne (1696–1752). Cormontaigne could not resist the urge to design a bastioned system of his own. In 1750 this was refined by General Noizet (head of the French Military Engineer School at Mezières). With minor changes the result was called *Modern French System* or *Improved System*, which — at first sight — differed little from Vauban's style. The principal features of Cormontaigne and Noizet's *Improved System* included a cavalier placed in the bastion, a redoubt on the re-entering place of arms, a redoubt in the ravelin, and a caponier leading from the wall to the redoubt in the ravelin. The principal things that remained were a *tracé en cremaillère* (saw-toothed-shaped with traverses) given to the covered way, and detached re-entering place-of-arms. After all,

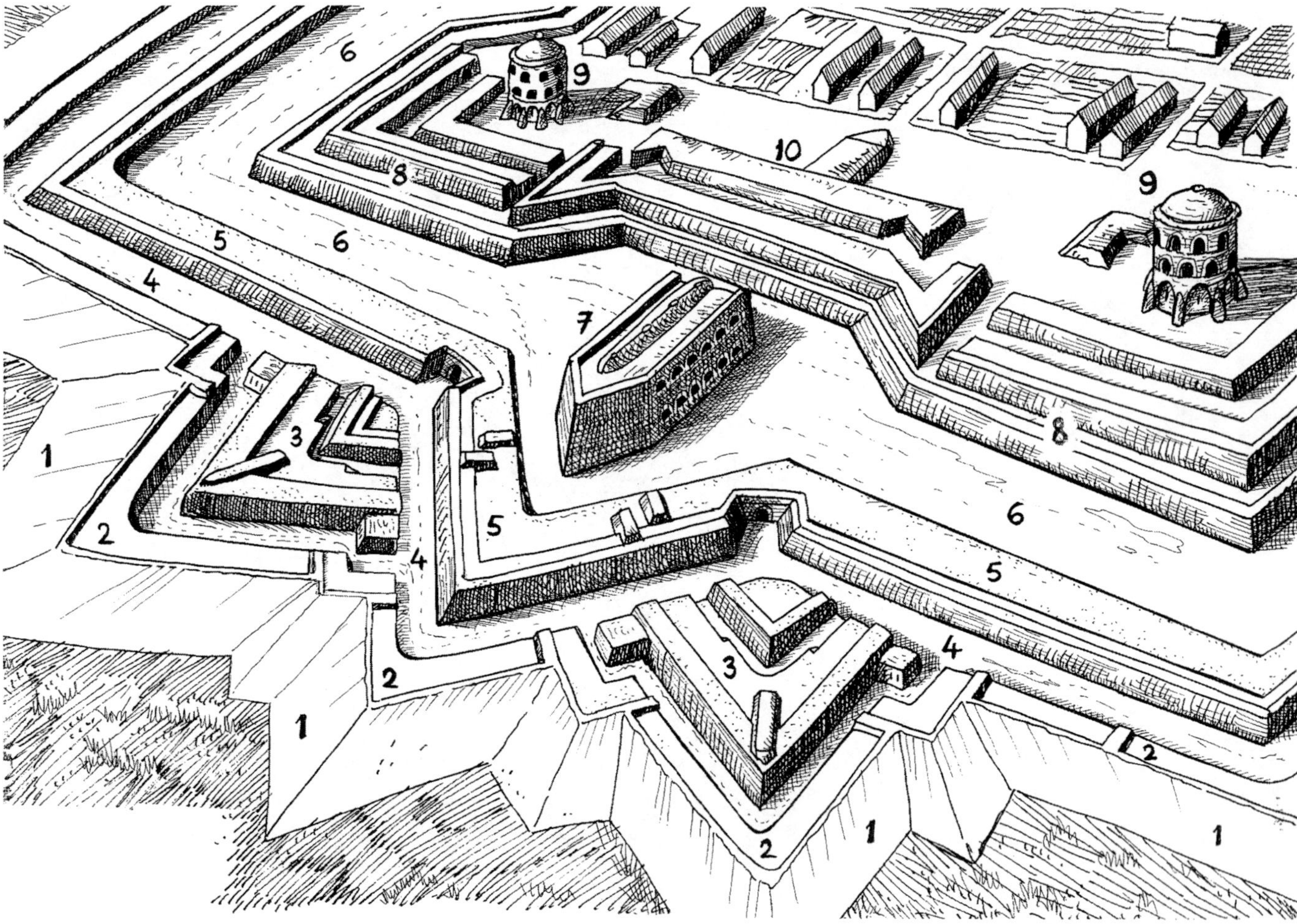

Montalembert's system of fortification. 1. Glacis. 2. Covered way. 3. Lunette. 4. First ditch. 5. Counterguard linked together forming a so-called envelop. 6. Main ditch. 7. Caponier. 8. Main enceinte (wall with parapet). 9. Three-story high round artillery tower. 10. Bomb-proof barrack and supply store.

nothing really new. Cormontaigne's fame largely rests on his posthumously published treatises, which were models of clarity and served as basic texts for successive generations of French engineers. Fortifications in Cormontaigne's style were made at Verdun, Longwy, Bitche, Thionville and Metz.

Montalembert

Significant suggestions were made by another Frenchman, the Marquis Marc-René de Montalembert (1714–1800). Originating from a noble family with a strong military tradition from Angoulême, Montalembert became a cavalry officer at the age of sixteen. In 1733, he was engaged at the siege of Kehl and at that of Philippsbourg a year later. He then saw service under the prince of Conti whom he followed in the wars in Austria, Bohemia and Italy. In 1747, he was elected to the French *Académie des Sciences* and dedicated himself to various studies. In 1752, he was appointed General-Lieutenant to the governor of his natal province of Saintonge. During the Seven Years' War (1763–1770), he served as military *attaché* in Sweden and Russia. He was also deeply interested in military architecture and searched for new means of defense with an original mind. On that subject Montalembert wrote eleven thick books— published between 1776 and 1784— developing a new method of fortification, which he called *Fortification Perpendiculaire* (Perpendicular Fortification). As an experienced man-of-war, Montalembert appears to have been one of the first engineers to realize that a siege was basically an artillery duel. He reasoned that the side with the most and the best artillery would carry the day and that the practice of standing a line of guns in the open on top of the exposed bastions and curtains was an invitation to defeat. To be short, Montalembert developed four important points.

1. A fortress must present its entire front toward the enemy. Montalembert objected strongly to Vauban's bastioned tracé, pointing out that curtain walls were useless

and that the bastions could easily be swept by enfilade fire. He thus advocated a simple front perpendicular to the enemy's approach, a front without bastion or a *tenaille tracé*, consisting of a series of triangular structures forming a continuous saw-edged front.

2. A fortress must have as many guns as possible in order to deliver a devastating fire able to crush the enemy before they could deploy their siege artillery. At the same time the defensive artillery had to be well protected. Montalembert thus preferred guns mounted in bombproof *casemates* (artillery chambers) with embrasures covered by solid shutters, instead of artillery exposed in open battlements. For this purpose, he proposed to revive a modernized form of artillery tower (notably the so-called *Bastei* designed by Albrecht Dürer at the end of 15th century): a large, high, round or U-shaped, multistory, stone-made artillery tower bristling with guns for long-range fire.

3. Weapons for close-range defense of the ditches would no longer be firing from the flanks of bastions, but from *caponiers*, large artillery towers, especially armed for this purpose, placed across the ditch; these works becoming strong points in their own right.

4. A bastioned enceinte was in due course vulnerable and practically always doomed to surrender — if attacked by an army employing Vauban's siege method. In fact, if a part of it was breeched, the whole system collapsed. Therefore Montalembert advocated the creation of rings of detached autonomous forts around cities and fortresses; so if one fort was conquered, it was bad but not a disaster, the other structures could still resist and continue the defense. It was, on a larger scale, the application of Vauban's principle regarding outworks and advanced works.

Montalembert's Influence

Montalembert's theory was both old-fashioned and backward (point 2) and visionary and well ahead of his time (points 3 and 4). On the whole, his system of fortification was rather sound, but it had two formidable disadvantages: it was extremely expensive to build; and it is doubtful whether it would have been possible to hold a sufficient garrison to man all that artillery, together with the necessary infantry and service troops and their stores and ammunition.

Like many 18th century innovators, his work could have passed unnoticed and his recommendations consigned to oblivion, but his suggestions were accepted later. Montalembert's main features (points 3 and 4) were taken up and developed with enthusiasm by the Germans and the Austrians in the 19th century. In fact, Montalembert's basic designs did become the blueprint for most European forts well into the 19th century.

In France, he had little opportunity to demonstrate his concept, and little came from his plans. Montalembert was sharply criticized and ignored by most of the French engineers who stuck with absurd obstinacy to the tradition of fortification evolved by Vauban, "The Master." Besides, Montalembert was not even a colleague; he was an outsider, he was a cavalry officer who dared criticize Vauban's bastioned system. The contemptuous conservative "professionals" were of the opinion that he dealt with matters he did not understand and that he should rather mind his own business. Montalembert's theoretical work had a modest influence on French fortifications at the time of Napoléon; but modern "polygonal" fortifications— which evolved from his designs— would not be introduced in France before 1874.

31

The Enceinte of the "Fermiers Generaux"

A Fiscal Barrier

Since 1670, when Louis XIV had ordered the destruction of its 16th century fortifications, Paris was an open, defenseless city. The limits of Paris were indicated by *bornes* (wooden marks) beyond which it was forbidden to establish new settlements. This interdiction was totally ignored, and Paris continued to grow outside the permitted limits. In 1639, the parish of Ville l'Evêque was integrated into Paris. In 1659 the village of Chaillot became a suburb, called Faubourg de Conférence. Between 1724 and 1728, Louis XV tried to stop the growth of Paris by ordering severe measures against illegal settlements. This regimentation ended in failure, and no one — including the king—could stop the chaotic and uncontrolled growth of Paris. In 1765, total freedom of construction was granted provided the width of street was respected and regulated to 9.72 m. From a population of about 260,000 in 1553, Paris grew to more than 600,000 inhabitants on the eve of the 1789 Revolution and about 800,000 in 1800, making it the most populated city in Europe.

As previously said, luxurious gates punctuated the limits of the city where fiscal posts were set for the collecting of taxes on imported and exported goods. Needless to say, smugglers could avoid these checkpoints by discretely entering the city through back streets. During the reign of Louis XVI (1774–1793), the fraud was so large scale and so much money was lost due to smuggling that the Parisian authorities decided on the creation of the so-called *Enceinte des Fermiers Généraux* (General Farmers' Wall).

Built at the request of Charles-Alexandre Calonne, General Controller of Finance from 1783 to 1787, this new wall was designed by architect Claude-Nicolas Ledoux (1736–1806) and built by the contractor C. P. Pécoul. It was not a military defense but a wall especially designed as a fiscal barrier. In addition, the wall clearly marked the administrative limits of Paris. Secondary advantages were that it offered the possibility for the police to control access to the town and an opportunity to give work to the jobless.

The term "fermiers généraux" deserves some explanation. To be short, a *fermier général* was not a *farmer* (strictly speaking this is a tenant renting land for cultivation) but a private person (often a rich financier or a very wealthy bourgeois), a contractor who leased from the crown the office of tax collector. This practice called *affermage* (farming lease) had been created by Henri IV and Sully and continued by Colbert. The acquisition of the charge was very expensive but it was a fruitful investment and an invitation to corruption, as the *fermier* levied taxes, gave a large part to the Parisian authorities, but pocketed for himself non-negligible illegal sums. For the king and Paris, it was a convenient system as the purchase of the office filled their coffers, and furthermore the authorities did not have to maintain a fiscal administration to pay salaries for official civil servants and tax collectors. For the common people, merchants and craftsmen, this private contractual system was expensive and thus particularly unpopular.

The Enceinte of the Fermiers Généraux was a prosperous private business at the service of the authorities; it made huge profits and employed about 1,000 people including security guards, controllers, tax collectors, assis-

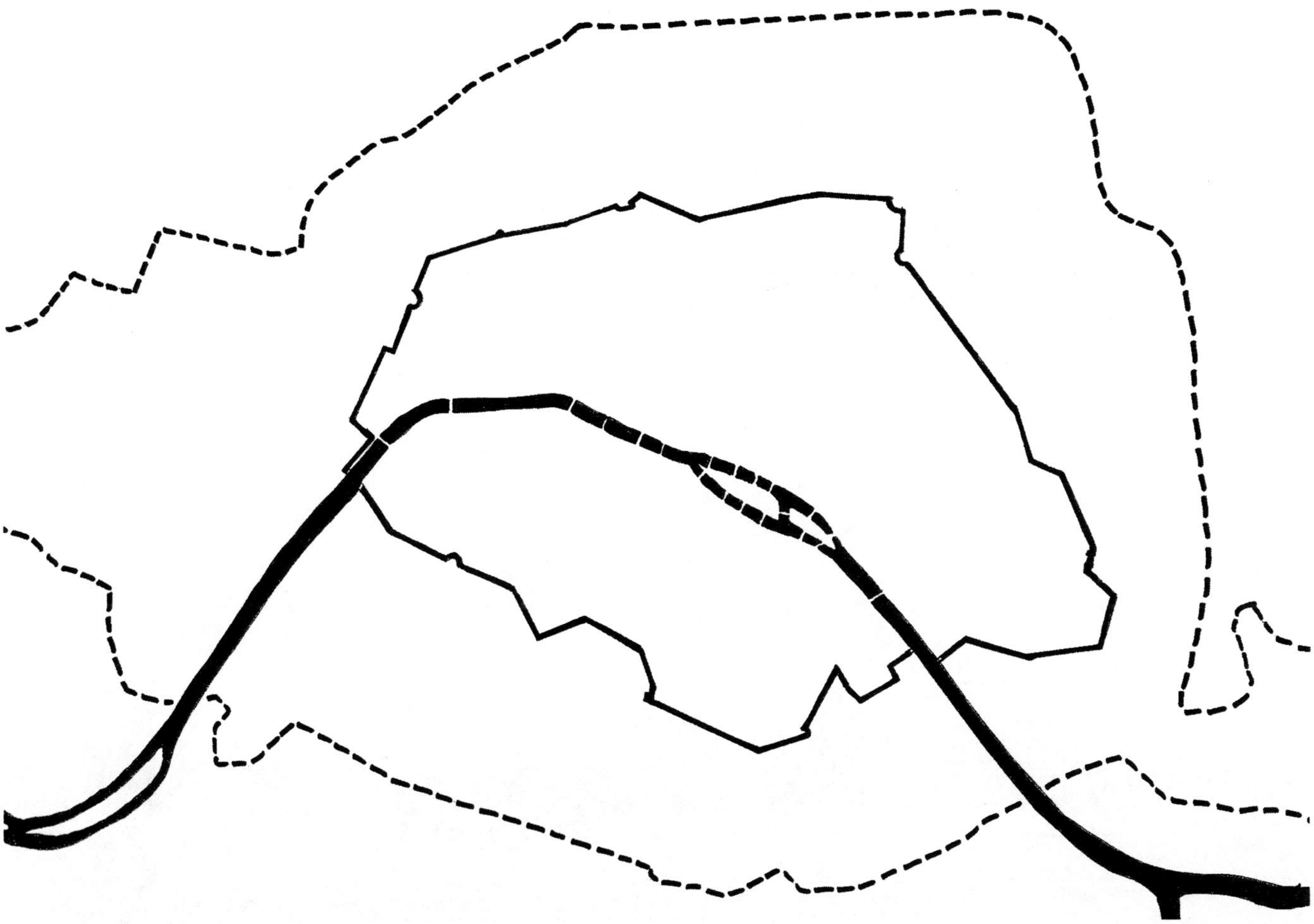

Fermiers Généraux' Wall. The ground plan shows the Enceinte of the Fermiers Généraux. The dotted line indicates the current administrative limits of Paris.

tants and supervisors. It had warehouses to store the confiscated smuggled goods. As a reaction, there was a proliferation of inns, open-air cafés and *guinguettes* (popular dance halls) right outside the Enceinte where the people of Paris came on weekends to have fun and where wine and beer were cheaper since taxes had not been paid on them.

The Farmers' Wall was very unpopular at large; there was a song going: *le mur murant Paris rend Paris murmurant!* (the wall enclosing Paris makes Paris moan). Another song went like this:

Pour augmenter son numéraire
Et raccourcir notre horizon
La Ferme a jugé nécessaire
De mettre Paris en prison
(To make big profit
And shorten our horizon
The Farm has judged necessary
To put Paris in prison)

A few years later, by the time of the French Revolution, many demanded the abolition of taxes and the destruction of the hated Farmers' Wall. In 1789, breeches were made in the wall and several tollgates were set afire by the angry populace. In 1791 the tax-collecting company was abolished, but as the revolutionaries—and later Napoléon—badly needed the money raised at the gates of Paris, the highly unpopular taxes levied at the enceinte were re-established in 1798. It continued to function until the demolition of the wall in January 1860.

The Wall

Built between 1784 and 1787, the enceinte enclosed the populated part of Paris in the second half of the 18th century and integrated several villages (now Parisian boroughs) including Chaillot, Le Roule, Montparnasse, Picpus and Gros-Caillou. Its layout roughly followed lines 2 and 6 of the present-day Parisian *métro* (underground railway). On the left bank of the Seine, it corresponded to the present-day *Boulevards du Midi* (Southern Boulevards) including Boulevard de la Gare, Boulevard de

Bonshommes tollhouse (from a photograph by Gouviot 1859)

l'Hôpital, Boulevard Auguste Blanqui, Boulevard Saint Jacques, Boulevard Raspail, Boulevard Edgar Quinet, Boulevard de Vaugirard, Boulevard Pasteur, Boulevard Garibaldi and Boulevard de Grenelle. On the right bank it coincided with, from the Trocadéro, to the present Avenue Kléber, Rue Lapérouse, Avenue de Wagram, Boulevard de Courcelles, Boulevard des Batignoles, Boulevard de Clichy, Boulevard Rochechouart, Boulevard de la Chapelle, Boulevard de la Villette, Boulevard de Belleville, Boulevard de Ménilmontant, Boulevard de Charonne, Boulevard de Picpus, Boulevard de Reuilly and Boulevard de Bercy. The total perimeter was 23 km in length (seven km on the left bank, and sixteen km on the right bank), enclosing a surface of 3,370 hectares.

Picpus tollhouse (from a painting by Palaiseau 1819)

The enceinte—financed by the General Farmers themselves—cost a fortune estimated at 17,000,000 *livres* (pounds). It was composed of a simple stone wall, 3 to 4 m high, crowned with a wallwalk and a breastwork where armed guards would patrol to thwart any attempt of smuggling; where the walls made an angle, observation posts were arranged for the same purpose. All along the wall, at the outer side facing the "country," there was a wide peripheral *promenade* (walk) bordered with trees, convenient for both public strolling and police patrol, but also very useful as a peripheral communication around Paris.

The Tollhouses

The most spectacular features of the enceinte were the *pavillons d'octroi* (tollhouses), designed by architect Claude Nicolas Ledoux. These were pieces of art, Athenian-styled *Propylaea* (monumental porches) intended to make a transition between city and countryside, beautify the enceinte, glorify the monarchy, and display the importance of Paris. There were 55 of them (seven were added in 1826), and all were different. They were characterized by a curious, rather difficult to define style combining neoclassical inspiration, Ancient Egyptian, Greek and Roman architecture to Ledoux's own original, sentimental, mysterious, pompous, romantic and lyrical visions. The architect made a wide use of arcades and massive columns, solid pillars, porticos, arches, porches, semicircular vaults, Roman bows, cornices, strong bossages, rotundas, cylindrical, square or Greek cross-shaped ground plans, rectangular façades, cubic forms, triangular frontons, flattened domes, and many other audacious combinations of volumes. Between 1775 and 1779, Ledoux built the royal salines (salt pans) of Arc-et-Senans near Besançon in the Doubs where he had already shown the measure of his confused utopism and how controversial his style was. In Ledoux's own words the wall and the impressive Parisian tollhouses also had a civic value: they were intended to educate people, to show them their duties and rights, to have them feel like honest, proud and good citizens, to have them accept paying taxes for the common good, to bring together people and the monarchy in a common idealized architecture.

Some specimens of tollhouses still remain today at the Nation Square, Denfert-Rochereau Square, the rotunda of the Saint Martin barrier and at La Villette.

32

The French Revolution of 1789

The Storming of the Bastille

It was again in Paris that one of the most important events of French history occurred: the Revolution of 1789. In the 18th century, France was still ruled according to discarded medieval laws, and society was based on a tripartite division: clergy, nobility and commoners. The institutions were no longer adapted to the changing world. The wealthy urban bourgeoisie had great economic power and counted among its members the liberal professions: lawyers, magistrates, etc. But, officially commoners, the bourgeois enjoyed no political power. They sought vigorously to rectify this state of affairs. In 1789, France was still profoundly monarchist, but everything was going to change in a few years. In 1788 King Louis XVI, unable to resolve the financial difficulties besetting the kingdom, decided to convene the States General. Paris became agitated as the citizens were concerned about the armed forces which had been sent to the capital. Alarming rumors began to circulate; there was fear of royal reprisals. On July 13, 1789, the masses seized a supply of muskets from the Arsenal and the Hôtel des Invalides. But as they had no gunpowder, they stormed the Chastel Saint Antoine, the notorious Bastille the following day. The governor of the fortress, De Launay, was killed. This was no longer a mere riot, it was a revolution. A National Assembly was set up to give France a constitution limiting the power of the king. The Constitutive Assembly did an enormous amount of work. It adopted the Universal Declaration of Human Rights, establishing Liberty, Equality and Fraternity thus abolishing the medieval system of social classes. It divided France into *départements* (administrative regions), and the old institutions, provincial parliament, and province were abolished. Civil servants were elected. Taxation was changed and better distributed. The French clergy was forced to independence from the Pope of Rome. Reluctantly, Louis XVI agreed to these changes and, in July 1790, it seemed that all Frenchmen were reconciliated.

In June 1791, the very convenient and logical *metric system* was adopted; based on *mètre* (distance), *litre* (volume) and *gramme* (weight), it was multiplied by deca (10), hecto (100), and kilo (1000); and divided by deci (0.10), centi (0.100), and milli (0.1000).

The stubborn and embittered Louis XVI could no longer bear the restrictions laid by the Assembly. He decided to flee abroad to place himself and his family under the protection of the partisans of monarchy. The escape failed and the king was brought back to Paris; henceforth he was a prisoner. Meanwhile the religious conflict between the Pope and the clergy grew more severe.

The idea of war began to gather momentum as the French wanted to spread the benefits of their Revolution through all the countries in Europe where the people were still the victims of tyranny. The ambitious and ideal principles they had created to rule themselves were recognized as worthy to be universally applied to the whole of mankind. In April 1792 war was declared on Austria. The campaign began with defeat, for the improvised French army was poorly organized and badly commanded. But on September 20, 1792, the victory of Valmy saved both Paris and the Revolution. A day later, France was proclaimed a Republic. Louis XVI, having proved that he had conspired with the invaders, was put on trial, condemned to death by a new assembly called the Convention, and executed on January 21, 1793.

The First French Republic

Now there was no turning back. The execution of Louis XVI gave rise to a great outburst of indignation from the European monarchies, and a joined force — led by Britain — declared war on revolutionary France. The coalition represented a grave danger, and a temporary dictatorial *Comité de Salut Public* (Committee of Public Safety) was set up. The French armies were reorganized by Lazare Carnot, and in 1794, France was victorious on all fronts. In 1795, peace was signed with the major powers but war against Austria continued. The Convention voted a new constitution, giving birth to a new regime, the Directoire (directory).

At the head of the army in Italy, a certain General Napoléon Bonaparte won several battles against Austria (Lodi, Arcole and Solferino), forcing his adversaries to sign the Treaty of Campo-Formio in October 1797. After an ill-fated campaign in Egypt in 1798, General Bonaparte put an end to the Directoire and seized power by force (November 9, 1799). He created a new regime inspired by Ancient Rome, called *Consulat*, and placed himself with full power at its head with the title of *Premier Consul* (First Consul).

French infantryman ca. 1792

33

Napoléon I and the First Empire

Napoléon Bonaparte

Napoléon Bonaparte was born on August 15, 1769 at Ajaccio (Corsica) in a middle class family. He attended military school, became a professional artillery officer, and took part in a number of engagements during the Revolution. While he earned a high reputation in 1793 at the siege of Toulon, his career was soon compromised by his association with the radical revolutionary Maximilien Robespierre. In 1795, he regained favor when he brutally suppressed a riot by force in Paris. The Italian campaign demonstrated the full measure of his military genius, which must surely rank among the greatest of all time. He was a remarkable organizer, a clear-minded, hardworking man with an exceptional memory. He was also stubborn, cynical, full of himself, only concerned with his own glory, incredibly ambitious, highly authoritarian, and could not bear to be contradicted.

When Napoléon Bonaparte came to power, France was deeply disturbed by divided factions and exhausted by war and internal revolts. In a few years, the First Consul Bonaparte made of France a powerful nation again. He reorganized financial administration by putting the currency on a sound footing. He appointed *préfets* (prefects) and placed them at the head of each *département* (territorial subdivision) representing his authority. After lengthy negotiations Bonaparte restored religious peace by signing a concordat with Pope Pius VII. He promulgated the *Code Civil*, which is still today the basis of French civil law.

The second anti–French coalition was defeated after the First Consul's victories at Marengo and Hohenlingen in 1800. France annexed Belgium and Piemond in Italy. In 1802 the treaties of Luneville and Amiens restored peace. As he badly needed money, Bonaparte sold *Louisiana* to the United States of America in May 1803; the purchase of this huge territory (stretching from the Great Lakes to the Gulf of Mexico) for $15,000,000 doubled the size of the USA.

Napoléon I, Emperor of the French People

Cunningly Bonaparte presented himself as the continuator of the French Revolution and, at the same time, a man guarantee the bourgeois order; he was acclaimed by all as the strong providential savior who had pacified and regenerated France after the previous chaotic period. In 1802, a referendum appointed the highly popular Bonaparte Consul for life. At this point, all his enemies were under control or unable to act against him. The competent, successful but megalomaniac First Consul found it not enough to be dictator for life, he also contemplated founding a dynasty. In May 1804, the Senate conferred on Bonaparte the dignity of Emperor. Pope Pius VII came from Rome personally to crown him. The ostentatious coronation took place on December 2, 1804 in the Notre Dame cathedral in Paris. The artillery officer from modest origins had made it; he was now Napoléon I, Emperor of the French People, and saw himself as the successor of the Ancient Roman emperors and the successor of Charlemagne. He took the role of emperor with great enthusiasm, organized an imperial court, and restored or created high offices and positions (e.g. the Legion of Honor) on

a strict hierarchical basis. France — and Europe — entered a new era.

The emperor worked actively to revive industry and trade. He also imposed strict censorship of the press and set up a strong police force headed by his minister of internal affairs, the inquisitive Joseph Fouché (1759–1820).

However peace did not last for long. Napoléon's prestige could only be maintained by war and conquest. In order to attack England, a large army was massed in the port of Boulogne in northern France, but the defeat suffered by the French fleet at Trafalgar (1805) put an end to the hope of invading the British Isle; Trafagar gave Britain an advantage at sea which lasted until 1914. Napoléon then turned his army against Austria, Russia and Prussia. By the end of 1807, after a series of astonishing campaigns marked by resounding victories at Ulm, Austerlitz, Jena and Friedland, Napoléon was the master of Europe. England, however, continued the struggle, and the emperor created the *Continental Blockade* to close all the ports of Europe to English vessels.

In Portugal and Spain the French encountered violent resistance and a savage, costly guerilla war, which they never succeeded in extinguishing. At that point, Austria decided to take advantage of Napoléon's discomfort by breaking the peace. The Austrians were defeated at the battle of Wagram in 1809, and Napoléon maintained his position.

Since she had failed to give him an heir, Napoléon rejected his wife Josephine de Beauharnais, divorced and remarried with Archduchess Marie-Louise, the daughter of the emperor of Austria. In March 1811 a son was born, the king of Rome or *Napoléon II*, also called the *Aiglon* (eaglet), who never reigned.

Zenith and Decline

In the meantime Tsar Alexander had broken the peace. Napoléon reacted by the gathering of the *Grande Armée* (a huge force composed of French and European conscripts) and foolishly decided to invade Russia. Napoléon's decline was begun. After the victory of the Moskva, the capital of Russia was reached on September 14, 1812. The burning of the town obliged the French to evacuate Moscow; the ghastly retreat from Russia began, and the Great Army melted away in cold, blizzard, snow and ice. For the French, army Spain had been an ulcer; Russia was a hemorrhage marking the beginning of Napoléon's end. All over Europe, there was great disquiet

Grenadier à pied Garde Impériale 1813 (Foot Grenadier of the Imperial Guard).

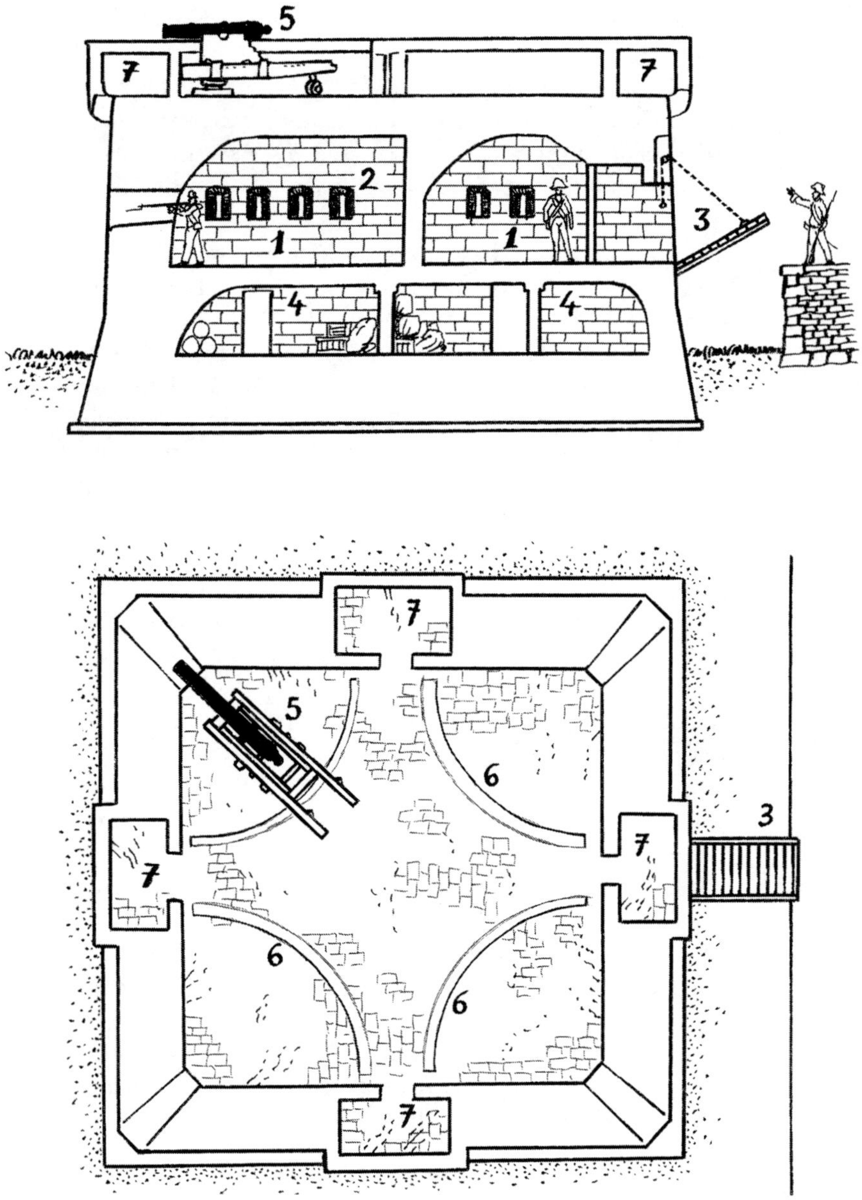

Cross section (top) and ground plan of the terrace (bottom) of a Tour Modèle 1. The standardized Tour Modèle 1 was designed by the Committee of Fortifications and issued in 1811. It was a small coastal fort including a troop chamber (1) fitted with loopholes for close-range defense (2), a drawbridge over the ditch (3), and a basement (4) for supply and ammunition. The top terrace was armed with one extra gun (5) mounted on a pivoting carriage by a portion of rail (6). Curiously there were balconies (7) fitted with medieval machicolations, probably more for decoration than for active defense.

and a great increase in the number of malcontents. The French domination, the Continental Blockade which was organized in an economic war against England, and the conscription of both French and foreign soldiers forced to fight Napoléon's wars, were highly unpopular. Even the French people were weary of endless wars. The Allies—England, Austria, Prussia and Russia — decided to put an end to Napoléon's yoke. The battle of Leipzig in October 1813 ended in a half-defeat for the emperor. Although Napoléon recovered the military genius of his earlier years and won delaying victories at Montmirail and Champaubert, he could not prevent the invasion of France and the Allied occupation of Paris. Recognizing his own defeat, Napoléon abdicated on April 4, 1814. The victors granted him the sovereignty of the derisory kingdom of the island of Elba (off the coast of Tuscany, Italy) with a small body of troops and a pension.

Louis XVI's brother, the count of Provence ascended the throne of France under the name of king Louis XVIII, since Louis XVII (Louis XVI's son) had died in 1795.

Everyone thought the Empire was over, when suddenly Napoléon returned from Elba, rallied troops and marched to Paris, which he entered on March 20, 1815. The *Cent Jours* (Hundred Days) came to an end when the Allies defeated Napoléon at the battle of Waterloo, June 18, 1815. The emperor was captured and deported to the cold and windy Saint Helena island in the Atlantic Ocean, where he died, a bitter, sick, and lonely man on May 5, 1821. Since 1840, the funeral remains of the emperor have rested in the crypt of the Invalids Church in Paris.

Curiously, in spite of the fact that Napoléon was more concerned with his own glory than with the welfare of the French people, in spite of bloody wars, suffering, and dictatorship, the Corsican emperor is still immensely popular in France today; France had experienced an exalting period, the bloody Napoleonic epic soon became an idealized legend, an illusionary tale of greatness and pride still vivid today. The "martyrdom" of Jeanne d'Arc and Napoléon, the defeats at Trafalgar and Waterloo, the recurrence of colonial rivalry in the 18th and 19th centuries, as well as the "perfid treachery" of Dunkirk (May–June 1940) and the destruction of the French fleet at Mers-el-Kebir (July 1940) form the epitome of the atavistic French conservative hatred against the British people.

Napoleonic Warfare

The era 1789–1815 changed the face of France and that of Europe as well. Warfare too was transformed. Before this period, international conflicts had been dynastic affairs and succession wars between quarreling aristo-

French 36-pound gun from 1802 on coastal mount. The gun carriage was mounted on a central pivoting swivel and could rotate owing to small wheels and a portion of rail. The recoil force was passed by means of two wooden curved cheeks.

cratic cousinages of emperors, kings and dukes. Their mutual relations and their wars were conducted by a precise diplomatic protocol and clear principles of international law. All this was called in question and changed. The French Revolution and the Napoleonic era (and before that the American Revolution) transformed passive subjects into active and passionate citizens. These events realized the ideal of the nation in arms driven by ideology, patriotism, and civic beliefs. The state ceased to be regarded as the "property" of dynastic princes, and instead became the instrument of powerful forces dedicated to abstract concepts, the embodiment of some absolute Good for which no price was too high, no sacrifices too great.

As the French state changed its nature, it changed its policy and the way war was conducted. The element of sheer ferocity in war, almost lost to sight in the 18th century, now became dominant. War was no longer to be either temperate or inconclusive, and terror was the order of the day. Voluntary professional enlistment and foreign mercenarism were replaced by national mass conscription. Henceforth it was the state who conscripted, armed, equipped, clothed and fed the drafted nation in arms.

The success of the French armies was due to the combination of the professionalism of the Ancient Régime and the enthusiasm of the Revolution. Napoléon inherited the legacy of the revolutionary army, including a flexible tactical system superior to those of France's enemies, a dedicated soldiery, and an officer corps based on talent; the young leadership generally had proved their worth, competence and courage in battle, weapons in hand at the forefront of their troop. Napoléon was fortunate to have young, fine and courageous generals—who he elevated to the dignity of Marshall—such as Berthier, Ney, Davout, Murat, Soult, McDonald, Cambronne and many others. Napoléon was also inspired by the advanced military theories by General Jacques-Antoine, count of Guibert and by the German military thinker Karl von Clausewitz. In addition Napoléon benefited from a spirited assault infantry, from the resurgence of impetuous French cavalry, and from a fine artillery which had been modernized and standardized by General Jean-Baptiste Vaquette de Gribeauval in the 1770s.

In the early 1790s France pioneered the use of strong units known as *combat divisions* that lived off the country and combined regiments of infantry, artillery and

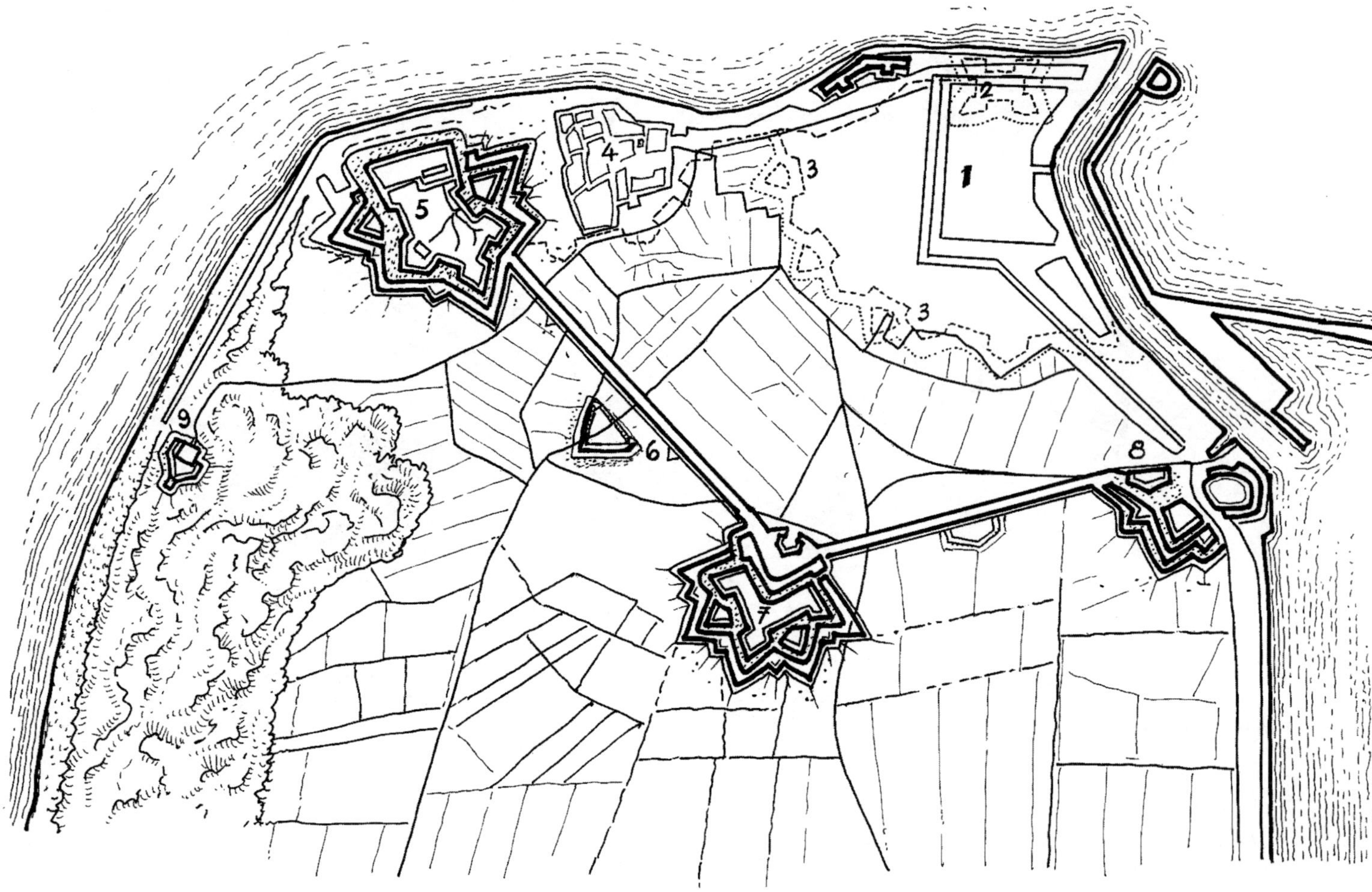

Den Helder (Holland). Den Helder — situated in the province of North Holland in The Netherlands — had been conquered by the French cavalry in January 1795. The small fishing village on the North Sea coast was chosen in 1811 by Napoléon to become a strong naval base facing England. It included an arsenal and a military port for the French navy (1). These would have been defended by a citadel (2) and a bastioned enceinte (3). The village of Den Helder (4) would also have been defended, but none of these projects were implemented. The maritime base was covered by a continuous earth wall, ditch and detached works: Fort Lasalle (5), redoubt Tolhek (6), Fort Ecluse (7) and Fort Dugommier (8). On the sea side, the coastal Fort Morland (9) defended the approach to the harbor. Today the maritime base and the forts are still used by the Royal Dutch Navy.

cavalry, enabling fire and shock power, rapid mobility and flexibility.

Disorganized by the Revolution, the French army was reshaped by Lazare Carnot and became an efficient and feared machine of war under the emperor's reign. However, no analysis of Napoléon's success can avoid the emperor's own personality. At least until 1812, he was a formidable leader, a military genius, and a superb master of tactics and operations, not aiming simply at defeating an enemy army, but at destroying it.

Uniforms, bright and colorful, were intended for recognition of friend and foe on the battlefield, but they also displayed the visual majesty of Napoleonic warfare that so easily captured the popular imagination. But we must not forget that colorful units and flags, grand strategy, courageous tactics, dramatic actions, and great victories constituted only a small part of reality; the other side of the coin was never ending casualties and endless suffering, bloody and ugly consequences of Napoléon's limitless ambition.

Napoleonic Fortifications

A rather unknown aspect of Napoleonic warfare was the renewal of French fortification. In July 1791, the Revolution had created the *Comité Central des Fortifications* (Central Committee of Fortification) allowing the Consulat and the Empire to develop a fine engineering corps mixing the tradition of Vauban and Cormontaigne to Montalembert's experimentations. Napoléon had good and modern-minded military engineers directed by the talented general Armand-Samuel Marescot (1758–1835). François-Joseph-Didier Liédot (1773–1812) designed

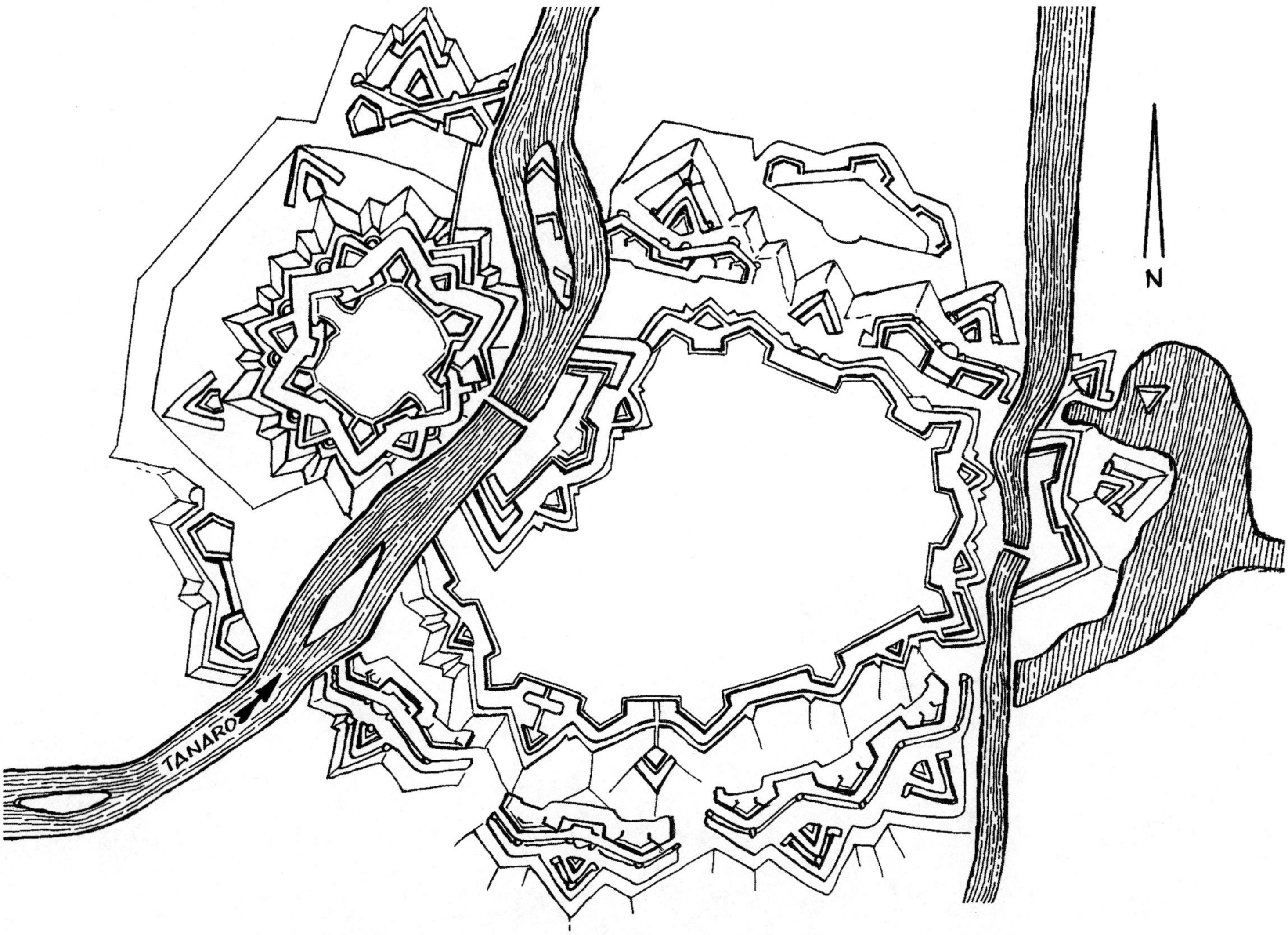

Alexandria (Italy). Situated in northern Italy, Alexandria was an important arsenal for the French armies. The city was militarized and heavily fortified by Count François de Chasseloup-Laubat (1754–1833) in 1801 as a logistical depot intended to supply the French armies in their campaigns against Austria. The impressive fortifications included a bastioned enceinte, detached fronts forming a first line of resistance, and a citadel on the left bank of River Tanaro. They protected supply, ammunition, equipment and food stores, barracks, a military hospital, and administrative buildings. The French fortifications were totally demolished after Napoléon's fall in 1815.

mountain fortifications, notably the Rocca at Anfo (Italy). Jean-Claude Eléonore Le Michaux d'Arçon (1733–1800) designed the so-called *Lunette d'Arçon*, a standardized triangular fortlet with back-fire casemates. Lazare Nicolas Marguerite Carnot (1753–1823) reorganized and actually created the army of revolutionary and imperial France; under Napoléon's reign he advocated the implementation of Montalembert's fortification, and designed the so-called *Carnot's Wall*, a detached wall with arched niches for infantry fire. François Haxo (1774–1838) developed casemated batteries and designed the so-called *Haxo casemate*, a well-protected arched masoned artillery emplacement, open at the rear and covered with earth. François de Chasseloup-Laubat (1754–1833) designed a totally original fortified front known as *Front d'Alexandrie*. Prominent engineers were Choumara, Rogniat, Montfort, Veilhan, Blanc, Decaux, Sorbier, Deponthon and many others.

Napoléon did little work in France because Vauban's lines of border fortifications were still reliable and because the Emperor's strategy was based on aggression and conquest: it was absolutely not envisaged to fight on French soil. The main Napoleonic fortifications were logistic bases and ports where French troops could be supplied and armed, strategic arsenals from where new offensives would be launched. They were constructed in the occupied European countries, principally in The Netherlands (Breskens, Amsterdam, Den Helder), Belgium (Antwerp,

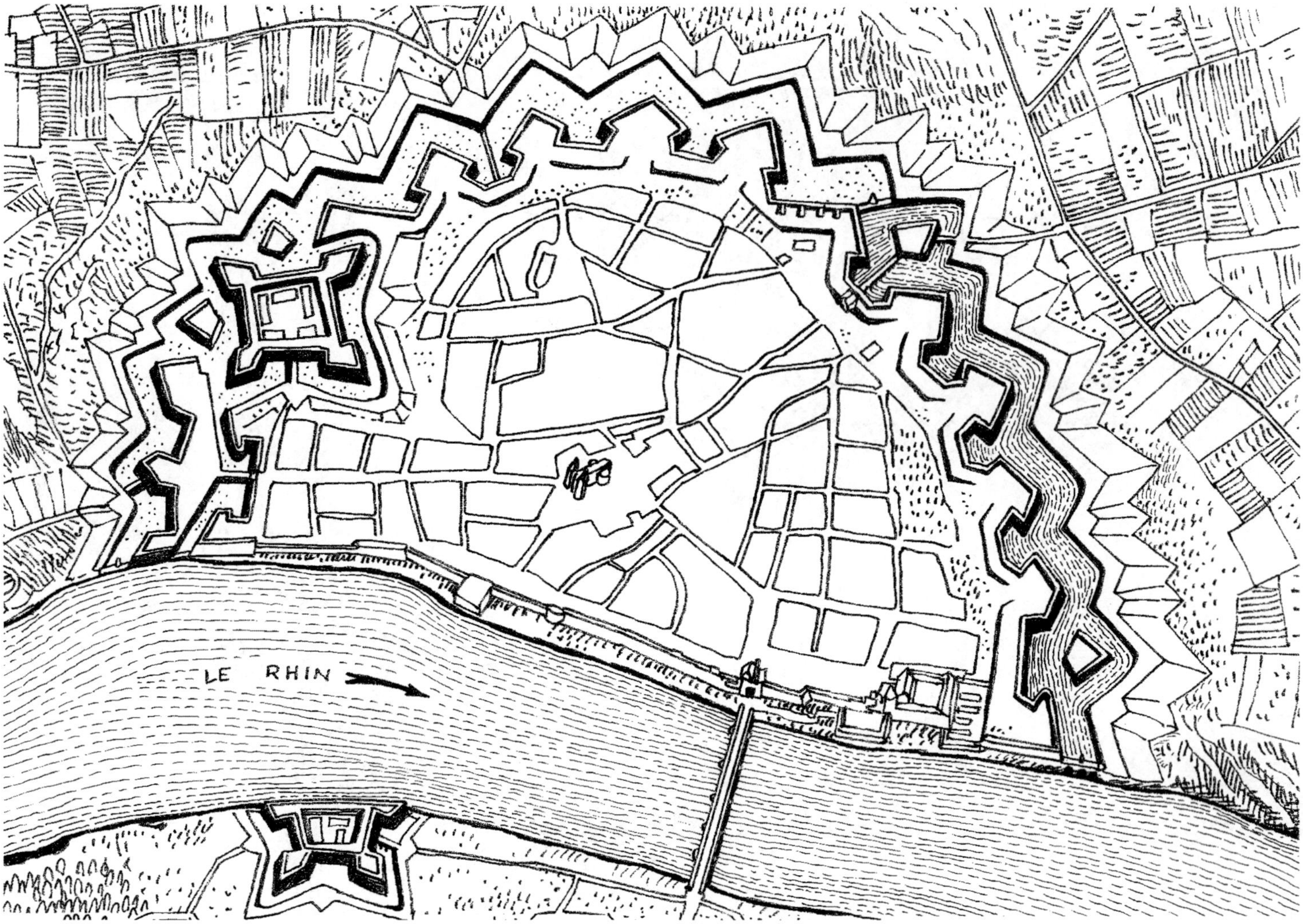

Mayence. Situated on the River Rhine in the province of Palatinate (Germany), Mayence became an important arsenal during the Napoleonic wars against Prussia.

Ostende), Italy (Alexandria, La Spezzia), and Germany (Wesel, Cologne, Mayence, Jülich). However, after Trafalgar, the British dominated the seas and could attack France from the sea wherever and whenever they wanted. As a result Napoléon ordered the reinforcement of the coastal defenses by the creation of standardized watch-towers, forts and batteries not only around the main French harbors (e.g. Toulon, Rochefort, Brest and Cherbourg), but also abroad (e.g. Willemstadt in The Netherlands and Raguse in Dalmatia).

34

Paris at the Time of Revolution, Consulat and Empire

Revolutionary Ambitions

In Paris the first gesture of the Revolution was the destruction of the Bastille prison, the symbol of arbitrary justice. Though they had other interests, the successive regimes of revolutionary France had great ambitions regarding the beautifying of Paris. A special committee, named *Plan des Artistes* (Artists Plan), was constituted and made designs from 1793 to 1797. The plans and suggestions by this group of artists, architects and urbanists—some of them totally utopian—were principally concerned with the improvement of social life, hygiene, urbanism, health and public facilities, but there were no concrete results. The social problems, the military situation, and the political instability brought too much pressure on the committee to achieve more than well-intentioned projects on paper. The Revolution had neither time nor means nor money to implement in buildings and monuments its Republican ideals.

Prestige Buildings

The Consulat and the First Empire were marked by both the pursuit of the prestigious work of the Capetian-Bourbon absolute monarchy and the creation of social urban facilities as advocated by the Revolution. Napoléon wished Paris to be not only the most beautiful city of France but also the glorious capital of Europe. It was his intention to make of Paris a "new Rome" where his victories and glory would be celebrated. The Napoleonic area was, above all, the expression of a will to grandeur. For this purpose, the Emperor created that heavy, ostentatious and pompous *Empire Style*, which imitated the Roman style without its suppleness and grace: massive colonnades, overabundant cornices and medallions, gilding etc. Among other grandiose schemes, plans were made for an Archives Palace, a University Palace, a Customs Palace and a Palace for the Emperor's son, the King of Rome. Another gigantic and extravagant plan was the creation of a huge roadstead in the plain of Grenelle; this *naumachy* (artificial lake) was designed by architect/urbanist De Naudie Perronnet in 1812; it would have been established along the Ecole Militaire (Military School) and would have stretched between the villages of Passy, Vaugirard, Issy, Meudon, Sèvres, Boulogne and Auteuil—covering with water approximately the present 7th, 15th and 16th arrondissements of southwestern Paris. The large lake would have served to regulate the flow of the River Seine and would have provided a large commercial and military port and a training place for the French navy.

Compared to Napoléon's great expectations and megalomaniac ambitions, the actual results may seem poor. Many of Napoléon grandiose projects never got off the ground, but several monuments were created.

At the emplacement where the Bastille fortress had stood, Napoléon contemplated creating a wide square in the middle of which a curious fountain would have been

Napoléon's Elephant Fountain on the Bastille Square, 1809

built in the form of a giant 24-m-high elephant made of bronze made of cannons captured from enemies. To judge the effect, an actual-sized model was erected in 1809. Made of timber and plaster by sculptor Bridan and architect Alavoine, the elephant of the Bastille Square collapsed in 1847 and was soon demolished.

The *Madeleine Church*, erected in the form of a huge Roman/Greek temple in honor of Napoléon's Great Army, was built between 1806 and 1814 by architect Vignon. After the fall of Napoléon, the immense and cold monument became a Catholic church dedicated to St. Mary Magdalene.

The *Carrousel Arch* in the Tuileries Garden was designed by architects Pierre-François Fontaine and Charles Percier; the Arch was built between 1806 and 1808 to celebrate the victories of Napoléon. An imitation of the Arch of Septimus Severus in Rome, the monument is made of red and white marble columns framing three vaults filled with bas-reliefs. On top of it were placed four gilded horses which were removed by order of Napoléon from the Venetian basilica of San Marco. The originals were returned in 1815 and replaced with copies to which a chariot and the statue of Peace were later added.

The most noteworthy Parisian monument dating from the Empire era is, of course, the *Arch of Triumph*, which was ordered by Napoléon as a memorial to his army. Placed at the end of the Champs-Elysees on top of the Chaillot hill (the present Place de l'Etoile–Charles de Gaulle), the Arch completed the great vista which started at the Louvre. The arch was designed in 1806 by architect Chalgrin and completed in 1836. It has a single barrel-vault and is 164 feet high and 147 feet wide. The faces of the arch have huge bas-reliefs, and the names of Napoléon's principal victories are sculpted in the high section. Under the Arch, the *Tomb of the Unknown Soldier* was placed in 1920 to commemorate the sacrifice of the soldiers of World War I (1914–1918). These monuments, offering a grandiose background to military reviews and parades, helped create strong patriot emotions and nationalist pride destined for a fine future.

Public Infrastructures

For various reasons, the reign of Napoléon was also marked by demolition: e.g. the medieval Grand Châtelet (which stood in the way) and the donjon of the Temple (to avoid the creation of a monarchist sanctuary). The main efforts of the First Empire were, however, concentrated on less spectacular infrastructures, especially

The Arc de Triomphe at Etoile Square (from Thérond)

bridges and quays: the Saint Louis Bridge connecting the Cité island to the Saint Louis island, the actual Pont des Arts, Pont d'Austerlitz and Pont de Jena. To Napoléon, we also owe the clearing of the parvis of Notre Dame cathedral, the laying-out of the present Rue de Rivoli and the completion of the Place de la Concorde with its fountain and Egyptian obelisk of Luxor. Among other contributions should be noted the construction in 1808 of the Canal de l'Ourcq, the abattoirs of Le Roule, Rochechouart, Ménilmontant, Grenelle and Villejuif—all of which were demolished in 1867 after the centralized abattoir of La Villette was founded. Also a legacy of the

Empire is the creation in 1804 of the Père Lachaise cemetery and Montparnasse cemetery, which was completed in 1824. During the Napoleonic period the population of Paris totaled 700,000. These lived in 27,000 houses, placed along 1,100 streets and 140 squares. They drank 600,000 hectolitres of wine per year and ate 100 million kilograms of bread, 80,000 each of cows, calves, and pigs, and 300,000 sheep. The total surface included 3,400 hectares.

Defenses of Paris in 1814 and 1815

In 1814 and 1815, the Parisians, who knew only the glamorous side of Napoléon's victories, discovered the horrors of war when they saw the flow of wounded and refugees and experienced the threat of invasion. When the Allies were close to capturing Paris, military engineer Joseph Rogniat was commissioned by Napoléon to fortify the highly vulnerable capital of France. Hastily the (previously described) enceinte of the *Fermiers Généraux* was militarized and reinforced with low earth-protected artillery combat emplacements. Field fortifications and temporary gun batteries—manned by Parisian volunteers—were placed in villages surrounding the capital. In spite of stubborn resistance by General Marmont at Romainville and Mortier at Pantin, Paris was captured in March 1814. After Napoléon's return from the island of Elba, and after Waterloo, Paris was once again put in a state of defense, but the Parisians did not defend the vulnerable town for fear of plunder and devastation. The Allies entered Napoléon's capital for the second time in July 1815 without any serious fight. After Napoléon's defeat, for the first time since the reign of Henri IV, Paris was occupied by foreign soldiers. The Allied force counted 110,000 troops: Russian Cossacks camped in the Champs-Elysées, Prussians in the Boulogne forest, and Germans in the Champs-de-Mars. The Prussian marshall Gebhart Blücher von Wahlstatt (one of the victors of Waterloo) established his headquarters in the castle of Saint Cloud, which he plundered.

Napoléon's defeat ushered in almost half a century of relative peace in Europe.

35

Monarchic Restoration (1815–1848)

Louis XVIII and Charles X

After Napoleon's Hundred Days, King Louis XVIII returned to a capital occupied by the Prussians and the Russians. The European powers worked to rebuild a Europe that had been totally changed by the French Revolution and the Empire.

The Treaty of Paris gave France her 1789 borders; the northern part of the country was occupied until a large sum of war damages had been paid. The monarchy was restored, and reprisals against former Revolutionaries and Bonapartists became increasingly commonplace. France was reintegrated into the system of European monarchies.

When Louis XVIII died in 1824, his 67-year-old brother, Charles X, succeeded him as king of France. Charles X was a pious and stubborn man, who failed to understand the changing ideas of his age. He wanted and acted to re-establish the anachronistic Ancient Regime. The ultraconservative measures he took caused resentment.

In July 1830, unrest led to riots in Paris. Once again, a Parisian revolution dictated the destiny of France. After three days of hard fighting on July 27, 28 and 29, 1830, known as the *Trois Glorieuses* (Three Glorious Days), Charles abdicated and had to flee; he died in 1836 in exile at Gorizia (Yugoslavia).

If the people of Paris had hoped for the re-establishment of the Republic, they were cruelly disappointed. Charles X's cousin, the duke of Orleans, became king under the name of Louis-Philippe.

Louis-Philippe

The new regime was called the *Monarchy of July* since it resulted from the Parisian uprising of July 1830.

The new king was a liberal prince, and his accession to power marked the triumph of the growing capitalist bourgeoisie. This social class became wealthier and began to occupy the most vital posts in government and administration. Large-scale industry began to make its appearance, and further aggravated the plight of the working class. Louis-Philippe's foreign policy was directed towards peace and reconciliation; he sought better relations with Britain and entered the *Entente Cordiale* (Heartly Friendship) with Queen Victoria. The tradition of the urbanism-minded Capetian kings was resumed by Louis-Philippe. The period between the revolutions of 1830 to 1848 was marked by a return to building. Under the leadership of both prefects of Paris Chabrol and Claude Berthelot, count of Rambuteau, several projects were completed: the church of Saint Vincent de Paul; new faubourgs (e.g. Saint Georges, Batignolles, Beaugrenelle); covered "passages" for elegant shops and trades; construction of the Seine quays and new bridges (e.g. Pont d'Arcole, Pont des Invalides, Pont du Carrousel); digging of the Canal Saint Martin extending the Canal de l'Ourcq; improvement of fountains, sewers and urban lighting; widening and creation of streets; and the creation of highly technically oriented schools and colleges e.g. Ecole Polytechnique (technical military engineer school), Ecole des Mines (mine school), Collège de France (senior teachers school), Ecole des Beaux-Arts (art school), and Ecole Normale Supérieure (teachers school).

36

Thiers's Fortifications (1841–1845)

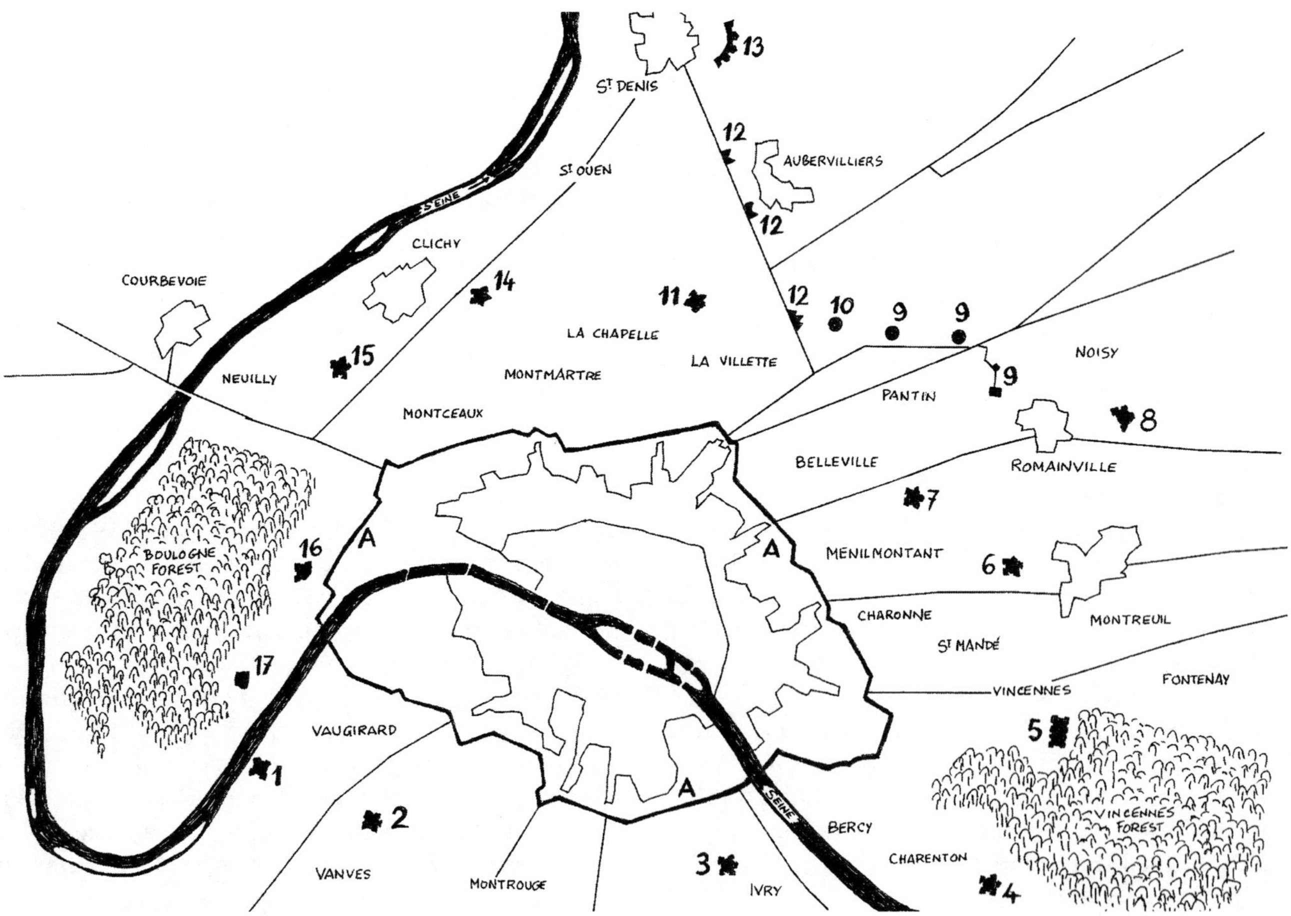

Project of new fortifications for Paris by general Valazé (1831). Valazé's design included the militarization of the wall of Fermiers Généraux (AAA) and the establishment of detached bastioned forts on the hills surrounding Paris. These included the following: 1. Fort of Javelle. 2. Fort of Vanves. 3. Fort of Italie. 4. Fort of Charenton. 5. Vincennes Castle. 6. Fort of Epine. 7. Fort of Bruyères. 8. Fort of Romainville. 9. Ouvrages of Pantin. 10. Fort of Orléans. 11. Fort (name unknown). 12. Ouvrages on the Saint-Denis canal. 13. Double crownwork of Saint-Denis. 14. Fort Philippe. 15. Fort of Clichy. 16. Redoubt of Passy. 17. Redoubt of Auteuil.

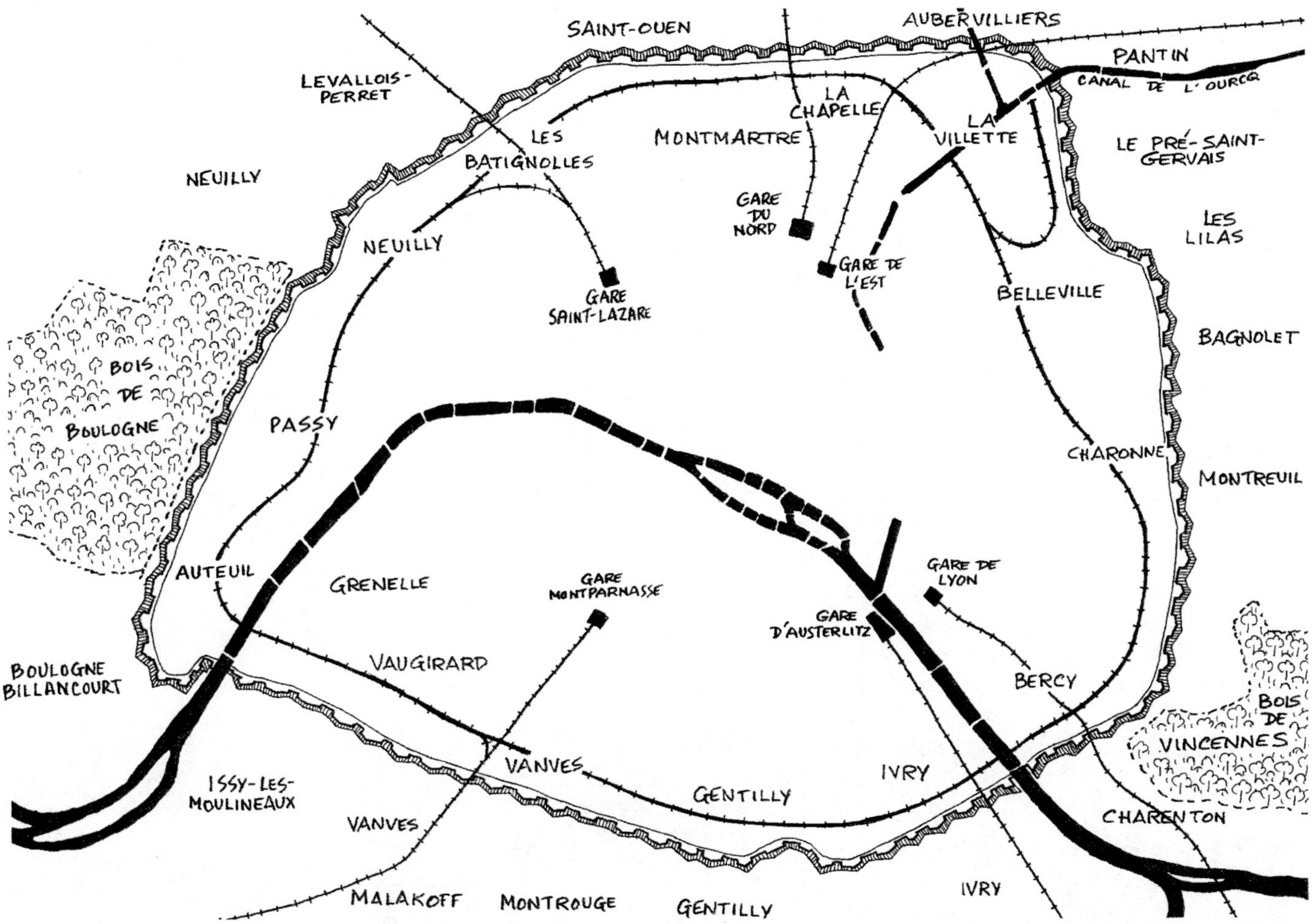

Map of Thiers's Enceinte 1841–1845. The map shows the bastioned enceinte, the main gares (railway stations) and the so-called Petite Ceinture, the internal military railroad intended to supply the fortifications.

The Necessity for a New Enceinte

Paris had not been occupied by a foreign power since the Hundred Years' War and by Spanish units during the reign of Henri IV. The occupation of 1814 and 1815 by the troops united against Napoléon had remained engraved in the city's memory. The capture of Paris had been felt as a supreme humiliation with traumatic results by the French at large. As early as 1818, Marshal Gouvion-Saint-Cyr, minister of War, appointed a commission charged to elaborate new defenses for Paris. In 1820, plans and surveys had been made to avoid any invasion in the future, but nothing happened under Louis XVIII's reign.

The idea for new fortifications of Paris, which had been a totally defenseless city since the reign of Louis XIV, was reactivated by the Monarchy of July after 1830. The project gave rise to boisterous political debates—the government stressing its purely defensive aspect, and the opposition fearing the danger of imprisoning the population of Paris behind walls and emphasizing the high cost. Some generals were also opposed to new fortifications, objecting to their cost and the fact that Paris was too large and too populated to be efficiently defensible and preferring to allocate funds to the constitution of a modern and mobile field army. Finally the upholders of new fortifications won the debates, and it was decided to transform Paris into a *camp retranché* (entrenched camp). The design of the new fortifications of Paris created a doctrinal quarrel among military engineers. Given the large surface of the city, the problem was should Paris be enclosed by a continuous Vauban-styled bastioned enceinte? Or should it be protected by a ring of detached forts as advocated by Montalembert?

In December 1831, general-engineer Valazé started a project in which the existing enceinte of Fermiers Généraux would be militarized, furnished with thick earth revetments and bastions; in addition forts and redoubts would be constructed on the hills at the northeast of Paris. This was more than a plan; some temporary detached structures were built e.g. at Romainville and Rosny-sous-Bois.

One year later, a project was designed by General Bernard who advocated the creation of a new, enlarged bastioned enclosure and a belt of forts. Other projects were made by Captain Delmas in 1832, Colonel Prévost de Vernois in 1833, and Colonel Paixhans in 1834.

Dode de la Brunerie's Design

Finally, in 1840, it was a more ambitious design by the president of the Committee of Fortifications, General Guillaume Dode de la Brunerie, which was retained. The political tension that occurred between France and Britain in 1840 spurred the implementation of the project. A war nearly broke out about the question of Egypt and the Ottoman Empire. It appeared that defending Paris had become a necessity. In April 1841, King Louis-Philippe and the Parliament, on the initiative of minister Adolphe Thiers (1797–1877), decided to protect Paris by a system of fortification and obtained a fund of 140,000,000 francs to carry it out.

Technically, the new Parisian defenses—designed by Dode de la Brunerie and known as *Enceinte of Thiers*—were a compromise between "monarchic" Vauban tradition and "imperial" Montalembert modernity. They included both a continuous bastioned enclosure and an outer ring of detached forts.

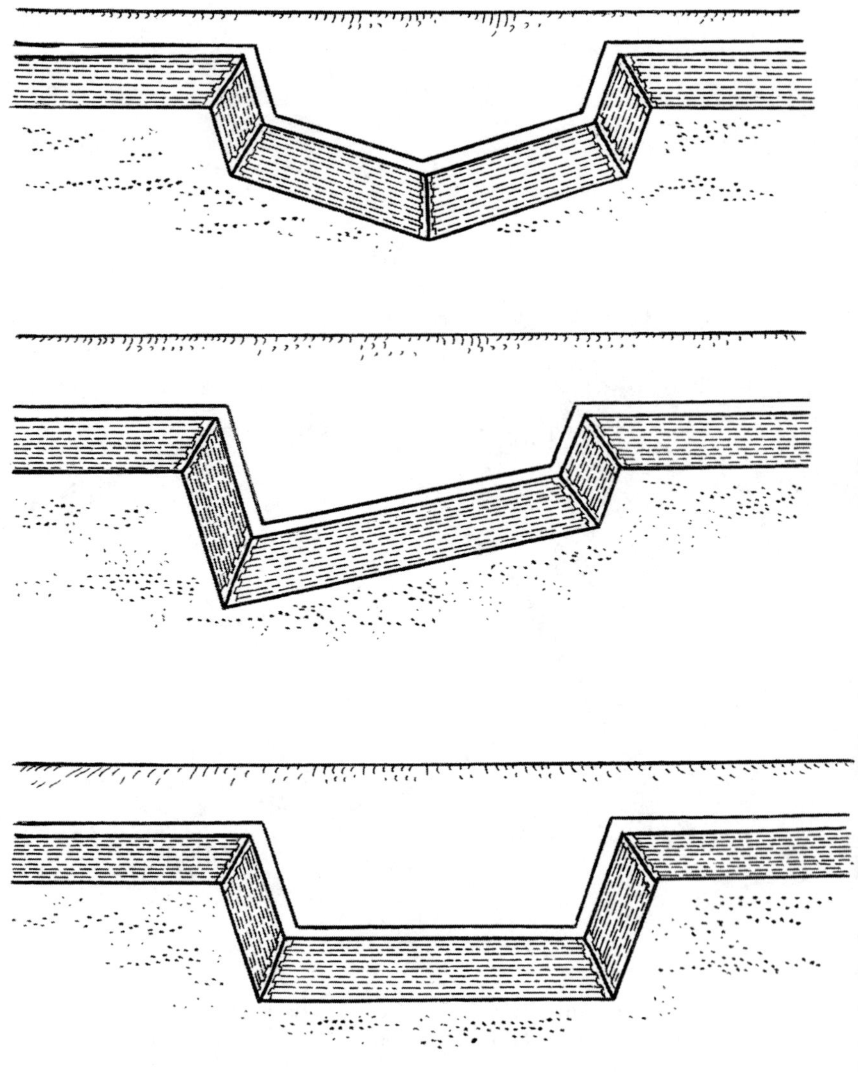

Shapes of bastions in Thiers's enceinte. *Top:* regular bastion with two faces and two flanks. *Middle:* half-bastion with two faces and one flank. *Bottom:* flat bastion with two flanks and only one face.

The Construction of the Fortifications

Before work could actually start, grounds had to be purchased under compulsion and compensations paid. Expropriation, disputes and land speculation gave rise to complicated proceedings and endless suing.

The construction—entrusted to the military Engineering Corps—represented a huge work which lasted from 1841 to 1845. It employed 47 senior officers who were at the same time architects, designers and treasurers, and who commanded 61 officers who directed and supervised 1,135 engineering soldiers/workers. The task was, however, so gigantic that the army staff soon had to employ common infantry soldiers and to subcontract private civilian building companies. In 1842, some 21,600 men—both military and civilian—were at work with tools which today would look ridiculous: shovels, picks, baskets, hampers, wheelbarrows and tip-carts. The construction of one front (composed of one curtain, two flanks and two bastion faces) represented 16,747 cubic m of foundations, walls and buttresses, 2,392 cubic m of revetments, 2,280 cubic m of flagstone for paving and the removal of 89,500 cubic m of *déblai* (earth dug from the ditch) which was transported as *remblai* (filling material) to build the rampart. The building site upset the entire Ile-de-France region. It necessitated an important infrastructure: stone quarries, transportation (wagons and carts for which roads had to be created), brick factories, chalk ovens, numerous tools, scaffold timber, shelters, sheds, barns etc. Furthermore, the mobilized workers needed food, camps and huts. Temporary accommodations were established in the villages of Courbevoie, Saint Denis, Saint Cloud, Vincennes, La Villette, Saint Ouen,

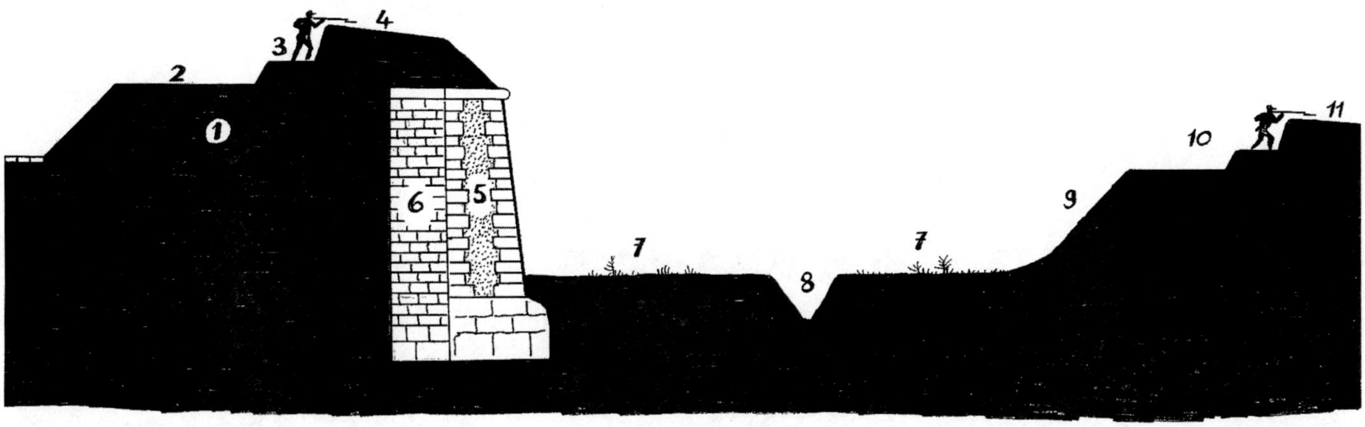

Cross section of Thiers's wall (1841). From left to right the cross section shows the rampart (1) with wallwalk (2), fire-step (3) and breastwork (4); the masoned scarp (5) with buttress (6); the ditch (7) with cunet (8); the sloping earth counterscarp (9); the covered way (10); and the glacis (11).

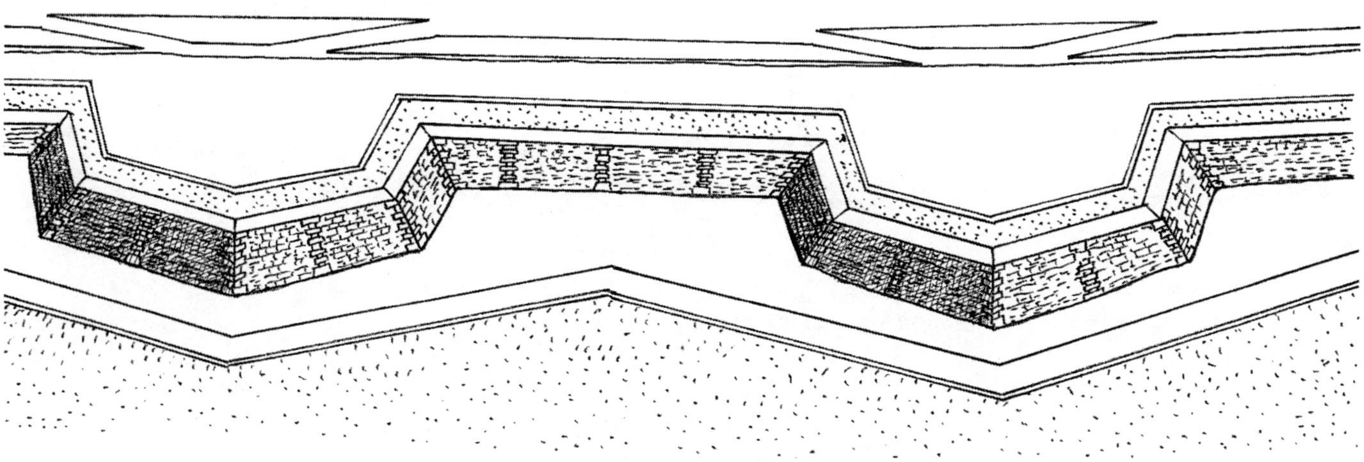

Thiers's enceinte: Bastions 27 and 28 between Pantin and La Villette.

Rosny, Romainville, Charenton, Fontenay, Ivry and Mont Valérien. Problems quickly arose between villagers and workers, between civilian workers and drafted soldiers (who were paid less), and between workers and authorities.

Several revolts and strikes occurred in 1842 and 1843. The *Gendarmerie* (police) had to be involved for repression before the Engineering Corps raised wages and improved living accommodations and working conditions. The works were also thwarted and slowed down by accidental collapses, geological problems, and grounds inappropriate for building. In spite of these difficulties, the bulk of fortifications was completed in November 1845; the forts could be armed and occupied by the garrison, but works continued until July 1847, and even until March 1848 with the planting of trees. By that time the total cost was 138,935,282 francs, a remarkable fact unique in the history of fortification and worthy of mention as the actual cost had not exceeded the planned funds of 140,000,000.

The Bastioned Enceinte

Contrary to former designs, Dode de la Brunerie's bastioned wall was large and extended well over the inhabited surface of Paris in the 1840s. Paris grew from 8,125 acres to 17,515 acres. Between Paris proper (still enclosed by the enceinte of the *Fermiers Généraux* which was demolished only in early 1860) and the new bastioned wall, there was a wide stoke of land called *Petite Banlieue* (small suburb). This included houses, small factories and workshops (mainly along the principal roads) as well as inns and dancing halls, and many farms, barns, fields and meadows. As a matter of fact, there were still agricultural activities *inside* Dode de la Brunerie's wall: grain on the

Gate in Thiers's enceinte

Grenelle plain, milk cattle being raised in Vaugirard, vineyards on the hills Montmartre and Belleville, truck farming, vegetables and fruit trees in the eastern part, as reflected by the present borough of *Maraîchers* (market gardening).

Indeed the new wall spread out greatly and amputated several neighboring villages such as Neuilly, Vanves, Gentilly, Ivry and Saint Mandé, parts of which were annexed to the municipality of Paris; the city was thus greatly enlarged and counted twenty *arrondissements* (administrative districts).

The tracé of the enceinte is clearly visible today: it corresponds to the current administrative limits of Paris marked by two circular driving rings, the so-called *Boulevards des Maréchaux* and the *Boulevard Périphérique* motorway. The enclosure also created a curious social standing barrier, which can still be felt today; inside the wall live the *Parigots* (glamorous real Parisians) and outside the *Banlieusards* ("common" suburb dwellers), both having contempt for each other!

Bastions, Ditch and Counterscarp

The enceinte was 140 m wide (including the glacis), and no less than 39 km long. It included a continuous ditch, a continuous scarp composed of straight curtains, and 94 bastions. The bastions had little salient, some were merely *half-bastions* (their faces being directly connected to the curtain without flanks), others were *flat bastions* fitted with only a single face. They were deprived of orillons, and some were surmounted with cavaliers. The average interval between two bastions (thus the length of the curtain) was about 350 m. Bastions and curtains were ramparted (built of masonry holding a thick mass of earth and rubble) and about 10 m high.

They were surrounded by a 37-m-wide dry ditch and a nonreveted 5-m-high sloping counterscarp, on top of which a covered way was established. There was also a glacis, and a 350-m-wide *non aedificanti* zone, which was forbidden to construction and vegetation. The artillery and musketry was placed behind a thick breastwork and protected from enfilade fire by thick perpendicular entrenchment known as *traverses*.

At the side of the city, there was a *rue de rampart* (a broad continuous communication lane), which constitutes the present Boulevards des Maréchaux.

There was also an internal, strategic railway running along bastions and curtains, called *Petite Ceinture*, with a length of 31 km and several stations, intended to rapidly transport supply, troops and ammunition.

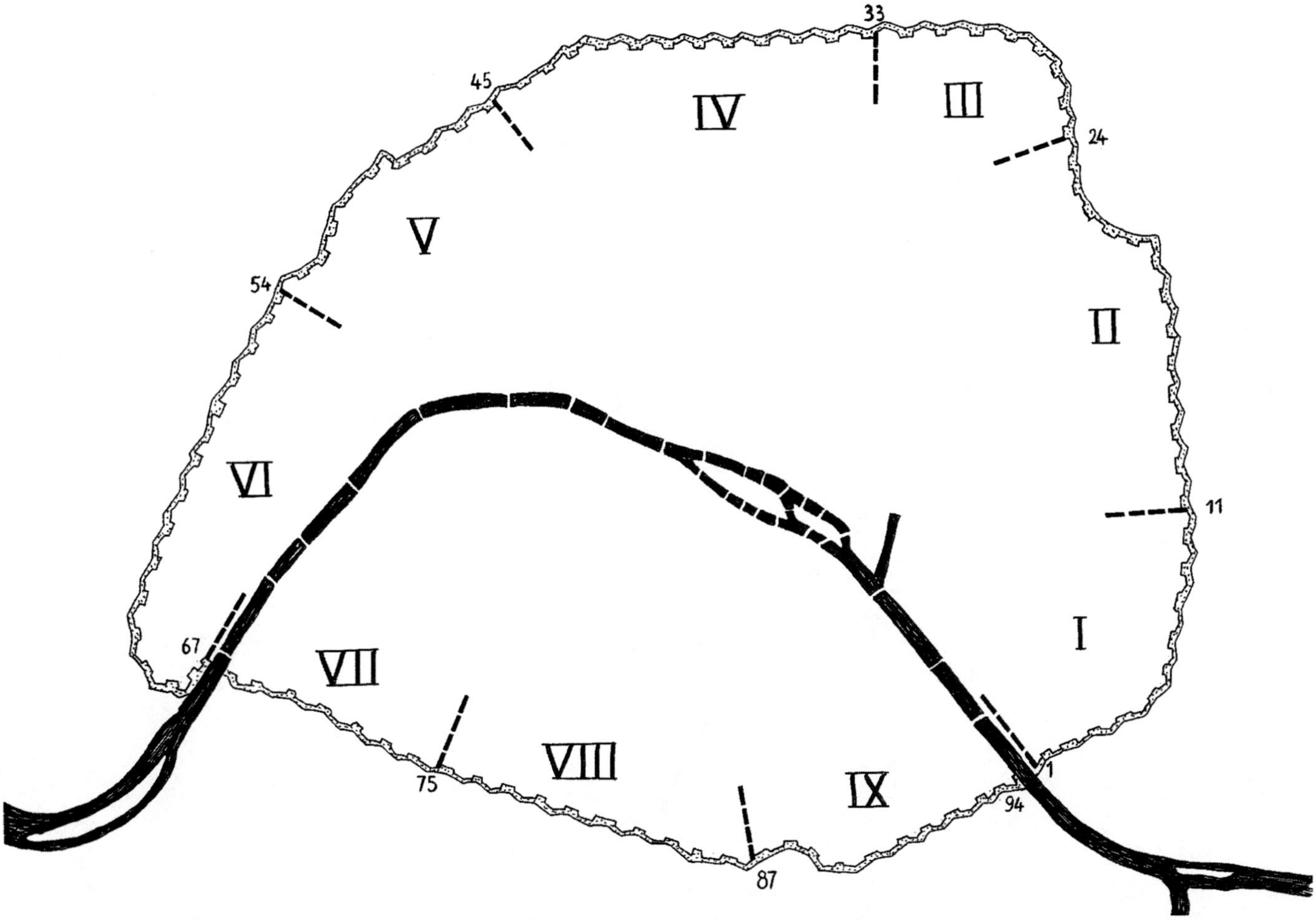

Map of Thiers's enceinte showing the nine military sectors.

Gates

Paris was accessible by means of no fewer than 52 gates.

There were 17 main gates for national roads, 23 secondary gates for *départementales* roads and 12 posterns for local access. Their names remain today as exits from and accesses to the Boulevard Périphérique.

The main gates were furnished with barriers, and some had swing-back drawbridges; they were also used as tollhouses for the collection of taxes. They were not defended by outer works (such as demi-lunes or hornworks).

The accesses were at the same time too numerous and not numerous enough; in wartime they did not provide an adequate sealed-off defense; and in peacetime they did not offer convenient and easy access to the town. Moreover there were several extremely weak gaps in the defenses: the River Seine as ever, but also the Canal de l'Ourcq, and soon large ill-defensible openings intended to let the railroad tracks through.

Division of the Bastioned Enceinte

Each bastion of the wall was given a number from 1 to 94. Bastion No.1 was placed in the east of Paris on the right bank; the numbering went on counterclockwise, so bastion No. 94 faced bastion No.1 on the opposite bank of the river. Tactically, the Enceinte was divided into nine military *secteurs* (sections):

Secteur I: Bastions 1 to 11 faced the suburban village of Charenton, Vincennes forest, Saint Mandé and Vincennes.

Secteur II: Bastions 12 to 24 faced Montreuil, Bagnolet, Romainville, Les Lilas, and Le Pré Saint Gervais.

Secteur III: Bastions 25 to 33 faced Pantin, Aubervilliers and Saint Denis.

Secteur IV: Bastions 34 to 45 faced Saint Ouen and Clichy.

Secteur V: Bastions 46 to 54 faced Levallois-Perret and Neuilly.

Secteur VI: Bastions 55 to 67 faced Boulogne forest and Boulogne-Billancourt village.

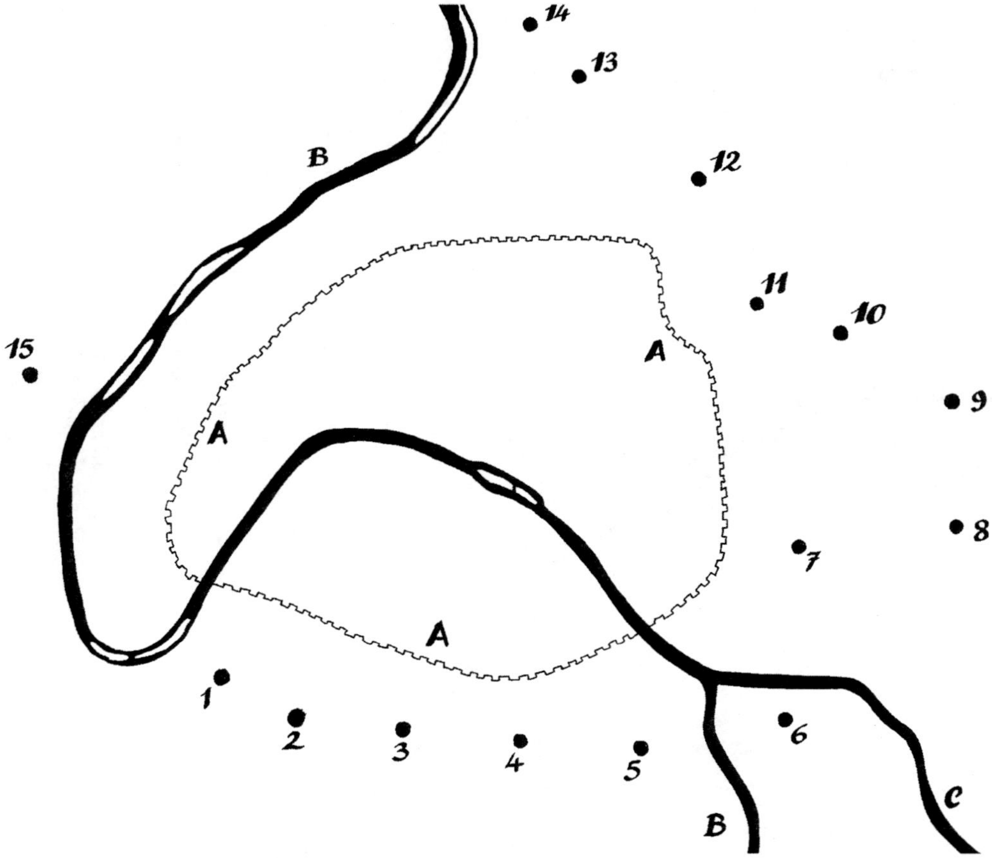

Map of Paris with the outer ring of forts. Only the main forts are indicated: 1. Fort of Issy-les-Moulineaux. 2. Fort of Vanves. 3. Fort of Montrouge. 4. Fort of Bicètre. 5. Fort of Ivry-sur-Seine. 6. Fort of Charenton. 7. Castle and fort of Vincennes. 8. Fort of Nogent. 9. Fort of Rosny-sous-Bois. 10. Fort of Noisy-le-Sec. 11. Fort of Romainville. 12. Fort of Aubervilliers. 13. Fort de l'Est. 14. Double crownwork of Saint-Denis. 15. Fort of Mont Valérien. A A A: Thiers's bastioned enceinte. B B: River Seine. C: River Marne.

Secteur VII: Bastions 68 to 75 faced Issy-les-Moulineaux and Vanves.
Secteur VIII: Bastions 76 to 86 faced Malakoff and Montrouge.
Secteur IX: Bastions 87 to 94 faced Gentilly and Ivry.

Detached Forts and Redoubts

The second part of the Parisian defenses was constituted by an outer ring of detached forts, lunettes, redoubts and batteries.

A *fort* was a strong permanent self-sufficient stronghold, a major artillery position with a permanent garrison.

A *lunette* was a defensive work, generally in the form of a ravelin flanking a fort. It could also be a detached work, in a bastioned form, a closed bastion, a large redan or a crownwork.

A *redoute* (redoubt) was a small fort or a large gun battery placed in intervals between major forts and usually manned only in wartime.

A *batterie* (battery) was a kind of redoubt, a fortified combat emplacement including several guns of the same type firing in the same direction.

These works were built on the heights and hills surrounding the city at a distance of 1.5 and 3 km from Paris.

The detached forts formed a wide arc from the southwest to the north including six *secteurs* (sections).

Secteur West
Fort of Mont Valérien
Secteur South
Fort of Issy-les-Moulineaux
Fort of Vanves
Fort of Montrouge
Fort of Bicètre
Fort of Ivry
Secteur Southeast
Fort of Charenton
Redoute of Faisanderie
Redoute of Gravelle
Fort Neuf of Vincennes
Fort of Nogent-sur-Marne
Lunette of Nogent
Secteur East
Redoute of Fontenay-sous-Bois
Redoute of Boissière
Redoute of Montreuil
Fort of Rosny-sous-Bois
Lunette of Rosny
Fort of Noisy-le-Sec
Lunette of Noisy
Redoute of Noisy
Fort of Romainville
Lunette of Romainville
Secteur Northeast
Courtine of Romainville
Batterie of Pantin
Fort of Aubervilliers
Ouvrage of Aubervilliers
Batterie of Aubervilliers
Batterie of Rouray
Batterie of Soissons
Batterie of Vertus

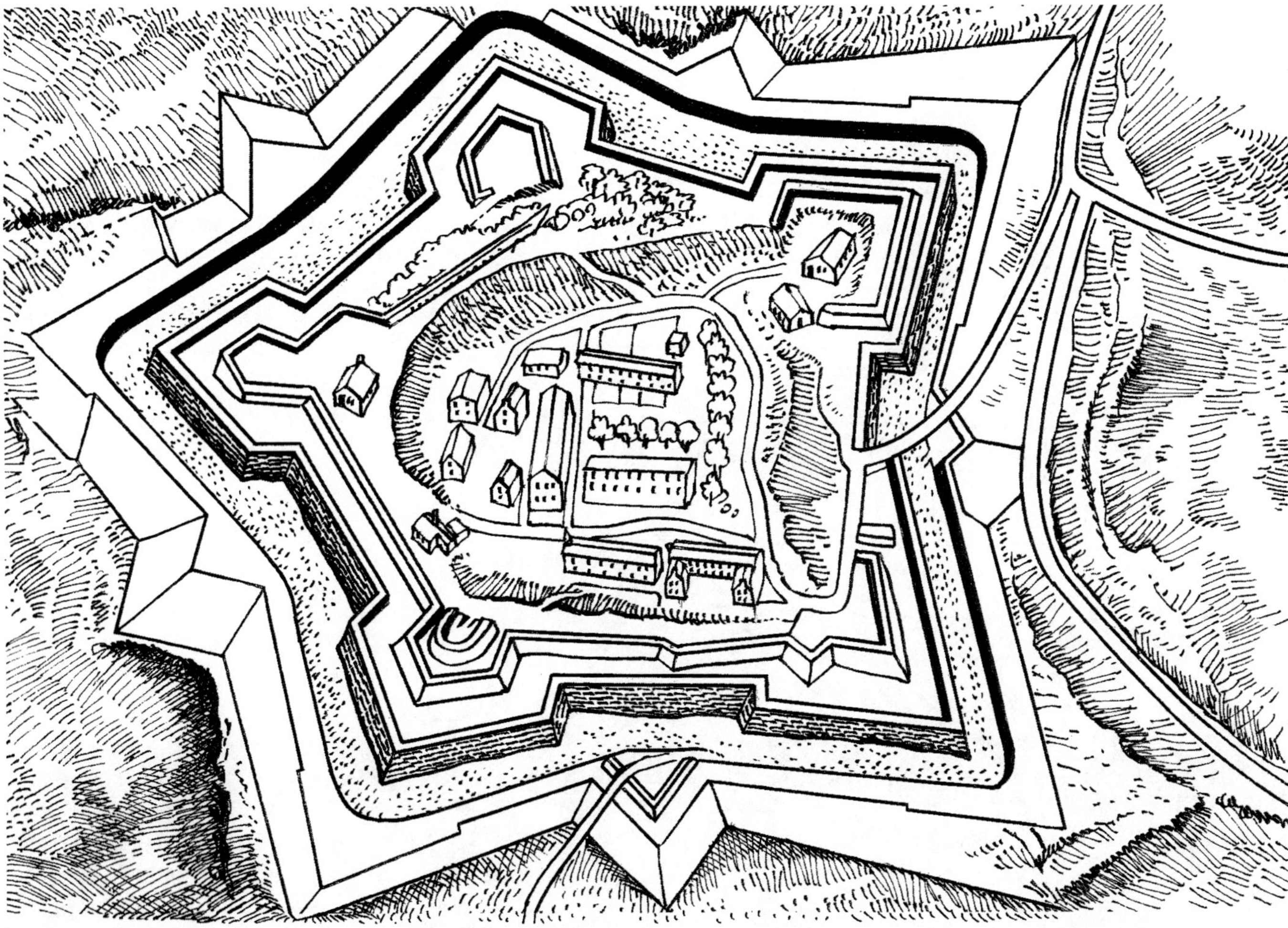

Fort of Mont Valérien. The western front of Paris was well-protected by a meandering River Seine. Moreover, an enemy attack was not expected on that sector so the western front was covered only by Fort de Mont Valérien. Placed on a 162-m-high hill with an extensive view over the country, the task of the fortress was covering the village of Gennevilliers, the main road to Cherbourg, and the hills of Sèvres, Saint Cloud and Montretout. The fort was a powerful pentagonal stronghold with glacis, covered way, ditch, curtains, and five bastions at the angles surmounted with cavaliers, enclosing a total surface of 23 hectares. The fortress of Mont Valérien — built between 1841 and 1845 — cost 4,500,000 Francs. It could accommodate a garrison of 2,000. Four bomb-proof powder houses contained 75,000 kilograms of explosives, and water was supplied by several cisterns.

Secteur North
Dike of Rû de Montfort
Fort of the Est
Dike of Croult
Double crownwork of Saint Denis
Rigole of La Briche
Fort of La Briche.

According to the site on which they were built, the forts had two main shapes: a quadrilateral tracé with four bastions at the angles; or a pentagonal outline with five bastions at the angles. Several forts diverged from these standards. The fort of Aubervilliers, for example, was a long rectangle with three bastions at the front and two half-bastions at the back. The fort of Vincennes—built next to the medieval castle of the same name—was an elongated rectangle with four bastions at the angles and two flat bastions in the middle of the long sides.

The forts could be reinforced by bastioned outer works including horn or crownworks, lunettes etc.

As for the other smaller detached works, their shapes varied from a simple square enclosure to a line of bastions.

Royal Citadels

The forts presented a curious style half way between classical Vauban and Napoleonic. All of them were different, though all had common elements. The most remarkable and striking feature was that they were built to be capable of all around defense; there was no strong

Gate fort of Mont Valérien

"face to the country" facing the enemy at the front and a relatively weak gorge facing Paris at the rear. The issue was not that the builders were pessimists who were resigned to a strong force penetrating between them and attacking in reverse. In reality the forts were built as much to defend Paris as to control the Parisians; they were designed to be capable of handling trouble from any direction, either from a siege by a foreign invader or from an uprising from the citizens. As the Republican opposition and Parliament had feared, the forts were royal citadels prepared for both foreign and civil war. The July Monarchy—which was overthrown by a Parisian uprising in 1848—was apparently determined not to tolerate the repetition of 1789 or 1830.

Description of the Forts

Each fort was detached, self-sufficient, and surrounded by a wide dry ditch which could be crossed by a bridge or a ramp ending with a drawbridge. On the outer side of the ditch was the usual counterscarp wall, surmounted by places of arms and a covered way reinforced by an earth breastwork or a palisade fence. On the outer side, the glacis could be arranged into a wide overgrown place of arms in the outline of a *redan*—a defensive work with two faces forming a salient angle. Opposite the center of each wall, at the foot of the scarp, was often a *tenaille*, a low breastwork to cover the ditch.

Internally the fort included bomb-proof accommodations and weapon and gunpowder stores arranged beneath portions of the ramparts. The forts were intended to be permanently occupied by Louis-Philippe's royal army, and there was invariably one or more barracks and various service buildings built on the bare terreplein. There was no systematic form of internal traversing so that buildings and terreplein were

Opposite, top: Fort of Vanves. A part of the southern sector, the fort of Vanves was built between 1841 and 1846. It was typical of the standardized rectangular work with four bastions. _Opposite, bottom:_ Fort of Nogent-sur-Marne. Fort of Nogent was built between 1841 and 1846. It was a rectangular structure with four bastions with a large demi-lune (called lunette) attached to one side.

rather vulnerable to enfilading fire and plunging mortar fire.

The flanks of the bastions were fitted with casemates for enfilading fire in the ditch. The long-range artillery was placed *en barbette* (firing over the breastwork) on the terraces of the bastions.

Percussion rifle (ca. 1860)

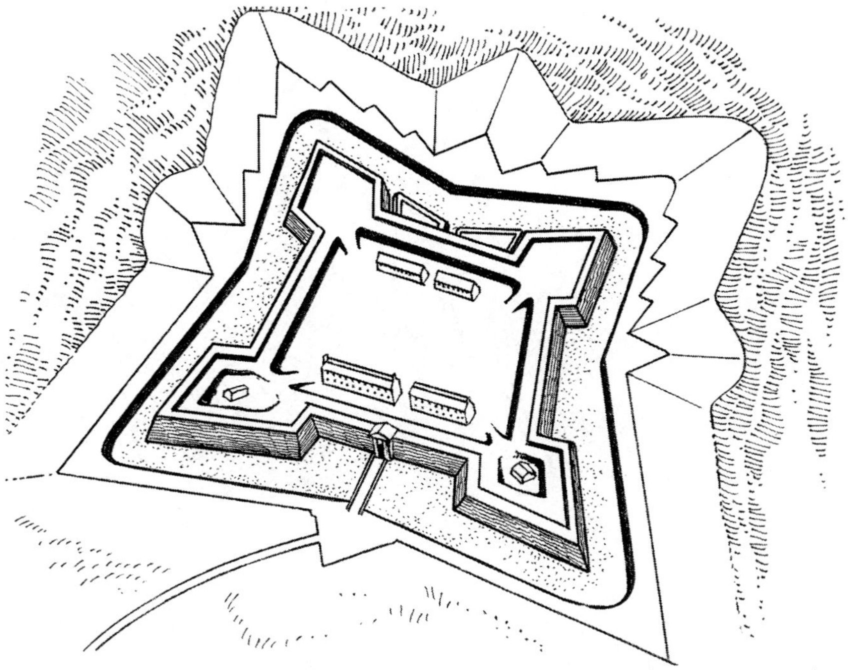

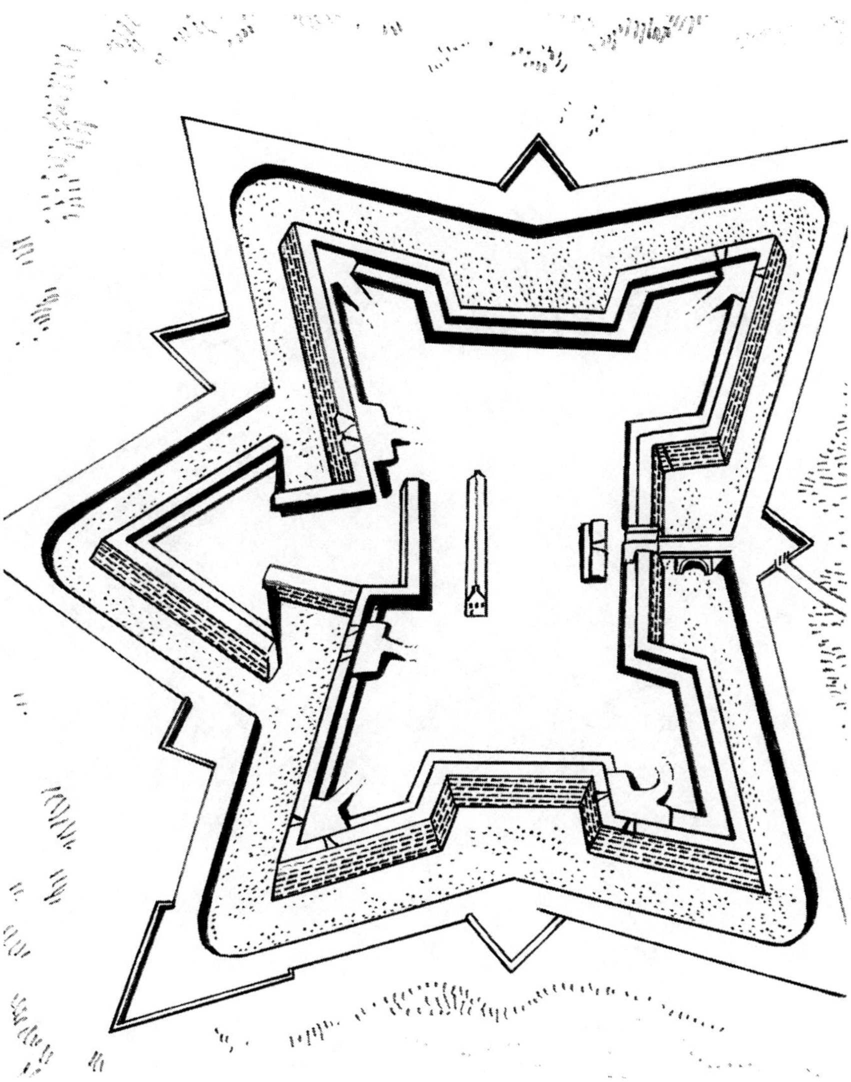

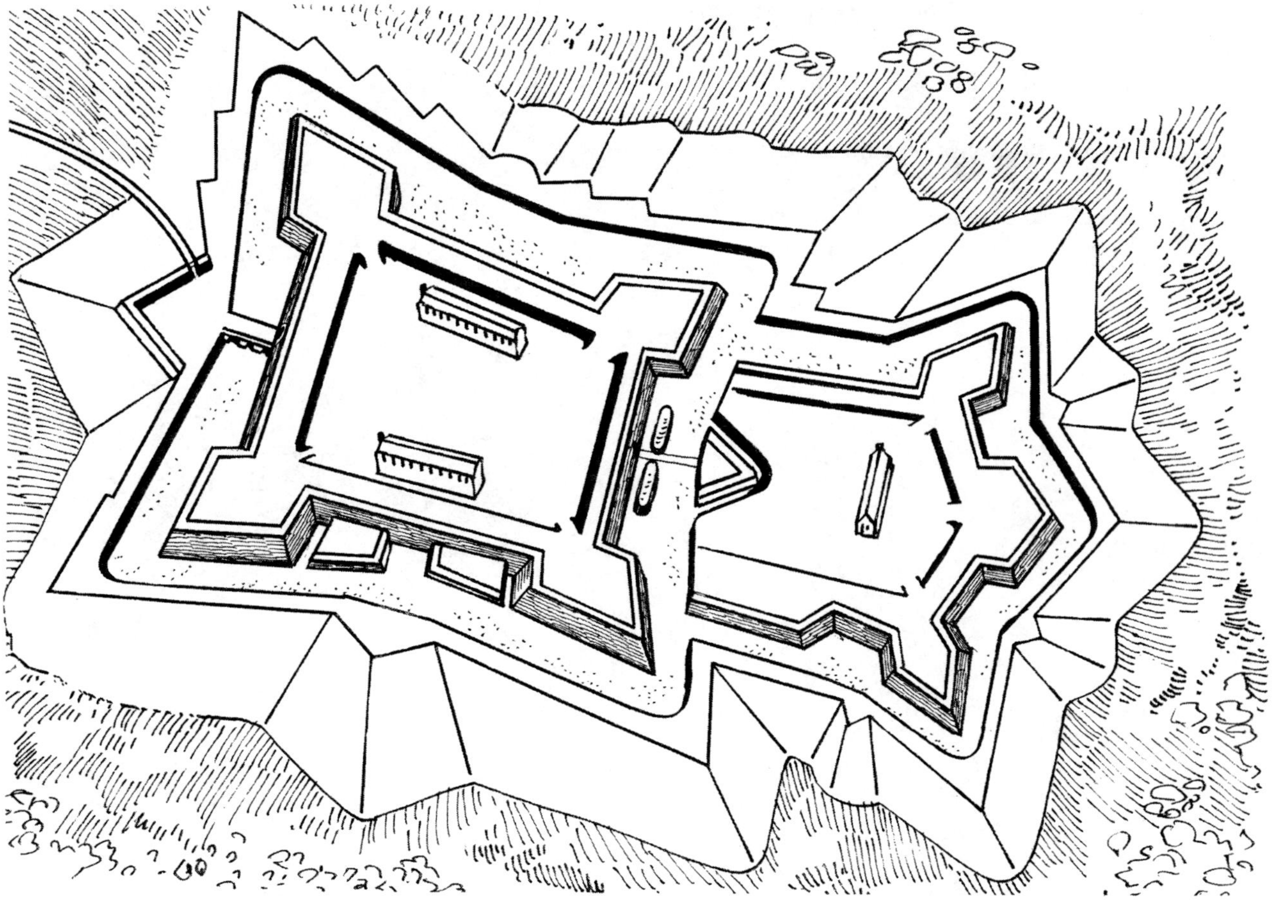

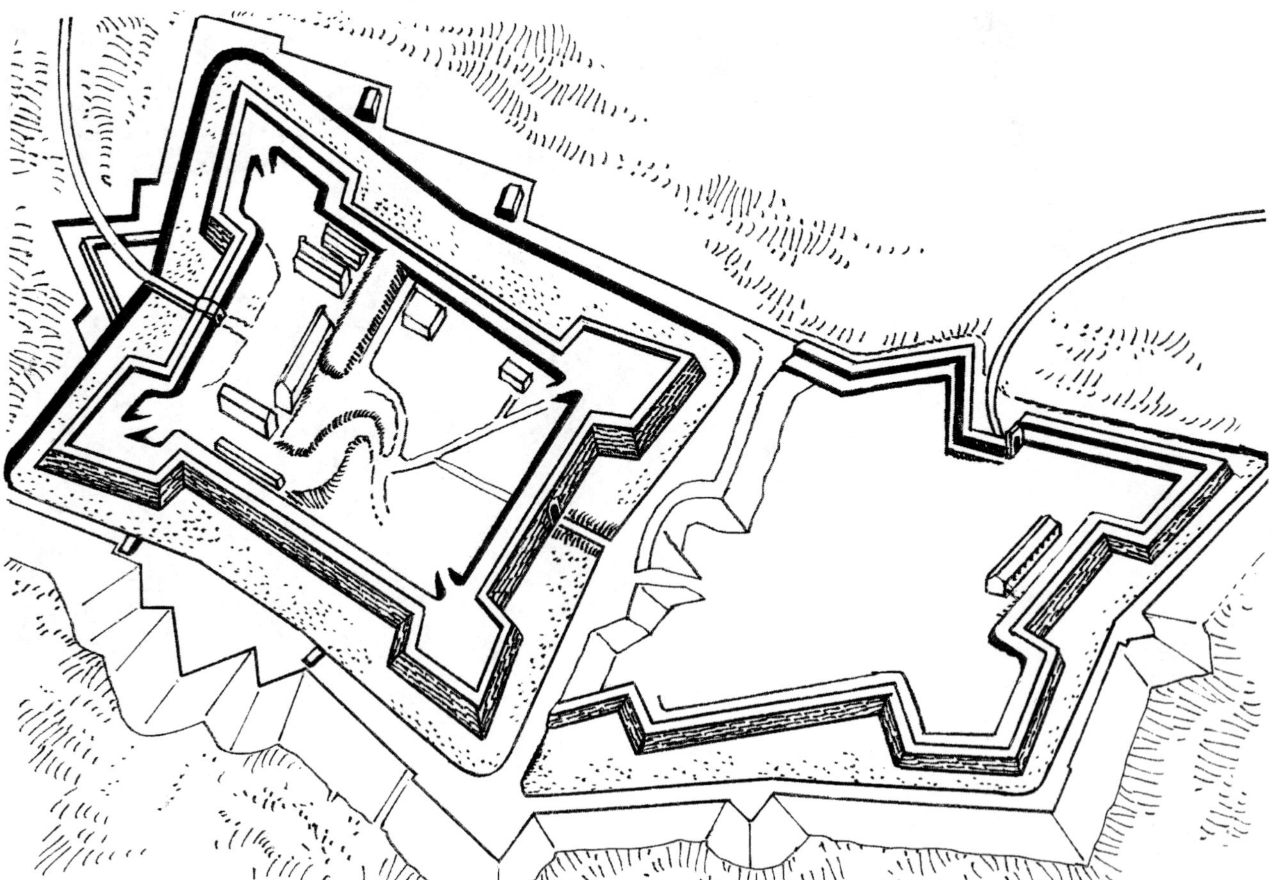

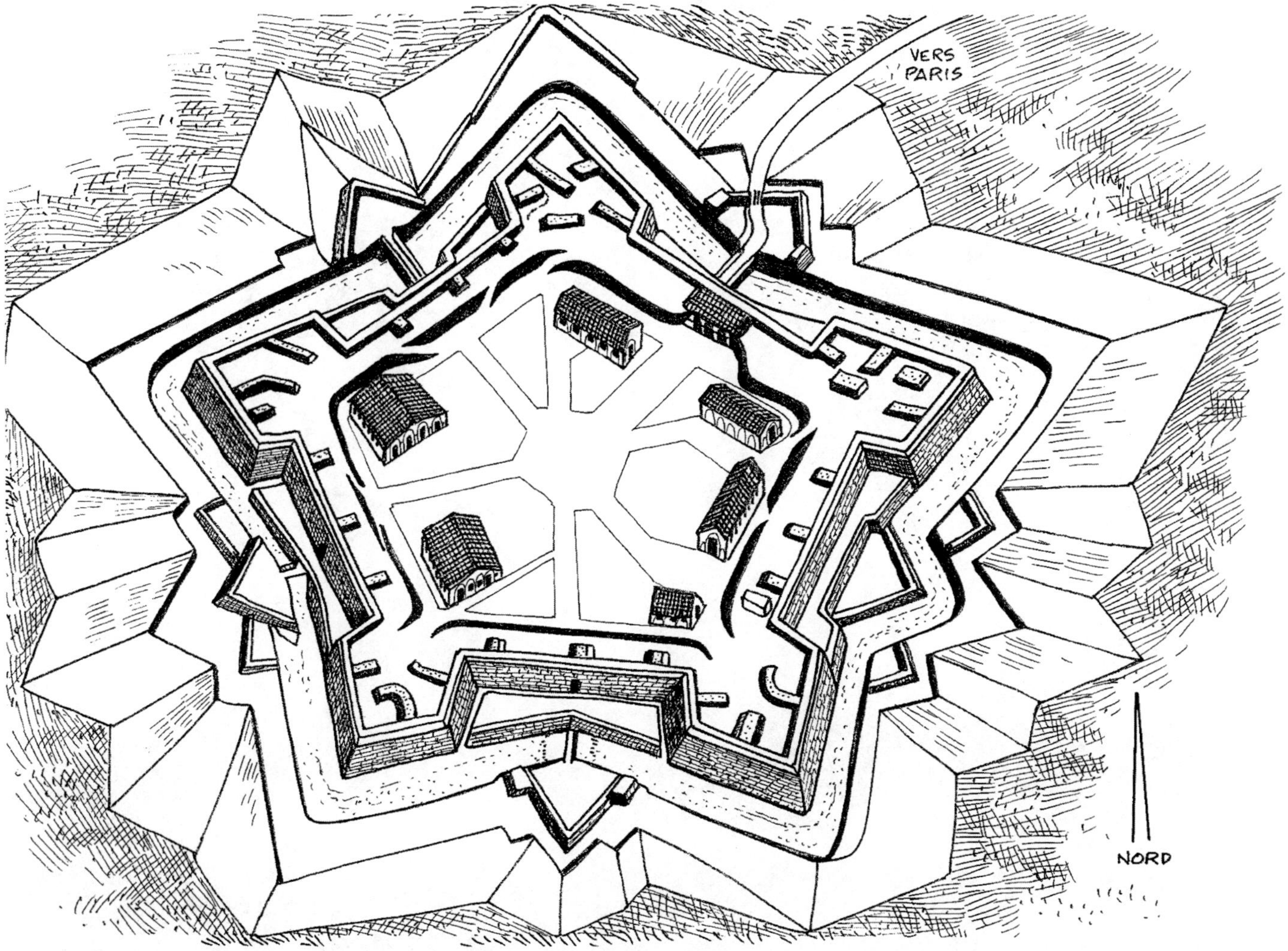

Fort of Issy-les-Moulineaux. Fort of Issy was built between 1841 and 1845. It represented the typical pentagonal type with five bastions.

The open gun emplacements were generally protected from enfilading fire by *traverses* and *parados* (thick mass of earth), forming compartments. The distance between each fort was calculated so that an attacked stronghold could be covered by fire coming from its neighbors; in theory there was a continuous line of fire around Paris.

Armament

By 1830 the flint-lock musket was superseded by a new infantry weapon with a new device for firing the gun, called a percussion or "detonating" system, based on an invention by Reverend Alexander Forsyth in 1807. The result was reliable handguns with an increased rate of fire. The French Army was equipped with the new 18 mm caliber *Fusil Modèle 1842,* with percussion, single action, a length of 140 cm, and a weight of 4.1 kg, produced by the Arsenal of Chatellerault. In 1846, this *fusil d'infanterie* (infantry rifle) was also produced in a short carbine version for artillery and cavalrymen known as *Carabine Thierry*.

After the Napoleonic era, the French artillery was modernized by General Valée in 1827. In essence the

Opposite, top: **Fort and lunette of Rosny-sous-Bois. Part of the eastern front where an enemy attack could be expected, the fort of Rosny was originally a temporary earthwork including five bastions, built in 1831 on a 115-m-high hill. In 1841 a new rectangular fort was built in stone and the old 1831 work was transformed into a crownwork — called Lunette of Rosny on the right side of the illustration — covering the new fort on the left.** ***Opposite, bottom:*** **Fort and lunette of Romainville. The fort of Romainville was placed on a 120-m-high hill dominating the village of the same name. It was originally an earthwork built between 1831 and 1832 (the lunette on the right of the illustration), which was enlarged from 1841 to 1845 by a stone-made rectangular work with four bastions (on the left). The northern front of the fort was covered by a line of detached work.**

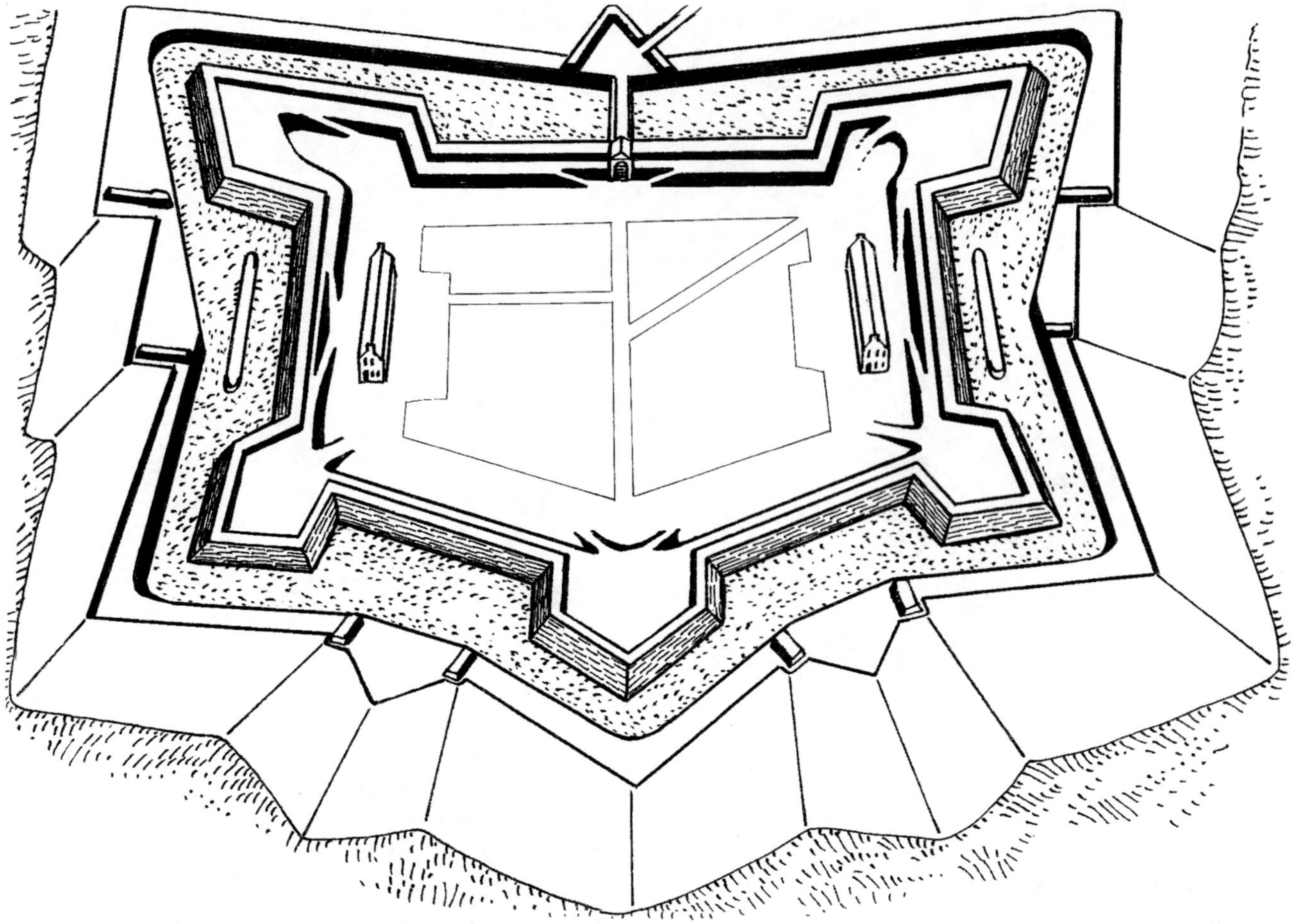

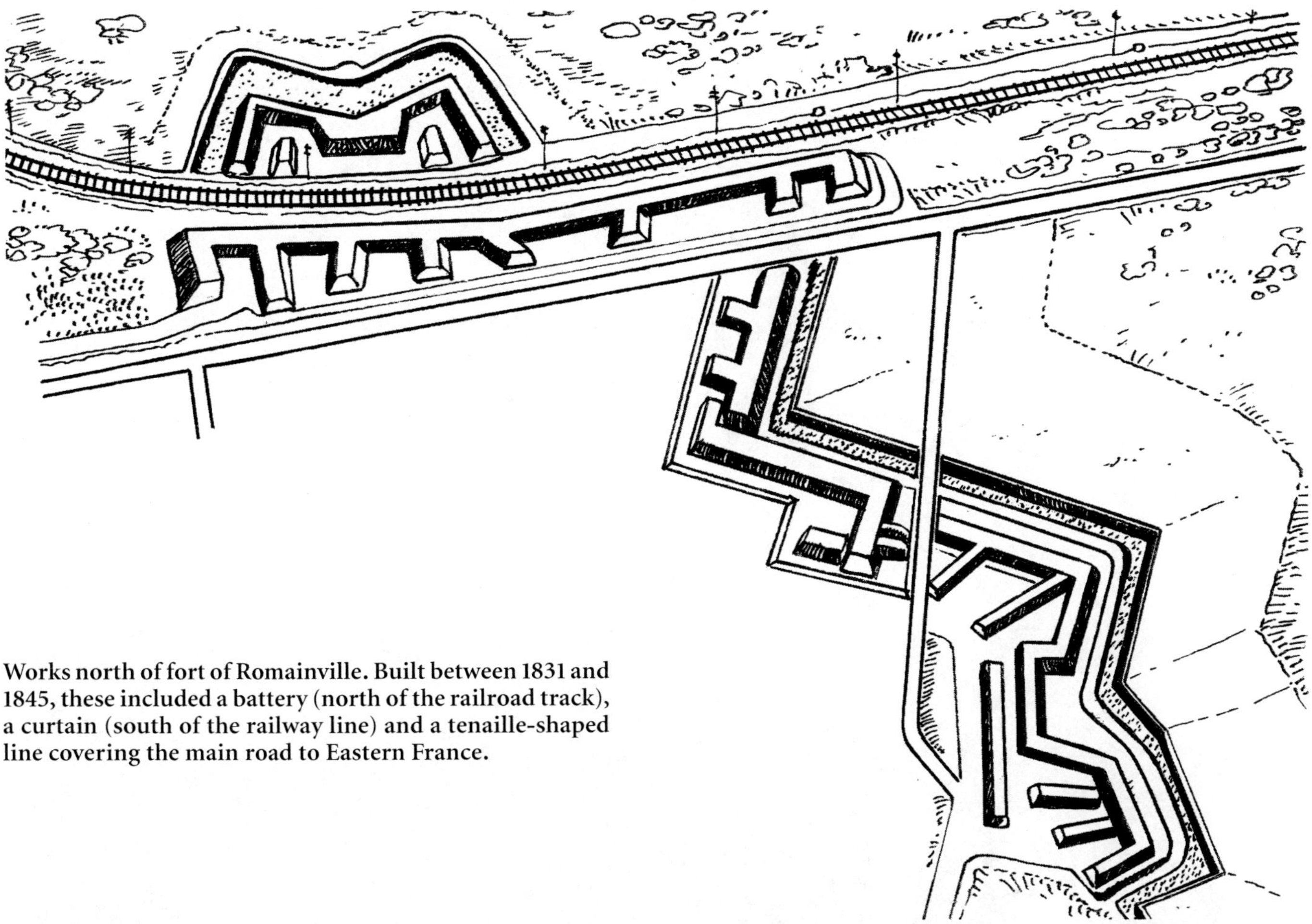

Works north of fort of Romainville. Built between 1831 and 1845, these included a battery (north of the railroad track), a curtain (south of the railway line) and a tenaille-shaped line covering the main road to Eastern France.

artillery remained composed of muzzle loading, solid shotted pieces, but an effort was made to increase mobility and efficiency by the standardization of gun carriages and ammunition carts. Field artillery was reduced to two main caliber (12 pounder and 8 pounder) and two caliber of howitzer (15 cm and 16 cm).

It was estimated that the defense of the bastioned wall enclosing Paris would demand a garrison of no less than 60,000 soldiers. Needless to say, the wall was not manned in peacetime.

The detached forts were permanently occupied by a professional military force including engineers (for maintenance), infantrymen (for close-range defense), artillerymen (for long-range action) and a few cavalrymen (for reconnaissance and carrying of dispatches and orders).

For example, in September 1870 during the siege of Paris, the fort of Rosny-sous-Bois was armed with 78 cannons including the following. On the bastions and curtains were deployed 58 guns, howitzers and mortars; the lunette ahead of the fort was armed with six cannons and six howitzers. In addition eight mortars were held in reserve. Each gun had about 200 rounds; the cistern in the fort contained 272,000 liters of water. The garrison comprised 797 sailor-gunners, 803 infantrymen, and 52 engineers; a part was housed in the fort and the others were accommodated in canvas tents. The countryside in the vicinity of the fort was defended by three infantry battalions of *Gardes Mobiles* (Mobile Guards) composed of Breton volunteers raised in the département of Côtes-du Nord (northern coasts of Britanny); the Breton guards occupied the village of Rosny-sous-Bois, which had been evacuated and barricaded; the volunteers also held the neighboring parc of Montreau Castle which had been transformed into a defensive position with fieldworks.

However, in peacetime, the forts were not armed with heavy weapons for political reasons. As a gesture of

Opposite, top: **Fort of Aubervilliers. The fort of Aubervilliers in the northeastern sector was built between 1843 and 1846. Note the Cormontaigne-style tracé en crémaillère (zigzag) given to the covered way. In addition, the fort was defended by two adjacent structures: a battery and an ouvrage (fortlet).** ***Opposite, bottom:*** **Redoubt of Fontenay. Built in 1832, the Redoubt of Fontenay was a small tenaille-shaped fort with walls forming re-entering angles. It was incorporated into the Dode de la Brunerie's project in 1841.**

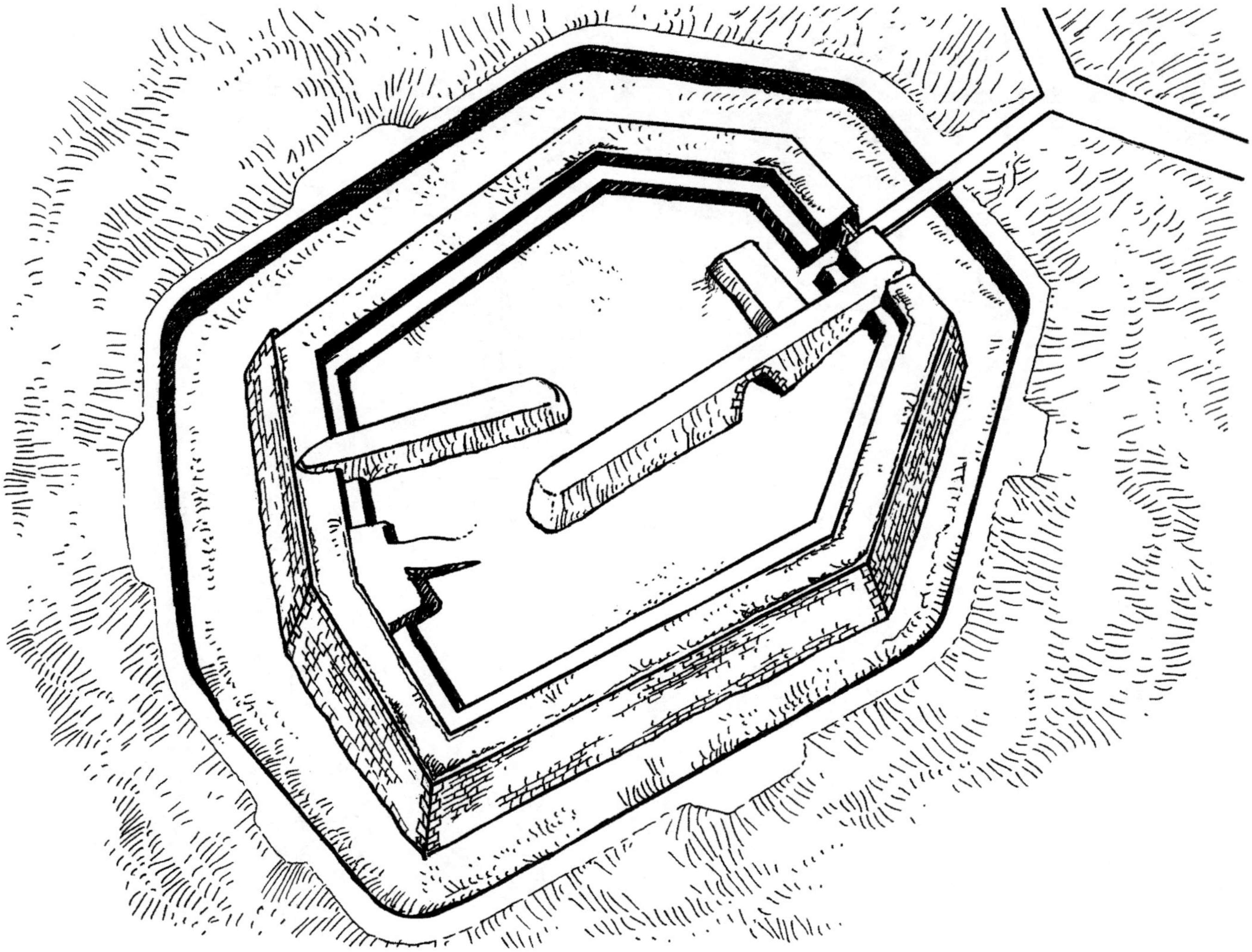

Redoubt of Montreuil. The redoubt of Montreuil was built in 1831 as a simple work without bastion. It was reshaped in 1841. Note the traversing (large and thick internal earth walls) intended to protect the work from enemy enfilading fire.

appeasement toward the parliament and the opposition who accused him of tyranny, Louis-Philippe agreed that the guns intended to arm the Parisian forts would be safely stored in the Arsenal of Bourges (in the province of Berry).

Paris counted about one million inhabitants in 1841, and the very expensive Enceinte of Thiers offered them the illusion of protection. As we are going to see, the Parisian fortifications were tested both for foreign and civil war during the tragic events of 1870 and 1871.

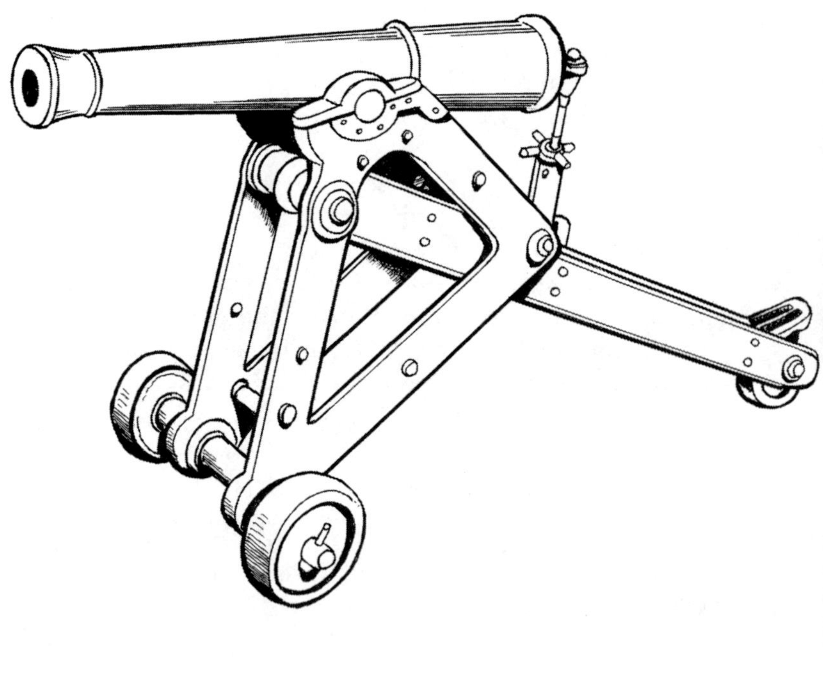

Cannon Model 1858 on casemate mount

37

Paris Transformed by Baron Georges Hausmann and Napoléon III

Napoléon III

The July Monarchy was a period of social conflict. At Lyon the silk weavers rioted in protest against their poverty. In Paris and everywhere in France, the low working class demanded liberty and decent living conditions. Despite repression and condemnation, the workers movement and trade unions developed. The July Monarchy failed to react when a serious economic crisis appeared in early 1847. The king refused to grant the people the reforms that they demanded; the entire country was dissatisfied by the king and his minister Guizot. Again agitation culminated in rioting in Paris, in which the police sided with the insurgents. The July Monarchy was swept away and Louis-Philippe decided to abdicate in February 1848; he went in exile to Britain and died in 1850. It was the end of the Capetian dynasty founded by Hugues Capet in 897.

The Republican bourgeois party took control, and the Second Republic was proclaimed on February 28, 1848. On December 10, 1848, Louis-Napoléon Bonaparte (Napoléon I's nephew) was elected president. When his term expired, president Louis-Napoléon seized power for himself on December 2, 1851. In 1852 with the support of the army, he set up a personal dictatorship and proclaimed the *Second Empire*. The new emperor called himself Napoléon III, since *Napoléon II* was Napoléon I's son, the king of Rome, who had lived in Austria since 1815 under the title of Duke of Reichstadt and who died in 1832.

Napoléon III was a social-minded prince; he sincerely wished to do good for his people, but in his own authoritarian way.

The Industrial Revolution

The remarkable thing about this period was the amazing economic expansion which occurred in France. The Industrial Revolution had arrived. There were 12,000 miles of railway in 1870, compared to some 2,000 in 1851. Railway exposed the countryside more fully to factory-produced goods, reduced the number of rural craftsmen, and thus furthered rural depopulation and the drift of workers to the towns. Railways permitted the development and the location of heavy industry in specialist towns, allowed a much larger market to be tapped by the new factories and allowed bulky raw materials to be brought in from increasing distances, both essential prerequisites for the growth of larger manufacturing units. The use of machine tools and heavy steam plants increased rapidly. Agriculture, business and public works grew apace. The urban population grew rapidly. Napoléon III surrounded himself with bankers and industrialists, and encouraged the formation of factories, trading companies, and banks and lending societies. More than ever all France lived under the stimulus of the capital. The political and administrative centralization, the political regime, the growing network of railroads and highways, the concentration of bank, education, scientific and technological research, publishing, press, culture and fashion assured the pre-eminence of Paris.

The Emperor also ordered the transformation of Paris. In the 1850s, the capital of France was a monstrous urban organism in its immensity, in the difficulties of supply and of traffic; it was also a city full of contrasts. The rich and wealthy lived in the *Beaux Quartiers* (beautiful boroughs) with broad lanes, wide streets, sunny squares, impressive monuments, parks, magnificent hotels, comfortable buildings, and villas with gardens, principally in the western part of the city. The eastern part, on the contrary, was still a dark medieval town with small, tortuous, badly lit streets, slums, unhealthy buildings, and ill-accommodated popular houses in which crowds of modest shopkeepers, craftsmen, small merchants, jobless, and a growing proletariat, working in small factories, were packed in very bad conditions and poor communication.

Within a few years from 1853 to 1866, *préfet* of Paris, Georges Eugène baron of Hausmann (1809–1891), radically changed the face of Paris and gave the city the appearance we still see today.

A New Face for Paris

Hausmann engineered a rebuilding program of monumental scale, his work was the greatest town planning scheme ever implemented in Paris. They improved urbanism, hygiene, public services, and mobility and encouraged economic development. Entire blocks of old Paris, some 19,718 houses, were destroyed to make space for wide streets, broad avenues and boulevards all through the center of Paris for the sake of mobility, easier traffic to such focal points as railway stations, without forgetting civic magnificence. New storied houses, apartment buildings and living accommodations in a somewhat uniform architecture were created along those axes. Among Hausmann's great achievements, we must mention the construction of the Halles food market and La Villette abattoir by architect Baltard, the total reshaping of the Cité island (now occupied by law courts, the Hôtel Dieu hospital, the trade courts and police headquarters), the continuation of the Louvre Palace, the construction of *gares* (railway stations), the creation of the magnificent Opéra house by architect Garnier, the layout of Châtelet Square with two theaters, the establishment of traffic circuits with radiating avenues (the present Place de l'Etoile-Charles de Gaulle, Place de la Nation and Place de la République), the continuation of the Champs-Elysés, and the construction of town halls for each of the twenty arrondissements.

The *octroi* (toll) had been transferred to the gates of Thiers's fortifications, making the enceinte of the *Fermiers Généraux* totally pointless. In January 1860, the wall and tollhouses were demolished and the stones were sold.

Hausmann continued the large and magnificent vista from the Arch of Triumph to the Louvre, notably by the continuing of the Rue de Rivoli — a broad, long street, parallel to the Seine, connecting Place de la Concorde to Place de la Bastille. It is one of Hausmann's greatest urban successes. The Rivoli street was designed by architects Percier and Fontaine. In the section that skirts the Tuileries and the Louvre, one can admire on the one side an elegant portico with, today, numerous clothing and souvenir stores.

The Paris opera house, designed by architect Garnier, was built between 1862 and 1875. It is one of the largest theaters for lyric opera in the world; it can accommodate 2,000 visitors and the stage has room for no fewer than 450 performers. Its façade displays a profusion of decorative elements, and the interior is just as highly decorated, with a monumental marble stairway and painted vaults.

Hausmann was assisted by two remarkable engineers, Alphand and Belgrand. The former was responsible for creating the parks of Montsouris, Monceau, and Buttes-Chaumont, and for laying out the forests/parks in Boulogne and Vincennes. The latter's contribution was the extension of a large sewer system (600 km long) as well as an important increase in the supply of drinking water.

The development of Paris caused the gradual decline in agricultural activities inside the 1845 wall and the increase of industrial and trading activities; Paris was — has always been and still is today — a place of great centrality, the heart of France; Hausmann's works also greatly contributed to the development of tertiary occupations, a sector of the economy including a wide diversity of jobs for the provision of services.

Hausmann's body of work represents considerable and admirable achievements. Paris was totally transformed into a modern capital, one of the most beautiful in Europe, but three points must be stressed.

First of all, Hausmann destroyed many remarkable, interesting and priceless vestiges of the Parisian past.

Secondly, the *préfet* was not interested in housing. The impact of the Industrial Revolution was tremendous, and Paris — within a few decades — became a large urban center attracting more and more people; the population increased by thousands of inhabitants every year, but demographic growth was not included in his plans. Behind the tall façades of the new buildings for the wealthy bourgeoisie in the broad and straight avenues, populous slums mushroomed, poor and unhealthy accommodations remained, and decaying poor boroughs developed. Small houses with their own gardens — taking up a great deal of space — were demolished to make room for more profit-earning multistoried buildings.

Hausmann virtually created two Parises, divided by social status and wealth: the western part of the city was intended for the rich; the eastern part, neglected and despised, was in fact a ghetto for the poor.

Finally, Hausmann's works reflected Napoléon III's fear of revolution. Significantly enough, the large squares, broad avenues and wide boulevards were also drawn for security reason; they were sufficiently wide to prevent the building of barricades— at least this was hoped; their width was also calculated to facilitate the deployment of infantry troops and the siting of guns and allowed cavalry charges against rebellious mobs. This strategic design was combined with the construction of *casernes* (barracks) housing antiriot troops, built at sites considered "dangerous" or deemed strategically important, e.g. Caserne Napoléon (near the Hôtel de Ville), Caserne des Célestins (near the Arsenal), and Caserne du Château-d'Eau (near the "boisterous" borough of Belleville).

38

The Franco-Prussian War and the Commune (1870–1871)

Tension between France and Germany

Napoléon III had always defended the principle of nationality and encouraged German unity, but soon he had to face Prussia which, having defeated Austria at the battle of Sadowa in 1866, was carving out a position for itself as a great military power and preparing for German unity with itself at the center. In spite of Napoléon III's early sympathy for Prussian ambitions, the German victory of 1866 suddenly gave rise to misgivings in France. As a result, tension increased between France and Prussia when a quarrel broke out with regard to Spain.

In 1868 Queen Isabella of Spain lost the Spanish throne following a military coup. The *Cortes* (parliament) of Madrid thereupon offered the crown to Prince Leopold von Hohenzollern-Sigmaringen, a relative of the king of Prussia. At the news, indignation swept France: a German on the throne of Spain would be like reconstructing the Hapsburg Empire of Carlos Quinto (Charles V). Leopold refused to become king of Spain, and the affair would have ended there, but France was so resentful that it demanded that Prussia pledge herself not to accept similar offers in the future. Anger at the Prussian court resulted in the sending of the famous "telegram of Ems," purposely written in a provocative, abrupt and impolite manner. The French felt humiliated, Napoléon III attempted to recover his waning prestige and fell into the trap designed by the German Chancellor Otto von Bismarck. Napoléon III — now fearing Prussia as the leader of a united Germany — made the foolish mistake of declaring war on Prussia on July 19, 1870. This was the war that Bismarck had long dreamed of, as war with France was seen as an opportunity to rally Germans to his program of unity.

The Prussians — under the competent leadership of Marshall Helmut von Moltke — were much better prepared for war than the French. They were well motivated, experienced and confident (notably by the victory over Austria); they had a well-organized intelligence service; and they were ready for mobilization, powerfully armed and equipped with modern rifles.

Rifled Weapons

Artillery pieces with rifled barrels were one of the most significant innovations in firearm warfare. The term *rifle* comes from the German verb *riffeln*, to groove, probably invented by Gaspard Koller, a gunmaker of Vienna, or August Kotter, an armorer of Nuremberg in the late 1400s.

Introduced about 1860, the rifling of the barrel with a groove gave the projectile a rotary movement which greatly increased its penetration and the stability of its trajectory and gave it the possibility of changing from the form of a solid sphere to that of a cylindrical hollow shell. In sending the projectile to the target loaded with a great quantity of explosives, it was no longer necessary to depend on heavy caliber guns. The weight of the shell was

French franc tireur, 1870

now independent of its diameter, and the cannon, of smaller caliber, was more manageable with a greater range. The rifled artillery (soon adapted to howitzers and handguns) was a true revolution in warfare. The average range of artillery suddenly increased from 1,000 to 6,000 m, precision became adequate and destructive potential became formidable. In the meantime the introduction of breech loading devices significantly increased the rate of

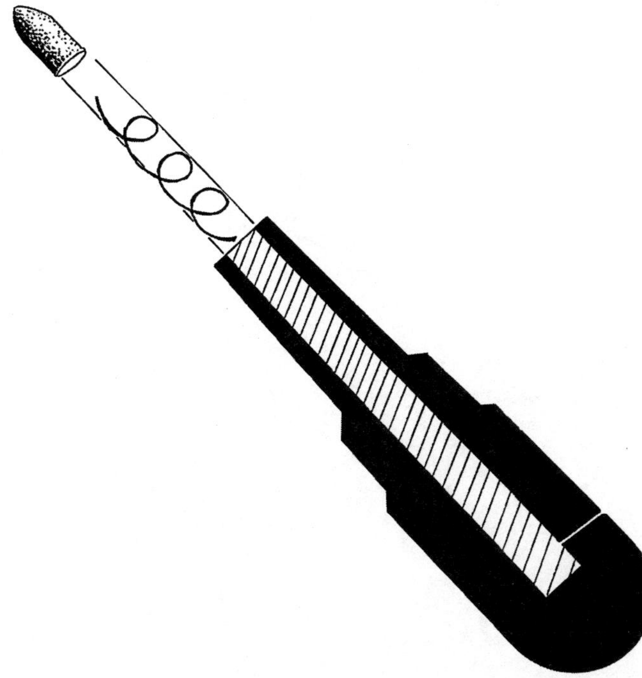

Cross section of a rifled gun. The rifle imparts a spinning motion to its projectile. It is caused by spiral grooves (rifling) cut into the inner surface of the barrel which engage with the projectile on its way to the muzzle. The rotation thus acquired continues during flight, giving gyroscopic stability which equalizes the tendencies to erratic flight, and thus increases accuracy.

fire. This increase of fire power marked a total change in warfare and also meant that—within a decade—17th and 18th century enclosing masoned bastions and walls totally lost their military importance.

The Fall of Napoléon III

The Prussians quickly seized the initiative of operations and invaded northeastern France. Marshall François-Achille Bazaine, put at the head of the most powerful French army, soon found himself blockaded in the city of Metz. French defeats followed in quick succession at Wissemburg, Froeschwiller and Forbach. General MacMahon, with another army, received orders to relieve Bazaine's forces and concentrated his troops around the fortress of Sedan. The battle of Sedan ended on September 1, 1870, with a negative outcome for the French. It was one of the greatest military disasters ever suffered by France. Bazaine and MacMahon's troops were forced to surrender, and—supreme humiliation!—Napoléon III himself fell prisoner and personally signed the act of capitulation. After a short custody in Germany, the emperor finished his life in exile in England where he died in 1873.

The principal reason for the fall of France can be

largely lumped together under the general heading "lack of preparation." In the face of a determined, well-prepared and skillful enemy, France could only oppose a scratch army with outdated armament, inadequate supplies, obsolete fortifications, and a leadership lacking forceful personalities of considerable military ability.

After Sedan, the Prussians had the way open to Paris where important events had happened. Indeed the defeat and capitulation of the Emperor had great political consequences. As soon as news of the capture of Napoléon III and the capitulation of Sedan reached Paris on September 4, 1870, crowds overran the Palais Bourbon. Gambetta made a speech at the City Hall proclaiming the fall of the Empire and the creation of the Third Republic. An emergency republican government of national defense was formed and presided over by Léon Gambetta, Jules Favre and General Trochu. Military defeat had annihilated a regime which — though strengthened by international prestige — had never been popular in hearts and minds.

The new French republican government decided to continue the war. Gambetta proclaimed a national war, with Paris as the symbol of national and republican resistance.

The problem for the French was that thousands of trained professionals were all in Prussian prisoner-of-war-camps, thus the new Republic had to create a military organization out of volunteers from the civilian society, with little professional expertise available. The 1870 war unleashed the full flood of nationalist feeling on both sides. Among the French civilian volunteers, the *franc tireurs* (literally "free riflemen") were among the most typical combatants of the Franco-Prussian War. Commissioned for the duration of the conflict, divided in autonomous units of several dozen men each, attired in picturesque uniforms and bearing evocative names, they included volunteers like Stefano Canzio and the sculptor Frédéric-Auguste Bartholdi, future designer of the Statue of Liberty in New York.

The Siege of Paris (1870)

Starting August 17, 1870, General Trochu (the military governor of Paris) and General Ducrot (his army

French Foreign Legion infantryman. The French Foreign Legion was created in March 1831 by Louis-Philippe. Originally, the intention was to have a small permanent professional elite army for colonial conquest. The Legion took part in all major conflicts in which France was involved, including the Franco-Prussian war of 1870, both World Wars of the 20th century (1914–1918 and 1939–1945), and colonial wars in Indo-China and Algeria between 1945 and 1954. Today the highly regarded Legion is composed of volunteers, both French and foreigners, who enlist for five years.

commander) acted to reinforce and arm the Parisian fortifications. A combat corps of civilian volunteers was raised to man the bastioned walls. In all about 400,000 men were mobilized for the defense of Paris, but these were mainly National Guardsmen who were poorly trained and militarily useless; moreover, Trochu and Ducrot considered them politically dangerous and unreliable. The main force was a detachment of 12,000 professional military sailors—experts in serving heavy artillery, who were placed under the command of Rear Admiral La Ronsière de Noury; they were assigned to the defense of the principal forts outside Paris. In the meantime the guns intended to arm the Parisian forts had been brought back from the Arsenal of Bourges, and the French had 1,964 guns. Around the city, work proceeded apace. To clear the field for cannon fire, trees were removed and houses demolished; a flotilla of gunboats was placed to defend the entrance and exit on the River Seine.

On September 12, 1870, the Prussian advance guards reached Château Thierry and proceeded with their plan of surrounding Paris. In spite of a counter-offensive led by General Ducrot near Châtillon-sur-Marne, the Prussian army crossed the Marne and Aisne rivers. On September 17, after bitter fighting, General Vogel von Falkenstein's forces occupied the heights of Villeneuve-Saint-Georges. Two days later, the encirclement of Paris was complete, and King Wilhelm I of Prussia established his general headquarters in Louis XIV's Royal Palace of Versailles. In the meantime the besieged fortresses of Toul, Strasburg and Metz had surrendered (only the fortress of Belfort resisted under the leadership of General Denfert-Rochereau), allowing the Prussians to make other forces available for a total and final attack. The siege of Paris had begun.

The Prussian army totaled 206,000 infantry, 34,000 cavalry, 900 field pieces and 240 siege guns. The Prussians entrenched themselves with formidable siege earthworks about fifty miles long and placed siege artillery batteries capable of battering down the Parisian fortifications and forts. Their plan was to take Paris not by assault, but by attrition. Although Bismarck was anxious for political reasons to end the war as quickly as possible, the affair could not be pushed with great urgency. One problem was the supply of ammunition, since their relatively rapid advance had overstrained the army supply system. It was not until a civil contractor was brought in that the movement of ammunition from Germany to Paris was sufficient to provide for a prolonged bombardment.

Day after day, the Prussian long-range rifled artillery fired at the city, inflicting grave damage and causing numerous casualties among both defenders and civilians. On October 28, 1870, the besieged made a successful sortie and captured the village of Le Bourget, which had little military significance but helped boost morale. On November 7, Léon Gambetta succeeded in leaving Paris by means of an adventurous hot air balloon flight, to lead the resistance from the province. He reached Tours, hoping to lift the spirit of the French through his energy, and formed a new army of volunteers to come to the rescue of the besieged capital. On November 29 and 30, the Parisians carried out another sortie in the plain of Avron; they destroyed a Bavarian unit, but a Prussian counterattack drove them back. In northern France, the French developed a guerilla war against Prussian supply lines, but these attacks failed to achieve their objective; instead of cutting the enemy's supply line, they angered the invaders and further embittered the war, as the Germans reacted with ruthless retaliations against civilians.

At the beginning of December 1870, the army raised by Gambetta, which was attempting to relieve Paris, was defeated, causing a great decline of hope. Meanwhile the Prussians had received heavy siege artillery and Paris was incessantly bombed, causing some 400 casualties. To relieve the pressure, a sally was launched on December 2. The French advanced toward the plateau of Champigny; facing too much fire, they had to quickly withdraw to Paris. Another sortie was launched on January 18 and 19, 1871; the garrison of Fort Mont Valérien attacked the Prussian positions established at Montretout, Buzenval and La Jonchère. This too was a failure. As all attempts to break through enemy lines had failed, the morale of the besieged collapsed. The effect of the shelling, together with the dreadful winter cold, fuel shortage, the repeated unsuccessful sorties, the loss of hope, fear and despair, and increasing sickness made the siege a terrible ordeal for the population. The lack of food caused a terrible famine, and the Parisians ate dogs, cats, rats and the animals of the zoo. The besieged city was also the scene of an internal struggle opposing moderate republicans to socialist revolutionaries. Completely exhausted, Paris held on two more months, but menaced by riots and starvation, the French were forced to surrender, and sued for terms. The revolutionary *levée en masse* (popular draft) had been defeated by an organized nation in arms.

On January 26, 1871, at 8:30 p.m. the firing stopped, the official capitulation was signed on the 28th followed by the occupation of the city by the Prussians. Ten days before this, in the Hall of Mirrors at Versailles, Wilhelm of Prussia was proclaimed Emperor of Germany by the assembled German princes; the greatest of the wars of nationality of the mid–19th century had achieved its goal: the creation of the Second German *Reich* (empire), marking the culmination of the movement for the national unity of Germany. The siege of Paris had cost the Germans 10,000 killed and wounded, and 2,000 missing. The

French had lost 16,000 killed and wounded, and 8,000 missing.

The armistice following the capitulation of Paris gave rise to the convocation at Bordeaux of a French National Assembly to discuss the peace conditions imposed by the Germans. The highly conservative assembly appointed Adolphe Thiers (Louis-Philippe's former minister, the very man who had commissioned the Parisian fortifications of 1841–1845) to the post of chief executive. Peace between the French Republic and the new German Reich was signed with the Treaty of Frankfurt on May 10, 1871. The peace that resulted had a number of unfortunate repercussions on the history of the 20th century, the seeds of World War I were sown.

The year 1870 had been a terrible moment for Paris and for France. However the long ordeal of the Parisians was not yet over, as France — militarily humbled — became divided by opposing factions.

The Commune (1871)

Almost as soon as the war with Germany was over, a violent and fearful civil war broke out. This revolution known as the *Commune* began in February 1871. This was principally the result of a spirit of anger and protest against the bourgeois class. The Parisians, who had withstood the siege despite extreme suffering, saw the capitulation as a terrible humiliation and an act of treachery. The lower social class of Paris, humiliated, Socialist and Republican in sentiment, and in great economic hardship, was handled maladroitly by the Thiers's government. A popular fury broke out against the minister. Anger reached its height when Thiers, fearing a spreading of uprising, ordered the dissolution of the National Guard composed of Parisian volunteers. Meanwhile the Germans left the town as they did not want to get involved in a Franco-French quarrel, but they occupied the forts to keep an eye on the situation. On March 18, 1871, the government tried to retake the guns placed on the Montmartre hill. Two senior officers were killed by the populace and riots broke out. The Parisian National Guard, about 30,000 strong, occupied the City Hall and forced Thiers and his government to retreat to Versailles while the Paris

Battalion commander Garde Mobile 1870

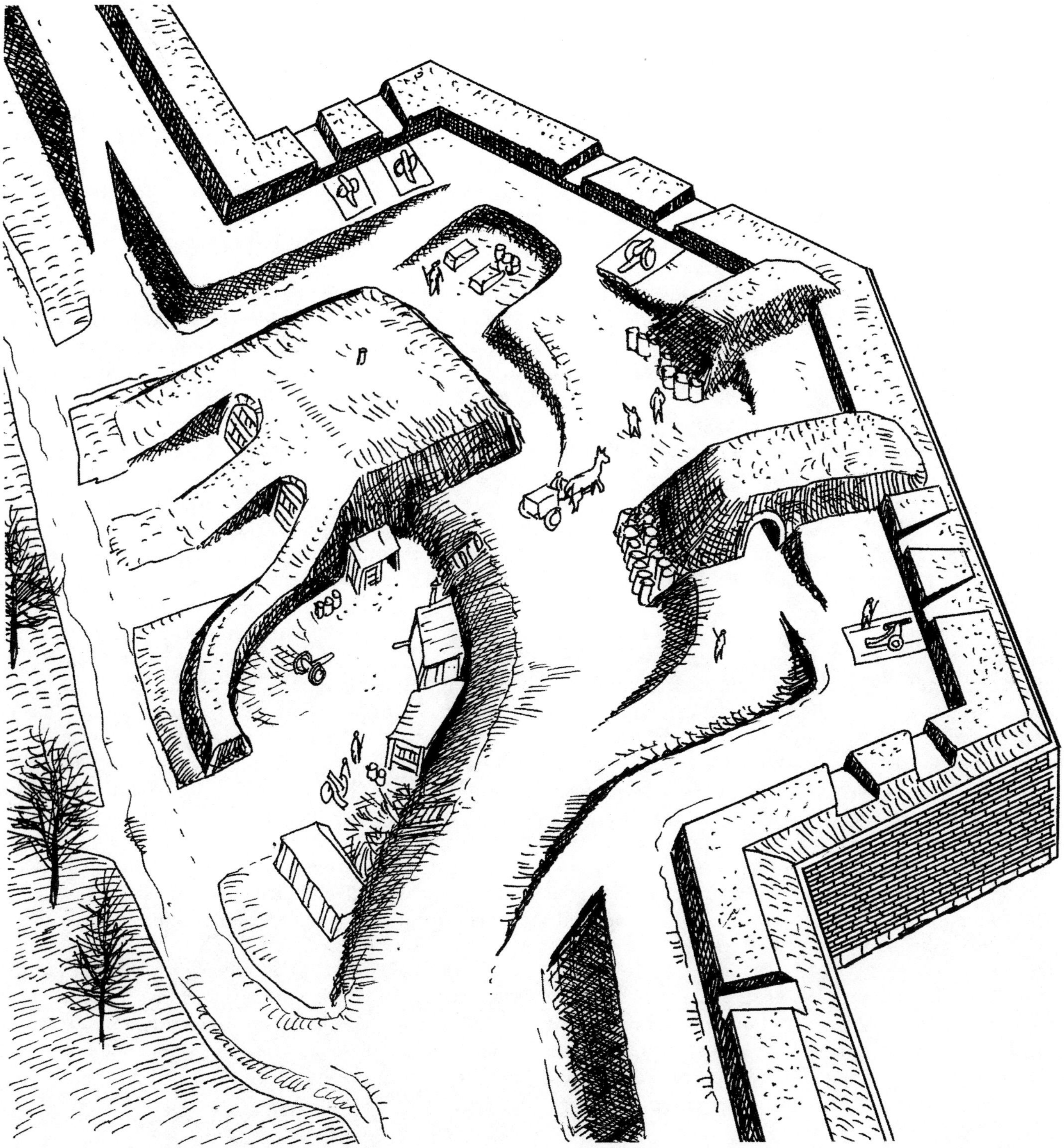

View of a bastion in Thiers's enceinte (1870). During the 1870 siege of Paris, the Parisian bastions were put in a state of readiness for war. The breastwork was fitted with embrasures. The terre-plein was arranged in different levels with huts for the garrison, sheds for materials, a powder house covered with earth and various protections, including thick traverses and gabions (open-ended woven brushwood cylinders filled with earth for reinforcement of breastworks and other entrenchments).

Commune organized itself into an autonomous workers government on March 26, 1871. This was overt rebellion and the start of a short but extremely bloody civil war, as Thiers preferred repression over negotiation.

The Commune of Paris has been variously described as a model of "Soviet," a forerunner of the Russian Communist Revolution of 1917. Governed by a group of revolutionaries, the Commune did not have a very precise political program — except for a few expressions, the most famous being "land for the peasants, tools for the workers, and work for all." Moreover they did not have enough time to make significant reforms. Symbolically, the

Commune adopted the red flag, it declared the separation of Church and State, abolished conscription and permanent forces, and adopted the principle of free, nonreligious and mandatory education. In the final analysis, however, social "communist" reforms were limited. As a matter of fact, the Commune of Paris seemed to have been more influenced by anarchist theories (developed by Bakounine and Proudhon) than by Karl Marx's communism. It was a valuable example of direct democracy, a government of the people by the people, and clearly showed that workers were perfectly capable of self-government. It all ended in bloody repression and martyrdom.

Thiers's government, after having secured Prussian neutrality, decided to recapture Paris by force. The regular French army (known as the *Versaillais*) under the command of General MacMahon blockaded the Parisian rebels (known as *Communards*). Paris suffered the ordeal of a second siege until the beginning of May when the Versaillais launched a large attack. After capturing the forts of Issy and Vanves, they assaulted the city at the Saint Cloud gate and took the boroughs of Auteuil, Passy and Vanves. From there they fought a violent urban warfare for the reconquest of Paris. The Communards had made numerous barricades in the streets which were taken one by one after bloody fratricidal combats, causing enormous casualties on both sides. Gradually the Communards were driven back to the eastern neighborhoods of Paris. They made the mistake of executing hostages (including the Archbishop of Paris) and set fire to public buildings such as the Palace of the Tuileries, the Palace of Justice and the City Hall, which were remorselessly and excessively avenged by fearsome reprisals. The final combats took place near the Père Lachaise Cemetery where the last Communard rebels were slaughtered by the Versaillais regulars during the "bloody week" from May 22 to May 28.

The Paris Commune fell on May 29, 1871. The defeat of the popular uprising was followed by an extremely bloody and harsh repression. The balance of the short civil war was catastrophic. According to some estimates, between 20,000 and 30,000 rebels were summarily executed, 45,000 were arrested and about 13,500 were sentenced to deportation and hard labor to the *bagnes* (penitentiaries) of Cayenne (Guyana) and New Caledonia. The repression reassured those who still feared the concept of a Republic. For the Socialists, the trade unions and the working class, the crushing of the Commune represented a missed opportunity for a popular revolution.

The lost war with Prussia was also a disaster. The two rich and industrially developed northeastern provinces of Alsace and Lorraine were transferred to Germany; the annexation of Alsace and Lorraine — against the will of the inhabitants—created an abyss between France and Germany. This hatred was one of the causes of the two world wars of the 20th century (1914–1918 and 1939–1945).

Moreover a war indemnity amounting to five billion gold francs was to be paid. The Germans occupied a large part of northern France until the reparations imposed by the peace treaty were paid. Apparently France was rich and prosperous. Indeed, by means of government loans, the indemnities were amazingly quickly paid, and in September 1873, the last German soldiers left French soil, while the French prisoners-of-war were liberated.

The Third Republic had begun in defeat, confusion, disaster and blood in 1870. Peace, law and order had been re-established at high human cost in 1871. The Third Republic was to be long-lived; it lasted until June 1940, and came to an end because of another successful German invasion.

After the disasters of 1870 and 1871, Parisian Catholics and conservatives decided to erect a church as a token of contrition and manifestation of hope. The result was the *Basilique du Sacré Coeur* placed on top of Montmartre hill. Built between 1876 and 1919, from a design by architect Lucien Magne, the imposing white silhouette of the Sacré Coeur, with its 80-m-high campanile, its huge dome and cupolas, and terraced garden, still dominates the Parisian townscape.

PART IV

MODERN FORTIFICATIONS (1874–1944)

39

New Weapons of War

Weapons Industry

The forty-three years between the Franco-Prussian War and World War I (1871–1914) constituted an unprecedented period of peace in Europe. This resulted partially from a common interest among the European nations in seizing areas of the world. Expansion of western influence in Africa, Asia, and the Pacific did cause considerable tension, but pursuit of colonial empire remained sufficiently distant to prevent a major European war. For the time being, Europeans drew the comforting illusion from their prosperity that they alone possessed the key to the future. But economic expansion placed enormous military power in the hands of these states and in the long run made war both inevitable and disastrous.

As we have seen, the Industrial Revolution had begun in Britain in the latter years of the 18th century, and industrialization developed throughout Europe and the United States in the 19th century. The competition of capitalist free trade was a forcing house for the development of new processes in mechanics, chemistry, textiles, food processing, communications, transmission of power, metallurgy and armament. The harnessing of steam power and its application to the mechanical processes of manufacture resulted in the hitherto unparalleled output of all types of weapons and equipment, especially after the widespread introduction of the machine manufacture of machine tools. As the 19th century wore on, the *Industrial Revolution* developed its own momentum. The civilian was now responsible for providing the industrial means of war, and workshops and factories became as vital parts of the struggle as the battlefield. Workers and combatants were now fundamentally dependent upon one another.

The American Civil War (1861–1865) was a colossal proving ground for new weapons of all kinds. For the first time the achievements of the Industrial Revolution were used on a large scale at war: rifled and breechloading cannons, repeating rifles, land and sea mines, armored and transport trains, submarines, surface torpedo boats, ironclad ships, the telegraph, balloons, raiding cavalry, trench warfare, and barbed wire. It was also the first war to be adequately photographed.

Some industrialists deliberately sought out military markets for their products, making contacts among those technologically minded officers who were reaching ranks high enough to authorize the purchase of modern equipment. The race of military development accelerated with each decade. In times of international tension, the demands for increased arms expenditure could reach a point almost of hysteria. The rapidly developing knowledge of science and technology combined with the factory system, born of the Industrial Revolution, provided the opportunity for the mass production of increasingly sophisticated and lethal weaponry. Both in the United States of America and in Europe, factories specialized in weapon production were created and became huge profit-making businesses. Friedrich Krupp (1787–1826) was the founder of a dynasty of German metallurgist. His successors, Alfred (1812–1887) and Friedrich-Alfred (1854–1902) specialized in producing heavy equipment, establishing at Essen in the Ruhr a powerful capitalist empire delivering weapons to the German armies during both world wars of the 20th century. In the United States, many private

Breechloading rifled cannon

companies were founded: Colt, Remington, Sharp, Spencer, Winchester, Smith & Wesson etc. In France were created the state-controlled Manufacture d'Armes de Saint-Etienne (MAS), Manufacture d'Armes de Tulle (MAT), and Manufacture d'Armes de Chatellerault (MAC).

In the late 19th century, the superior weapons of European forces enabled them for the most part to score easy victories in Africa and Asia over native armies many times their own size. Colonial conflicts also offered opportunities for lethal experimentation with new weapons.

Artillery

In 1815 a smooth bore muzzle loading cannon was only slightly better than pieces used in the 16th century. It could fire a solid ball weighting 10 kilograms over a distance of 2,500 m, or one weighting 30 kilograms over a range of 800 m.

In 1914, a rifled breech-loading ordnance could hurl explosive shells weighing 800 kilograms over a range of 20 km — and with a potentially greater accuracy than its predecessors of the Napoleonic era. What happened in this lapse of time was the great development of artillery, which rested upon three things:

- First the science of ballistics, which developed slowly and quite independently of the art of war in the research of Galileo, Descartes, Newton, and their followers;
- Second, the science of chemistry, which was not really born till the 18th century;
- And third, the technological developments in manufacturing, which came only with the Industrial Revolution.

In 1897 the French army revealed a new weapon, the 75 mm gun model 97, which became so well known as the French *Soixante-quinze* (seventy-five). This piece introduced the concept of the quick-firing field gun. It had on-carriage hydraulic recoil control (ensuring that the gun stayed in the same place when firing), a rapid-acting breech mechanism (adding to the speed of loading), a one-piece round of ammunition (a metal cartridge including both projectile and propellant charge), and a shield (protecting against enemy fire). The French 75 could fire about 18 aimed shots a minute; it made other artillery field pieces in the world obsolete overnight, and — with the addition of pneumatic tyres — stayed in service until 1945.

Rifles

Small arms had developed from the smooth bore musket firing a single ball every minute to sophisticated rifles and fully automatic machine guns spitting out bullets at the rate of 600 rounds per minute.

Rifles were largely improved. The French MAS Chassepot fusil d'infanterie M66 was designed by Antoine-

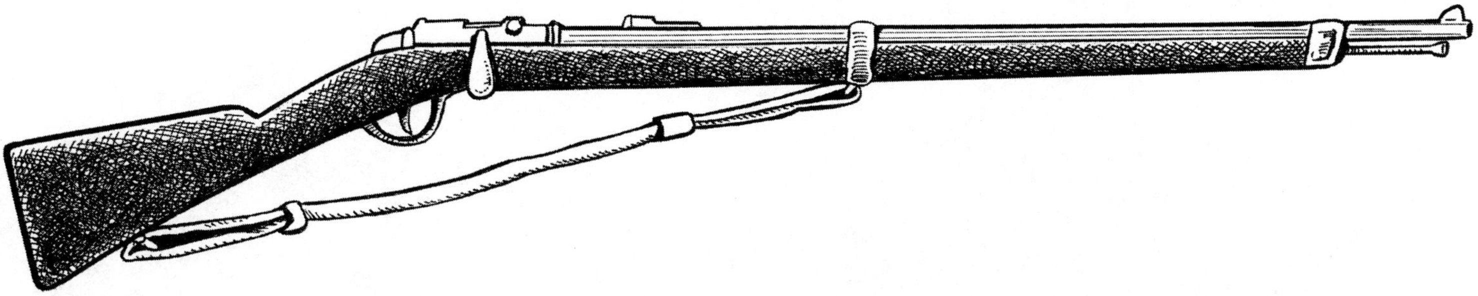

French MAS Gras rifle model 1874

Alphonse Chassepot (1833–1905); it was issued to the army in 1866 and used until 1874; with a caliber of 11 mm (0.43"), single action, and a weight of 4.1 kg (9.13 lbs), it was an excellent infantry weapon. The improved MAS Gras—designed by General Basile Gras—was introduced in 1874; the small caliber repetition Lebel rifle, designed by the officer Nicolas Lebel, was introduced in 1886. The British Lee-Enfield (introduced in 1895) and the German Mauser K98 (introduced in 1898) were used in both world wars of the 20th century, a record of durability and reliability that must rank them as very successful weapons. Those rifles gave a squad of infantrymen more fire power than a whole battalion of 18th century musketeers.

Machine Gun

This period also saw the appearance of a formidable weapon: the machine gun. Since the invention of firearms, every weapon designer's idea had been to make them fire faster. As early as the mid–14th century organ guns had been experimented with. In 1718, James Puckle invented a portable gun firing 63 shots in seven minutes. A machine gun designed by Richard Gatling, firing 300 rounds per minute, was used with devastating effect during the American Civil War and by the British army in the Zulu wars in South Africa.

During the Franco-Prussian war of 1870, the French had Montigny *mitrailleuses* (machine guns). The weapon,

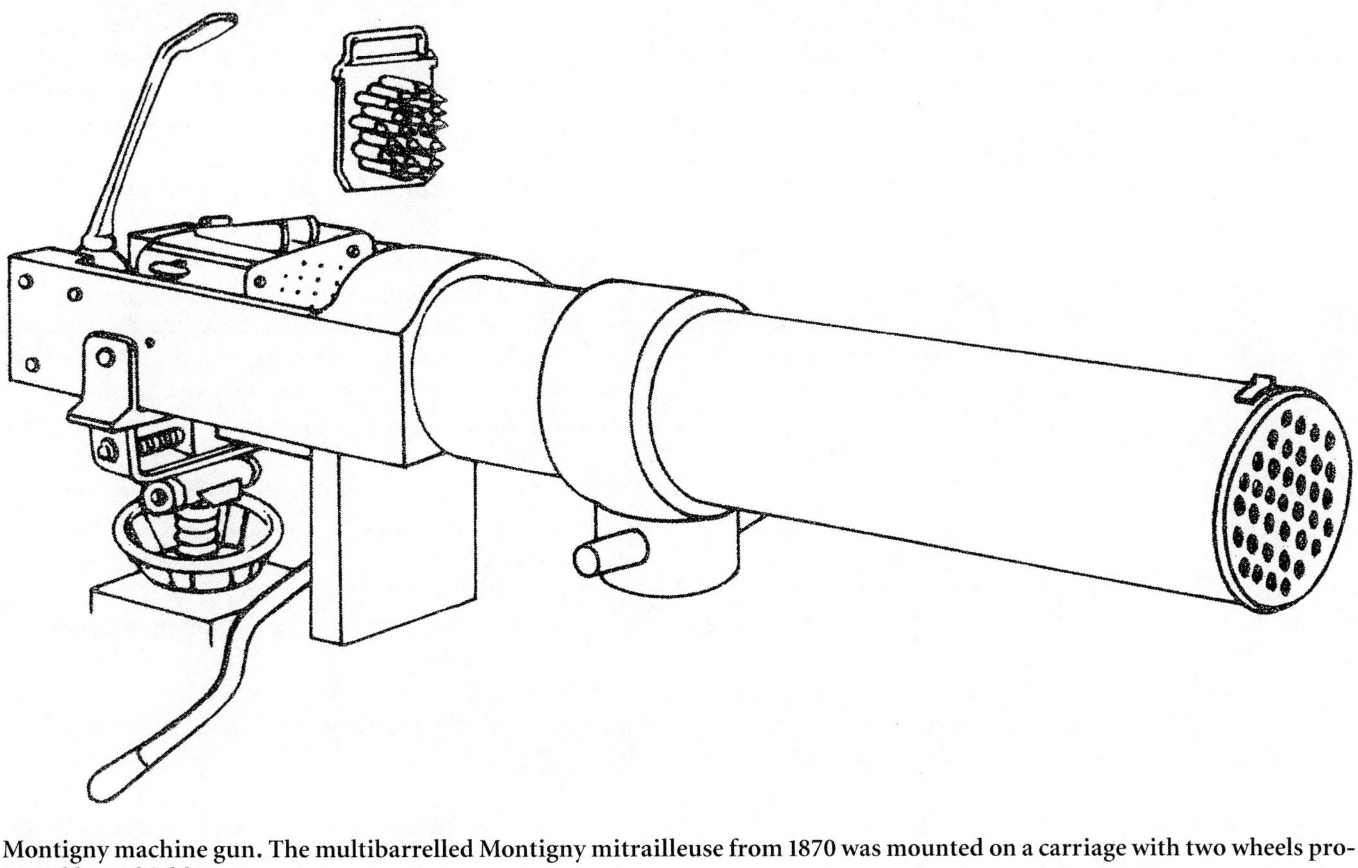

Montigny machine gun. The multibarrelled Montigny mitrailleuse from 1870 was mounted on a carriage with two wheels protected by a shield.

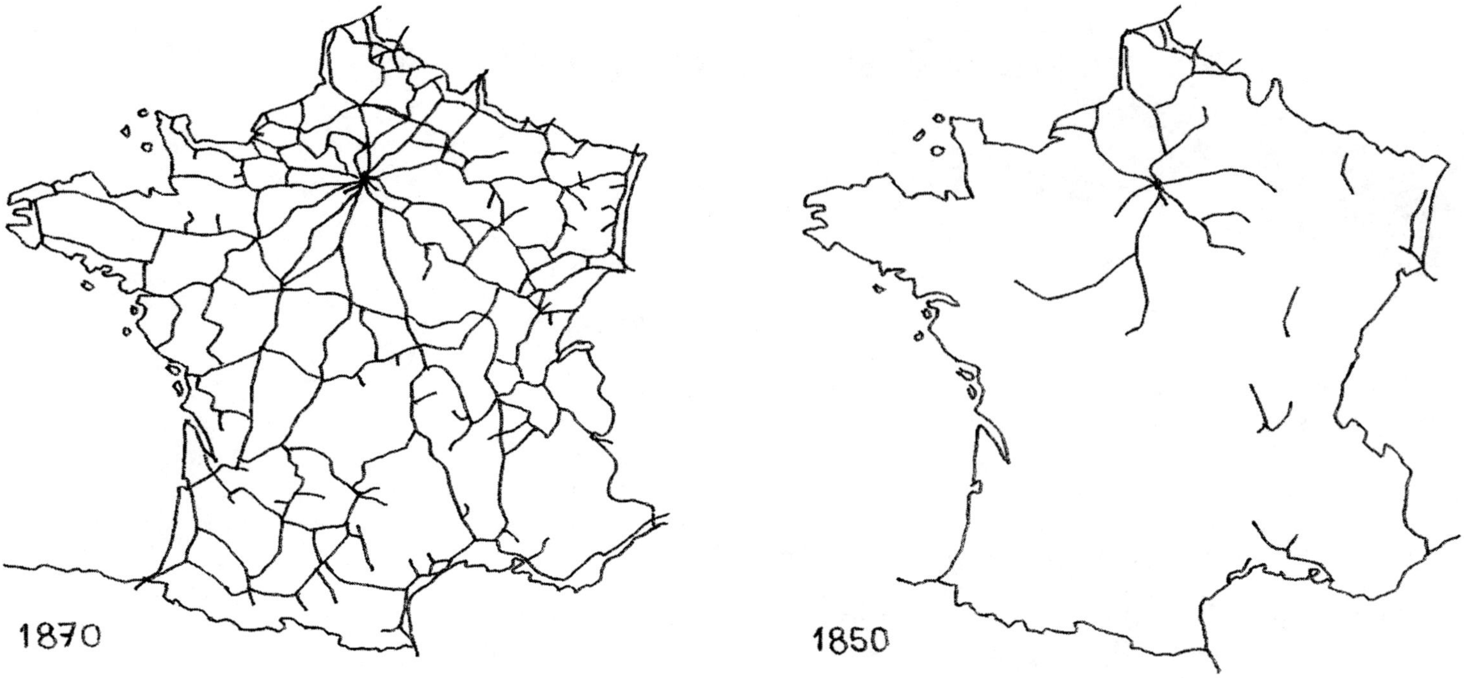

French railroad mileage in 1850 (right) and 1870 (left)

developed between 1851 and 1869 by engineers Faschamp and Montigny, had thirty-seven barrels, which were mounted on a field gun carriage and pulled by four horses. The magazine consisted of a metal plate, perforated to contain a number of cartridges, that slotted into the breech block; these were fired in succession by rotating a handle.

The Montigny quick-firing cannon could deliver the content of ten magazines, about 370 shots, in one minute with a range of 1,000 yards. The weapon was extremely effective at close range, but the French kept news of it so secret that their own men were insufficiently trained in its use. The French generals missed the significance and persisted in thinking of it as an artillery piece. As a result, the deadliness of the machine gun would not be convincingly demonstrated until World War I.

Other multibarreled designs were made: the Nordenfelt-Palmcrantz from 1873 and the Gardner machine gun. The first fully automatic machine gun was designed in 1883 by the American Hiram S. Maxim; it used its own recoil energy to load itself, fire, and eject empty shells; the gunner had only to squeeze and hold the trigger. It had a rate of fire of 650 rounds per minute.In 1897 the French adopted the Hotchkiss machine gun. The gas-operated and air-cooled Hotchkiss machine gun was mounted on a tripod; it weighed 23.58 kg (52 lb) and had a rate of fire of 600 rounds per minute; the ammunition system used metal strips holding thirty 8 mm rounds, fed in horizontally from the left.

Railway

The second half of the 19th century also saw the tremendous development of the railroad. The impact of railways on warfare was significant. It revolutionized strategy, increased the pace and power of maneuver on the field, made armies more massive and more mobile, and stimulated a whole science of logistics; the debilitating long marches of the past which wasted the soldiers' strength before battle disappeared. It maintained troops in good condition; the sick and wounded could be evacuated to base hospitals and replaced by fit men.

In the late 19th century, the increased mobility offered by the world's ever growing rail network allowed nations both to maintain smaller standing armies, and at the same time to greatly expand the possible theater of war.

The American Civil War demonstrated the strategic importance of the railroad. Organized by David C. McCallum and Herman C. Haupt, the United States military railroads allowed the North to launch the massive attacks in Tennessee and down the Mississippi that broke the Southern Confederates. General W.T. Sherman's amazing campaign in the summer of 1864 from Chattanooga down to Georgia would have been impossible without the use of railway.

Military transport over great distances by rail played a major role during the Austro-Prussian war of 1866 and in the British expedition against Magdala in 1867–68. In 1870 the Prussians were able to transport troops, horses,

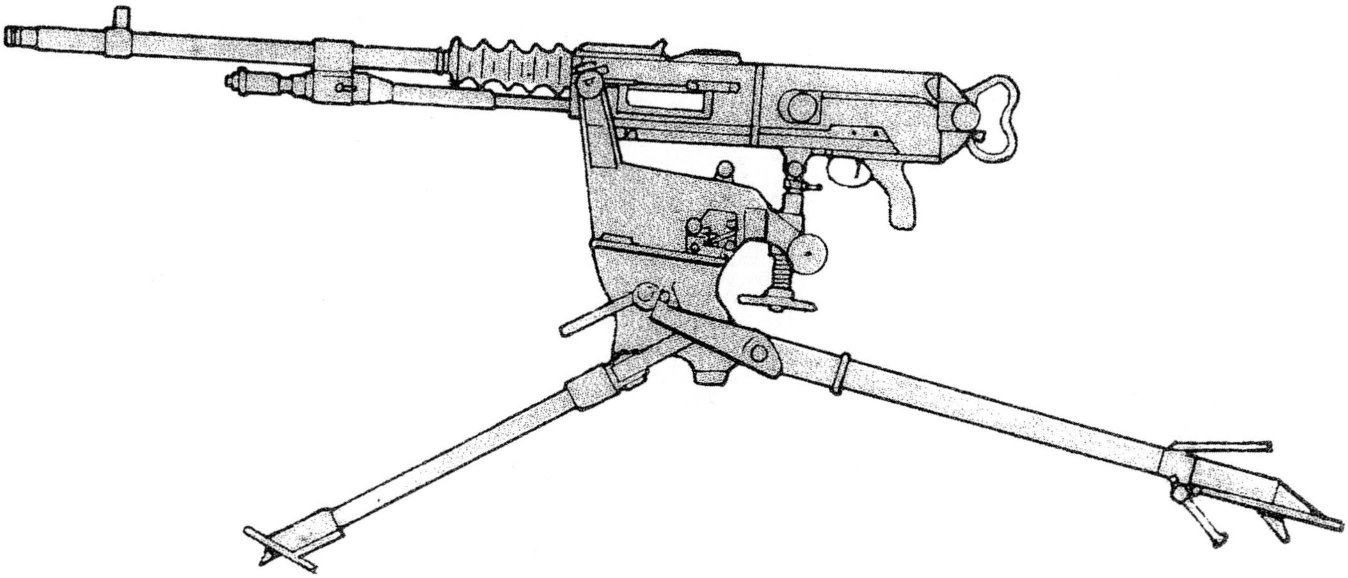

French Hotchkiss machine gun Model 1914

ammunition, artillery and equipment by train, a decisive trump for their victory over the French.

Trains were not only employed for transport. Soon they were used as weapon carriers armed with huge navy-like long-range artillery and heavy mortars, cannons so heavy that they could not be transported by road and operated on land. Armored trains soon appeared too: protected with thick steel plates and bristling with weapons, they formed mobile fortresses.

The development of railway and telegraph (apparatus for sending messages long distance by electric signals) came close together, and the telegraph office was almost invariably at the train station. Electrical communication began with the theory of Faraday, continued with the experiments of Joseph Henry and Charles Wheatstone and culminated in the invention of Samuel F.B. Morse. Telegraph was of great strategic value, for it practically obliterated the factor of time in long-distance communications. After 1900, the wireless radio, using electromagnetic waves, made communication even more reliable, flexible, and rapid since sender and receiver were no longer tied to systems of cables and wires.

40

New Systems of Fortification

German Developments

One of the most obvious effects of the Industrial Revolution in the second half of the 19th century was the simultaneous development of new weapons systems and of the defense against them. New methods of fortification were created.

As ever, the problem was twofold: how to keep out the projectiles launched by the new weaponry and how to install and operate that very same equipment. Given the long range of the new artillery and the destructive power it had, it was henceforth pointless to protect a city at close range with ditches, bastions and walls. The rifled gun had finally ended the long reign of the bastioned fortification. The defenders' best response was to direct as many guns as possible on the enemy force from simple works. What was needed were new fortresses which were artillery strongholds of the kind advocated by Montalembert in his *Fortification Perpendiculaire* developed in the years 1776–1784. What was needed were bases of operations, not for columns of infantry or cavalry but for heavy artillery covering a wide radius of fire. Properly sited (on a hill for example), each fort could defend a large area and help to cover its neighbor with overlapping fields of fire. A ring of such forts could defend a city. A line of them could protect a whole frontier. Defense in depth, made up of a series of parallel lines of fortresses, strengthened by fortified complexes around manufacturing cities and communications centers, could turn the whole state into one impregnable stronghold.

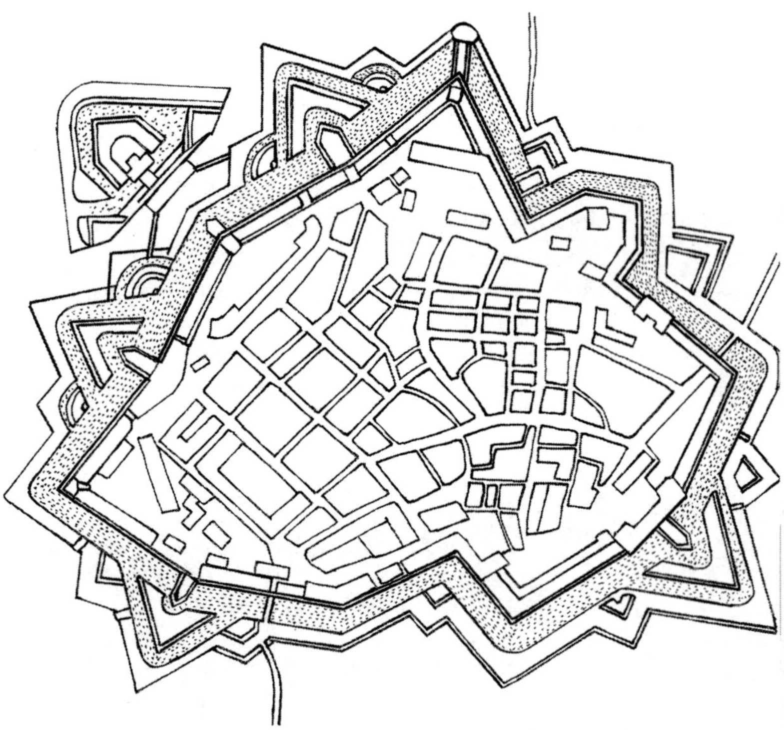

Ground plan of Germersheim. Germersheim, situated on the River Rhine in the province of Palatinate (Germany), was fortified between 1834 and 1855 by the engineer von Schmauss following the so-called Old Prussian System, based on Montalembert's theory. The fortifications included fronts defended by large caponiers as well as a ring of detached forts.

This was the theoretical reasoning behind the American, German, Belgian and Dutch military constructions of the second half of the 19th century. Indeed, every industrialized European power subscribed to this strategic

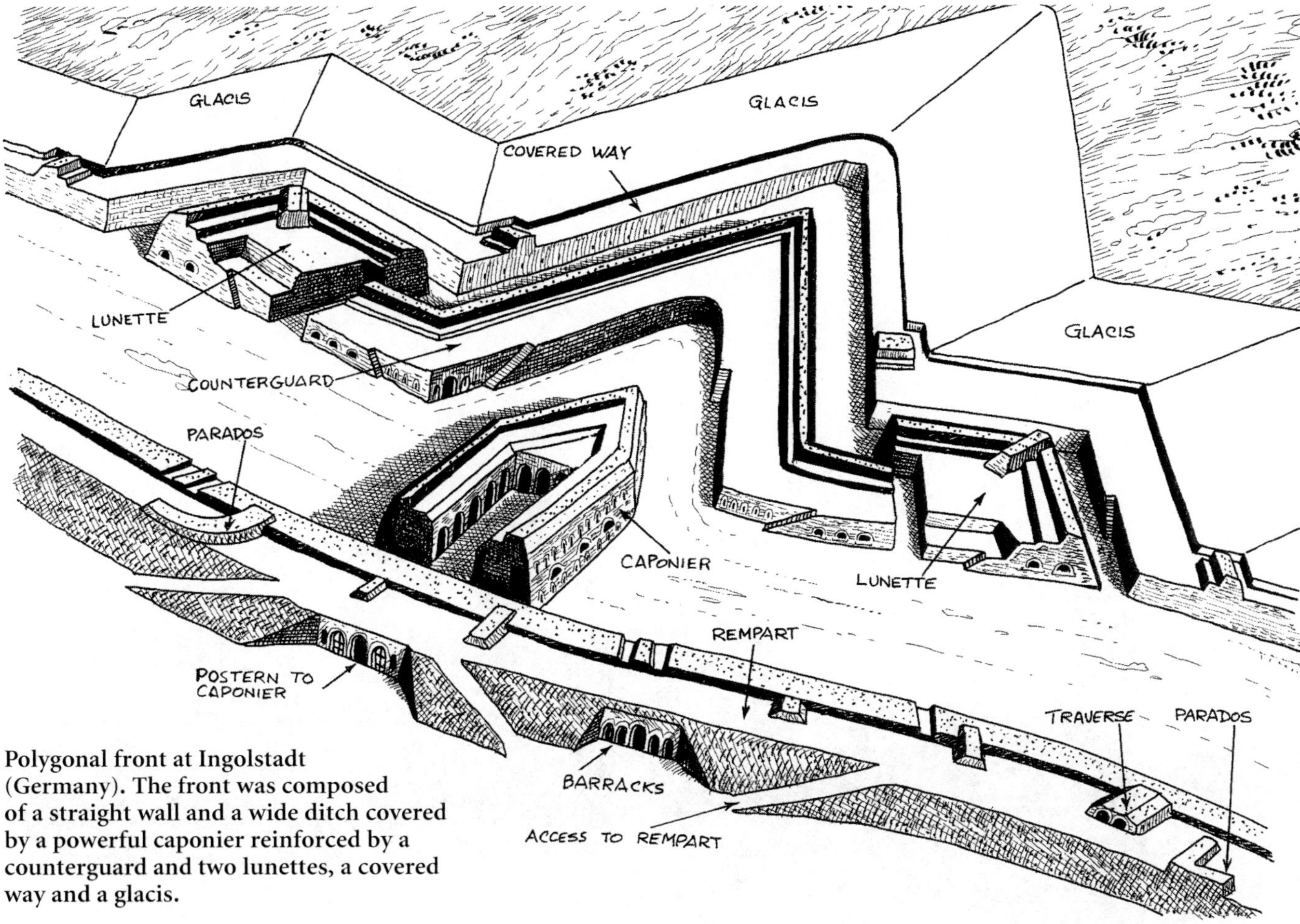

Polygonal front at Ingolstadt (Germany). The front was composed of a straight wall and a wide ditch covered by a powerful caponier reinforced by a counterguard and two lunettes, a covered way and a glacis.

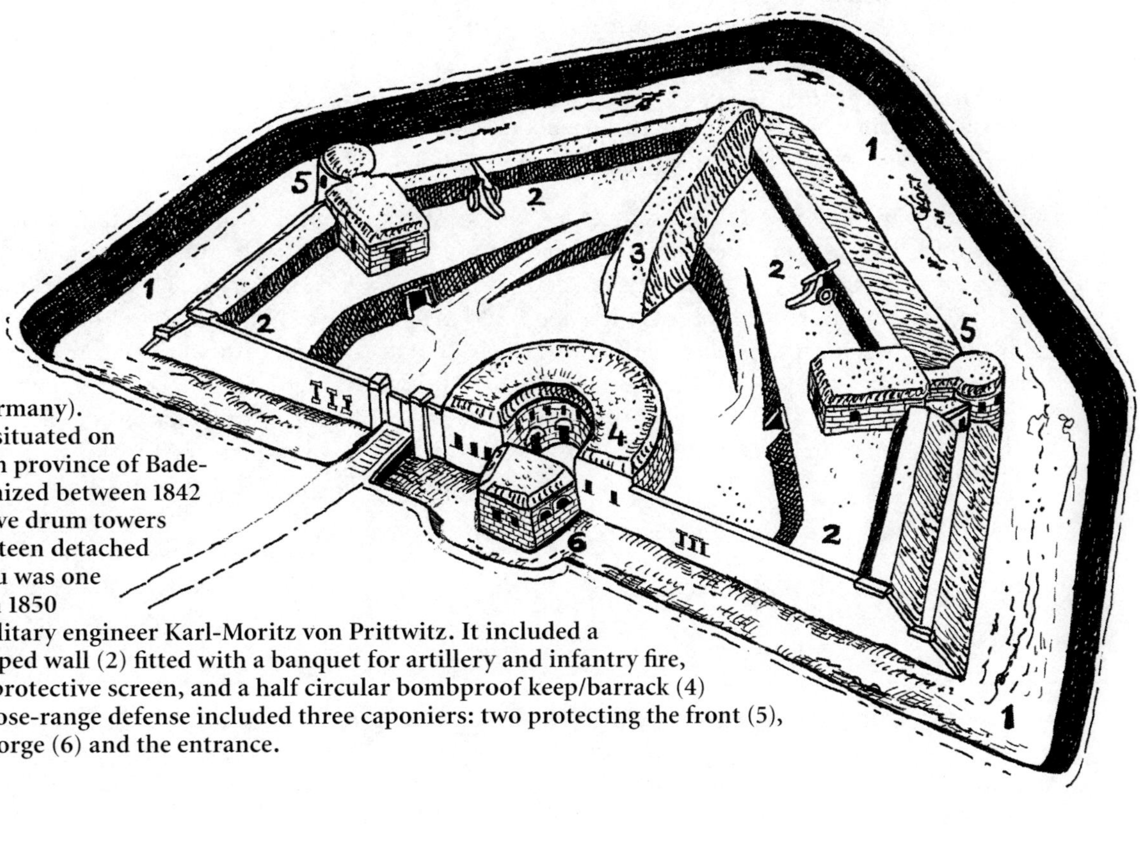

Fort Friedrichau (Ulm, Germany). The fortifications of Ulm, situated on the Danube in the southern province of Bade-Wurtemberg, were modernized between 1842 and 1859 with walls, massive drum towers and an outer girdle of fourteen detached forts. The fort Friedrichsau was one of them. It was designed in 1850 in Prussian style by the military engineer Karl-Moritz von Prittwitz. It included a ditch (1), a pentagonal-shaped wall (2) fitted with a banquet for artillery and infantry fire, a traverse (3) serving as a protective screen, and a half circular bombproof keep/barrack (4) placed in the gorge. The close-range defense included three caponiers: two protecting the front (5), and another flanking the gorge (6) and the entrance.

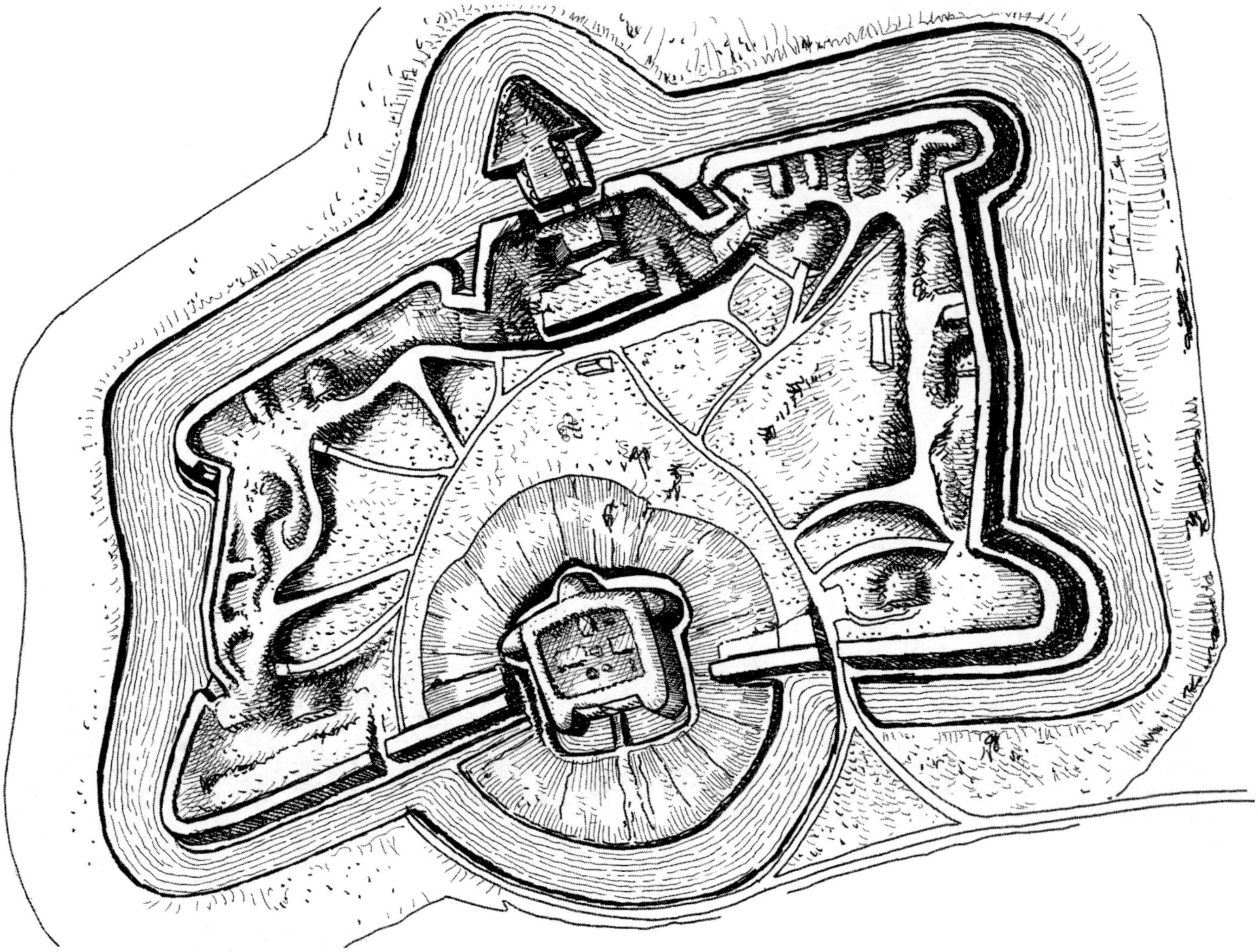

Fort Rijnauwen (The Netherlands). The Dutch Fort Rijnauwen was part of a ring of forts built between 1867 and 1881 to defend the city of Utrecht. The other forts were Ruigenhoek, Voordorp, Hoofddijk, Vechten and Hemeltje. It used a 30-m-broad wet ditch, ramparts bristling with gun batteries, a front caponier, and a powerful réduit (keep) placed in the gorge of the fort.

thinking in some way. Besides, forts, together with steam battleships, size of army, heavy artillery and railway mileage, were symbols of national status.

The Germans were prompt to design and build new fortifications based on Montalembert's theory. Modern works appeared as early as 1834 at Germersheim (south of Mannheim). A new system called the "Old Prussian Method" was employed at Koblenz, Mainz, Ulm and Ingolstadt.

Belgium and The Netherlands

About 1860, the Prussian system was improved and applied in Belgium by General Henri Brialmont. This method of fortification was often referred to under the generic term of *Polygonal System* because of the pentagonal form of the fort. The neutral Belgian nation had embarked upon a fortification program of staggering magnitude for such a small country. The whole of Antwerp was enclosed by a linked system of forts forming a "National Redoubt" if the rest of Belgium had been overrun. Antwerp was protected by a formidable system of fortification. The northern part formed a citadel with batteries overlooking the Scheldt estuary, it also served as headquarters and formed the defenders' last refuge. Then came a ring of eighteen forts, redoubts and earthworks. Eleven km beyond that came another outer ring of 31 detached forts. The largest forts could accommodate a thousand soldiers, plus 135 guns and mortars up to 21 cm (8.3 inches) in caliber. If fully equipped (which never happened), the places could have had 9,000 pieces of artillery operated by 70,000 soldiers plus a garrison of 10,000 infantrymen. The suspected German passage through the Meuse valley was blocked by outer rings of forts defending Namur and Liège.

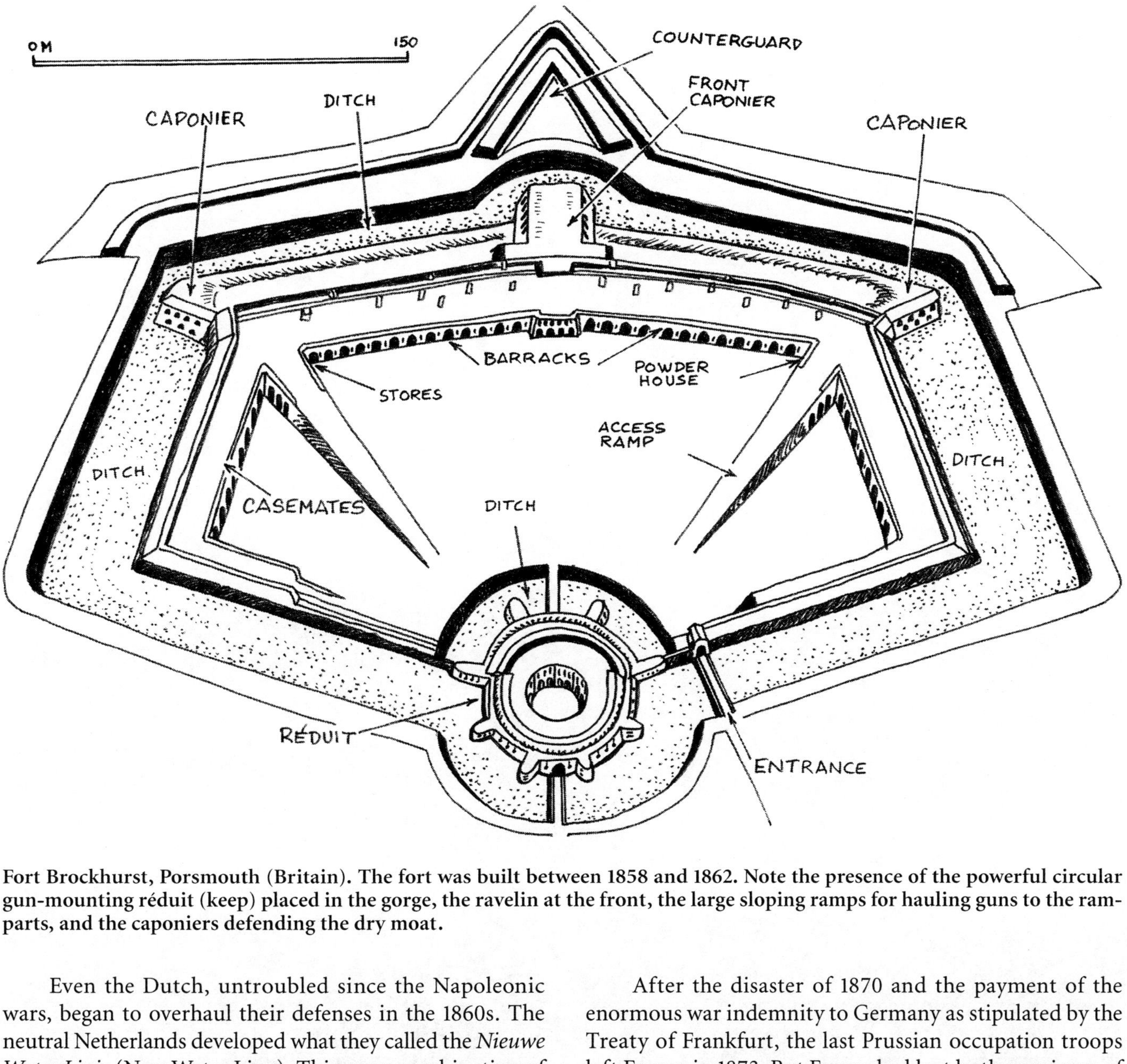

Fort Brockhurst, Porsmouth (Britain). The fort was built between 1858 and 1862. Note the presence of the powerful circular gun-mounting réduit (keep) placed in the gorge, the ravelin at the front, the large sloping ramps for hauling guns to the ramparts, and the caponiers defending the dry moat.

Even the Dutch, untroubled since the Napoleonic wars, began to overhaul their defenses in the 1860s. The neutral Netherlands developed what they called the *Nieuwe Water Linie* (New Water Line). This was a combination of floodable areas and rivers running from the Rhine to the Zuiderzee, and fortifications and detached forts placed on the main strategic passages e.g. around Utrecht to stop any enemy advance towards the capital, Amsterdam.

In the period 1860–1870, the British heavily fortified the Royal Navy harbors (notably Portsmouth and Portland) with a series of detached forts and coastal batteries.

General Séré de Rivières's Forts

The French were late to adopt the new polygonal fortification, and undertook a program of modernization only after 1874.

After the disaster of 1870 and the payment of the enormous war indemnity to Germany as stipulated by the Treaty of Frankfurt, the last Prussian occupation troops left France in 1873. But France had lost both provinces of Alsace and Lorraine including the fortresses of Thionville, Metz, Bitche, Phalsburg, Strasburg and Neuf-Brisach, leaving the northeastern border of France totally unprotected. At last, the French had drawn a certain number of conclusions regarding the new technique of warfare, notably the introduction of the powerful rifled artillery. The newly founded Third Republic decided to rebuild the defensive border system.

Raymond Adolphe Séré de Rivières (1815–1895) was born in Albi in southern France. He took part in the conquest of Algeria in 1841 and in the campaign of Italy in 1859. As a military engineer, he worked on the fortifications of Toulon between 1843 and 1847, Metz from 1864 to 1868, and Lyon between 1868 and 1870. During the

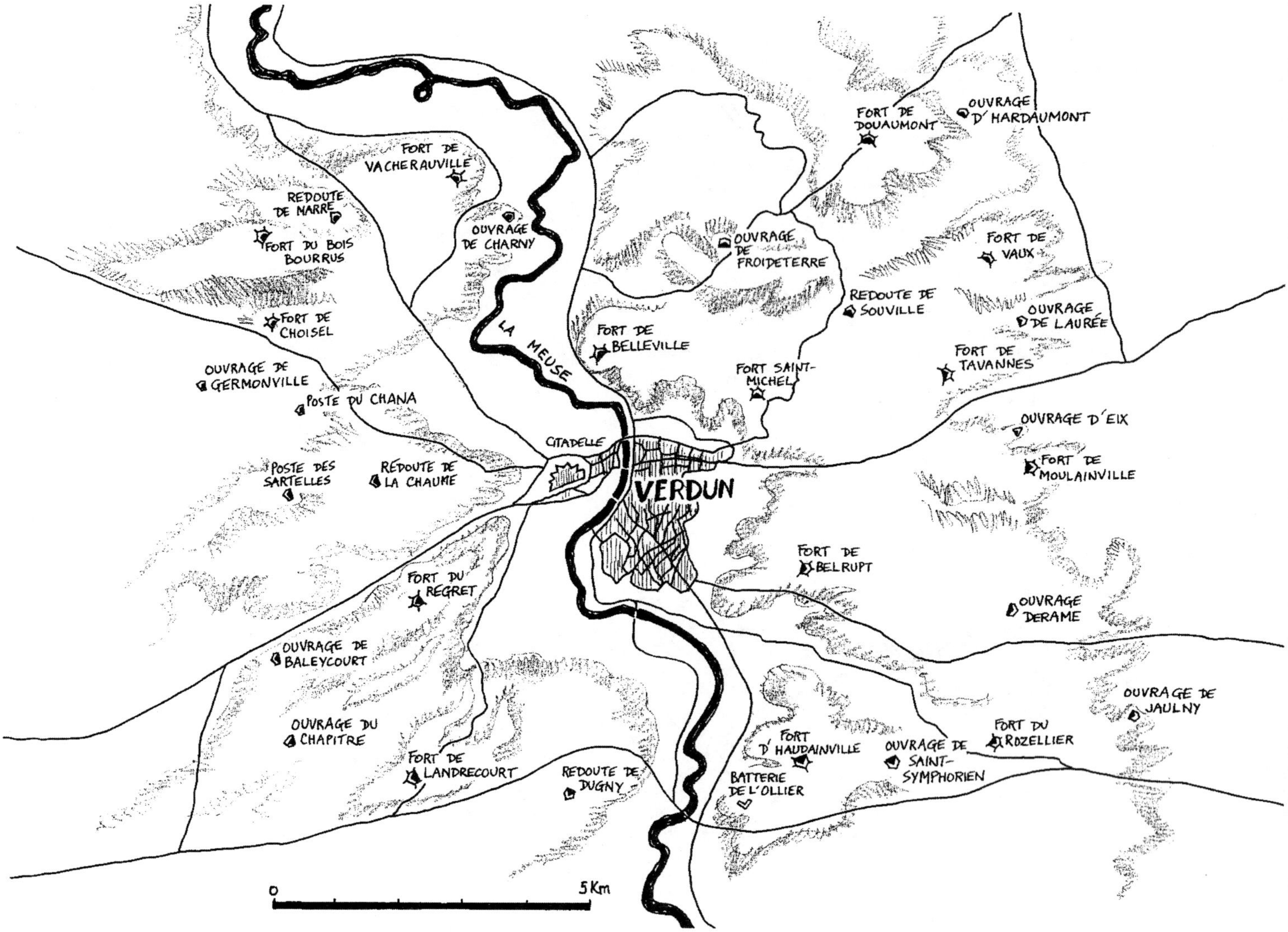

Verdun. The map shows the "camp retranché" of Verdun on the eve of World War I.

Franco-Prussian War of 1870, he was appointed engineer-general of the Eastern Army commanded by Bazaine. During the Commune of Paris he was placed at the head of the 2nd Engineer Corps of the "Versailles" army.

In July 1872 the Defense Committee was created in order to reorganize the defense of France after the disastrous 1870 war, and Séré de Rivières was placed at its head. From 1874 to 1880, he occupied the role of Director of Military Engineering Works and was tasked to reorganize the defense of France. At great cost a gigantic military program was launched in order to fortify the most important French border cities, including Boulogne-sur-Mer, Calais, Lille, Maubeuge, Nancy, Laon, Lyon, Besançon, Briançon, Dijon, Langres, and Paris. The northeast border—facing a dangerous, aggressive and hated Germany—received special attention. Four large defensive positions were established around the cities of Belfort, Epinal, Toul and Verdun. Those cities were transformed into *camps retranchés* (entrenched camps) with rings of forts around them. Between them, *rideaux défensifs* (defensive curtains) were established, composed of lines of isolated forts and gun batteries covering major crossroads, passes, river valleys, railroad lines and other weak or strategically important points. Intended to avoid the repetition of the invasion of 1870, the new fortified places were also planned to serve as offensive bases for the future reconquest of the lost provinces and to revenge the humiliation of 1870.

The new fortifications of France were a immense enterprise which took years to build and swallowed gigantic state funds, estimated at the colossal sum of 460 million Gold-Franks between 1874 and 1886. The forts were designed by the Technical Section of the French Engineer Corps and built by the *Génie* (the Engineer Corps), but private building companies were also subcontracted. Séré de Rivière's program was impressive. By 1885, 166 major forts, 43 smaller ones and about 200 batteries had been built.

41

The Second Parisian Ring of Polygonal Forts

With the tragic siege of 1870 fresh in mind, and the fact that Paris was henceforth only 250 km away from the new border with Germany, it was decided to reinforce the defenses of the capital. The existing fortifications, the enceinte of Thiers and the forts built during the period 1842–1845 having proved unable to hold the enemy at bay in 1870, a new ring of forts was planed around Paris. Built between 1874 and 1881, the new Parisian fortifications were composed of various forms of defenses with a somewhat unclear terminology.

As we have already explained, a *fort* was a strong permanent self-sufficient stronghold, a major artillery position with a permanent garrison.

A *réduit* was a complex of several defensive works, a group of strongholds to which troops could withdraw.

The difference between a *redoute* (redoubt) and an *ouvrage* (work) is not always clear; both were small forts or large gun batteries placed in intervals between major forts and usually manned only in wartime.

A *battery* was a kind of redoubt, a fortified combat emplacement including several guns of the same type firing in the same direction.

A *coupure* (cut) was probably a small battery designed to cover a vulnerable part of a fort.

The Parisian fortified belt was composed of three main strategic sections.

The *Position du Nord* (Northern Position) formed a barrier on the northern front including the following:

- Fort of Cormeilles-en-Parisis
- Ouvrages on the plateau of Cormeilles composed of battery of Borne de Marbre, battery of Moulin de Risquetout, battery of Etang, battery of Cotillons, battery of Rond Point, battery of Chapeau Rouge and redoubt of Franconville
- Fort of Montlignon
- Fort of Domont
- Battery of Blémur
- Fort of Montmorency
- Fort of Ecouen
- Redoubt of Moulin
- Battery of Sablons
- Redoubt of Butte Pinçon
- Battery of Pierrefitte
- Battery of Stains
- Fort of Stains.

The *Position de l'Est* (Eastern Position) constituted a long line of protection at the east of Paris including the following:

- Forts of Vaujours with two neighboring batteries: batterie de courtine Nord and batterie de courtine Sud
- Fort of Chelles
- Fort of Villiers-sur-Marne
- Fort of Champigny
- Fort of Sucy-en-Brie
- Battery of Limeil
- Fort of Villeneuve-Saint-Georges.

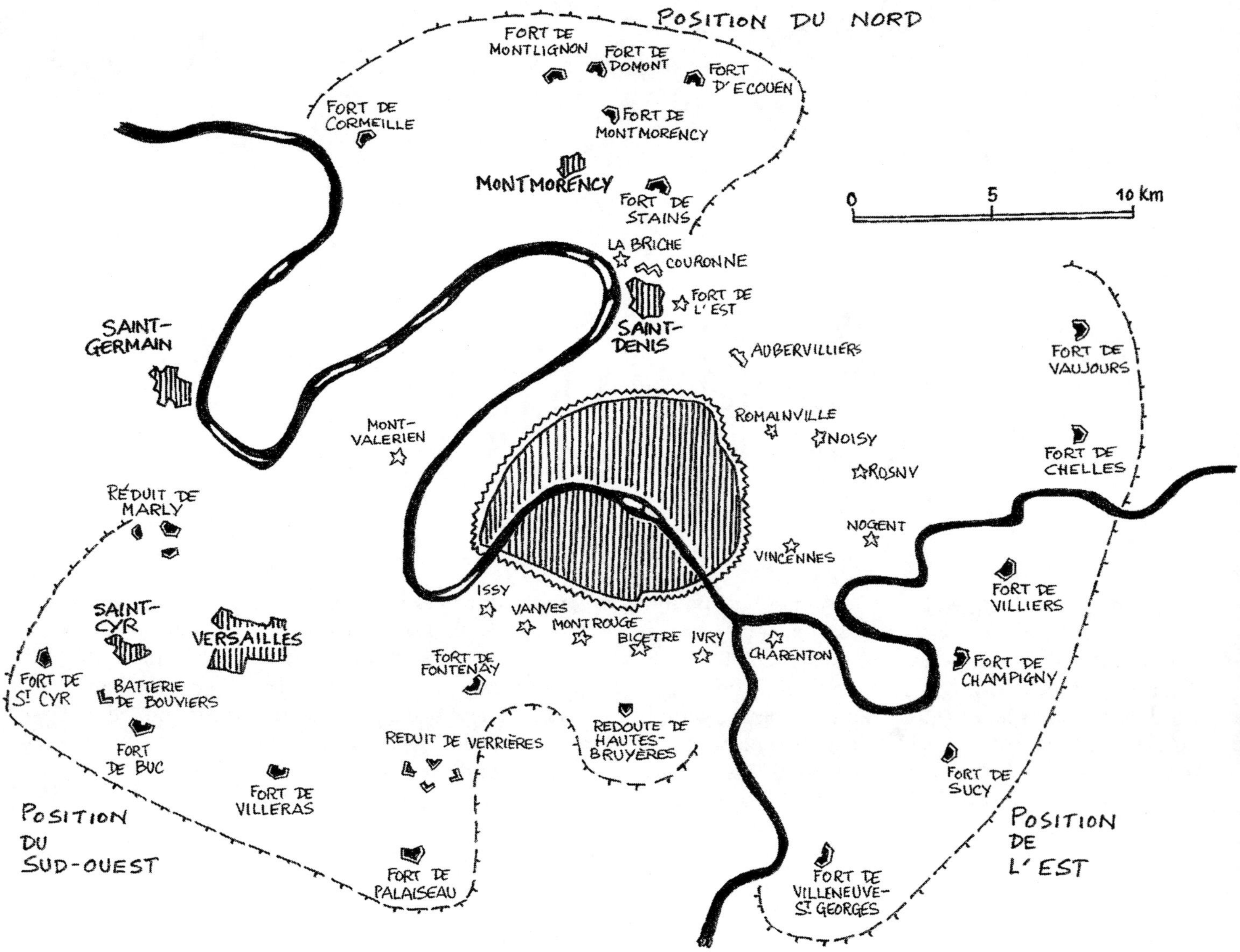

Map of the outer ring of forts (1874–1881)

The *Position du Sud-Ouest* (Southwest Position) described a large curve including the following:

- Redoubt of Hautes Bruyère (built in 1870 modified in 1874)
- Fort of Chatillon (built in 1870 modified in 1876)
- Coupure of Chatillon
- Réduit of Verrières composed of battery of Chataigneraie, battery of Terrier, battery of Gatines, battery of Igny, battery of Bièvre, fort of Palaiseau, battery of Yvette, and battery of La Pointe
- Fort of Villeras
- Fort of Haut-Buc
- Ouvrages on plateau of Satory composed of battery of Porte du Désert, battery of Station saint Cyr, battery of Ravin de Bouviers, work of Docks du Génie, and battery of Bouviers
- Fort of Saint Cyr
- Battery of Chapelle de Bois d'Arcy
- Réduit of Marly-le-Roi composed of fort of Trou-d'Enfer, battery of Arches, battery of Réservoir, battery of Noisy-le-Roi, battery of Auberderie, battery of Marly-le-Roi, and battery of Champs-de-Mars.

General Séré de Rivieres's forts were established on the heights surrounding Paris, on the very hills which the Prussians had positioned their long-range artillery during the 1870 siege. The interval between the 1842 older bastioned forts was only 3 to 5 km; the intervals between the new polygonal forts was about 12 to 20 km (that was the range of the new rifled artillery). There was no gap in the system, and each fort could cover its neighbors with its guns.

A special military strategic railway, named *Grande*

Ceinture, was established all around Paris to supply the forts with men, heavy equipment and supplies.

The forts were all different with various capacities as given by the few following examples. The fort of Chelles, built between 1876 and 1879 cost 1,260,850 francs, had a garrison of 363 soldiers serving 29 pieces of artillery. The fort of Vaujours built between 1876 and 1882 totaled 691 men serving 48 guns. The fort of Champigny, built from 1878 to 1880, cost 1,850,700 francs and had a garrison of 388 men serving 31 guns. The fort of Domont, built between 1874 and 1878 counted 1,174 soldiers serving 74 cannons.

42

Description of a Polygonal Fort

All polygonal forts were different. Either French, Dutch, Belgian, American or British, no two of them were the same as they were adapted to their local situation. The size too varied a lot depending on their task and on the terrain in which they were established. However, all of them — at least in the period 1860–1885 — had common features and consisted of the same basic elements in varying combinations.

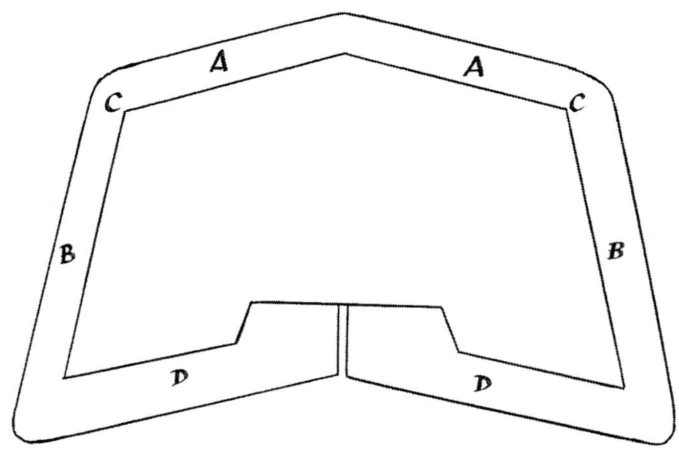

Basic elements of a polygonal fort. The sketch shows the main parts of a polygonal fort including: A A: the front turned toward the enemy. B B: the flank of the fort. C C: the shoulder, the point of junction of front and flank. D D: the "pseudo-bastioned" gorge, the rear of the fort with the entrance.

General Outline

The French polygonal forts built around Paris were of two sorts.

The first kind was a large pentagonal (five-sided) gun battery, in fact a large bastion composed of a *front* displaying two faces forming an obtuse angle turned toward the enemy and two *flanks* (sides); to this category belonged the forts of Chelles, Vaujours, Châtillon, Saint Cyr and Domont, for example.

The second sort had various regular forms: rectangle or trapezium with two caponiers, e.g. the forts of Montmorency, Montlignon, Stains, Sucy-en-Brie, Villeneuve-Saint-Georges, Palaiseau, Villeras, Buc, and Trou-d'Enfer.

In both cases, front and flanks formed a thick rampart furnished with a wallwalk and a breastwork; the combination of masonry and solid earth heaped up in front and on top of the stonework acted as a burster layer, detonating shells before they struck the fabric of the fort. Ramps gave access from the low terre-plein to the rampart.

The rear side, called the *gorge*, was the back façade of the fort turned towards the friendly side. Therefore the gorge was generally less fortified than the front and the flanks. It had, however, to be strong enough to be defensible against an enemy attacking from the back; and if the fortress was taken it was through the gorge that it would be reconquered. The gorge could have the outline of a bastioned front (called *tracé pseudo-bastionné* by the French engineers) with small flanks from which the entrance and the rear ditch could be defended. The gorge could also be a straight wall defended by a projecting caponier.

Ditch and Caponier

All forts were surrounded by a *ditch*. The Parisian forts were built on hills so the ditch could not be filled with water. Just like in the bastioned fortification, the inner wall of the ditch was called *scarp* and the outer wall was the *counterscarp*. The width of the ditch could vary from 10 to 20 m, and the depth could be between 7 and 10 m. Scarp and counterscarp walls were very often masoned, and the excavation could be fitted with various obstacles such as *abattis* (felled trees with their trimmed and sharpened branches facing the enemy), fences of strong metal bars or — later — barbed wires.

The ditch was defended by caponiers. A *caponier* was a vaulted chamber extending into the ditch fitted with loopholes enabling fire to be brought to bear on the width of the ditch. The form and the function of the caponier recalled the 15th century *moineau* or *moyenau* (an indentation with flanks placed in the middle of an overlong medieval wall) and the 16th century Italian bastion with ears. The caponier was connected to the inside of the fort by means of an underground gallery. There were often three caponiers: One *double caponier* placed at the middle of the front covering both faces; and one or two *simple caponiers* placed at the *shoulder* of the fort, at the point of junction of face and flank, each covering the flank ditch. In addition there could be a fourth caponier placed in the gorge, when the latter was not given a bastioned outline.

The defense of the ditch could also be made by means of *créneaux de pied* also called *goulottes à grenades* (hand grenade launchers), which were vertical pipes placed in the scarp to drop grenades on attackers. These apertures can be compared to the medieval *machicolations* (openings between corbels placed at the top of a wall through which missiles or other defensive material might be dropped).

Covered Way and Glacis

Just as in the bastioned fortification, the counterscarp of the polygonal fortification could be fitted with a *covered way* (for advanced defense, sortie and patrol).

There was always a broad and bare *glacis*, a long slope extending beyond the counterscarp to the natural countryside, capable of being swept by fire from the fort. The glacis could also be covered with sharp abattis and barbed wires. In addition, as the range of rifles had considerably been increased, there was a wide *nonaedificandi zone*— a wide area around the fort in which was forbidden any buildings or vegetation. In case of mobilization and war, anything interfering with the radius of fire was removed, trees cleared off, and houses and barns destroyed.

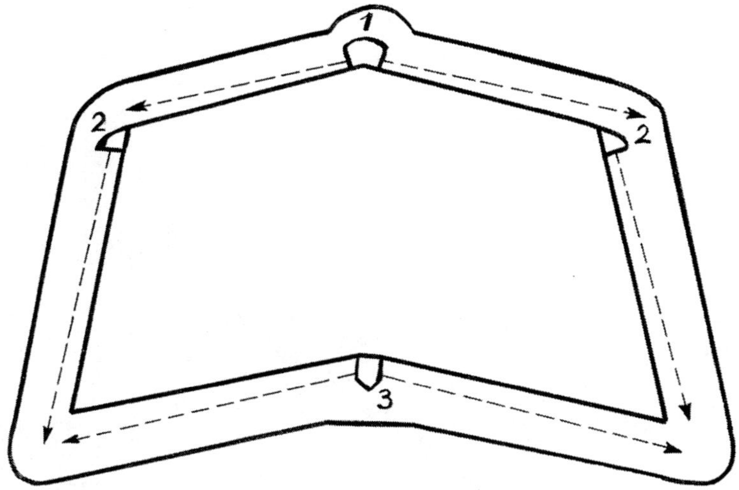

Schematic view of the caponiers. The sketch shows the places of the caponiers and their fields of fire intended for the close-range defense of the ditch including: 1: the double front caponier covering both sides of the front. 2: the shoulder caponier covering the side of the fort. 3: the gorge caponier covering the rear and the entrance to the fort.

The forts were not camouflaged, their presence was evident to anyone — including enemy intelligence — and it was also hoped that this knowledge would be a deterrent.

Gatehouse

The entrance to the fort — the most vulnerable part of the fortress— was obviously placed in the gorge, at the rear. It was defended by a caponier or a casemate placed in the flanks of the rear scarp, controlled by a guardhouse placed in a gatehouse. The gatehouse was generally soberly decorated with pilasters, a cornice and a fronton sometimes bearing the name and the date of construction of the fort.

The gate was composed of strong armored metal doors, and its access was by means of a bridge across the rear ditch. The last section was a drawbridge. To remove it, several variations were used such as lifting (vertically with chains), rolling (the roadway moving horizontally), equilibrium (with counter-weight) or swinging back in a pit.

Accommodation

The forts were not permanently occupied or armed. In peacetime only a small garrison of engineering and artillery troops maintained it. When maneuvers were held, when international tension or war demanded it, the

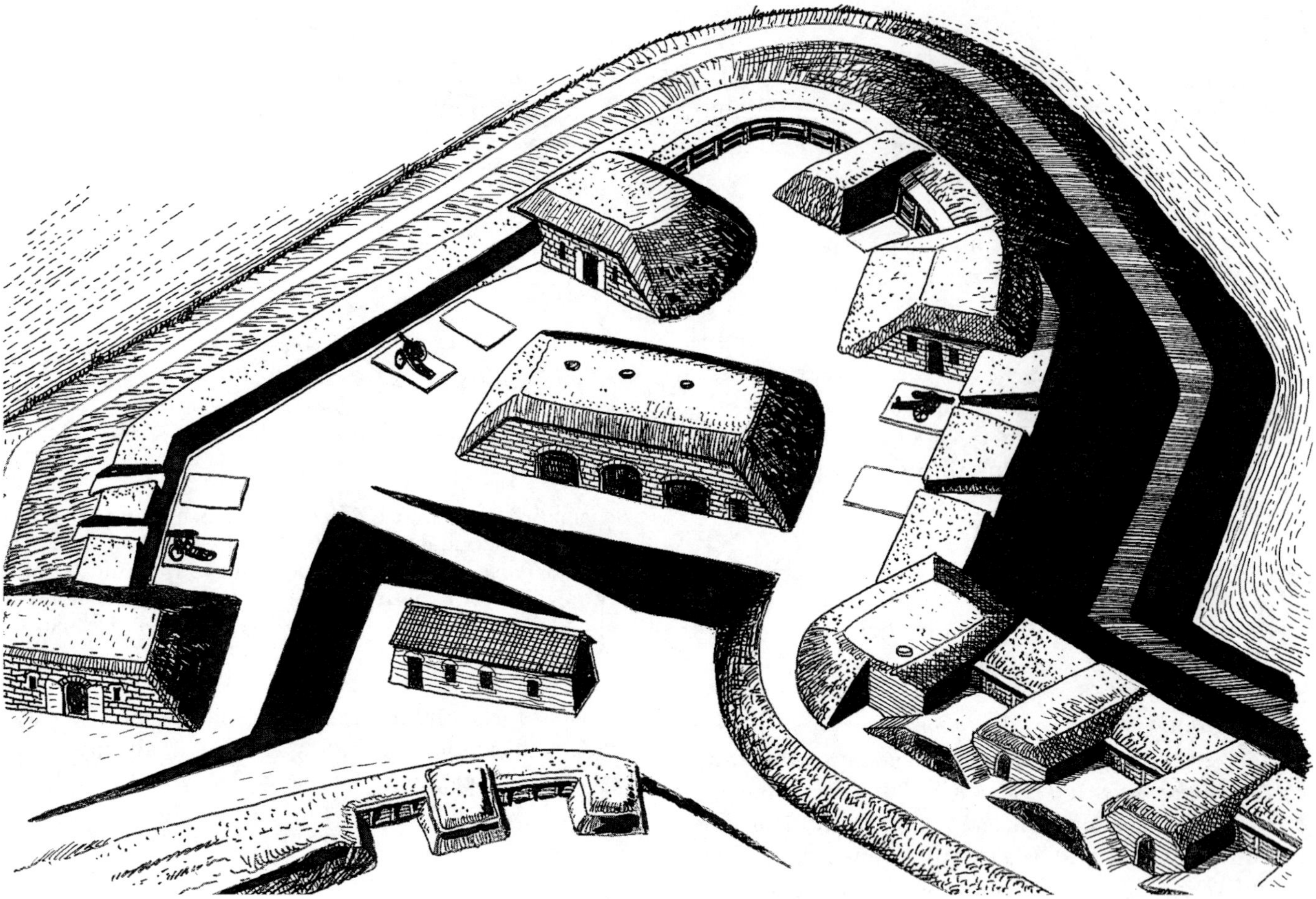

Traverses and parados

fort was put in a state of readiness, and the garrison could hold hundreds of soldiers. Each fort had to be a self-containing structure with everything prepared for a very moderately comfortable life and survival of the community, and for operation of the armament.

Bomb-proof barracks were built for the troops. They sometimes included one or two stories. They were divided into vaulted dormitories with bunks for privates and sleeping rooms for NCOs, while senior officers and the commander had their own rooms. The living quarters were heated by stoves and linked with corridors, galleries and staircases. The living quarters were placed in the gorge of the fort or on the terre-plein in its middle. Of course they were made of strong masonry covered with a thick layer of piled earth, up to five m thick, which offered good protection against enemy projectiles but made ventilation difficult. To reduce this problem, ventilation shafts and pipes were built. In some cases, the barracks opened out to a narrow yard, called *puits de lumière* (light well), and the chambers were fitted with small windows providing a minimum of light and ventilation. Close to living quarters, facilities existed such as a lavatories and washing rooms, a bakery, a kitchen, food stores, water supply (cisterns or a well), and an infirmary for small injury and light casualty. In addition, the commanding officer had a headquarter, an office for administrative affairs, and a telegraph exchange (later telephone). There was also often a *poste de police* (a prison cell) to punish undisciplined soldiers.

The façades of barracks, stores and service rooms were soberly decorated with patterns of bricks framing the few openings; some had curious "neo–Gothic" decorations. All service and living buildings were *défilés*, which means positioned in such a way as to escape from enemy view and fire as much as possible.

Powderhouse

Each fort had one or more powder houses where explosives and ammunition were stored. For safety reasons, the powder house was placed as far away as possible from the living quarters, heavily constructed, with heavy doors, strong masoned walls and a roof covered

Lahitolle Model 95 gun (1880). The breech-loading gun was mounted on a special fortress carriage for barbette fire, that is firing over the high parapet instead of firing through an embrasure. The term barbette (small beard) is said to come from the French, due to the resemblance of the parapet to a beard beneath the gun muzzle.

with a very thick layer of earth. The powder casks rested on wooden shelves and narrow shafts permitted ventilation. To prevent fire, serious measures were taken: all metal parts (e.g. locks, hinge-pins of doors) were made of bronze (which does not spark); men working in the powder house wore wooden clogs; light was provided by petroleum lamps placed in small recesses fitted with thick glass windows (these were later replaced by electric lamps). The fort also included an armory or a small arsenal where ammunition was stored, shells and cartridges were filled, and where small weapons were stored, maintained or repaired.

Artillery Emplacements

The garrison was composed of engineering troops for maintenance, artillerymen for offensive long-range firing, and riflemen for close-range defense, who were trained and drilled to closely operate together.

The pieces of rifled artillery were mounted on a metal carriage with two big wheels. They were intended for long-range firing at the enemy and—should it be needed—to support by their fire a neighboring fort being attacked. In peacetime the guns were stored in garages and shelters. In operation they were hauled along shallow ramps and placed on the rampart in the open, which allowed the fumes of a discharge to clear quickly. They were protected at the front behind the *parapet*, a breastwork made of masonry and thick earth. The gun emplacements were divided into compartments so that, in case of a direct hit, the damage was limited. For this purpose emplacements were fitted with *traverses* (raised earth banks placed at the sides) to protect from enfilade and raking fire, and *parados* at the back, which were traverses protecting from splinters and fire from the rear. Parapets, traverses and parados were made of masonry holding a thick layer of earth; they could also be reinforced with various revetment e.g. *fascines* (large bundles of brushwood), *gabions* (large wicker baskets filled with earth), sod, sandbags, hurdles and planks.

Another possibility was to place guns mounted on a swiveling carriage within a so-called *Haxo casemate.* Named after the inventor—the French general and military engineer François-Nicolas Haxo (1774–1838)—such a gun emplacement combined good protection and good

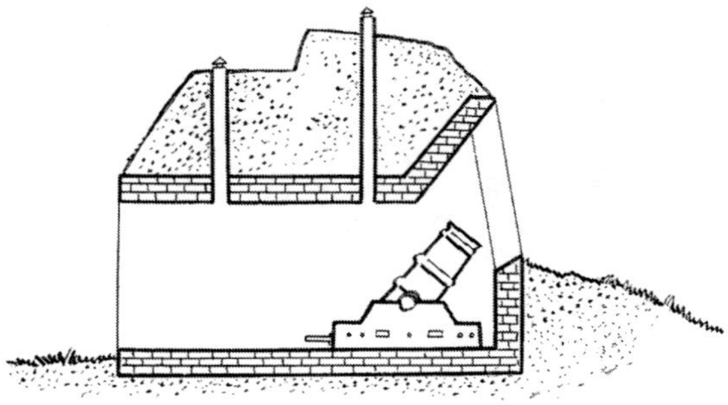

Cross section of a Haxo casemate for mortar

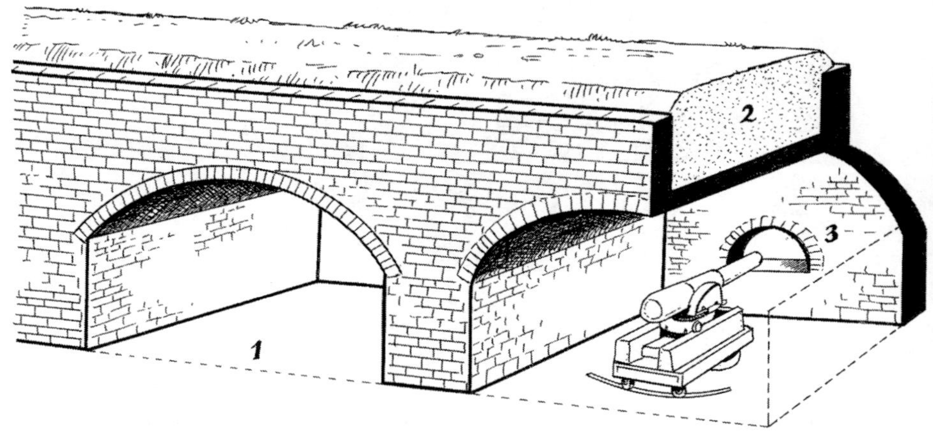

Haxo casemate. The so-called Haxo casemate was generally 3 m high and 8 m long. It was opened at the rear (1), masoned, and covered with earth (2). The firing chamber was of course fitted with a gun port (3).

Fort of Chelles (1876)

Haxo casemate (back view)

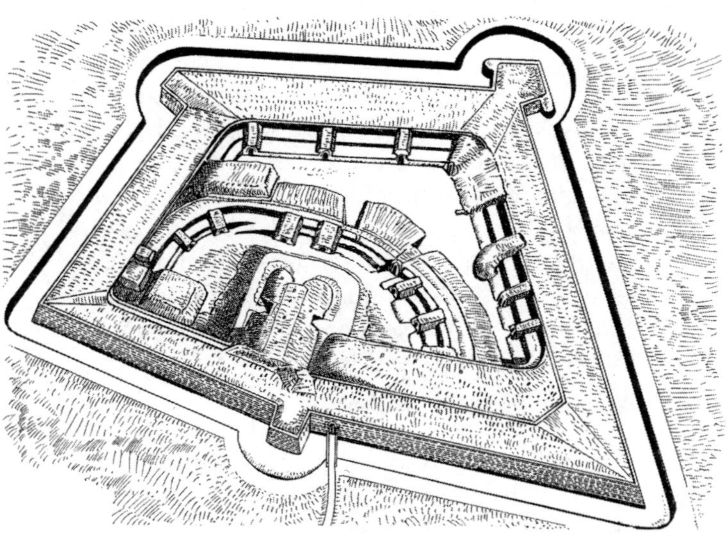

Fort of Montmorency (1875)

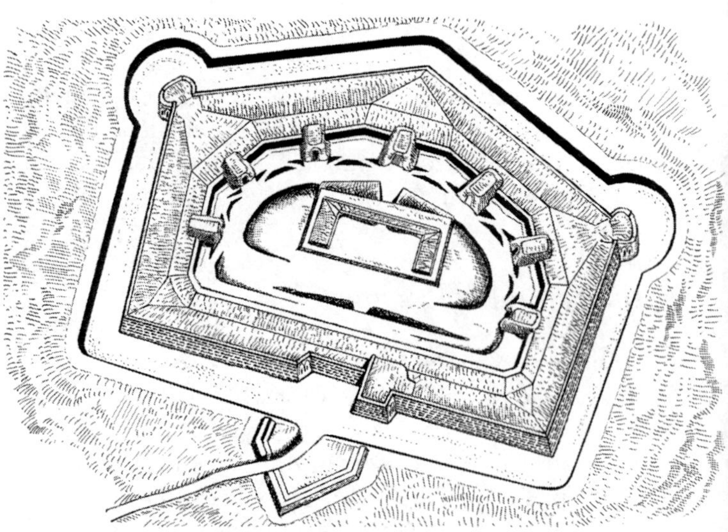

Redoubt of Verrières (1875)

ventilation. The Haxo casemate was a vaulted fire chamber formed in the rampart under the parapet; it was fitted at the front with an opening, named *embrasure*, through which the gun was fired; it was built in masonry and covered with a thick layer of earth; the back of the casemate was fully open, permitting the smoke of the discharge to clear rapidly. The Haxo casemate could also house a heavy high-angle firing mortar; in that case the sole (bottom surface) of the embrasure was sloped upwards.

Some French forts included a *cavalier*, an additional raised wide terrace — higher than the parapet — where the guns were placed in order to have a larger command of the surrounding countryside. However, the drawback was that the high cavalier was conspicuous and could present an easy target to enemy artillery. This was why, after 1880, the cavalier was abandoned and the forts were given a very low profile, slightly higher than the surrounding ground, to limit the vulnerability.

Cross section infantry parapet. The schematic view shows the following:

1. Ditch.
2. Scarp of the fort.
3. Parapet.
4. Fire-step.
5. Abri-traverse (shelter).

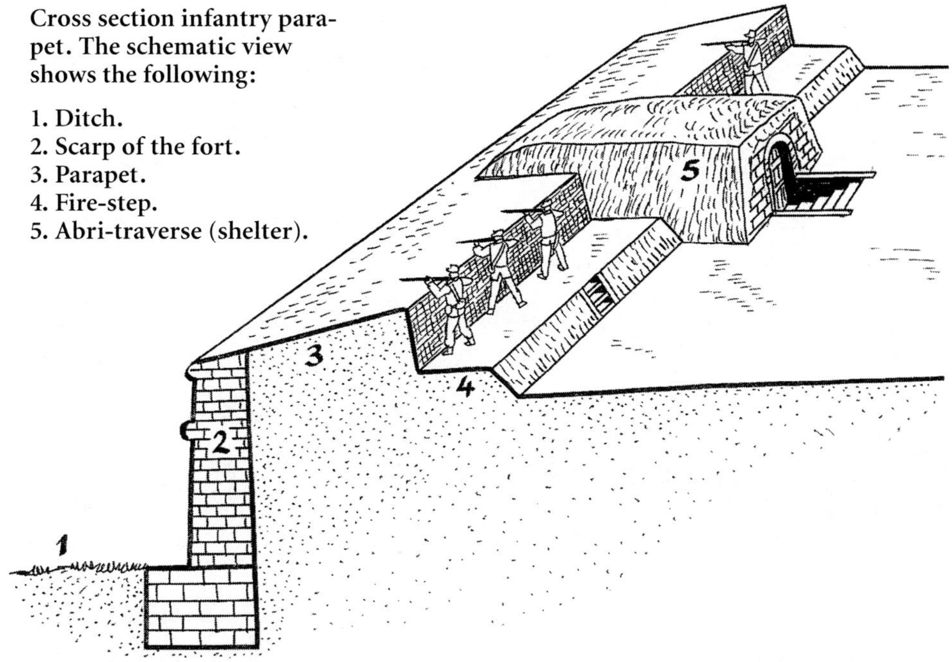

Infantry Positions

The riflemen manned the caponiers in the ditches and were deployed in the open for close-range defense. They were protected by a thick breastwork furnished with a *banquette* or *fire-step*, a narrow platform on which they stood to fire; after shooting they could step down and thus were completely protected by the parapet.

At regular intervals along the parapet perpendicular *abri-traverses* were built. These were small shelters made of masonry covered with earth inside which riflemen and gunners could seek refuge (e.g. when the fort was heavily shelled prior to an assault). The shelters also provided cover against enfilade and raking fire, and they could be used as ammunition stores.

Réduit

In the polygonal forts built in the period 1850–1885 in Britain, The Netherlands, Belgium and Germany, there was quite often a *réduit* (redoubt), a closed independent self-defensible work, a stronghold within the fort to which the garrison could retire when the rest of the fort was taken. Of various size and strength, the réduit was always placed in the gorge. It can be compared to the medieval *keep*, the residential and strongest tower of the castle of the Middle Ages. The réduit was often used as quarters for the garrison, and headquarters and administration place for the commander. It included many facilities such as kitchen, troop chambers, rooms for officers, supply stores, infirmary, ammunition store and arsenal, observatory, own glacis and ditch, own gate, and close-range combat emplacements etc.

Opinion was divided regarding the last stand keep. Some military engineers maintained that the keep stiffened resistance and allowed the garrison to withdraw to a position from which it might later sally out and recapture the fort. Others felt it encouraged the idea of retreat. In the French forts of the same period, the réduit was always omitted for psychological reasons: the French high command considered that without a safe place to withdraw the defenders had no other choice than to fight to the bitter end or to abandon the work and retreat at the right time. In the end, the French were right. As a matter of fact, if the attacking party got this close, the fort and its keep were as good as lost. Depending on tactical conditions of course, it is well known that a withdrawal in good order is often a better move than a desperate fight till the last man. After 1885, attached réduits were abandoned as relics of old-fashioned thinking.

Redoubts and Batteries

The intervals between the new forts was about 12 to 20 km, and — to fill the gaps in the defensive system,

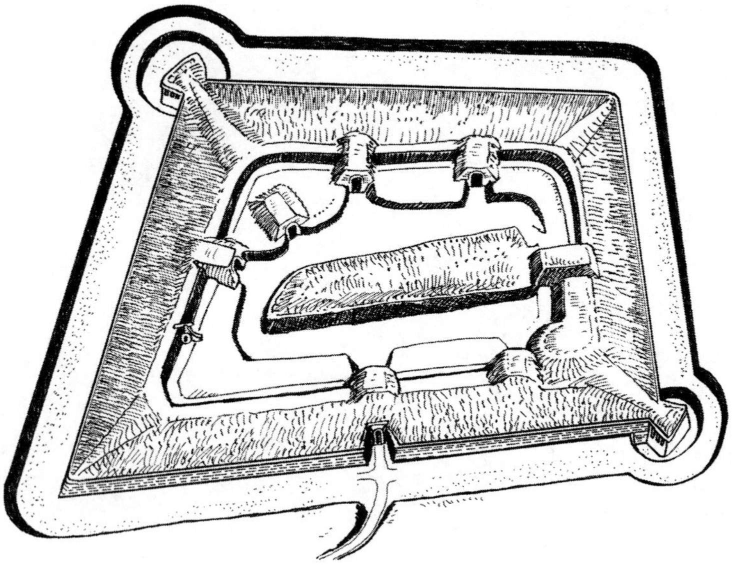

Redoubt of Franconville (1875)

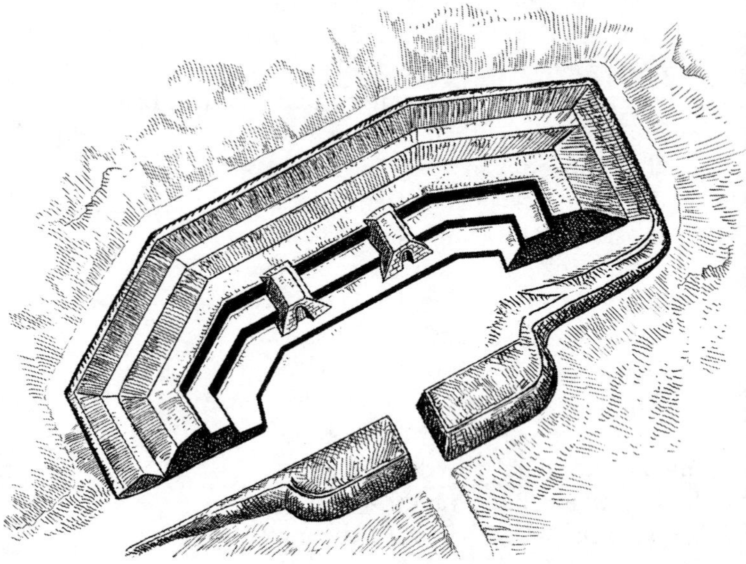

Battery of Champs-de-Mars (1876)

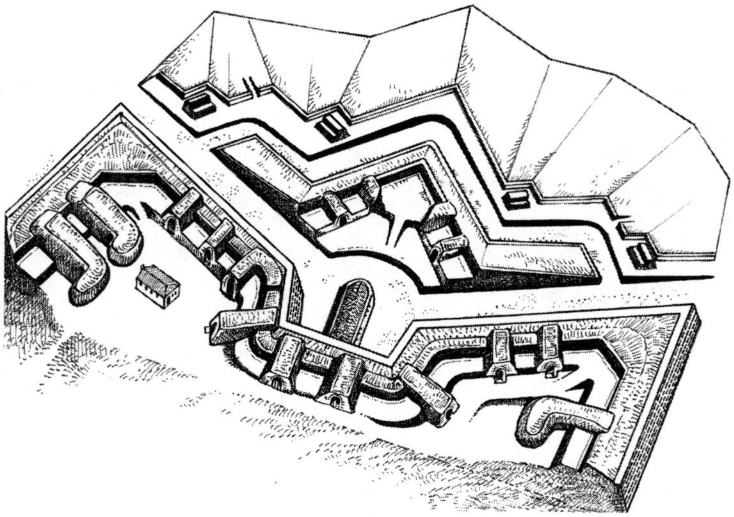

Ouvrages des Docks du Génie (1875)

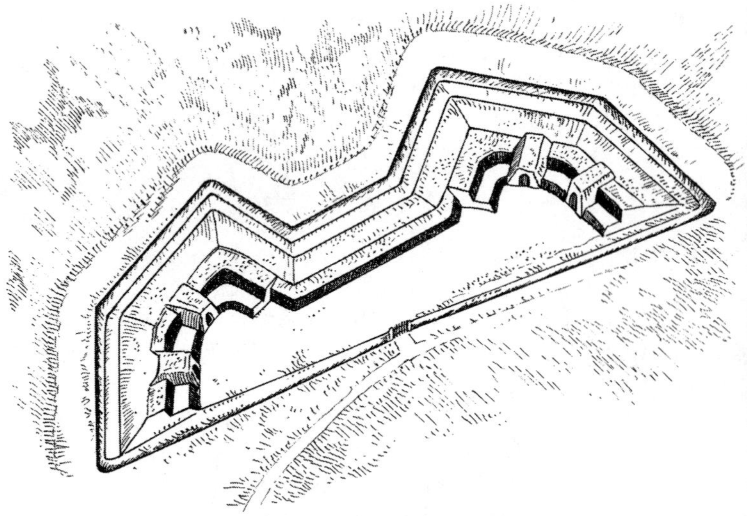

Battery of Terrier (1875)

according to local situation — redoubts and batteries were built as reinforcement; so each fort with its annexes could cover its neighbors with its guns.

Shapes, degree of protection, armament and garrison of redoubts, ouvrages and batteries varied a lot according to the task they had to perform and depending on the local situation. Some were small independent enclosed pentagonal fortlets with a ditch defended by caponiers (e.g. redoubt of Verrières, battery of Chataigneraie, battery of Gâtines, battery of Bièvres). Other were trapezium shaped (e.g. battery of Limeil, battery of Bouviers, battery of Bois-d'Arcy). Others were very simple earth entrenchments composed of a main front and no or little protection at the back (e.g. battery of Terrier, battery of Champs-de-Mars).

In times of war, notably during the 1914 German offensive that threatened Paris, redoubts, ouvrages and batteries were reinforced with improvised fieldworks including trenches, concrete infantry shelters, and barbed wire networks.

43

The Crisis of the 1880s

New Projectiles

In the early 1880s, fortress engineers must have believed that they had so refined the design of defensive structures that the ideal of the impregnable fortress had been achieved. Those who thought so were wrong. Although artillery had improved in the period 1860–1880, recoil mechanisms were primitive, good fire-control instruments were as yet unknown, high explosive and slow-burning powders had scarcely been tried.

The rapid development of artillery and projectiles at the end of the 19th century turned the contest between attack and defense into a desperate race. While France and the major industrialized nations spent enormous fortunes to protect their frontiers with masoned polygonal forts, a crisis suddenly broke out.

About 1880, appeared antipersonnel projectiles such as the *shrapnel shell*, which exploded in the air in numerous deadly balls with devastating effects for non-fully protected soldiers. In 1884 a French chemist, named Vieille, invented the first satisfactory smokeless powder which neither gave away the gun's position nor obscured battlefields and casemated firing chambers with clouds of toxic fume.

By 1885, new chemical propellant appeared, replacing the traditional black gunpowder. The new substances (nitro-lignose, cordite, nitro-cellulose, pitric acid under various names such as lyddite, melinite or shimose etc.) were smokeless and far more powerful than the traditional corned black gunpowder. The new high explosives underwent molecular disruption and chemical recombination, detonating as a disruptive wave moving at 3,000 m a second or more. They permitted the development of shells with an enormous penetration and an extremely high shattering effect. In 1886, significant experiments were performed by the French army at Fort Malmaison near Soissons. The damage done was amazingly extensive and the results seemed quite conclusive: the new ammunition — soon fitted with a fuse in the nose — could plunge through earth and smashed masonry, exploding inside the fortifications, stripping away whole sections of retaining wall, blasting away the guns placed in casemates while soldiers would be pulverized, entombed and poisoned with fumes. Larger and more powerful guns could be built, and advances in weapons rapidly and dramatically increased the lethality of the battlefield. In less than a decade, high explosives made existing fortifications obsolete.

Concrete Protection

The tremendous improvement of artillery in the late 1880s resulted in a policy of burying everything possible and relying on armored steel turrets (some being retractable or "disappearing") and concrete casemates to deliver the fire necessary both to deal with an enemy at a distance and protect the immediate environs of the work from assault. Fortification entered into the age of concrete and metal armor.

Liquid concrete — a mixture of cement, water, sand and gravel — was poured between wooden shuttering around an internal skeleton of iron rods; when solidified, concrete walls and roofs could be as thick as 1 or 2

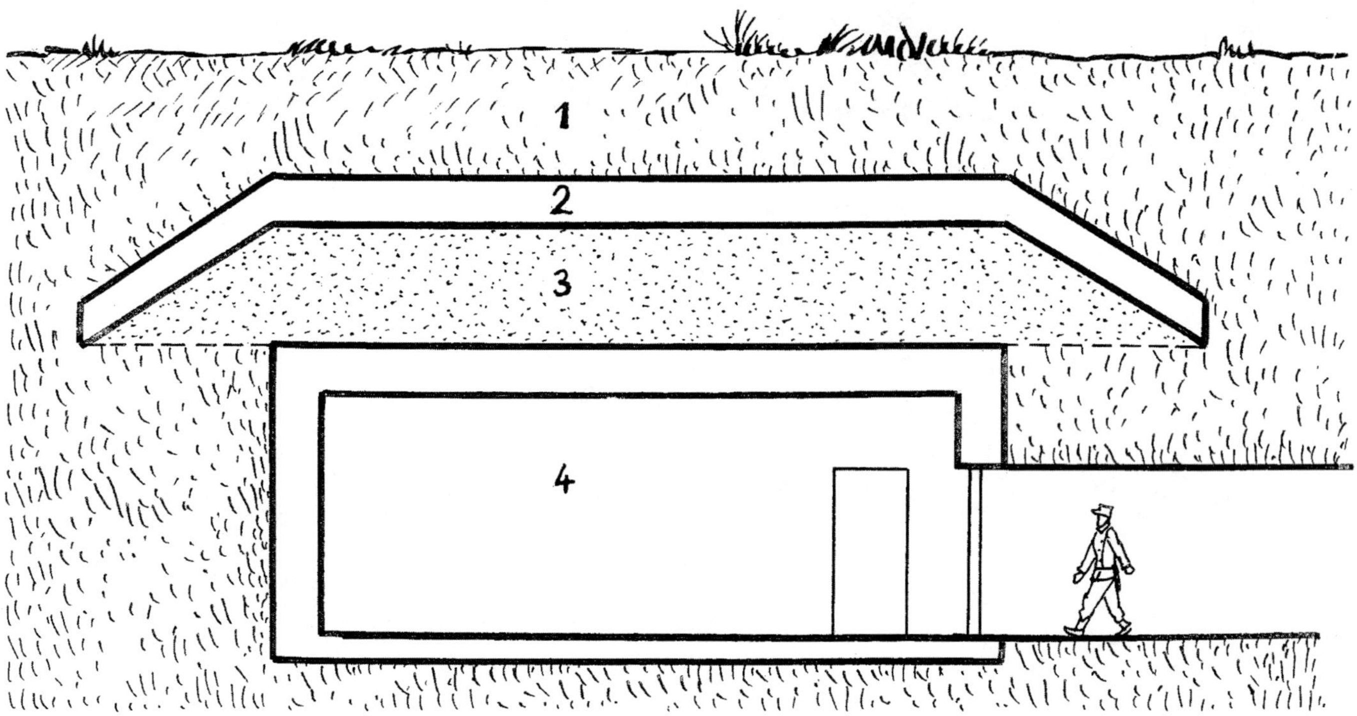

Cross section concrete reinforcement. 1. Earth cover. 2. Concrete burster layer. 3. Bed of sand. 4. Original masoned chamber.

m, overhead protection and camouflage being further enhanced by a layer of earth and grass.

The French developed a special form of armor, a sort of "second skin" over many of their existing forts, principally those located near the border with Germany. This skin — placed above an existing masoned chamber for example — consisted of a 3-m-thick layer of earth, then a 1-m-thick concrete burster layer (extending well beyond the underground chamber to guard against oblique shots), then a 1-m-thick layer of sand. The projectile would be slowed down by the earth and stopped and burst by the concrete and the sand would absorb the explosion wave and prevent the destruction of the substructure.

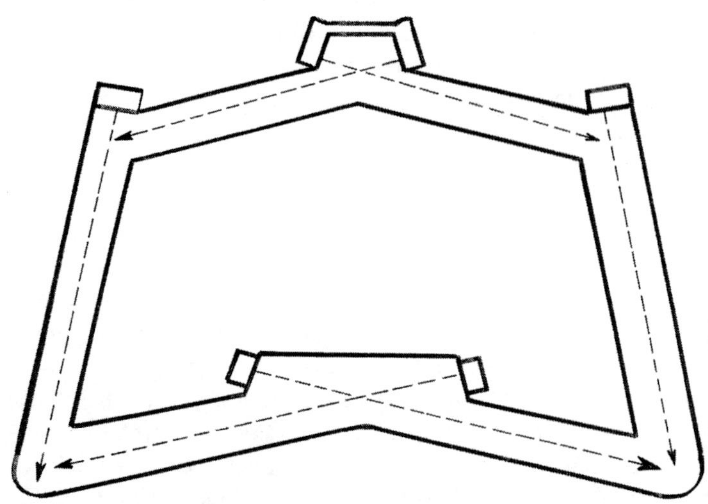

Schematic view of the "coffers." Placed under the counterscarp, the so-called coffers were much less vulnerable than the previous caponiers.

Counterscarp Coffer

The masoned caponiers for close-range defense of the ditch, proved extremely vulnerable to the new high explosive projectiles. They were replaced by concrete casemates, named *coffres de contrescarpe*, placed under the counterscarp at the angles of the front ditch. They were fitted with embrasures and their own ditches. They were manned by soldiers armed with modern rifles, machine guns or quick-firing guns. The communication between the counterscarp coffers and the core of the fort was done via an underground tunnel.

Gradually, the glacis of the fort was covered by a thick and impassible network of barbed wires and later antipersonnel mines.

Armored Turret

The devastating effect of the new projectiles made open-air artillery unsuitable. Guns had to be placed in totally protected emplacements.

One solution was the "disappearing" or articulated

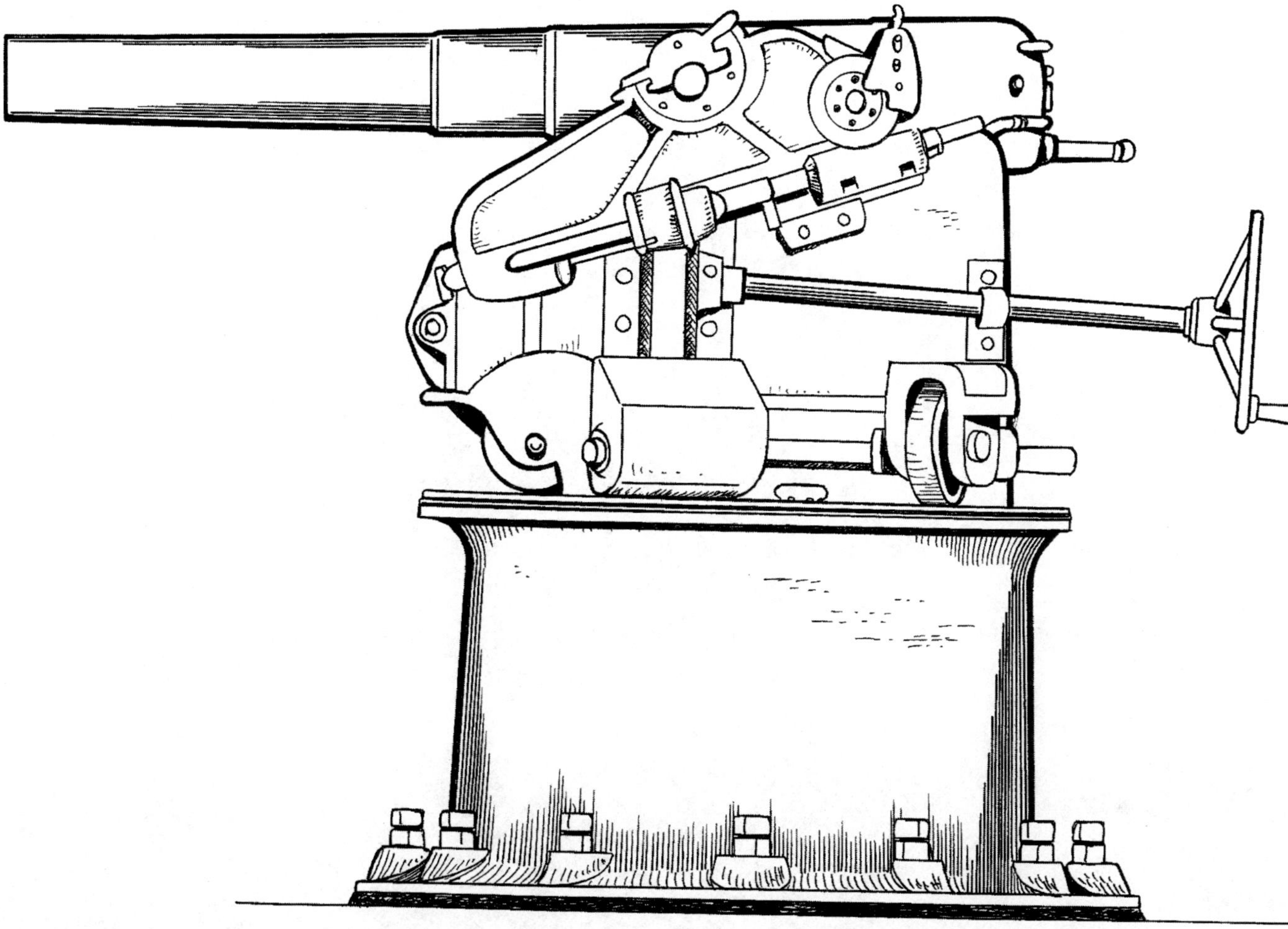

Six cm Schneider casemate gun (1908). This breechloading rifled gun, used in the period 1900–1914, could be placed either inside a casemate or in an armored turret. It was served by one NCO and three gunners. It could fire either a high explosive shell of 2.7 kg or an antipersonnel shrapnel round containing 80 balls.

mounting in which the gun popped up, banged away and disappeared by force of its own recoil below a sunken concrete pit for covered reloading, thus not presenting a permanent target to enemy fire. Whether accurate or not, this mounting was expensive and offered only frontal protection; guns and servants were still vulnerable to plunging high trajectory fire from mortars.

A solution was to place guns in a concrete casemate whose embrasure was covered by a thick plate of steel. Tested at Bourges in 1889, these sorts of firing chambers (called *casemates de Bourges*) were placed for flanking role at the rear of a fort, thus concealed from enemy view and fire.

Rapidly it appeared that the best solution was to mount guns on armored turrets, a practice already applied to modern battleships. This was pioneered by the Prussian Lieutenant-Colonel Shumann and developed in Germany by engineer Hermann Gruson of Krupp's Steel Company and by the French engineer Mougin from the Saint Chamont Armament Company. The result was a new trend in military architecture featuring a breechloading rifle ordnance mounted in revolving armored cupolas— something like an upturned metal saucer. The armored cupola had an all-around traverse (moving and able to fire in any direction); its rim was concealed beneath a monolithical apron of thick concrete, further shielded by a thick pack of earth, grass and bushes. A more refined system was the "disappearing" armored turret, which — provided with short guns— was retractable: the device was raised by counterweights for firing and lowered for reloading or when not in operation. As a result, the only visible feature from a distance was a grassy mount with a few turret roofs flush with the surface.

The targets did not even have to be within sight of the fort. Thanks to accurately printed maps, fire-control instruments and communications, it was possible for a garrison of gunmen and signal troops— expert in serving modern guns and modern communication means— to completely dominate large portions of the surrounding countryside. But the increase in protection offered by

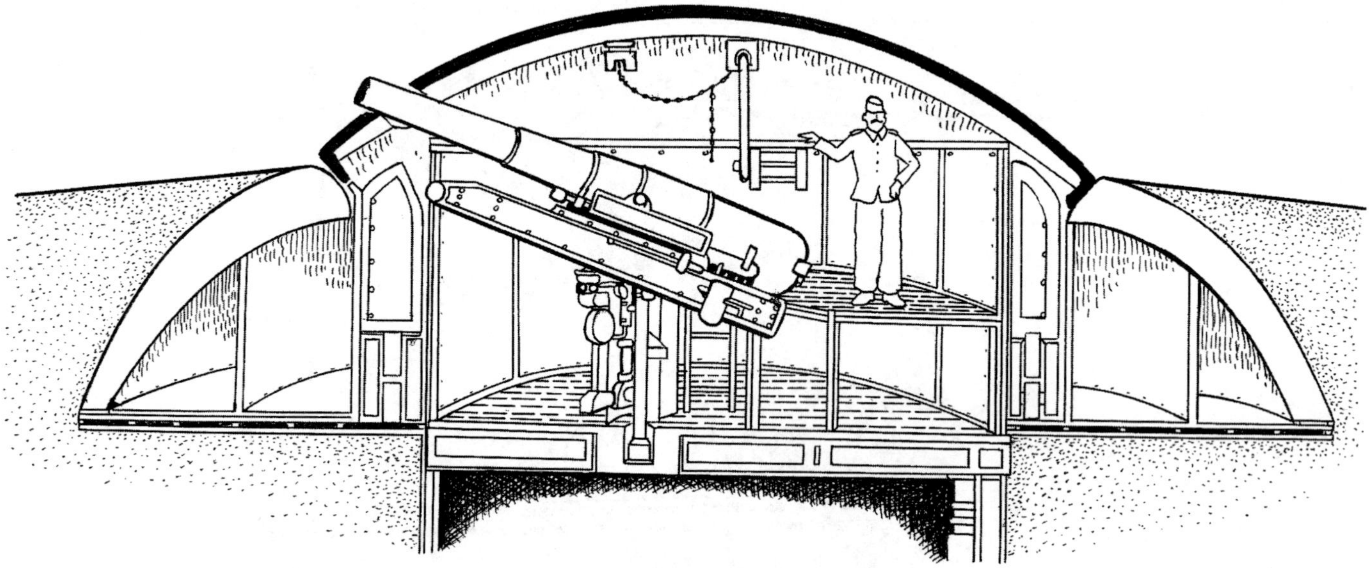

Schneider Le Creusot armored turret (ca. 1900). The turret is seen here in cross section. Under the fully rotating turret were mechanisms for operating, an ammunition store (with lift), crew quarters, and communication tunnels with the rest of the fort.

revolving armored turrets was not without disadvantages; due to their high cost, forts saw their fire-power vastly reduced from that considered advisable in previous years. Moreover turrets could only be armed with comparatively light guns, which could engage only one target at a time.

Dessus and Dessous

A modern fort at the close of the 19th century was like a land warship. From then on, it was divided into two parts. Parapets and traverses, open artillery emplacements were all removed; the *dessus* (top structures) were the only visible things at its top, including the low armored artillery turrets, a few armored observation cupolas, the entrances, and the occasional ventilator, air shafts and rifle port. The *dessous* (underground structures) were all buried as deep under the ground as possible; the ammunition magazines, stores, workshops, headquarters, telephone exchange, infirmary, plants to move the turrets, barracks and accommodation for the garrison were connected by passages, tunnels and galleries. Indeed all was subterranean, illuminated by electricity produced by internal combustion engines, electricity which also powered all the machinery necessary for living in and operating the fort — notably the ventilation system, and the power-driven hoists supplying guns with rounds. Fortress troops became troglodytes.

A New Era

Military architecture had entered a new era, and needless to say it was a very costly era as such sophisticated forts with all their refinements cost a fortune to build and to maintain. The gigantic cost, the increasing complexity of equipment demanding specialist technicians, the mass production, accumulation and maintenance of reserve stockpiles of equipment and supplies, the development of communication systems, and the speed at which new devices were designed, updated and introduced determined that the wars of the first half of the 20th century would be what the Germans called *die Materielschlacht* (the Battle of Material).

The French — who had invested colossal funds in Séré de Rivières's masoned fortification — could not update all their defenses. The 1874 forts around Paris were left as they were. The gigantic funds demanded for modernization were employed to readapt the forts near the frontier with Germany.

Opposite: **Fort of Douaumont (Verdun). Part of the position of Verdun, the fort of Douaumont was built in 1882. After the introduction of new explosives about 1885, the fortress was reconstructed and improved between 1899 and 1914. The original "polygonal" design was modified. All service facilities were made of concrete and buried under the ground, well able to withstand shell fire. The armament included one 75 mm gun (1), one 155 mm gun (2), and machine-guns (3), all placed in armored turrets. Quick-firing guns were placed in casemates de Bourges at the rear (4). Close defense depended upon belts of barbed wire, and the ditch was covered by machine guns placed inside counterscarp coffers (5), replacing the vulnerable caponiers. The coffers were linked to the fort by galleries passing under the ditch. Fort Douaumont was captured by the Germans in February 1916, and retaken by the French in October 1916.**

44

Paris at the Close of the 19th Century

World Exhibition Fairs

After healing the terrible wounds inflicted by the Franco-Prussian War and the Commune, Paris developed towards the west along Boulevard Malesherbes, Park Monceau, in Chaillot, Passy, along the Champs-Elysées, Invalides and Champs-de-Mars. The Industrial Revolution reached its zenith, and France was passing through a phase of economic prosperity which was given a concrete expression in several impressive buildings.

The *Hôtel de Ville*, in the center of a huge square near the Seine (Place de Grève, used as a port) was for ages the site of public executions. Over the centuries, the City Hall has been the scene of major events with historical significance for both Paris and France. Previously built in Gothic style in the Middle Ages, it was rebuilt in a 16th century Renaissance style by architect Domenico da Cortona. The building was intentionally destroyed by fire during the Commune insurrection of 1871. The actual City Hall was rebuilt in 1882 after a design by architects Deperthes and Ballu. It is an imposing and original building with pavillions surmounted by domes in the shape of truncated pyramids and decorated with a forest of 136 statues.

Other marks of prosperity were industrial and world exhibitions. Those of 1889 and 1900 were an opportunity for great works, some elements of which have been preserved, such as the Eiffel Tower, the Grand Palais, the Petit Palais, the bridge Alexander III and the Orsay railway station for example.

The *Eiffel Tower* is truly the symbol of Paris. Originally it was temporarily erected for the World Fair of 1889 to be a witness of man's inborn will to build something capable of demonstrating the measure of his genius. In the Industrial Revolution, a time of progress and scientific conquest, architecture had undergone radical changes; glass, steel, iron and concrete were the new construction materials, suitable for making buildings lighter and more dynamic. Designed by engineer Gustave Eiffel, the Tower is 300 m (1,050 feet) high, and at the time of its construction was the highest building in the world. It is, however, extremely light (7,000 metric tons) as it is an interlaced structure comprising some 15,000 pieces of metal welded together. It rests on four enormous pilons with cement bases, and participates as one of the most beautiful sights of Paris, stretching from the Palais of Chaillot, the Jena bridge, the Eiffel Tower, the Champs-de-Mars and the Ecole Militaire. It has three floors: the first at 187 feet, the second at 377 feet and the third at 899 feet; on each of them there are bars and restaurants allowing tourists to pause and enjoy the unique breath-taking panoramic view over the whole of Paris.

The World Fair of 1900 was an important step in the history of the architecture of Paris. For the occasion, monuments of art were created, with huge dimensions and characterized by ample colonnades, friezes and sculptural compositions. The *Grand Palais*, designed by architects Deglane and Louvet, has a Ionic façade, is 787 feet long and 65 feet high. Part of it is permanently occupied by the *Palais de la Découverte* (Discovery Palace), cele-

Opposite: **Eiffel Tower**

brating man's conquest in science, another part is used for important artistic events, fairs, motor shows and similar major exhibitions.

The *Petit Palais,* designed by architect Charles Girault in 1900, consists of a monumental portico crowned by a dome and flanked by colonnades. It contains the collections of the City of Paris formed by numerous 19th century paintings and sculptures.

In 1899 work started on the *Métropolitain* (underground railway) designed by engineer Fulgence Bienvenüe; the first subterranean *métro* line, from the Porte-de-Vincennes to the Etoile Square was completed in 1900.

La Belle Epoque

The second half of the 19th century saw the constitution of a French colonial empire comprising Algeria, Tunisia, and Viet Nam, as well as territories in Africa including Senegal, Sudan, Dahomey, Congo, and Madagascar; the French regarded themselves as modern and advanced people bringing *the* civilization everywhere they ruled.

The years before 1914 were called the *Belle Epoque* (Good Time) during which the bourgeoisie considered themselves quite happy and respectable. Before the first world war, a cultivated and wealthy Parisian bourgeois was an elegant gentleman who lived in nice apartments in one of the Beaux Quartiers, invested his savings in industry, trade and Russian shares, shopped in the Galeries Lafayette or the Printemps warehouses, drove a Peugeot or Delahaye automobile, admired impressionist and fauvist paintings, read literature by Verlaine and Maupassant, listened to music by Debussy and Ravel, attended the Comédie Française theater where actress Sarah Berhard performed, and at night went to a Café-Concert to enjoy girls dancing the French Cancan, or an opérette with dynamic music by Jacques Offenbach, after which he and his joyful friends had supper with champagne at Maxim's restaurant.

The working class, however, did not benefit very much from all this prosperity and social laws were still rather half-hearted. Strikes and violent incidents took place with increasing frequency and were harshly repressed by the mounted gendarmerie and the army.

At the limits of Paris, Thiers's wall and grassy embankments gradually lost their military character and were transformed into a promenade. The ditch and the glacis turned into a true slumbelt, popularly known as the *Fortifs* (short for fortifications), covered with shabby plank huts and carts surrounded by gardens and occupied by tens of thousands of jobless, social drop-outs and Gypsies. The *Fortifs* were a place of prostitution and at night a very unsafe area infested with *Apaches* (criminals), *mauvais garçons* (bad boys) and other thugs.

There was a terrible flood of the Seine River in 1910.

A Fragile Peace

During the peace of the late 19th century, uncertain and unstable as it was, wealth had accumulated prodigiously, machinery had vastly improved and activity of every kind had developed. The world was dominated by Europe, and above all by Great Britain, but, in spite of the "European Concert," the seeds of world conflict were maturing. The Russo-Japanese War, the collapse of the Ottoman Empire, agitation in Austria-Hungary, tension between France and Germany about Morocco, wars in the Balkans, growing aggressive nationalism everywhere, feverish rearmament with weapons of mass destruction, and the constitution of large alliances led to an explosive situation. August 1914 marked the end of an era.

45

The First World War (1914–1918)

The Early Stage of the War

The pretext for war was the assassination of Archduke Franz-Ferdinand, heir to the throne of Austria-Hungary, on June 28, 1914, in Sarajevo in Bosnia. The Austrians held Serbia responsible. The interplay of alliance brought all the leading European powers into war in August. Russia mobilized to defend its ally Serbia, involving France and Great Britain, while Germany went to war to support its ally Austria.

France mobilized 3,600,000 men and Germany rather more. French soldiers wore red trousers and blue coats, which were far too easily seen, while the Germans had adopted *Feldgrau* (verdigris or greyish green) as the color of their uniform. Both sides had excellent rifles, Lebel and Mauser. The Germans had powerful, heavy guns; France boasted good light artillery, notably the famous 75 cm with recoil system.

On August 2, 1914, the German army invaded neutral Belgium, smashed the Belgian forts of Liege and Antwerp with huge mortars and menaced northern France. Meanwhile the French made a generalized attack through Alsace, an offensive quickly blunted. In the north, the battle of Charleroi went badly for France, Belgium was entirely occupied and the Germans swept on towards Paris. The French commander in chief, General Joseph Joffre, ordered a wide retreat and—with reorganized forces—launched his great offensive on the Marne. After several days of fierce combats (September 7–11, 1914), the Germans were stopped and had to retreat. In order to get fresh troops to the front, the French army had mobilized the taxis, busses and private trucks of Paris, which thus contributed to the successful outcome of the battle. The victory of the Marne had saved Paris, indeed, France, but the war was not over. After savage fighting, each army trying to turn its adversary's flank, the front stabilized without any decisive victories from Belgium to the Vosges mountains in an enormous arc. The rich and industrialized northern departments were all in German hands. Each camp had believed that the war would be of short duration; in fact it continued for four years in extremely harsh and difficult conditions.

The men who led the armies of all combatants in World War I were unable to cope with a war which produced such tactical innovations. Matters were simply beyond their competence; they had to deal with problems for which their experience and training had not equipped them, and few military leaders displayed much imagination in tackling them. The rate of technological advance, exceeding military authorities' ability to understand it, resulted in enormous butchery on the battlefield.

Trench Warfare

The next stage of the conflict was a terrible war of attrition with opponents entrenched in large field fortification networks. In order to maintain their positions in the face of the enemy, the armies dug in, in trenches set out in parallel lines linked by narrow zigzagging communication sappes. They were protected by mines and barbed wire, while the no man's land was swept by deadly fire of rifle and machine guns. For attacks, equipment was to become increasingly important, with the use of machine guns, mortars and guns that fired shells in a curving trajectory, poison combat gases and flame throwers. Men were slaughtered on a scale hitherto unknown. By the end of the conflict, the face of war had been changed by the introduction of tanks and by the use of airplanes for reconnaissance, observation, aerial combat and bombing raids. This meant mobilizing all the economic forces of the nation involved, and women often had to replace men in the fields and factories. The war took on a worldwide scope.

The French military operations were inspired by the disastrous doctrine of the offensive at all costs. In 1915, Joffre attempted two major offensives in Champagne and Artois which producing pointless slaughter (400,000 casualties) for ridiculous results— a move of only 4 km. In 1916, it was Germany's turn to launch a gigantic attack against the *camp retranché* of Verdun in order to shatter French morale and force the collapse of the French army. Verdun saw large-scale carnage, exhausting both opponents. In the end, the unswerving determination of General Philippe Pétain, who established the Voie Sacree (sacred path)— maintaining the communication with Bar-le-Duc — in order to get supplies through to his troops, caused the failure of this large-scaled offensive. After heavy fighting, in which 240,000 Germans and 275,000 French were killed or reported missing in action, the Germans had to abandon their plan. The battle of Verdun was a pointless and criminal butchery, which was seen as a great victory and was taken as a symbol of French resistance.

In late 1916, Joffre was thoroughly exhausted and replaced by General Robert Georges Nivelle. In April 1917, the new commander launched another offensive on the Chemin des Dames in Champagne. This attack too proved costly and pointless and was stopped after a few days. The result of three years of war with extreme casualties and suffering for meager results caused the undermining of the French soldier's morale. Defeatism spread, and mutinies occurred in a growing number of regiments; there were similar movements in the German army. Nivelle was dismissed and replaced by the victor of Verdun, Philippe Pétain. The C-I-C saved the situation by harsh measures. He did not hesitate to execute men as an example to others, which re-established respect for authority, but he also did his best to improve the daily lot of the rank-and-file, which restored confidence.

After the Bolchevik Revolution of October 1917, Russia withdrew from the war, thereby releasing several hundreds of German divisions, which were promptly

French infantryman 1914. The mantle was dark blue and the trousers were red. This old-fashioned conspicuous uniform was soon replaced by a blue-grey uniform with a steel-crested helmet.

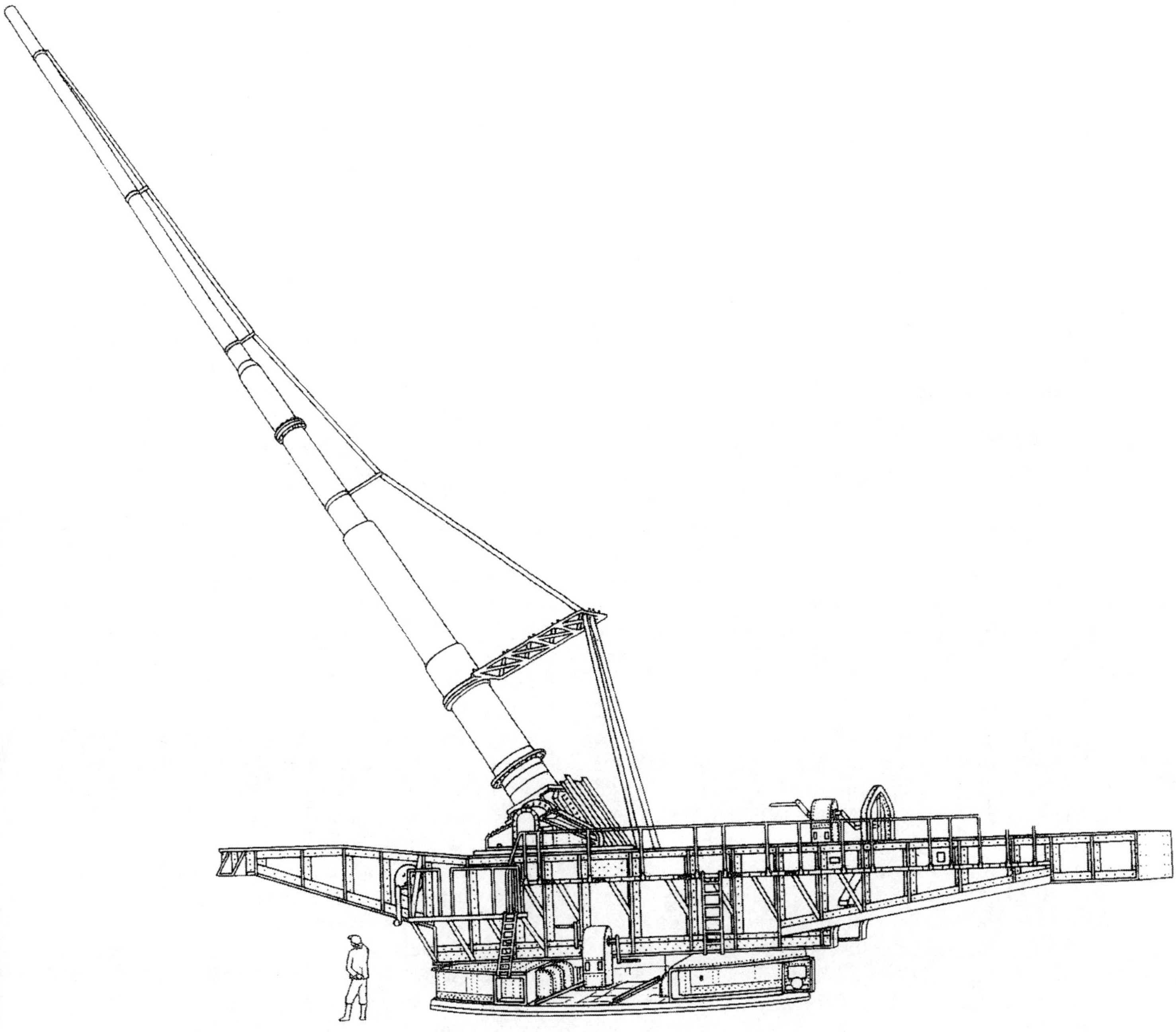

Paris Gun

shifted to the western front. Fortunately for the Franco-British allies, the United States had declared war on Germany in April 1917. This was the result of German all-out submarine warfare in the Atlantic Ocean against Britain and her main commercial partner. The American forces of General John Joseph Pershing were gradually beginning to land in France.

In March 1918, the Germans launched an offensive at Amiens, breaking through the Anglo-French lines, and in May, they menaced Paris again. The Allied High Commander, Marshall Ferdinand Foch succeeded in halting the attack, and in July the Germans were brought to a stand still. Their army was now exhausted, and in September 1918, its was Foch's turn to attack on all fronts, taking advantage of the decisive assistance provided by one million American soldiers. All the German lines collapsed one after another, the troops retreated in good order, abandoning northern France and Belgium. Germany found herself under threat of invasion and called for an armistice; a revolution broke out and the Kaiser was obliged to flee to neutral Holland. The armistice was signed on November 11, 1918. After a pointless conflict, which claimed some 37 millions European casualties, victory had come at last.

The Bombardment of Paris in 1918

During the war, the Parisian population had suffered a lot. As many peasants and workers were drafted to the front, as the industrial northern region was occupied by the Germans, and as the transportation system was totally employed for military purposes, there was a severe shortage of goods, food and fuel. At the end of 1917 a terrible epidemic, called the Spanish influenza, had taken the lives of about 210,000 people.

The town had also been attacked several times by German air raids of *Zeppelin* (large dirigible airships) and *Gotha* bomber airplanes. Though casualties were relatively light, the terrifying manifestations of a wholly new type of warfare made a deep impression on the Parisian public. Suddenly and unexpectedly, a new threat appeared. At a little after 7:20 on the morning of March 23, 1918, a violent explosion occurred at 6 Quai de Seine in the 19th arrondissement. No one was injured. Fifteen minutes later a second explosion occurred, striking a building near the Gare de l'Est. Later, further explosions followed spattered around Paris, and several people were injured and killed. It was assumed that it was another air raid, but no air alert had been sounded and no aircraft was to be seen in the clear sky. Actually the explosions were caused by shells fired by huge German super-cannons.

In the spring of 1916, the German army had ordered from the Krupp factories extraordinary guns with a range of 75 miles, with the intention of launching a terror bombardment on Paris and breaking the morale of the French. The gun took two years to design and manufacture and was extremely complicated, relying on very high muzzle velocity, an incredible trajectory and tortuous mathematical calculations. After feverish efforts by a team directed by the Austrian ballistics experts Doktor Eberhardt and Professor Rausenberger, Krupp issued in late 1917 the big *Kaiser Wilhem Geschutz* (Emperor William's Gun), popularly known as *Paris Guns* or erroneously called *Grosse Bertha* (Big Bertha). Actually *Big Bertha* was the designation of a powerful 42 cm (18-inch) German siege mortar, relatively short ranged, used successfully early in the war, in 1914, at the sieges of Liège, Namur, and Antwerp, and somewhat affectionately called Big Bertha by gunners in honor of the ample lady who had recently inherited leadership of the house of Krupp.

Three monster cannons were produced, and the battery was set up in great secret, carefully camouflaged (by netting, wire mesh and foliage, in clear day by artificial fog), in the forest of Crépy-en-Laonnais, near Laon, 120 km (70 miles) from the heart of Paris. Each cannon was transported by rail, assembled with cranes, and placed on a firing platform consisting of a circular casing, mounted by a turntable fitted with ball bearings on which the gun could traverse; the lot rested on a solid concrete foundation. Each gun barrel had a total length of 34 m (112 feet), and an overall weight of 138 tons. Their shells of caliber 21 cm were propelled by a charge of 250 kg (550 lbs). They left the barrel at a speed of 5,280 feet per second, a velocity allowing passage into the stratosphere; they reached an altitude of 12 miles in 24 seconds; a maximum height of 24 miles was reached in 90 seconds, at which point the projectiles were traveling at 2,250 feet per second. On their downward curve, speed increased to over 3,000 feet per second, and—after a flight of 92 miles in 179 seconds—the shells exploded in Paris on its unaware citizens. During firing, gunners and engineers got out of sight, seeking cover in large concrete shelters. Such was the formidable arrangement designed to demoralize the French.

Over 20 projectiles fell on Paris each of the first two days of the bombardment. One of the Paris Guns exploded accidentally, killing most of its crew, and there was a lull for three days until firing resumed on Good Friday, March 29, producing the greatest slaughter so far. At 4:30 p.m. a shell struck the Saint Gervais church in the Rue Miron, near the City Hall, where several hundred people were praying. The explosion destroyed a pillar and a great chunk of the vaulting, so a large area of the roof fell down on the congregation, killing 90 people and injuring 70. The firing continued with more or less intensity in April, May, June and July. On Friday August 9, 1918, the last shell fell in Rue Saint Denis at Aubervilliers.

In all, after four intermittent bombardments, 367 shells were fired on Paris, being directly responsible for 250 deaths and a further 620 wounded.

In the balance of effort, time and money expended versus damage done, the *Paris Guns* were a waste, but as propaganda weapons they had immense value. They surprised the world, and the shelling had a corrosive effect on the morale of the Parisians who experienced the terror of being struck in the heart of their city from behind an enemy line supposed to be a safe 70 miles away.

In September 1918, the advancing allied troops found traces of the firing installations, but the guns had been removed as carefully as they had been assembled months before in preparation for the attack. After the war, no Allied Armistice Commission was ever able to find the secret monster guns in defeated Germany. They had probably been demolished with oxy-acetylene cutting torches, and the parts scattered and then disappeared.

46

The Maginot Line

Demolition of the Thiers Enceinte

In April 1919, it was decided to demolish the useless Enceinte of Thiers from 1845, which anyway was neglected and abandoned by the military. The demolition lasted from 1919 to 1924. Their removal allowed the development of more space-consuming plans. The City of Paris bought up these lands, a quarter of which was to be reserved for building low-rent apartments, while the other three quarters were to be laid out as public walks, sporting grounds, games areas, parks, cemeteries, various railroad installations (e.g. marshalling yards), private buildings, a University (Boulevard Jourdan), an exhibition hall (at Porte de Versailles), and later (in the 1950s) a convenient peripheral highway all around the city.

New Plans for the Defense of France

France had suffered hideously in World War I. In the post-war period, the military authorities saw the task of the French army to be not so much to defeat the enemy (Germany of course) as to prevent another invasion. The French, who had suffered from German invasions in 1870 and 1914, were convinced that a line of fortification built along the border with Germany would prevent any such event in the future and that there would never be fighting again on French soil. That was the theoretical reasoning behind the construction of the so-called Maginot Line.

In the 1930s, every European country still had faith in continuing belts of fortification as the best means of defending their frontiers. Buried and scattered fortifications in the form of deep dug outs and subterranean forts were a logical development resulting from the new warfare experienced during World War I: aircraft, tank, guns of larger caliber concentrating fire, and poison gas.

After 1918, the French did not immediately fortify their new border with the defeated Germans since the occupation of the Rhineland and the demilitarization of Saarland made it unnecessary. The treaty of Locarno made it clear, however, that the situation along the Rhine was not to be a permanent one. Remembering how the forts at Verdun had successfully withstood bombardment in 1916, the French High Command felt renewed confidence in permanent fortification. Differences of opinion occurred over details and these were resolved in 1929, when the National Assembly voted on the construction of a heavily fortified line of defense along the border with Germany for a scheme proposed by the then Minister of War, André Maginot (1877–1932). The growing ambition of Mussolini's Fascist Italy induced the French government to build additional fortifications in the Alps to protect the Franco-Italian border.

Surveys were effected in 1928–1929. Work at the so-called Maginot line started in early 1930 and continued until 1940. The strategic concept behind the Maginot line was that in any future war with Germany, no more blood should be shed on French soil and that vital industries situated in the northeast would be protected. Tactically when the French military authorities analyzed the warfare of World War I, they remembered the strongholds and the trenches; even if fluid situations did develop, they had been brought to a full stop by the simplest of earthworks,

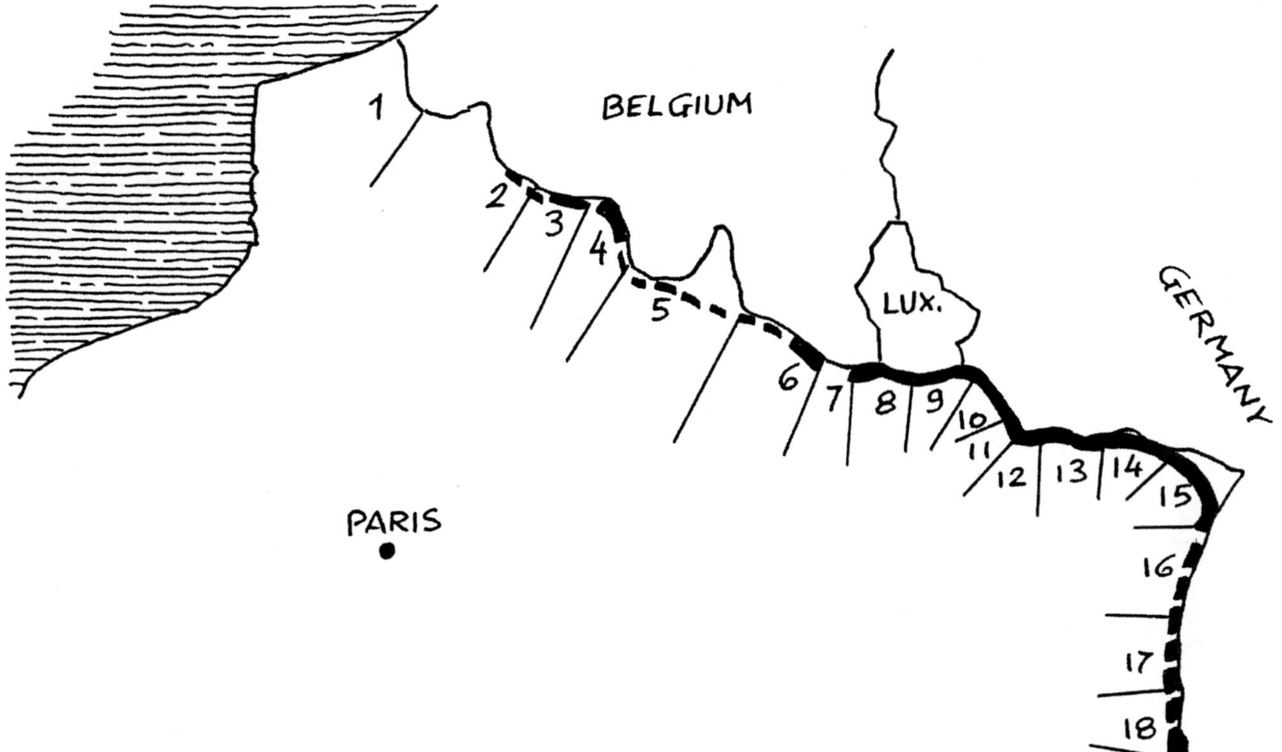
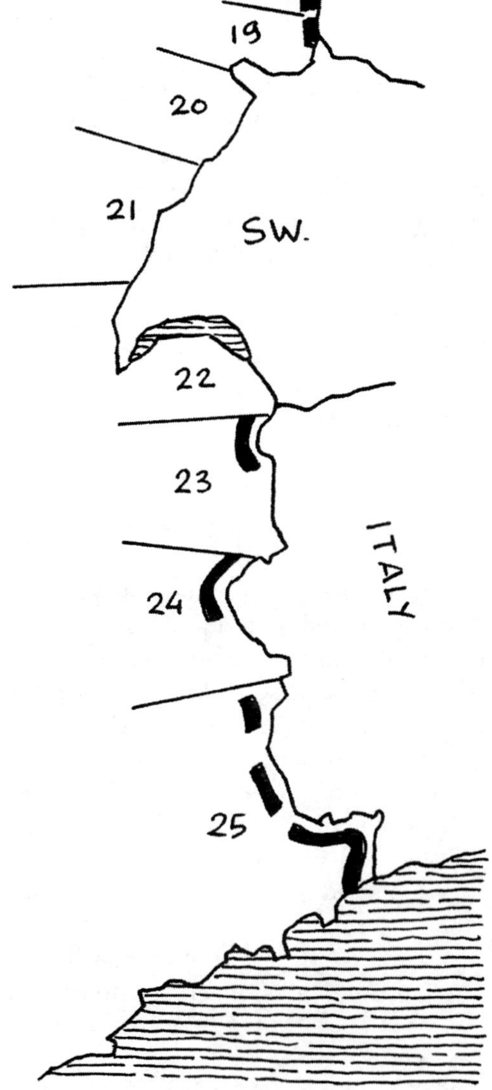

Map of France showing the main defenses in 1940. From Duinkirk in the north to Menton in the south, the eastern borders of France were divided into *Secteurs Fortifiés* (SF, fortified sectors) as follows:

1. SF Flanders
2. SF Lille
3. SF Escaut
4. SF Maubeuge
5. SF Ardennes
6. SF Montmédy
7. SF Merville
8. SF Crusnes
9. SF Thionville
10. SF Boulay
11. SF Faulquemont
12. SF Sarre
13. SF Rohrbach
14. SF Vosges
15. SF Haguenau
16. SF Lower Rhine
17. SF Colmar
18. SF Altkirch
19. SF Upper Alsace
20. SF Montbéliard
21. SF Jura
22. SF Rhône
23. SF Savoy
24. SF Dauphiné
25. SF Alpes Maritimes

Sectors 1 to 7, facing allied Belgium, were hastily established in 1939 and weakly defended. The strongest section, the Maginot Line proper, included sectors 8 to 18 facing the (German-speaking) Grand Duchy of Luxembourg and Nazi Germany. Sectors 19 to 22, facing neutral Switzerland, were almost defenseless. Sectors 23 to 25 were intended to repulse Fascist Italian attacks on the Alps passes.

trenches, barbed wires and machine gun nests. In that case, they imagined how effective a wide zone of carefully designed, well-sited, purpose-built and permanently constructed defenses and strongholds would be. No aggressor would be able to break through; caught out in the open, the assaulting army would be massacred. Established on the frontier, such a defense zone would make France impregnable. The line—with a relatively modest garrison—could protect the whole frontier, absorb the initial shock of attack and provide time for the full mobilization of the French army. The line would thus afford greater mobility to the rest of the French army.

That was the theory.

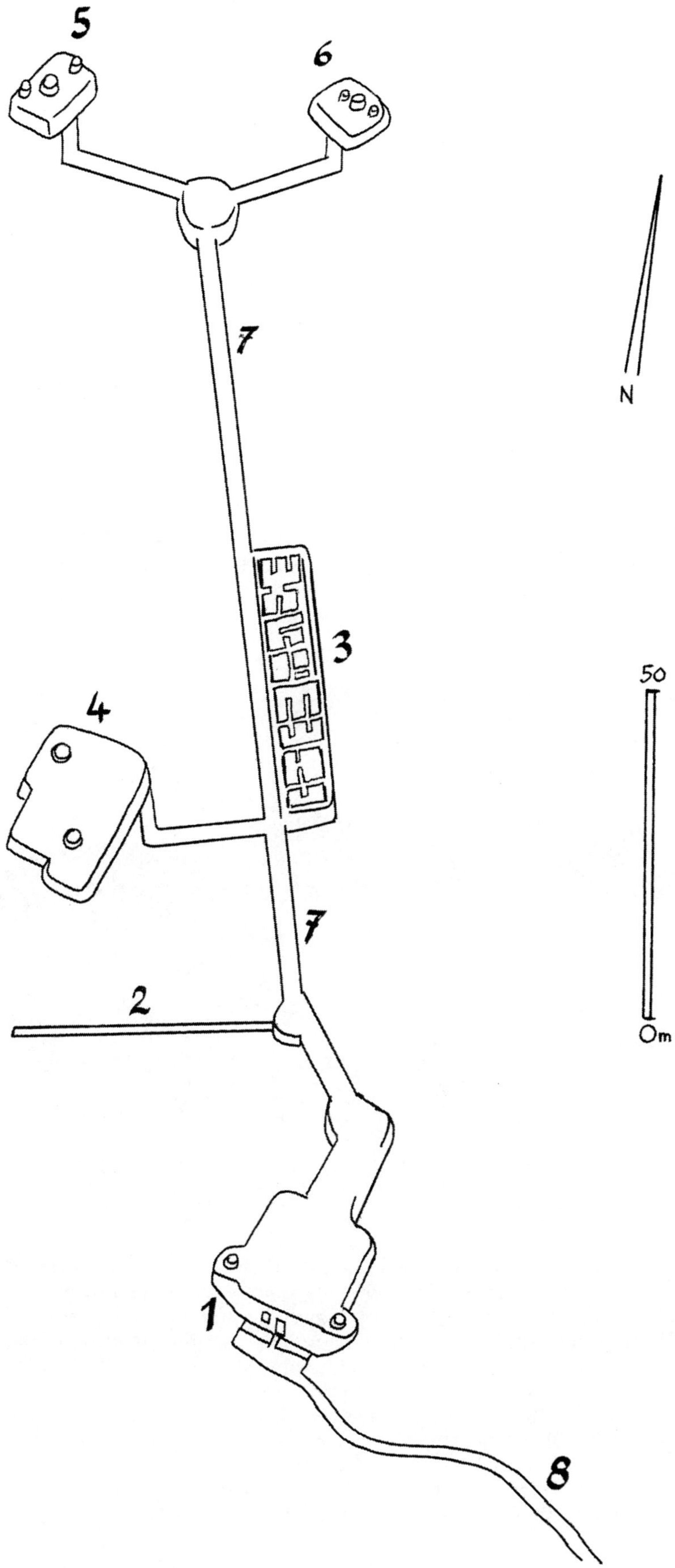

Fort Immerhof (Maginot Line). The small Fort Immerhof is situated near the village of Hettange Grande, north of Thionville (Lorraine). Its task (and that of its neighbor fort Soetrich) was to defend the main road (today Highway A31) and the railroad track running from Metz to Luxemburg City. The fort, built between 1930 and 1935, included the following elements.

1. **Entrance block. The façade was protected by a 3-m-deep ditch, crossed by a movable footbridge leading to a gate reinforced with armored doors. The block housed the radio central, a supply store, and an ammunition store. It was defended with two armored cupolas equipped with automatic rifles and 50 mm mortars and one 47 mm anti-tank gun placed inside a casemate.**
2. **Sewer for draining off infiltration and used water.**
3. **The totally subterranean "usine," the heart of the unit, included a power plant, a workshop, a ventilation room with filters and a pumping station, a kitchen, an infirmary, quarters, toilets and washing facilities for troops, NCOs, officers, and the commander, and a headquarters with telephone exchange and map room.**
4. **Mixed combat block No. 3 equipped with two breech-loading 81 mm mortars placed in an armored turret, a firing casemate armed with one 47 mm anti-tank gun (never delivered), and 7.5 mm twin machine guns, two crenels for automatic rifles, and an ammunition store.**
5. **Combat block No. 2 (western armored turret) armed with 7.5 mm Mack 31F twin machine guns, two observation cupola armed with automatic rifle for close-range defense, and an ammunition store.**
6. **Combat block No. 1 (eastern armored turret) symmetrically identical to western turret.**
7. **Underground communication tunnel linking elements.**
8. **Military road to Hettange Grande.**

The fort was surrounded by a barbed wire network and anti-tank obstacles. Its garrison totaled 198 men including infantrymen, gunners, electromechanics, telegraphists etc. Fort Immerhof was a "Petit Ouvrage" (PO small work); as a comparison, Fort Hackenberg counted nineteen combat blocks and a garrison of 1,034 men. The small Fort Immerhof is perfectly preserved and open to the public from April to September.

Composition of the Maginot Line

The Maginot line was the most ambitious and the most thorough piece of permanent fortification the world had ever seen. It was an expensive program which swallowed huge sums of money from the French budget in the pre–World War II period. The basic design was worked out by General Belhague, Inspector General of Fortifications, with the help of engineer Froissard. The Maginot line was the culmination of the long process of development which had evolved from the post–1886 concrete forts and the German *Feste* at Metz. It was built in two main phases.

During the first phase, between 1929 and 1938, the fortifications were designed and constructed under supervision of the *Commission d'Organisation des Régions Fortifiées* (CORF fortified regions organization committee). The CORF, in order to speed up the construction, employed soldiers of the engineering corps but also subcontracted civilian companies. The CORF works included expensive, powerful and high quality forts following a route that would take advantage of the strategically most useful natural features. Each individual concrete fort was adapted to the topography of the terrain. At the surface, the ouvrage included observatories, artillery and machine gun blocks, disappearing gun turrets, and anti-tank and anti-personnel obstacles at the front. In some sectors, the defenses included flooded areas. At the rear, back behind the firing zone, there were fortified entrances for men and ammunition which were connected to the combat emplacements by underground passages—some wide enough to house narrow-gauge electric trains. The entrance blocks were protected with armored doors, machine gun posts, and ditches with drawbridges. There were also false entrances designed for deceiving purposes. The largest forts could house 1,200 soldiers. For instance, the Ouvrage of Simserhof near Bitche in Lorraine totaled a garrison of 28 officers and 792 troops. Between the entrances and the combat emplacements, there were underground barracks, ammunition stores, filter and ventilation rooms, emergency hospitals, telephone exchanges, command posts, power plants, kitchens, and water and food supplies. Some forts even had sun-lamp rooms. All these facilities, allowing an autonomy of about three months, were protected by concrete structures buried deep underground. At various positions along the tunnels, there were ambuscades and hidden mines to entomb unwary invaders, while the defenders had their own secret exits and sally ports. Everywhere there were fireproof and gas-tight doors, exhaust vents and air intakes fitted with anti-gas filters.

Casemate of Bois de Beuveille. Situated near Metz (Lorraine) in Sector La Crusne, the self-containing Casemate d'Intervalle (interval casemate) of Bois de Beuveille included two stories. The ground floor was occupied by the combat chamber, ammunition store, ventilation and anti-gas filters. The basement included a generator, supply store (diesel oil, drinking and cooling water, ammunition etc.), crew quarters, a toilet, and a room for the commanding officer. The concrete walls and roof were 2.25 m thick. The depicted aerial view seen from the rear included the following: 1. Fixed twin machine gun armored turret; 2. Mixed weapon and observation armored turret fitted with periscope, light machine gun, and 50 mm mortar; 3. Flanking firing chamber armed with twin machine gun and a 47 cm anti-tank gun; 4. Armored searchlight; 5. Entrance with armored door and removable footbridge over the narrow and deep concrete ditch.

The second phase of the construction of the Maginot line was designed and completed between 1935 and 1940 by the so-called *Main d'Oeuvre Militaire* (MOM military manpower) provided solely by the French *Génie* (engineering corps). Due to a reduction in the budget resulting from the difficult economic climate which prevailed in the late 1930s, the numerous MOM works were lighter bunkers and interval casemates of different sizes and shapes with a reinforced field fortification character, sometimes named "camelote" (junk) fortification.

It is worth noting that the British Expeditionary Force, stationed in the northern province Picardy from September 1939 until May 1940, built several hundred concrete pillboxes based on their own design.

Small machine gun bunker at Holving (Lorraine). This bunker was typical of the MOM construction built in the last phase of Maginot Line. On the left side of the bunker was the armored entrance with a close-range defense crenel. On the right side (facing the enemy) there were two embrasures for firing with automatic Fusil-Mitrailleurs (light machine guns).

Fermont: Entrance block for ammunition. Fort Fermont, situated near Longwy (Lorraine), had seven combat blocks manned by 19 officers and 553 soldiers. The depicted entrance for ammunition was placed at the rear of the position, and tunnels linked it with the advanced combat blocks. Should the enemy attack from the rear, the entrance was protected by barbed wires and anti-tank obstacles and armed with a 47 mm anti-tank gun and several machine guns. Note the 60 cm narrow gauge railroad track used to supply the fort. The façade of the building was painted in motley camouflage color or covered with a large camouflage net.

By 1939, the Maginot line was 1,500 km (930 miles) long. Officially it was continuous and complete from Dunkirk (in the north near the English Channel) to Menton (at the border with Italy on the Mediterranean coast), but there remained many gaps, many structures were incomplete, and in certain sectors the "line" was hardly even started. The defensive units were organized in 25 *Secteurs Fortifiés* (SF, fortified sectors). The line consisted of 5,800 defense structures of various sizes, as follows: 39 ouvrages (forts with artillery and entry blocks); 246 interval bunkers; 52 heavy artillery casemates; 205 artillery bunkers; 3,216 machine-gun pillboxes; 472 anti-tank gun bunkers; 936 combined machine gun and anti-tank gun bunkers; 222 artillery casemates with armored revolving turrets; and 94 observation posts. The Maginot line proper extended from Basel to Longwy, and it was the most powerful in the sectors facing Luxembourg and Germany (Metz, Lauter and Belfort) where the bulk of the heavy CORF ouvrages and forts were built. The other zones (including the extension in the Alps) had various strengths. Some sectors were only lightly fortified with a majority of MOM works, notably along the weak Belgian border, deprived of natural barrier. The planners, in consideration of cost and in deference to Belgian sensibilities, curtailed the construction of the Maginot Line at the tip of the Ardennes, precisely where the Germans chose to align the axis of their effort in May 1940.

The Maginot Line Myth

The Maginot line captured the imagination of the world in the 1930s. Several nations had been convinced of the validity of the Maginot line, and the French fortification technique was widely copied throughout Europe — notably in Czechoslovakia. Right before World War II, military construction was in full swing all over Europe, and the concrete mixers were working overtime. All those believers were fated to be disappointed. There were indeed two Maginot lines: the real one, which was a great technical and military achievement, and the other one, which was a myth created by optimistic apologists.

The French propaganda and the press put the emphasis on the CORF works and complaisantly presented the Maginot line as an impregnable military wonder. This gave birth to a dangerous myth of invincibility and security in the French population.

If detail arrangements were subject to strict security, the purpose of the Maginot line was to deter Germany from making a surprise attack, and no attempt was made to keep the fortifications such a secret. The Germans were perfectly aware of the power of the line. They knew it would be a hard nut to crack. They did not make direct assaults on the Maginot Line, only a few ouvrages were attacked — notably that of La Fertée, in the northwest part of the line. Instead they just ignored it; they crossed the Meuse at Sedan and penetrated into France via the Ardennes mountains, The Netherlands and Belgium. Moreover they had airplanes and judiciously used their tanks in mass surprise attacks.

In spite of the Anglo-French counterattack in Belgium, the Western front rapidly collapsed. The French armies were encircled or defeated or withdrew in panic. The British could, however, save the bulk of their expeditionary force, which re-embarked at Duinkerk.

Six weeks after the start of the war in the West, France was obliged to capitulate. The Maginot line proved impenetrable, but it has often been blamed for the collapse of France; the latter was caused by the defensive mentality and the blindness of the French military authorities to the development of modern warfare in the late 1930s. Some sectors of the ill-fated Maginot Line — encircled and attacked from the rear — were still fighting, but their crews had to surrender after the armistice had been proclaimed on June 25, 1940.

47

The Chauvineau Line

Conception of the Chauvineau Line

During the first world war, the German offensives in August 1914 and July 1918 towards Paris had clearly shown that the capital of France could still be threatened by a brusk attack. As early as 1920, Marshall Joseph Joffre (1852–1931)—the prestigious victor of the Battle of the Marne in September 1914—proposed without success to promote the creation of an advanced line of defense. The idea was, however, reconsidered in 1931 and, with Hitler's rise to power in January 1933, various plans were made.

One had to wait until 1937, before the Grand Headquarters of the Paris region admitted the necessity of some kind of defense around the capital. In September 1938, General Narcisse Chauvineau (1874–1969) was commissioned with the elaboration of a defensive plan. Since 1936 Chauvineau had been retired; he had been a staff officer during World War I and had been a teacher of fortification at the Application School for Artillery and Engineering. He had published a work entitled *Une Invasion, est-elle encore Possible?* (Is an invasion still possible?) in which he developed personal concepts over continuous fortified lines based on anti-tank defenses. In December 1938, Chauvineau's plan was ready and submitted to the military authorities. The plan was intended to protect Paris from long-range guns and from a rapid penetration by armored vehicles.

Composition of the Chauvineau Line

The line was placed in the north and northeast of Paris. It was based on the use of natural obstacles (river, hills and forests) and artificial hindrances (inundation, anti-tank obstacles and weapons emplacements). The shortage of workers and the unknown importance of the garrison of the line had as a result to limit the main weapon emplacements: machine guns against the infantry and anti-tank guns against armored vehicles. Three to four concrete bunkers, able to resist 105 mm shells, were planned for each km of front. In order to reduce the construction delay, Chauvineau proposed using standardized bunkers already used in the Maginot line, the so-called MOM works (Main d'Oeuvre Militaire or military works). The MOM bunkers with their reinforced field fortification character were criticized and nicknamed "junk fortification." Chauvineau's project was accepted in its principles, but the military authorities insisted that the bunkers should resist 150 mm shells, resulting in precious time wasted. Studies went on and the conception was accelerated during the mobilization of September 1939 and during the *Blitzkrieg* (Lightning War) in Poland. In his order of September 9, 1939, General Héring, military governor of Paris, confirmed Chauvineau's defensive disposition.

The safety line, about 250 km long, covered the northern part of Paris (enclosing three regions of the Isle-de-France: the Val-d'Oise, a part of the Valois and the Multien) from Conflans-Sainte-Honorine in the west up to La Ferté-sous-Jouarre in the east. It was based on natural obstacles offered by the rivers Oise (in the west) and Nonette (in the north), a wooden zone near Retz, and River Grivette, and rivers Ourcq and Marne (in the East). The "Line" was of course not a continuous wall but a succession of strongholds. The rather well-protected

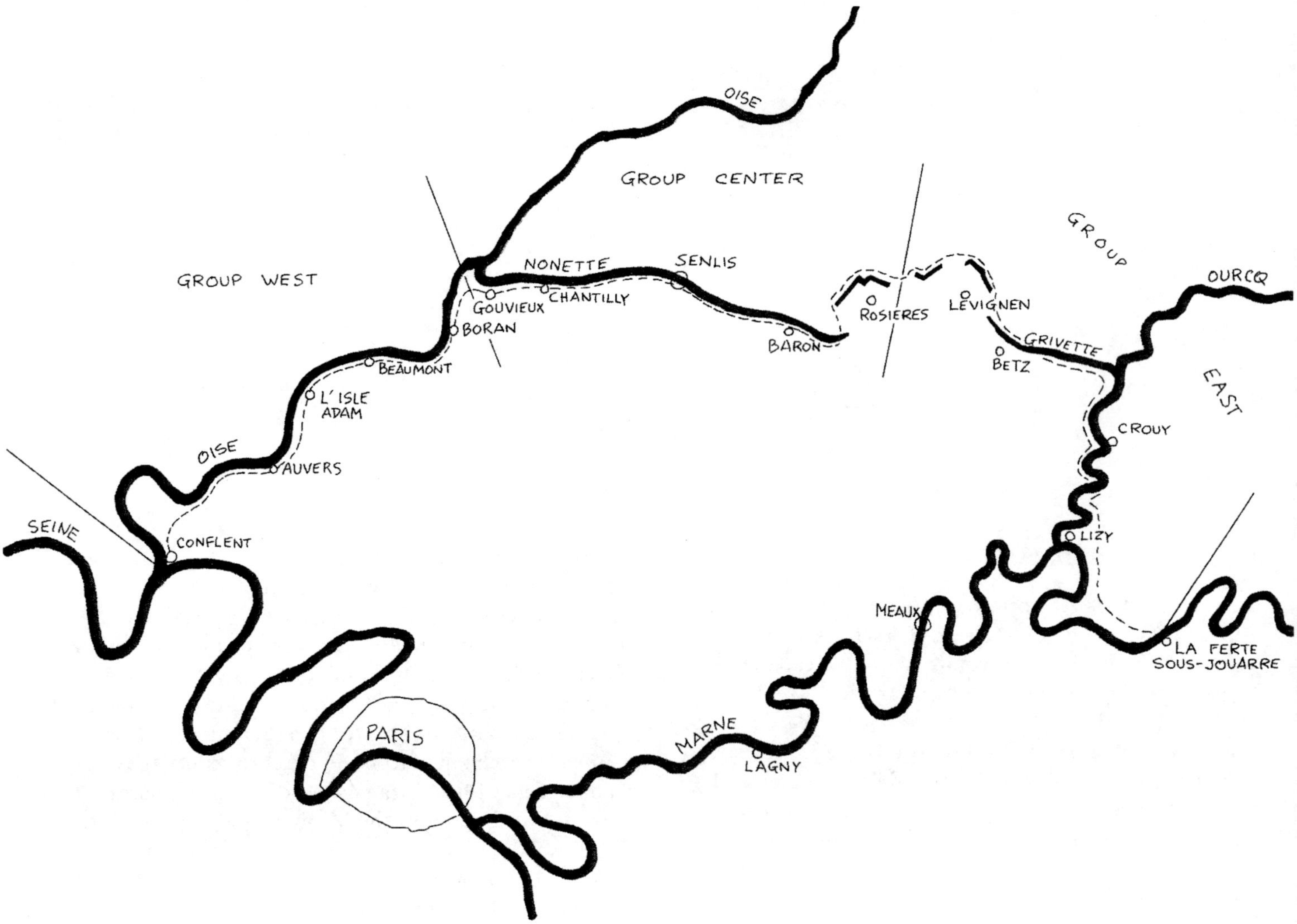

Map of the Chauvineau Line in June 1940. The Chauvineau Line had a total length of about 250 km. Its western front followed the river Oise from Conflent-Sainte-Honorine (at the junction of the rivers Seine and Oise) to Boran. The northern front followed the small river Nonette, which runs in an eastern direction along Gouvieux, Chantilly, Senlis and Baron. Between Rosières and Levignen, there was no natural obstacle, and to fill the gap anti-tank ditches were excavated. The eastern front of the line then followed the small River Grivette, River Ourcq and River Marne from Betz down to Crouy-sur-Ourcq and Lizy-sur-Ourcq and finished at La Ferté-sous-Jouarre in the East.

western and eastern flanks were defended by concrete works only at the passage points (bridges and crossroads). The northeastern section of the line, lacking an important natural barrier, was composed of groups of concrete artillery bunkers and machine gun pillboxes reinforced by barbed wires, anti-tank ditches and mines. In addition the old and neglected forts of the Northern Position built by General Séré de Rivières in the period 1874–1884 (including fort of Cormeille, fort of Montlignon, fort of Domont, fort of Montmorency and fort of Ecouen) were hastily refurbished to be used as support positions.

The conception of the Chauvineau line was, on the whole, rather sound and could be expected to offer comparatively good resistance to infantry and armored vehicles, but it had a very weak drawback: it had no defense against enemy aircrafts.

Construction of the Chauvineau Line

The direction of the construction of the Line was entrusted to General Chauvineau himself who was promoted to the rank of Engineering Commander of the Region of Paris. The line was divided into three main tactical sections: Group West, Group Center and Group East. These were divided into thirteen sectors, each commanded by a colonel/work-director. Each colonel in his sector had a headquarters, a transport company and a

Cross section machine gun pillbox. This small bunker was more a concrete shield than a proper bunker as its rear was covered by wooden poles and earth.

Above: **Front view anti-tank concrete pillbox.**

Right: **Ground plan bunker for 25 mm anti-tank gun. The bunker was composed of a single firing-chamber with a rear door to let the gun in. It was also fitted with a flanking concrete wall at the side where the enemy was expected.**

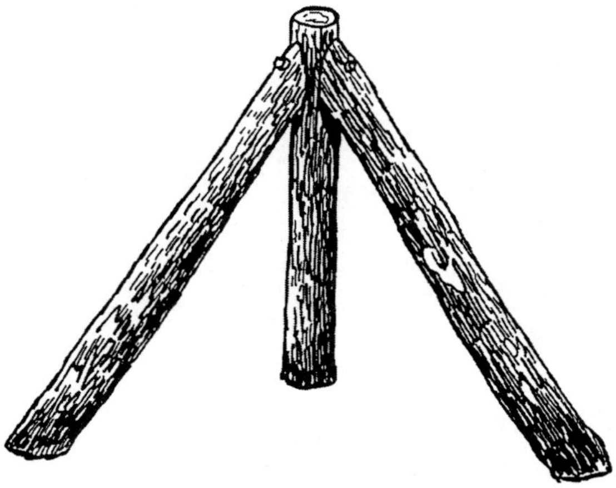

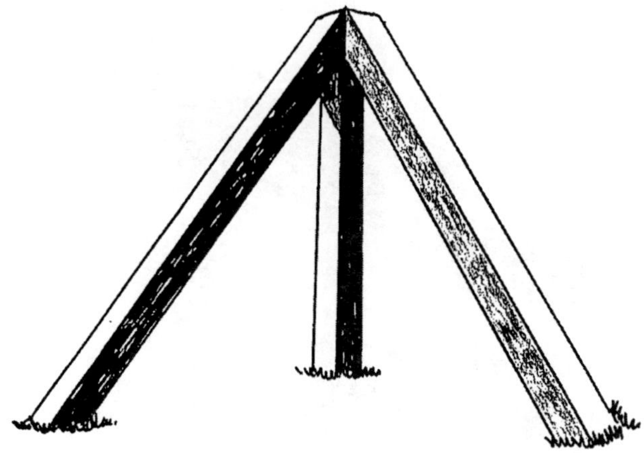

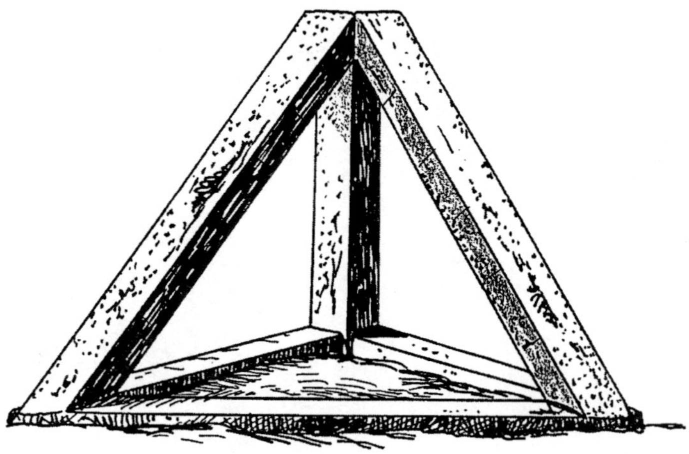

Tetraeder. These anti-tank obstacles were able to stop or hinder the progression of light tanks such as the German PzKw I and II used at the beginning of World War II. They were composed of three (about 2 m long) beams forming together a pyramid. They could be made of wood, concrete or steel. The base could be strengthened for additional strength, and several obstacles could be coupled together to constitute a line. Another French anti-tank obstacle, widely used in the Maginot Line, was composed of rows of steel rails encased in concrete blocks pushed in the ground.

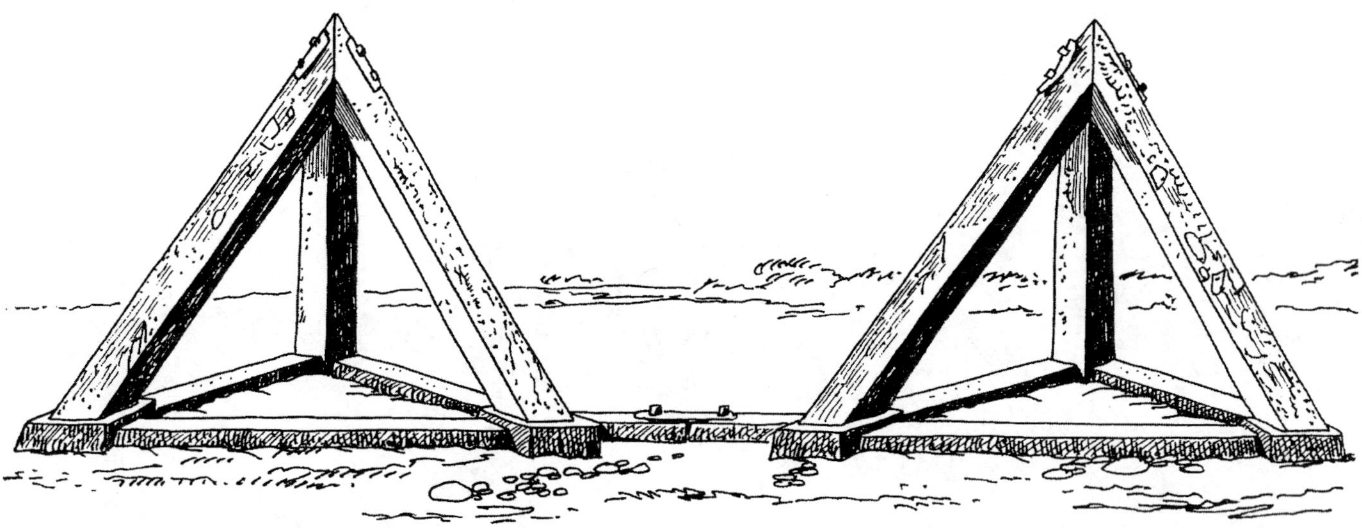

construction material dump. Ten regiments of engineering workers were put at their disposal and several private civilian building companies were also contracted to carry out the works. The construction began on October 6, 1939, by the establishment of weapons emplacements. There were several models of standardized bunker. The lightest of these was intended to protect a machine gun or a 25 mm anti-tank gun. Needing only 12 cubic m of concrete, this structure was actually more a shield than a proper bunker. It could only resist small arms, and its rear was open. Another machine-gun/anti-tank gun structure — needing 25 cubic m of concrete — was similar but more elaborate with walls and roof having a thickness of one m, able to resist 105 mm shells. A reinforced model of 140 cubic m of concrete, called *blockhaus*, included two firing apertures, one for a machine gun and

Anti-tank ditch. Anti-tank ditches were generally dug using an excavating machine *(top)*. The profile *(bottom)* clearly shows the effectiveness of the obstacle.

Tirailleur indochinois (1939). In both world wars of the 20th century, France raised troops from its colonies. Important contingents of colonial troops included men from North Africa (e.g. Spahis, Zouaves, Tirailleurs, Algerians and Moroccans), Senegalese riflemen from Black Africa (Tirailleurs Sénégalais), and the depicted Indochinese tirailleur from Viet Nam. Tirailleur means infantryman or skirmisher.

French infantryman (1940). The depicted private of the 2nd Battalion of Chasseur à Pied wears the 1926-pattern "Adrian" crested helmet, the 1920-pattern khaki capote (great coat), the 1936-pattern dark blue trousers, and the 1935-pattern equipment including leather cartridge pouches, gasmask bag and rucksack. He is armed with the 1907/15 M16 rifle with bayonet.

Profile French S-35 tank. At the outbreak of World War II, the French had good tanks such as the H-39, the heavy Char B and the depicted S-35. The S-35 was designed by the Société d'Outillage Militaire et Usinage d'Armement (Military Tools and Armament Factory or SOMUA). It was armed with one 47 mm turret gun and one front hull machine gun. The French tanks were not less effective than the German PzKfw Mark II, III and IV, but the difference was in the use of the armored power. The French persisted in a policy that compelled tanks to act merely as an adjunct to the infantry. As for the Germans, they introduced a new dimension to warfare known as Blitzkrieg. They used tanks in concentrated Panzer divisions directed against the enemy's weakest spots and brought a brutal combination of surprise, speed and mobility which gave them uncontested victory in 1940.

the other for an anti-tank gun. A fourth model was called *encuvement* (bedding); intended for 47 mm or 65 mm army field guns. It was composed of a roofless open concrete platform allowing a wide arc of fire but offering poor protection.

Working on the line did not go without problems of course. Half of the engineering units were withdrawn and deployed at the borders of France; there was thus a shortage of man power, of skilled fortification building officers, worsened by lack of transport vehicles, materials and supplies. In May 1940 about 300 concrete bunkers were built and about fifteen km of anti-tank ditches had been dug. A dam established in the valley of River Nonette created thirteen km of impassable inundation. About 800 tetraeders (anti-tank metal obstacles) had been placed as road hindrance, and many bridges had been prepared for demolition. The whole line demanded the use of 6,000 tons of concrete, 180 tons of metal bars and 21 tons of explosive.

The Battle of France (May–June 1940)

Clearly the French were not ready for war, and their unreadiness was more psychological than military. They had been bled white in World War I, and they hoped to confine the 1939–1940 war to proper limits, i.e. behind the protection of their formidable Maginot Line. Many pre-war military analysts expected the war on the Western front to revolve in static operations around the French Maginot Line and the German Westwall. As history has shown, this did not happen. The *Phoney War* ended dramatically on May 10, 1940. The Germans concentrated their efforts on a revised version of the Schlieffen Plan, designed by General Manstein. The campaign in the West fell into two parts: the battle of The Netherlands and the battle of France.

The first phase began on May 10, 1940 when the Germans struck with air attacks and parachute landings on Dutch airfields and bridges, and their troops moved into Holland and Belgium. Both countries called for help from France and Britain, and the Allies began their planned move forwards, the so-called *Dyle Plan*, which was a counterattack in Belgium. The Dutch were swiftly forced back and capitulated on May 15. Meanwhile a party of audacious German glider-borne paratroopers had captured the Belgian fort Eben-Emaël on the 11th, and their Panzer divisions had thrust through the "impassable" Ardennes mountains to reach the River Meuse. Bridgeheads were secured by May 14, and a breach was established between Sedan and Dinant. In the night of May 15/16, began the battle of France.

The German Panzers moved forwards heading behind the British Expeditionary Force and the French armies, which were forced to fall back from Belgium. By May 20, 1940, the Germans had reached the North Sea at Noyelles and established a corridor between the Allied forces. The next day, the Anglo-French made a vain attempt to cut this corridor near Arras, but this failed. On May 22, the Germans turned north to drive towards the Channel ports. As Hitler still had hopes to make peace with Britain, he ordered a halt and did not permit his forces to move forward until the 25th. The Allies fell back to Dunkirk where most of the British troops could be evacuated by sea. During this respite, General Weygand attempted to regroup the French armies on a defensive line running along the rivers Somme and Aisne, but the majority of the French soldiers had lost confidence in their leaders and themselves.

As early as May 14, 1940, the uncompleted Chauvineau Line was put in a state of readiness. Commanded by General Lanoix, the line was manned by three legions of *Gardes Mobiles* (Police Units), infantry mounted on bicycles, twenty tanks, a few 75 mm anti-tank guns and various infantry troops drawn from reserve forces. On May 17, the working sites were bombarded by the German *Luftwaffe* (air force), and the troops were placed in a state of alarm. Some 80 bridges were prepared for demolition with explosives, and anti-tank and anti-personnel mines were placed. After June 7, reinforcements came to the line with the deployment of North African colonial infantry units armed with additional anti-tank guns. On June 9, remnants of the French VIIth Army, headed by General Frère, withdrew to the Chauvineau line. The following day, about 30 bridges were destroyed on rivers Oise and Nonette. On June 11, the Germans progressed south of the rivers Seine and Marne and heavy fighting took place in the north of the Chauvineau line around the villages of Isle Adam, Ormoy Villiers and Levignen. Several assaults were repulsed, causing many casualties on both sides but these were rear guards fighting for the honor. In the evening of June 12, the garrison of the line received the order to withdraw.

Paris, declared an open city, was taken by the Germans on June 14, 1940. By that time Mussolini declared war and, on June 21, 1940, Italian troops moved a short way into southern France meeting stubborn resistance in the Alps. In spite of this local victory, elsewhere all French troops collapsed, resulting in the fall of France. On June 22, 1940, Marshall Philippe Pétain accepted an armistice with the Germans. The Third Republic, founded in 1871, was abolished and the prestigious victor of Verdun, Marshall Philippe Pétain (aged 84 in 1940) became the leader of a highly conservative authoritarian state whose motto was *Travail-Famille-Patrie* (Work-Family-Fatherland). The French people were stunned by the suddenness and thoroughness of the defeat which overwhelmed them.

48

Occupation and Liberation (1940–1944)

Vichy

After the defeat of June 1940, every French citizen was caught up in the conflict. France was divided into two zones, separated by a line of demarcation difficult to cross without German permission. All northern France—including the Channel and the entire Atlantic coastlines—north and west of a line running from the Swiss border at Geneva, via Bourges, to Saint-Jean-de-Luz was occupied and ruled by the German Army from Paris. The *zone nono* (nonoccupied southern "Free Zone") was ruled by Marshall Philippe Pétain's puppet government, the so-called *Etat Français* (French State) with its capital at Vichy. Both provinces of Alsace and Lorraine were annexed to the Reich, and the northern departments were incorporated to occupied Belgium. A million and a half prisoners of war were locked up in camps in Germany, held as hostages brooding over their powerlessness in morose ill temper.

Hitler's orders were to run the country in order to ensure that nothing happened to impede the German armed forces and that France should contribute whatever was available, in the form of labor, industrial production, or raw materials, to the German war effort. Soon a million workers and youths were rounded up and deported to Nazi Germany to furnish the industrial labor for an enormous war machine. The huge majority of the French population resigned themselves to their fate, adopted a "wait and see" attitude, and some supported the *National Revolution* initiated by Pétain. The French State's motto was *Travail, Famille, Patrie* (work, family, country). It sought to "regenerate" France but had to accede to the demands of the Nazi occupying power. All Frenchmen tried to survive as they could in a land where everything was rationed and lacking because of the German pillaging. The Parisians lived in a world of basic privation, shortage of food, clothing and other necessities of daily life. There was famine in urban areas, particularly in Paris. Housewives stood in the long ration lines for hours, hoping there would be something left in the shop when their turn arrived. As a result there were large-scale illegal black market dealings. It was the time of *système D*, which stood for the French verb *se démerder*, which literally means "to get out of that shit," or "making do," or "solving any difficulties under any circumstances." Only a small fringe of the population either chose to resist the occupiers (Gaullists and Communists) or to collaborate and serve the Germans (Fascists and pro–Nazis).

Pétain trying to alleviate the suffering of the French people, pursued a policy of foot dragging but could not avoid a criminal collaboration with the Germans, which cost him the support of many Frenchmen. In Drancy, a suburb north of Paris, the French authorities had established a huge improvised prison, which was used as a *Durchganglager* (transit camp). Drancy was the antechamber to the Nazi concentration hell. Conditions in the camp were atrocious with overcrowding, scarce food, poor living accommodations, and little or no medical aid. To keep the Germans friendly, the French authorities had ordered harsh measures against the Jewish community, many of whom were arrested and rounded up by the police, detained in Drancy, delivered to the German SS and deported to various *Vernichtungslager* (extermination camps)—notably Auschwitz where they were mass

Left: **Organisation Todt worker. The Organisation Todt (OT) was a semimilitary Nazi government unit set up in 1938 for the purpose of building military installation, special highways, and — during World War II — bunkers and fortifications. The OT was led by Dr. Fritz Todt until his death in 1942 and then by Hitler's architect Albert Speer. As many Germans were drafted in the Wehrmacht, the OT widely opened its ranks to volunteers from Nazi occupied nations, among which was a certain number of Frenchmen. The OT also made wide use of slave laborers drawn from prisons and concentration camps. The depicted volunteer wears the German two-piece field fatigue suit with two armbands, one displaying a swastika and the other bearing the label Org. Todt.** ***Right:*** **Luftwaffe Helferin (ca. 1943). The depicted Luftnachrichtenhelferin (air force signal auxiliary) wears the normal blue-grey service dress with the German airforce "diving" eagle insignia, specialty badge (qualified radio operator) and a sleeve chevron of rank. Female auxiliaries — employed in Luftwaffe administration duties — were a common sight in occupied Paris. Because of the color of their uniform, they were nicknamed "souris grises" (grey mice) by the population.**

German pillbox

murdered. Communist and Gaullist resistance members, "terrorists," Allied spies and agents, as well as many people supposed to be the enemies of the Nazi Reich — after being tortured — were also shipped from Drancy to German *Konzentrationslager* (concentration camps) from which very few came back in 1945.

In November 1942, the Allies landed in Algeria and Morocco; the Germans responded by invading the so-called southern Vichy Free Zone. Now the whole of France was occupied, while the number in the Resistance movement grew constantly. Many Frenchmen refused to accept defeat and joined the Resistance. Inspired by General Charles de Gaulle, who from London led the Free French, they took part in the fight by making hit-and-run raids against enemy forces and by transmitting information.

German Bunkers in Paris

Throughout 1943, the German armies were bled white on the Russian front, and the Allied strategic bombing offensive moved steadily towards its terrible crescendo. The signs announcing the opening of a new front in the West could not be misread: 1944 would be the year, France the place and the spring or summer would bring the hour.

As early as 1942, Hitler had anticipated the threat and ordered the fortifying of the Atlantic coasts from Norway to southern France against an Allied landing; the so-called *Atlantic Wall*— built between 1942 and 1944 — was a juxtaposition of defensive "hedgehogs," a girdle of infantry positions, machine guns and mortar nests, anti-tank guns emplacements, medium and long-range coastal artillery batteries, observation posts, radar stations, mine fields and beach obstacles. In addition the Germans held several armored divisions as mobile strategic reserves. In reality, the much-vaunted Atlantic Wall, against which the invading Allies were intended to dash themselves into ruins, was only a figment of Hitler's imagination. Despite Marshall Erwin Rommel's frantic efforts to create a strong defense system, it was only in the Pas-de-Calais (the northern part of France facing the Straight of Dover) that the "Wall" existed in anything like its intended form.

In Paris, the German army used the forts of both outer rings for various purposes: store place, barrack, training ground, telephone exchange, weather station, observation post, and various other military roles. Some of the forts were used as prisons and execution places. In the fort on Mont Valérien, about 4,500 résistants were shot by the Germans, and the *Mémorial de la France Combattante* (Memorial of Fighting France) was erected in 1946 to commemorate their sacrifice.

The Germans did not fortify Paris, but they erected various concrete bunkers in and around the buildings their administration occupied, e.g. the *Kommandantur* (administration office) opposite the Opera, the Hôtel Meurice on Rue de Rivoli, the Hôtel George V on the Place de la Concorde, and the Hôtel du Prince de Galles, which were used as headquarters. In Saint-Germain-en-Laye (a smart suburb west of Paris), the *Oberbefehlhaber West* (Ob-W, Chief-Commander of the West), *Generalfeldmarschall* (Field-Marshal), Gerd von Rundstedt, had a fortified headquarters established in the Lycée Claude Debussy and Lycée M. Roby. Those headquarters were guarded and lightly defended by check points and concrete pillboxes armed with machine guns.

In 1943 and particularly in early 1944, as a preparation for the June 1944 invasion in Normandy, the Parisian factories working for the German war industry (e.g. the Renault automotive plants at Boulogne-Billancourt), and the railway communication centers (e.g. the marshalling yards of Achère and Porte de La Chapelle) were repeatedly bombarded by the RAF and the USSAF. By that time the Germans were forced to build underground concrete shelters and *Flakstände* or *Flak-Bettungen* (anti-aircraft gun emplacements). Allied bombing raids over France and Paris caused thousands of victims, a necessary tragedy which was used by the Vichy's propaganda and the Paris press, which was entirely in the pay of the Nazi occupiers.

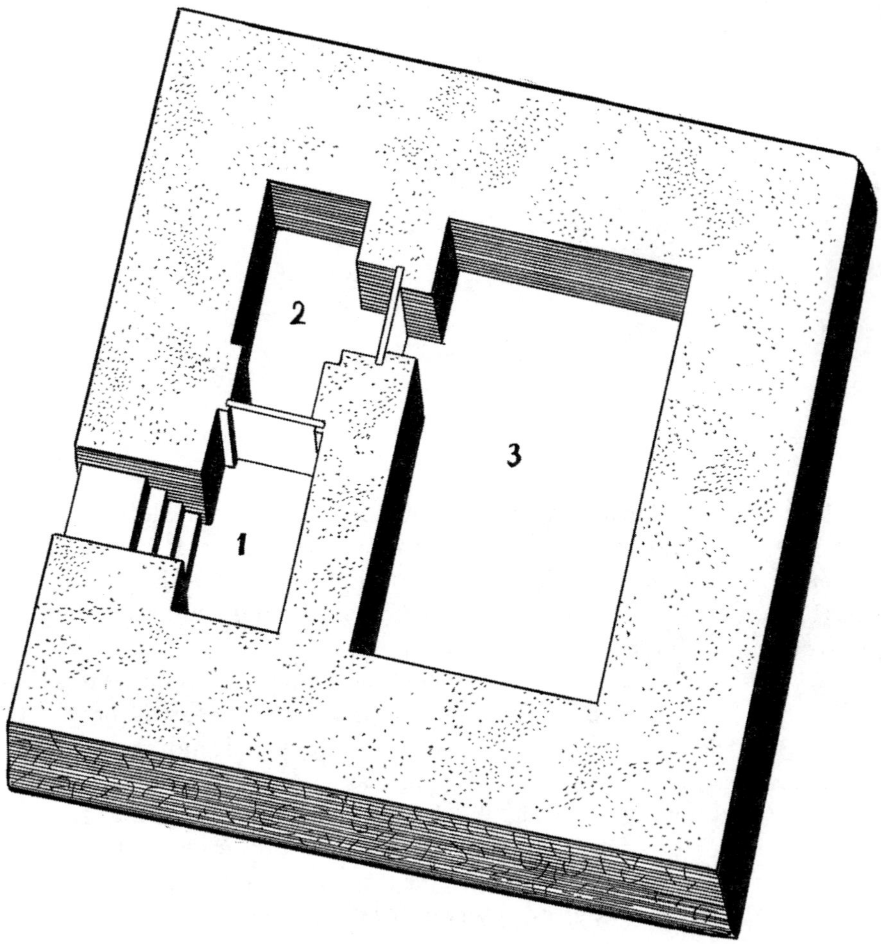

German bunker SO-150. This air raid concrete shelter, located at Boulevard Victor Hugo at Saint-Germain-en-Laye, was part of the German headquarters in France. The roof has here been taken away for the purpose of showing the entrance (1), the gaslock (2) and the troop chamber (3) measuring 2.80 x 4.65 m. The bunker was camouflaged and fitted with a ventilation system and telephone; it was square (7.65 x 7.65 m), the roof was 2 m thick and covered with earth, and the walls were 1.50 m thick.

The Liberation of Paris (August 1944)

On June 6, 1944, the Allies landed on the beaches of Normandy. After a hard battle in the bocage, the German forces were pocketed around the city of Falaise. The remnants of the 5th and 7th Armies retreated in the northeast direction. On August 15, the Allies landed on the French Riviera at Saint Tropez, and the main German forces in the south of France were rapidly ordered to withdraw northwards.

In this context of victory, the *Comité de Libération de Paris* (Paris Liberation Committee) organized by the French Resistance became impatient. On August 17, 1944, the Resistance decided to liberate Paris in an armed uprising. The *Forces Françaises de l'Intérieur* (FFI, French Interior Forces) seized control of the Police Headquarters and turned the Cité island into a fortress. Several government buildings were occupied, including the City Hall, the Palace of Justice, and the Ministry of War. At the same time, about 600 improvised barricades were erected in the streets to hinder German movement. The Parisian uprising did not, however, suit

Flakstand type L 422A. This bunker, designed and issued by the German Luftwaffe in February 1943, was intended to shelter gunners and house an 8.8 cm or a 10.5 cm heavy anti-aircraft gun for firing against high-flying airplanes. The terrace, arranged as a gun platform, was placed on top of a bunker composed of an ammunition store, a gaslock, and troops quarters. Its length was 11.720 m, its width was 11.10 m, and its height was 6.30 m. Walls and roof were 2 m thick, and the construction of the bunker demanded 850 cubic m of concrete.

Left: Communist FTP. The French Communist Party had its own armed force known as Francs-Tireurs-Partisans (FTP, Free-Riflemen-Partisans). The partisan is armed with a captured German MPi 40 submachine gun with ammunition pouches fixed on the waistbelt. Both FFI and FTP took part in the fight against the Nazis by making hit-and-run raids. After the liberation of France in autumn 1944, all volunteer civilian militias (both Gaullist and Communist) were disbanded for political reasons and incorporated into the Free French Regular Army to continue the war against enemy forces until Germany's surrender in May 1945. ***Right:*** French FFI maquisard (1944). The Forces Françaises de l'Intérieur (FFI, French Interior Forces) were the armed militia of the Gaullist Résistance. They did not wear uniforms but were distinguished by an armband bearing the initials FFI. The depicted man is armed with a grenade and a British Sten submachine gun.

Eisenhower's plan; the Field Commander of all Allied Troops intended simply to bypass Paris in order to spare lives and because he felt that the German garrison was impotent and could safely be left alone until later. General de Gaulle asked the 2nd Free French Armored Division under General Leclerc's command to be sent to help take the city lest the Paris Resistance Movement should be wiped out by the remaining Germans. Skirmishes and sniping took place everywhere in Paris, notably in the center of the town, at the Place Saint Michel and in the Quartier Latin; the combats caused about 2,000 casualties on the side of the insurgents.

Hitler's orders to the *Militärbefehlhaber* (German Military Governor at Paris), General Dietrich von Choltitz, were clear: destroy Paris if you cannot defend it. Von Choltitz was not a fanatical Nazi, but a ruthless soldier who did what he could in a dramatic situation. He ordered the crushing of the uprising, but in the end he could not do otherwise than disregard Hitler's criminal order: instead of repressing the gallant but poorly armed and improvised uprising, he asked for a truce allowing the German forces to withdraw. The truce ran until noon on August 23, but sniping and skirmishing continued. When von Choltiz realized that the uprising had spread too far to be checked by force, he was forced to admit his defeat. He then decided to avoid a tragic and hopeless blood bath and surrendered his garrison to the Allies on August 24, 1944. The day after, General Leclerc's 2nd Free French Armored Division and the 4th US Infantry Division drove toward the heart of Paris with a delirious joyful welcome. By August 25, all organized German opposition had ended. The joy and pride of the Parisians were great because they had fought to recover their own freedom, as General Charles de Gaulle triumphantly announced in a famous speech held in the City Hall after he had entered his country's capital after four years of exile in London, "...*Paris brisé! Paris meurtri! Mais Paris libéré par lui-même!...*" (Paris broken! Paris bruised! but Paris liberated by itself!...). The truth is that Paris—and France—were liberated by the Allies, more particularly by the Americans. The myth of "Paris liberated by the Parisians, the FFI and Leclerc" was a convenient tale, created for national purposes, which contributed to show the rebirth of France, to emphasize the pride of de Gaulle's Free French movement, to revenge the defeat of 1940, and to bring France back into the victorious Allied camp. The myth was an attempt to reconcile the French people, but the heroic liberation of Paris and General Charles de Gaulle's glorious speech were only one side of the coin.

The other side was a brutal and popular *épuration* (purge or "cleansing") directed against the so-called *collabos*: those who had overtly collaborated with the Germans, those who had profited from the Occupation, the *Pétainistes* (Marshall Pétain's followers), who had delayed too long to turn coat, and women who had slept with the Germans. In the confused situation following the liberation of August 1944, many people settled old scores: retaliation, political differences, class hatreds, but also—as always happens in periods of chaos and a vacuum of authority—private quarrels, individual revenges, and criminal actions. After four terrible years of Nazi occupation, the festering hatred burst forth and was sinking Paris (and France as well) in blood and terror. The purge was a particularly ugly page of French history; it often went under illegal conditions with improvised court-martials, firing squads, and even lynching and individuals dealing out summary punishments. According to the French historian Robert Aron, the toll of the purge that took place in France was estimated at 30,000 or 40,000 summary executions: an estimate clearly incomplete, and a toll exceeding that of the 1789 Revolution.

The war went on until the capitulation of Germany on May 8, 1945. The old Marshall Philippe Pétain was tried and condemned to death for treason but promptly pardoned by de Gaulle; he was imprisoned in a fortress on the windy and small Atlantic island of Yeu where he died in 1951.

The country had suffered a lot as a result of World War II, a total of 600,000 people had lost their lives. The economy had been pillaged by the Germans. In liberated France many towns, bridges, roads, and railroads had been destroyed and had to be rebuilt. Essential supplies were hard to get; reconstruction was slow. Paris fortunately had received relatively little damage, but France had economically and socially to be reconstructed.

Appendix: Vestiges of the Parisian Fortifications

Gallic Period

All vestiges of this period, which were made of earth and perishing wood, have vanished. None of the wooden architecture that prevailed before the Roman conquest has come down to us.

Roman Wall

From the Roman stone wall, only a few remnants were ever found in the Cité island e.g. on the Notre Dame parvis, in the foundations of the present Préfecture de Police, and parallel to the Quai de la Corse and Quai aux Fleurs. They were once excavated and now are buried in the ground again.

Middle Ages Period

From the medieval era, we still have the Château of Vincennes, the Conciergerie towers (in the Cité island) and basements of towers of the Louvre fortress in the entrance of the present-day art museum.

From Philippe Auguste's enceinte, the following remnants are visible today.

- A portion of an 80 m curtain and two towers in the Rue des Jardins-Saint-Paul;
- A tower at 55 Rue des Francs Bourgeois;
- A tower at 20 Rue Etienne Marcel;
- A well-preserved tower at 29 Rue Guénégaud;
- The remnant of a tower at 13 Rue du Louvre;
- A well-restored tower in the School of Languages, at Passage Dauphine;
- The rest of a tower in a shop at 4 Cour du Commerce-Saint-André;
- A fragment of wall at 47 Rue Descartes;
- A fragment of wall in the hall of a building at 48–50 Rue Cardinal Lemoine;
- A portion of wall and the basement of a tower in an underground parking lot at 27 Rue Mazarine;
- A cross section of the wall on Rue Clovis;
- A 16-m-long fragment of wall at 9 and 11 Rue d'Assas.

From the enceinte of Charles V, there is a fragment of scarp wall at Boulevard Bourdon (northern part of the basin of Arsenal) and a piece of counterscarp wall in the garden of Carrousel. As for the Bastille, its outline is shown on the ground north of the present Place de la Bastille.

Fossés Jaunes

From the enceinte of Fossés Jaunes, only a fragment is still visible today the northern flank of bastion No. 1, which is used to support the terrace of the Tuileries Garden.

Enceinte of Fermiers Généraux

From the Ancient Régime's tax-barrier, there are still four tollhouses built by Ledoux:

- The rotunda of Porte de la Villette;
- The barrière du Trône with its two high columns at the Place de la Nation;
- Two symmetrical pavilions at the Place Denfert-Rochereau;
- And the rotunda of Chartres Boulevard of Courcelles.

Bastioned Enceinte of Thiers

The bastioned enceinte was totally demolished between 1919 and 1924. Today all one can see is two busy, noisy, and smelly ring motorways. There is very little left, though some fragments of wall have been incorporated into later buildings, and some gatehouses have been preserved and today are still used by the French army or the Gendarmerie (e.g. 54 Boulevard Davout and 50 Boulevard Lefebvre). The bastion No. 45 (72 Boulevard Berthier) has been transformed into a warehouse for storing costumes and sets of the Opera House. Publicly visible today are the following:

- The northern face of Bastion No. 44 at the rue André Suarès near Porte de Clichy;
- The west flank of bastion No. 28 near Porte of La Villette;
- A part of bastion No. 1 at Boulevard Poniatowsky near Porte of Bercy;
- The postern of Peupliers;
- And the Porte of Arcueil in the Rue Emile Deutsch.

Most of the detached forts of the period 1841–1845 are still preserved today. They are completely swallowed up in the urban landscape, but they cannot be visited as they are still used by the French Army, fire brigades, police force and other administrative organizations. The fort of Ivry today houses the ECPAD, the Documentation Center of the French Defense. A part of Fort Mont Valérien is open to the public with the *Memorial de la France Combattante,* which was erected in 1946 to commemorate the sacrifice of 4,500 résistants who were shot by the Germans in 1944. The Fort of Nogeut-sur-Marne is now the Poste d'Information et de Recrutement de la Légion Etrangère (Information and Recruitment Center of the French Foreign Legion).

Polygonal Forts

Most of the Séré de Rivières polygonal forts built after 1873 still exist today. They are either phagocyted in the suburbs or left alone to waste in the forests surrounding Paris. They form green oases and paradises for lizards, birds and bats. Some are still used by the Army as training grounds and as store places for fire brigades and police. A few of them have been sold to local associations and may be visited (e.g. Fort of Domont and Fort of Chelles).

Chauvineau Line

From the Chauvineau Line, only a few abandoned concrete blocks can be seen in the forests; two monuments have been erected at l'Isle Adam and Ormoy Villiers to commemorate the battles of 1940.

German Bunkers in Paris

Most German pillboxes built during the 1940–1944 Occupation have been demolished. Some larger bunkers were preserved and used as shelters or store places until the mid–1960s. None of them can be visited as they are now private state property.

Glossary

Abbaye abbey
Allée lane
Arc arch
Arrondissement each of the twenty wards or main administrative subdivisions of Paris
Avenue avenue
Banlieue suburb
Barrière tollgate, turnpike
Bastille a large medieval stronghold defending a gate
Bois wood, forest, park
Boulevard originally a *bulwark* (artillery emplacement), now a wide lane
Château castle
Châtelet a small castle, a stronghold or a gatehouse
Chapelle chapel
Cité city, the oldest part of a town
Colline hill
Eglise church
Faubourg suburb
Forêt forest
Fossé moat, ditch
Gare railway station
Halle covered market
Hôtel a rich noble residence, a private or royal palace
Hôtel de Ville city hall
Isle or **île** island
Ile de la Cité the "City Island," the oldest part of Paris
Ile-de-France the region around Paris
Ilôt islet, a small island
Jardin garden, park
Etoile a wide star-shaped square at the junction of several main streets
Lycée grammar school
Marais marsh
Métro short for *Métropolitain*, underground railway, also known as RAPT, Régie Autonome des Transports Parisiens (Autonomous Company of Parisian Transports)
Mont mount, hill
Palais palace
Parc park
Passerelle footbridge
Place public square, plaza
Pont bridge
Porte gate
Quai quay, wharf
Quartier neighborhood, borough
Rive bank of a river; *rive gauche* (left bank) is the southern part of Paris; *rive droite* (right bank) the northern
Rue street
Ruelle small street, back street
Square public garden
Tour tower
Ville city, town
Village village

Bibliography

Association des Amis de la Maison Vauban. *Vauban: sa vie, son oeuvre.* Yonne, France: Saint-Léger-Vauban, 1984.

Bainville, Jacques. *Histoire de France.* Paris: Librairie Plon, 1933.

Baron, Etienne. *La France.* Paris: Editions Magnard, 1947.

Benevolo, Leonardo. *De Europese Stad.* Amsterdam: Agon BV, 1993.

Blockmans, Wim. *Oorlog door de Eeuwen heen.* The Netherlands: HD Uitgeverij Hilversum, 1977.

Bornecque, Robert. *La France de Vauban.* Paris: Arthaud Editions, 1984.

Cetekk, Claude. *Nous avons bâti Paris.* Paris: Interlivre Editions, 1997.

Diderot, Denis, and Jean LeRond d'Alembert, eds. *Encyclopédie, Arts Militaires.* Reprint, Paris: Interlivre Editions, 1986. (orig. pub. 1751–1772)

Dropsy, Christian. *Les Fortifications de Metz et de Thionville.* Published by the author, Metz, France, 1998.

Eydoux, Henri-Paul. *Monuments et Trésors de la Gaule.* Paris: Librairie Plon, 1958.

Gaber, Stéphane. *La Route des Fortifications (Lorraine).* Metz, France: Editions Serpentoise, 1999.

Gaxotte, Pierre. *Histoire de France.* Paris: Hachette Editions, 1960.

Groetschel, Yves, and Guy Le Hallé. *Les Enceintes de Paris.* Paris: Village Communication, 1997.

Harmand, Jacques. *La Guerre Antique de Sumer à Rome.* Paris: Presses Universitaires de France, 1973.

Harouel, Jean-Louis. *Histoire de l'Urbanisme.* Paris: Presses Universitaires de France, 1981.

Hartink, Tom. *Antieke Wapens Encyclopedie.* Lisse, The Netherlands: Rebo International BV, 2001.

Histoire du Mont Valérien. Paris: Cogery Editions, 1939.

Hughes, Quentin. *Military Architecture.* Hants, England: Beaufort Publishing Ltd., 1974.

Koch, H.W. *Het Krijgsbedrijf in de Middeleeuwen.* Amsterdam: Elsevier BV, 1980.

Lebas, A., *Places Fortes et Fortification Pendant la Guerre de 1914–1918.* Paris: Editions Payot, 1923.

Le Hallé, Guy. *Précis de la Fortification.* Paris: PVC Editions, 1983.

Lepage, Jean-Denis. *Castles and Fortified Cities of Medieval Europe: An Illustrated History.* Jefferson, NC: McFarland & Company, 2002.

_____. *The Westwall (Siegfried Line) 1938–1945.* West Chester, OH: The Nafziger Collection, Inc., 2002.

Marchand, Bernard. *Paris, Histoire d'une Ville (XIXe–XXe) siècle.* Paris: Editions du Seuil, 1971.

Mathiex, Jean. *Histoire de France.* Paris: Hachette Editeur, 1981.

McNair, Ronald. L'Ob-West à Saint-Germain-en-Laye. *39–45 Magazine No. 123,* Editions Heimdal, September 1996.

Meurer, Peter H. *Das Festungsbuch des Nicolas Person.* Germany: Verlag D. Pfähler, Bad Neustadt, 1984.

Monnier, Gérard. *Histoire de l'Architecture.* Paris: Presses Universitaires de France, 1994.

Montanelli, Indro. *Histoire de Rome.* Paris: Editions Mondiales, 1959.

Neumann, Hartwig. *Festungbaukunst.* Bonn: Bernard & Graefe Publishers, 1988.

Parker, Geoffrey. *Warfare.* Oxford, England: Cambridge University Press, 1995.

Poppema, Simon, and Jean-Denis Lepage. *Historische Verdedigingswerken.* Amsterdam: Stichting Open Monumentendag, 1995.

Rocolle, Pierre. *2000 Ans de Fortification Française.* Paris: Editions Lavauzelle, 1989.

Rorive, Jean-Pierre. *La Guerre de Siège sous Louis XIV.* Brussels: Editions Racine, 1998.

Siegner, Otto. *Frankreich ein Bildwerk.* Munich: Verlag L. Simon, n. d.

Singman, Jeffrey. *Daily Life in Medieval Europe.* London: Greenwood Press, 1999.

Thevenot, Emile. *Les Gallo-Romains.* Paris: Presses Universitaires de France, 1978.

Thevenot, Emile. *Histoire des Gaulois.* Paris: Presses Universitaires de France, 1976.

Viollet-le-Duc, Eugène. *Histoire d'une Forteresse.* Paris: Berger-Levrault Editions, 1978.

Virilio, Paul. *Bunker Archéologie.* Paris: Editions du Demi-Cercle, 1996.

Volkmann, Jean-Charles. *Chronologie de l'Histoire de France.* Paris: Editions Gisserot, 1997.

Wenzler, Claude. *Architecture du Bastion.* Rennes, Editions Ouest-France, 2000.

Index